Operations Research/Computer Science Interfaces Series

Volume 59

Series Editors:
Ramesh Sharda
Oklahoma State University, Stillwater, Oklahoma, USA

Stefan Voß
University of Hamburg, Hamburg, Germany

More information about this series at http://www.springer.com/series/6375

Gabriella Dellino • Carlo Meloni
Editors

Uncertainty Management in Simulation-Optimization of Complex Systems

Algorithms and Applications

Springer

Editors
Gabriella Dellino
Istituto per le Applicazioni del Calcolo "Mauro Picone"
Consiglio Nazionale delle Ricerche
Bari, Italy

Carlo Meloni
Dipartimento di Ingegneria Elettrica e dell'Informazione
Politecnico di Bari
Bari, Italy

ISSN 1387-666X
Operations Research/Computer Science Interfaces Series
ISBN 978-1-4899-7961-2 ISBN 978-1-4899-7547-8 (eBook)
DOI 10.1007/978-1-4899-7547-8

Springer New York Heidelberg Dordrecht London

Softcover reprint of the hardcover 1st edition 2015

Printed on acid-free paper

Springer Science+Business Media LLC New York is part of Springer Science+Business Media (www.springer.com)

Foreword

The importance of methods and models to address uncertainties in optimization and simulation of complex systems is evident by the great plethora of books and papers recently dedicated to this subject. When optimizing systems' performances, accounting for or neglecting uncertainty may lead to completely different results; therefore, uncertainty management is a major issue in simulation-optimization. Such methods find a lot of applications in almost any area of human endeavor, from engineering to science, from business to healthcare and transportation, among others. At the same time, however, there is some ambiguity in how these methods are developed and applied.

This editorial project on "Uncertainty Management in Simulation – Optimization of Complex Systems" is a bright example of a valuable book in this fast emerging multi-disciplinary field. The book aims at investigating strategies to account for uncertainty in complex systems described by computer simulations. It originated from an interdisciplinary meeting, held in Rome, in May 2012, promoted by the European Science Foundation as a Strategic Workshop in the framework of emerging fields requiring action at a European level, as the Horizon 2020 research program. The workshop, organized under the patronage of AIRO (The Italian Operations Research Society), was aimed to foster the exchange of knowledge between European research teams, to establish new research networks, and to explore the possibilities of future collaborative actions.

Following up these activities, this book focuses on the mathematical and algorithmic aspects of uncertainty management in simulation-optimization of complex systems. The 11 chapters are authored by a number of distinguished scholars from different European countries and discuss the most critical subjects in this area. Each chapter balances in-depth scientific investigation with a clear and easy to understand style.

The book highlights that a very promising research direction is the development of methods able to combine the most powerful characteristics of various approaches.

I wish to express my thanks to the Editors, two renowned scholars, Drs. Gabriella Dellino and Carlo Meloni, for their effort in the realization of this volume. This book is very valuable to all practitioners and researchers working on different fields but unified by the need to address uncertainty management issues in Simulation-Optimization. Along with this contribution, further studies combining algorithmic developments and applications in a similar way would be highly beneficial to the field. Such an effort would enhance the cooperation among researchers and enforce the impact of mathematics on innovations in key technologies.

Genoa, Italy
May, 2015

Anna Sciomachen
President of the Italian Operations Reseach Society (AIRO)
Full Professor of Operations Research
Department of Economics and Business Studies
University of Genoa
Genoa, Italy

Preface

Several optimization problems arise in production, transportation and logistics, energy management, finance, engineering, and applied sciences; in all these contexts, managers carry on a decision-making process, which is usually affected by uncertainties, so the final outcome can be noisy. There are applications in virtually any area of business and management, government, science and engineering, so methodologies to support decisions in uncertain environments are urgently needed.

This book aims at illustrating strategies and methods to account for uncertainty in complex systems described by computer simulations. When optimizing the performances of these systems, accounting for or neglecting uncertainty may lead to completely different results; therefore, uncertainty management is a major issue in simulation-optimization. Because of its wide field of applications, simulation-optimization issues have been addressed by different communities with different methods, and from slightly different perspectives.

The literature shows that alternative approaches have been developed, also depending on the application context, without any well-established method clearly outperforming the others. An internet search using a popular web browser with the keyword "Simulation Optimization" returns about two hundred thousand pages, while the more focalized Google Scholar gives about twenty four thousand pages mainly containing scientific and technical articles, conference publications, research reports, and academic manuscripts. Clearly, Simulation-Optimization is a field that stimulates growing interest among researchers and simulation practitioners dealing with real problems. As one result of this great deal of work on Simulation-Optimization in the literature, dedicated optimization routines have been recently incorporated into several commercial simulation software packages. One important reason for this popularity is that many real-world optimization problems are too complex to be addressed directly through analytical mathematical formulations while simulation models avoid major simplification (e.g., stochastic issues can be taken into account). Consequently, a common goal in both the optimization and simulation communities is to develop methods to guide and help the analyst to produce high quality solutions, in the absence of tractable mathematical structures.

It is worth noting that several issues and topics emerge in the area of Simulation-Optimization to enlarge the number of problems that can be handled using this approach and to improve the existing methodologies. They include: multi-response simulation-optimization; random constraints management; best solution assessment; definition of effective neighborhoods for local-search based optimization; effective schemes for sampling and exploration of the experimental area of interest; management of computational costs for functions estimation (via simulation) with respect to optimization efforts; inclusion of Simulation-Optimization in decision support and/or control systems; specific methods for combinatorial problems (e.g., scheduling and planning); distributed or parallel Simulation-Optimization techniques; web- and cloud-based Simulation-Optimization.

This volume brings together—as chapter contributors—researchers from different (though interrelated) areas; namely, statistical methods, engineering and economics modelling, experimental design, stochastic programming, global optimization, metamodeling, and design and analysis of computer simulation experiments. Editors' goal is to take advantage of such a multidisciplinary environment, to give readers a much deeper understanding of the commonalities and differences of the various approaches to simulation-based optimization, especially in uncertain environments. Editors aim to offer a bibliographic reference on the topic, enabling interested readers to learn about the state of the art in this research area, while also accounting for potential real-world applications to improve the state-of-the-practice as well. Besides researchers and scientists of the field, the primary audience for the book includes Ph.D. students, academic teachers, as well as practitioners and professionals.

We received significant contributions from the authors, all being very active and talented researchers in the area; further, the resulting interdisciplinary background across them definitely provides an added value to the whole editorial project.

This editorial project is a follow-up action of a European Science Foundation granted strategic workshop proposed and organized by the editors (ESF AWARD: STRAT01-EW11-068: PEN—formerly PESC—Strategic Workshop) "Uncertainty Management In Simulation-Optimization Of Complex Systems: Algorithms And Applications"—held in Rome (Italy), 9–12 May 2012—during which many of the book contributors had the opportunity to discuss the topic from complementary aspects. Additional information can be found on the web at the following link:

http://www.esf.org/hosting-experts/scientific-review-groups/physical-and-engineering-sciences-pen/activities/pesc-strategic-initiatives.html

The volume is organized in three thematic parts, namely Advanced Tutorials, Uncertainty Management Approaches, Methods and Applications. They contain 3, 4, and 4 chapters, respectively, making a total of 11 contributed chapters. Each chapter—in general—reports on a co-authored work as the result of a research group, and has a specific bibliography.

The first part of the book, devoted to Advanced Tutorials, starts with a chapter authored by Russell Cheng reviewing recent research on the use of simulation in random search optimization of system performance to aid time-critical decision making, assuming the availability of a simulation model that can be run sufficiently quickly. The following chapter, by Gabriella Dellino, Jack P.C. Kleijnen, and Carlo Meloni, offers an overview on metamodel-based robust simulation-optimization methods, reviewing the current state of the art, focusing on methods to tackle robustness issues using metamodels in general, and Kriging in particular. The first part of the volume ends with a chapter by Leonidas Sakalauskas exploring simulation-based modeling to study a stochastic equilibrium.

The second part of the volume focuses on uncertainty management approaches in simulation-optimization. The chapter by Thomas Bartz-Beielstein, Christian Jung, and Martin Zaefferer starts this part and deals with sequential parameter optimization methods for handling uncertainty, also discussing how they can be applied to real-world cases. The following chapter is authored by Bertrand Iooss and Paul Lemaître and presents a thorough and careful review on global sensitivity analysis methods. The third chapter of the second part of the book is contributed by Saverio Giuliani and Carlo Meloni and investigates the connections between optimization models with uncertainties, activity-based costing, and resource-based view of the firm. The successive chapter is by Piergiuseppe Morone and Valentina Elena Tartiu and analyzes how different types of uncertainty can affect the quality of decisions taken in the bio-based products market, its further development and, more generally, the shift towards a bio-based economy.

The third part of the volume deals with methods and applications and starts with an in-depth chapter by Giampaolo Liuzzi, Stefano Lucidi, and Veronica Piccialli on the class of global optimization approaches for simulation-based complex systems. The second chapter of this part proposes a simulation-optimization study by Mieke Defraeye and Inneke Van Nieuwenhuyse on shift scheduling in queueing systems characterized by time-varying arrival rates. The following chapter by Ebru Angün describes the solution of a disaster preparedness and short-term response planning problem through a multistage stochastic optimization model. The fourth and last chapter describes a research work by Annalisa Cesaro and Dario Pacciarelli addressing a problem of costly spare parts allocation in a single echelon inventory system with complete pooling characterized by long repairing time and severe service constraints.

The editors acknowledge the European Science Foundation who supported this editorial project. Moreover, they wish to thank the Foundation C.D. Tardini-NPO (Rome, Italy) for its support in hosting and organizing the related workshop and following activities. We would like to thank all those who have contributed to this editorial project by their support, advice, and contributions. First among these are all the contributing authors for submitting their recent research results and all the participants to the workshop held in Rome (including those who do not appear as authors in this volume). We are deeply grateful to the authors for bearing with our repeated requests for improvements and revisions to meet the high scientific standard required by Springer's Operations Research/Computer Science Interfaces Series. The reviewers for their time and efforts spent to help improving the manuscripts are also gratefully acknowledged. Thanks are also due to Professors Ramesh Sharda and Stefan Voss, Editors in Chief of this Springer Series, for supporting our editorial project, and to Springer editorial office and managers for their permanent help. We hope that the chapters included in this volume will stimulate further research in the growing area of Simulation-Optimization and contribute to address new challenging problems. A final word of thanks is kindly dedicated to all those who supported our editorial work without even knowing it: our families and our friends, who were always on our side.

Bari, Italy
May, 2015

Gabriella Dellino
Carlo Meloni

Contents

Part I Advanced Tutorials

1 **Supporting Time-Critical Decision Making with Real Time Simulations** 3
Russell C.H. Cheng

2 **Metamodel-Based Robust Simulation-Optimization: An Overview** 27
Gabriella Dellino, Jack P.C. Kleijnen, and Carlo Meloni

3 **Simulation-Based Modelling of a Stochastic Equilibrium** 55
Leonidas Sakalauskas

Part II Uncertainty Management Approaches

4 **Uncertainty Management Using Sequential Parameter Optimization** 79
Thomas Bartz-Beielstein, Christian Jung, and Martin Zaefferer

5 **A Review on Global Sensitivity Analysis Methods** 101
Bertrand Iooss and Paul Lemaître

6 **Connections Among Optimization Models with Uncertainties, ABC and RBV** 123
Saverio Giuliani and Carlo Meloni

7 **Addressing Uncertainty in Complex Systems. The Case of Bio-Based Products Derived from Urban Bio-Waste Valorisation** 151
Piergiuseppe Morone and Valentina Elena Tartiu

Part III Methods and Applications

8 Global Optimization of Simulation Based Complex Systems 173
Giampaolo Liuzzi, Stefano Lucidi, and Veronica Piccialli

9 Personnel Scheduling in Queues with Time-varying Arrival Rates: Applications of Simulation-Optimization 203
Mieke Defraeye and Inneke Van Nieuwenhuyse

10 Stochastic Dual Dynamic Programming Solution of a Short-Term Disaster Management Problem 225
Ebru Angün

11 Optimal Stock Allocation in Single Echelon Inventory Systems Subject to a Service Constraint 251
Annalisa Cesaro and Dario Pacciarelli

Contributors

Ebru Angün is an Associate Professor of Operations Research in the Department of Industrial Engineering at Galatasaray University (Istanbul, Turkey), where she has been since 2004. From September 2008 to September 2009, she was a Visiting Scholar in the Department of Industrial & Systems Engineering at Georgia Institute of Technology. She received a B.S. degree in Industrial Engineering from Istanbul Technical University in 1995, and an M.S. degree in Industrial Engineering from Bogazici University in 1998. She carried out her Ph.D. research in Tilburg University, which she joined in 2000, and she received her Ph.D. degree in 2004. Her research interests center on stochastic optimization (i.e., simulation-based optimization, stochastic programming, and chance-constrained optimization) and applications in the disaster management, logistics, and healthcare. She has published papers in Probability in the Engineering and Informational Sciences, European Journal of Operational Research, Journal of the Operational Research Society, INFORMS Journal on Computing, and Simulation Modelling Practice and Theory. She has been serving as a referee to the following journals: European Journal of Operational Research, INFORMS Journal on Computing, Simulation Modelling Practice and Theory, and Journal of Simulation.

Thomas Bartz-Beielstein became professor for Applied Mathematics at CUAS (Cologne University of Applied Sciences) in 2006. Since then, he has built a research team of international status and visibility. He is speaker of the research center CIplus (Computational Intelligence plus), head of the research team CIOP (Computational Intelligence, Optimization & Data Mining), and initiator of the SpotSeven team (www.spotseven.de). His expertise lies in optimization, simulation, and statistical analysis of complex real-world problems. He is one of the leaders in the field of statistical analysis of optimization algorithms and the inventor and the driving force behind SPOT (Sequential Parameter Optimization Technology). Thomas has more than 100 publications on computational intelligence, optimization, simulation, and experimental research.

Annalisa Cesaro earned her Ph.D. in Computer Science and Automation (Operations Research) from the Roma Tre University. Since 2010, she has worked as researcher for Data Management.spa in collaboration with Roma Tre University. Currently, she is a technologist at the Italian National Institute of Statistics. Her research interests are in areas involving tactical and operative management of cooperative systems, both in case of materialized (physical resources) or dematerialized (web) services, thus designing and/or evaluating efficient/optimal ways of consuming resources, computer algorithms, and technologies. The main practical areas of application are spare part management, census systems, population and business registers.

Russell C.H. Cheng is Emeritus Professor of Operational Research at the University of Southampton. He has an M.A. and the Diploma in Mathematical Statistics from Cambridge University, England. He obtained his Ph.D. from Bath University. He is a former Chairman of the U.K. Simulation Society, a Fellow of the Royal Statistical Society and Fellow of the Institute of Mathematics and Its Applications. His research interests include: design and analysis of simulation experiments and parametric estimation methods. He was a Joint Editor of the IMA Journal of Management Mathematics. His email and web addresses are R.C.H.Cheng@soton.ac.uk and www.personal.soton.ac.uk/rchc.

Mieke Defraeye obtained her Ph.D. from the Research Center for Operations Management at KU Leuven, Belgium. She received her M.Sc. degree in Business Engineering at KU Leuven in 2009. Her research interests include service systems with non-stationary arrivals, capacity planning and scheduling under uncertainty, and operations management in healthcare settings.

Gabriella Dellino graduated in Computer Science Engineering at the Polytechnic of Bari, in 2005. In 2009, she earned her Ph.D. in Applied Mathematics from the University of Bari. During the Ph.D., she was a visiting fellow at the CentER—Tilburg School of Economics and Management (The Netherlands). Then she joined the research group of Decision and Management Methods of the University of Siena, while in 2011 she became assistant professor in Management Science at IMT Institute for Advanced Studies (Lucca). Currently, she works at the Istituto per le Applicazioni del Calcolo "Mauro Picone" of the National Research Council of Italy. Throughout these years, she has been involved in several national and international research projects funded by academic organizations and private companies, including the recent cooperation in the FP7 STAR*AgroEnergy research project, led by University of Foggia. Her research mostly focuses on designing mathematical models and computer simulation models for complex systems investigation, with a specific focus on metamodelling approaches and uncertainty management, the final aim being the development of a Decision Support System, supporting managers and stakeholders from the relevant domain(s) in their decision-making processes. Applications of the designed methodological frameworks spread from engineering to management, economics, and health care. This research activity resulted in several publications on international journals and books.

Saverio Giuliani graduated in 2001 in Statistics and Economics at the Sapienza University of Rome. He achieved a post-graduate specialization in Economy and

Statistics for Territorial Analysis and then a Master in Management Accounting. In 2010, he got a Ph.D. in "Economy and Finance" at the University of Foggia in cooperation with the Vilnius Technical University. His professional career started in 2003 as a consultant in management accounting, decision support systems, and data warehousing for health care. Since 2004, he is officer of the Italian Ministry of Economy and Finance, working mainly on guidelines and monitoring performance management of public administrations. Currently, he is also working at the National Anticorruption Authority on anticorruption strategies and risk management. His research and professional interests include: activity-based costing methodology, performance management, statistical data analysis, stochastic programming, and multi-criteria optimization. His works have been published on different journals and conferences.

Bertrand Iooss obtained a Master in Statistics and Random Models in Finance in 1995 from University Paris VII. Further, he defended (1998) his Ph.D. thesis in Geostatistics at the Paris School of Mines on the subject of wave propagation in random media for seismic exploration problems. From 2000 to 2002, he worked as a research-engineer at the Institut Français du Pétrole in the Geophysics Division on wave tomography problems. From 2002 to 2010, he was a research-engineer at the Nuclear Energy Division of CEA Cadarache, working mainly on safety applications and developments of sampling strategy and uncertainty/sensitivity analysis methods. In 2009, he obtained his habilitation thesis in Statistics at Toulouse University. Since 2009, he is the co-leader of the French research group (CNRS) on "Stochastic methods for computer experiments" (http://www.gdr-mascotnum.fr). At the present time, he works as a senior researcher and project leader at Electricité de France (EDF), Research and Development Division, Industrial Risk Management Department. He is also a Research Associate at the Institut de Mathématiques de Toulouse (Université Paul Sabatier, France). His research interests involve the design, analysis, modeling, and uncertainty management in computer experiments, related to nuclear engineering and environmental problems.

Christian Jung is a Ph.D. student at CUAS (Cologne University of Applied Sciences). He is doing his Ph.D. studies in cooperation with TU Dortmund University. His research interests include process optimization and modeling of complex real-world problems. Christian studied Electrical Engineering and works at SMS Siemag AG. He joined the SpotSeven team in 2011. Christian has a strong background in simulation and industrial optimization and excellent programming skills.

Jack P.C. Kleijnen is Emeritus Professor of "Simulation and Information Systems" at Tilburg University, where he is still a member of both the Department of Management and the Operations Research Group of the Center for Economic Research (CentER) in the Tilburg School of Economics and Management. His research concerns the statistical design and analysis of experiments with simulation models, in many scientific disciplines including management and engineering. He was a consultant for several organizations in the USA and Europe, and served on many international editorial boards and scientific committees. He spent several years in the USA, at universities and private companies. He received a number of national and international awards; e.g., in 2008, the Queen of the Netherlands appointed him a Knight in the Order of the Netherlands Lion and in 2005 the INFORMS Simulation Society awarded him the Lifetime Professional Achievement Award (LPAA). Currently, he is writing the second version of 'Design and analysis of simulation experiments' to be published by Springer in 2015, and has been supervising the Ph.D. thesis by Ehsan Mehdad, defended in April 2015. His e-mail address is kleijnen@tilburguniversity.edu, his publication list is available on https://pure.uvt.nl/portal/en/persons/jack-pc-kleijnen(da721b00-b03f-4c42-98fe-55e593f541a8)/publications.html and his web page is: http://www.tilburguniversity.edu/webwijs/show/?uid=kleijnen.

Paul Lemaître graduated as a statistical modelling engineer, having obtained an M. Eng. in Mathematics and Modelling at the Institut National des Sciences Appliquées, Toulouse (France) and an M.Sc. in Applied Mathematics at the University of Toulouse, France, both in 2010. He then defended a Ph.D. thesis Applied Mathematics in 2014 in the ALEA Lab of the French Institute for Research in Computer Science and Automation (INRIA). The Ph.D. was also conducted in partnership with Electricité de France (EDF), Research and Development Division, Industrial Risk Management Department. This applied PhD's main topic was sensitivity analysis when the quantity of interest is a binary function—mainly failure or non-failure of the modelled system. He now works for a young start-up in Lyon, France (The CoSMo Company) which aims at delivering a predictive analytics platform for complex system. His research interests involve data mining, design of experiments, surrogate modelling, optimization, and sensitivity analysis.

Giampaolo Liuzzi was born in Rome, Italy, in 1972. He received the M.Sc. degree in Computer Science Engineering (summa cum laude) and the Ph.D. degree in Operations Research from the University of Rome "La Sapienza," Rome, Italy, in 1997 and 2001, respectively. Since 2010, he has been a research scientist at the Institute for Systems Analysis and Computer Science "Antonio Ruberti" (IASI) of the National Research Council (CNR). He has authored or coauthored about 30 papers on international journals.

Stefano Lucidi received the M.S. degree in electronic engineering from the University of Rome "La Sapienza," Italy, in 1980. From 1982 to 1992, he was Researcher at the Istituto di Analisi e dei Sistemi e Informatica of the National Research Council of Italy. From September 1985 to May 1986, he was Honorary Fellow of the Mathematics Research Center of University of Wisconsin, Madison, USA. From 1992 to 2000, he was Associate Professor of Operations Research of University of Rome "La Sapienza." Since 2000, he is Full Professor of Operations Research of the University of Rome "La Sapienza." He teaches Operations Research and Global Optimization Methods in Engineering Management. He belongs to the Department of Computer Control and Management Engineering "Antonio Ruberti" of the University of Rome "La Sapienza." His research interests are mainly focused on the definition, study and application of nonlinear optimization methods. This research activity has produced 78 papers published in international journals and 20 papers published in international books.

Carlo Meloni is an Assistant Professor of Systems Engineering and Optimization at the Politecnico di Bari (Italy). His main research and professional interests concern the theory and the applications of optimization, simulation, and other OR/MS methodologies. He took part in research projects promoted by the MIUR (Italian Ministry of Education, University and Research), academy, research centers, companies, and organizations from both for-profit and nonprofit sectors. His works have been presented in several international conferences and published on different international journals and volumes. Carlo Meloni is member of the Italian Society of Operations Research (AIRO), INFORMS (The Institute for Operations Research and the Management Sciences), and IMACS (International Association for Mathematics and Computers in Simulation). He is also active in different EURO (The Association of European Operational Research Societies) working groups. Currently, he is a researcher affiliated with INDAM (Istituto Nazionale di Alta Matematica "F. Severi," Italy) and CNR-IAC (Istituto per le Applicazioni del Calcolo "M. Picone," Italy). He was the recipient (with Gabriella Dellino) of an ESF (European Science Foundation) award for the organization of the Strategic Workshop "Uncertainty management in simulation-optimization of complex systems: algorithms and applications," which was held in Rome from 9th to 14th May 2012.

Piergiuseppe Morone is professor of Economics at Unitelma Sapienza—University of Roma (Italy). He obtained a Ph.D. in Science and Technology Policy at SPRU-Sussex University (UK) in 2003 and an MA in Development Economics from the same University in 1999. His research interests range from knowledge and innovation economics to behavioral economics and biobased economy. He has published on several international journals and has recently edited a book on *Knowledge, Innovation and Internationalisation* (Routledge).

Dario Pacciarelli is a professor of operations research in the Department of Engineering at Roma Tre University. His research interests are in areas involving efficient utilization of resources, computer algorithms, and discrete optimization. The main contributions are to the design, analysis, and evaluation of heuristics and exact algorithms for planning and scheduling problems, including real time control of railway traffic, airport supply chain management, air traffic management, production scheduling in the pharmaceutical industry. He is author or co-author of more than 80 publications in top international journals (including *Operations Research*, *Transportations Science* and *Transportations Research Part B*), books, and conference proceedings.

Veronica Piccialli was born in Naples, Italy in 1975. She received the M.Sc. degree in Computer Science Engineering (summa cum laude) and the Ph.D. degree in Operations Research from the University of Rome "La Sapienza," Rome, Italy, in 2000 and 2004, respectively. In 2006, she was a post doc at the Combinatorics & Optimization department of the University of Waterloo, Canada. Since 2008, she is Assistant Professor at the Engineering Faculty of the University of Rome Tor Vergata, where she teaches Optimization in Management Engineering. In 2013, she got the national scientific qualification as Associate Professor. She has authored and coauthored 16 papers in international journals and 2 book chapters published in international books.

Leonidas Sakalauskas is a Head of Operational Research Division of the Institute of Mathematics Informatics of Vilnius University. He is active in science from 1980s and has published about 250 scientific papers in reviewed scientific journals. He is a main organizer of more than 20 scientific conferences and workshops, among them he chaired the XXV EURO Conference "OR Connecting Sciences," July 8–11, 2012, Vilnius (Lithuania) which attracted more than 2000 participants.

Valentina Elena Tartiu is Research Fellow within the interdisciplinary research unit—STAR*Agro Energy, headquartered at University of Foggia (South Italy) and is currently working on issues regarding the new value chains of the renewable resources based on biomass (e.g., the bio-waste streams valorisation) and their role in the shift towards a bio-based economy. She holds a Ph.D. in Management (2011) at the Bucharest University of Economic Studies. Her research interests bridge between mathematical modeling of complex systems and sustainability issues, specifically around sustainable waste management, sustainability transitions, environmental behavior.

Inneke Van Nieuwenhuyse is Associate Professor at the Research Center for Operations Management, KU Leuven, Belgium. Her research interests include operations management, more specifically the design and analysis of stochastic manufacturing and service systems. She has been involved in applied research projects for industrial and consulting companies as well as hospitals. Her work has been published in a.o. European Journal of Operational Research, IIE Transactions, and International Journal of Production Economics.

Martin Zaefferer is a Ph.D. student at CUAS (Cologne University of Applied Sciences). He is doing his Ph.D. thesis in cooperation with TU Dortmund University. Martin works in the SpotSeven team since 2009. From 2010 until 2012, he was a master student of Engineering in Automation & IT. He studied electrical engineering with a focus on automation at CUAS and graduated in 2010 (diploma). His outstanding theses received several awards from industry (Erzquell Brewery, Ferchau Engineering, Aggerverband). His research interests include computational intelligence, applications of knowledge discovery, and sequential parameter optimization. Martin is an experienced programmer with a strong background in R and Matlab.

Part I
Advanced Tutorials

Chapter 1
Supporting Time-Critical Decision Making with Real Time Simulations

Russell C.H. Cheng

1.1 Introduction

This chapter discusses random search optimization where a simulation model is used to explore different ways of running a given complex system with the objective of finding a good way to operate the system. There are many situations where a computer simulation model can be used in this way. For example Mousavi et al. [1] give case studies arising from healthcare and manufacturing and Huang et al. [2] describe use of simulation to estimate system performance when managing surface transport systems.

Many decision making problems reduce to being an optimization problem where the objective is to find a good way of operating the system. One version of the problem is where the system performance can be regarded as being a smooth function of a number of continuously varying decision variables and the problem is to find those values of these decision variables that will optimize system performance. This is essentially the classical optimization problem. Another version is where the system can be operated in a finite, but large, number of distinctly separate ways and the problem is to choose a good way, possibly the best, of operating the system. In this latter version of the problem the number of distinct ways can be combinatorially large, when we have what is known as a combinatorial optimization problem. The distinction between the two types of problem can become blurred in particular instances.

In a series of papers Cheng [3–6] discusses both types of problem, but where it is assumed that a simulation program can be used to analyse the different ways of operating the system. In all these papers Cheng considers the case where the

R.C.H. Cheng (✉)
School of Mathematics, University of Southampton, Southampton SO17 1BJ, UK
e-mail: R.C.H.Cheng@soton.ac.uk; cheng@btinternet.com

G. Dellino, C. Meloni (eds.), *Uncertainty Management in Simulation-Optimization of Complex Systems*, Operations Research/Computer Science Interfaces Series 59, DOI 10.1007/978-1-4899-7547-8_1

different ways to be compared are selected at random. Simulation runs are then made to see how the system performs under each, to see which is best. In this chapter we summarise the methods discussed in two of the papers, Cheng [3] and Cheng [5], which cover the situation where, in one case, a simple statistical model based on the *full* normal distribution is used to represent the output of simulation runs, and in the other a *partial* normal model is used. The statistical analysis of the output when such a normal statistical model can be used is relatively straightforward and, when applicable, can be implemented relatively easily.

We assume that our objective is to identify a way of operating the system being studied which yields good system performance as measured by a given performance measure. For simplicity we assume that this performance measure is a cost so that, ideally, it is to be minimized, but if not minimized, at least where a solution can be found for which the cost is relatively small compared with the range of values it might take.

If the decision on how to operate the system has to be based solely on the results of the random search, then it is very natural to use the way that corresponds to the lowest performance measure found amongst those randomly selected for consideration. We will use the term *search point* or *design point* to indicate the particular settings of those quantities under our control and which define how the system is run in a particular way. The random search is thus simply a search of a number of randomly selected design points, and we will use $W_{(1)}$ to denote the best performance measure value obtained amongst the design points selected for consideration. We will fully define the terminology and notation in Sect. 1.2, but it will be convenient to use this terminology and notation immediately.

There are two main aspects of RSO that are of interest: (i) the experimental procedure used in carrying out the random search itself leading to the identification of $W_{(1)}$, and (ii) establishing how good the system performance actually is corresponding to this solution, typically involving calculation of a confidence interval for this quantity.

The papers by Cheng cited above discuss both aspects, in the first focusing on how best to balance the number of points searched in the RSO and the simulation effort used at each point. Cheng also discusses the second aspect, including the use of mainly computer intensive methods for calculating quantities like confidence intervals. We shall discuss both these aspects, however the main purpose of this chapter is to focus on how use of a full or partial normal statistical model simplifies the consideration of (ii). In particular we discuss two situations: (a) the situation where the performance measure, as estimated in the simulation runs, is a random variable whose distribution is normal, and (b) the partial normal case, where the performance measure does not have a distribution that is completely normal, but where the distribution of the lower end of the range of values, i.e. the more desirable values, can be approximated by the left tail of the normal distribution. This second situation is the more generally applicable, but the analysis is more technically difficult; where the first situation is appropriate the analysis applicable in that case is preferable.

For the full normal case the analysis of output can be carried out sufficiently quickly not to add a significant overhead to computing time. Thus, if simulation runs can be carried out sufficiently quickly, it is possible to complete a simulation based evaluation of system performance sufficiently fast to allow it to support real time decision making. We will give such a realistic example involving the handling of large incidents in the fire and rescue service.

In the next section we describe RSO in general terms whilst in Sect. 1.3 we discuss the case where a full normal model is used to represent the output obtained from an RSO. In Sect. 1.4 we show how to fit this normal model to results obtained by RSO. In Sect. 1.5 we describe the "cover moves" problem encountered by the fire rescue service when dealing with large incidents, and carry out the analysis of output from an RSO in this problem using the full normal model. In Sect. 1.6 we discuss the partial normal model, and use of this model is illustrated in Sect. 1.7 by its use in a travelling salesman problem. Some conclusions are provided in Sect. 1.8.

1.2 Optimization and Random Search

1.2.1 Classical and Combinatorial Optimization

Consider first optimization in the deterministic case. Let $J(\theta)$ be the system performance measure. We suppose that it is a continuous function of a vector θ of d continuous decision variables, where θ can be selected from a compact region Θ of R^d. We seek the value of θ which minimizes $J(\theta)$ and write the minimum expected performance as

$$\delta = \min_{\theta\in\Theta} J\left(\theta\right). \tag{1.1}$$

We shall only consider the case where this is obtained at an interior point $\theta_{\min}$ of Θ. In classical optimization $J(\theta)$ is assumed to possess smoothness conditions which allow it to be approximated by a quadratic function of θ in the neighborhood of $\theta_{\min}$. Convergence properties of numerical search procedures are then relatively easy to establish.

In a combinatorial optimization problem we can still let $J(\theta)$ be the system performance measure, with θ being a vector of d decision variables. However we do not regard the components as being continuous, but as being discrete. A simple but typical case is where $d=1$, with θ representing a *permutation* of N objects on which system performance depends.

Cheng [6] conjectures that there are combinatorial problems where results from classical optimization theory may be applicable, with d assumed large and moreover where a normal statistical distribution may be a reasonable representation of the variability of the simulation output. This viewpoint of combinatorial optimization problems is somewhat speculative at this juncture and we not to try develop rigorous theory to support this view. However our numerical example does give an indication of the effectiveness of use of a normal statistical model in a genuine application.

The following formulation of RSO is based on that given in Cheng [6].

1.2.2 Random Search Optimization

Random search can be thought of as being a simple way of exploring the region Θ, supposing that this region does contain $\theta_{\min}$. This immediately makes the problem stochastic, even if our problem had been initially deterministic. We consider the statistical model of random search optimization (RSO) considered by Cheng [4] in which simulation runs are made to explore the behaviour of $J(\theta)$. We begin by assuming that the random search is carried out as follows. This will not be the final version of the search that we will be discussing in more detail, but allows us to set out the issues.

First sample m mutually independent values of θ:

$$\theta_1, \theta_2, \ldots, \theta_m, \tag{1.2}$$

which we shall call *search* or *design* points, from some continuous distribution with density $g(\theta)$, $\theta \in \Theta$. We allow for a general density rather than sampling from a uniform distribution to enable sampling to be focussed in the most promising regions of Θ based on prior information.

Then for each θ_i we make n simulation runs, each of some predetermined and fixed standard length t. We shall not discuss how individual runs are conducted. For example, if a warm up period is needed in each run, we assume that this has already been considered and dealt with. If the total time available allows a maximum of c simulation runs, we have that

$$c = nm.$$

It will be convenient to write the performance measure as $J(\theta) = \mu + X(\theta)$ where μ is a constant to be defined and $X(\theta)$ is the part depending on the decision quantities θ. We write J_i for $J(\theta_i)$ and X_i for $X(\theta_i)$. The important point to note is that because the θ_i are randomly sampled, the J_i and X_i are *also* random variables. In all that follows we shall use the notation $J(\theta)$ and $X(\theta)$ when we are regarding J and X as deterministic functions of θ, and the notation J_i, and X_i, when regarding J and X as a random variables resulting from the random sampling of the θ_i in (1.2). The constant μ can be viewed as the mean of the random variables J_i, and the X_i as having mean $E(X_i) = 0$.

An *additional* random variation has to be allowed for when simulation is used to assess system performance. This is because each simulation run will typically involve random variation so that the observed performance measure $J(\theta)$ will include random error, even when θ is being regarded as fixed. We assume that the *observed* performance measures, obtained from simulation runs, take the form

$$Y_{ij} = \mu + X_i + \eta_j + \varepsilon_{ij}, \quad i = 1, 2, \ldots, m;\ j = 1, 2, \ldots, n. \tag{1.3}$$

Here we distinguish between two random 'error' quantities appearing in a simulation run, even when θ is fixed. The quantities ε_{ij} are assumed to be all mutually independent random errors arising from random numbers sampled independently over all the different design points and replicates. We assume the ε_{ij} have mean zero and variance σ^2. The quantities η_j are random errors which arise from the use of common numbers. Let $\mathbf{z}_j$ be a set of random numbers used in the jth run made at a given design point, and suppose this *same* set is used in the jth run of all the m design points, i.e. the set $\mathbf{z}_j$ comprises random numbers *common* to all the jth runs across all design points. They therefore give rise to the same random error η_j in the simulation output irrespective of the design point θ_i.

The averages of the observations at each θ_i are

$$W_i = n^{-1}\sum_{j=1}^{n} Y_{ij} = \mu + X_i + n^{-1}\sum_{j=1}^{n} \eta_j + n^{-1}\sum_{j=1}^{n} \varepsilon_{ij} = \mu + X_i + \overline{\eta} + \zeta_i,$$

$$\text{for } i = 1, 2, \ldots, m, \tag{1.4}$$

where the averaged errors ζ_i have mean zero and variance:

$$\mathrm{Var}\,[\zeta_i] = \sigma^2/n = \sigma_n^2, \text{ say.} \tag{1.5}$$

We include the suffix n as a reminder that $\mathrm{Var}[\zeta_i]$ depends on n.

The effect of using random numbers is to add the *same* random error, $\overline{\eta}$, to all the W_i. This shows the benefit of using random numbers when we compare different W_i, as the $\overline{\eta}$ random error then cancels out.

Equation (1.4) shows that there are therefore two sources of variation in RSO: the *search induced variability* of the X_i and the *simulation induced variability* of the ζ_i, which is independent of that of the X_i. We shall write $F_X(\cdot)$, and $F_\zeta(\cdot)$ to denote the cumulative distribution functions (CDF) of X_i and ζ and $f_X(\cdot)$ and $f_\zeta(\cdot)$ for their probability density functions (PDF).

It will be convenient to assume that the observations W are put in ranked order

$$W_{(1)} < W_{(2)} < \cdots < W_{(m)}.$$

It is natural to take the decision $\theta_{(1)}$ corresponding to $W_{(1)}$, the minimum observed value of the W_i, as the best available of those points searched. Note that, because

$$W_{(1)} = \mu + X_{(1)} + \overline{\eta} + \zeta_{(1)} \tag{1.6}$$

involves a random error $\zeta_{(1)}$, it may be that $X_{(1)}$, the *actual performance achieved* corresponding to $W_{(1)}$ is not the best amongst the decisions examined. As $X_{(1)}$ is never directly observable it is therefore of particular interest to estimate its distribution. One of our objectives is to show how this can be done. Moreover it is of particular interest to see if this can be done sufficiently quickly so that it can be obtained in time-critical decision taking. In the next section we consider a statistical model that allows us to do this.

1.3 The Full Normal Model

1.3.1 RSO When Search Points Have High Dimension

Under the classical assumption that $X(\theta)$ is a quadratic function of θ near $\theta_{\min}$ it is known, see Chia and Glynn [7], Cheng [6], that $W_{(1)}$ has minimum variance when

$$m \sim rc^{d/(d+4)}, n \sim r^{-1}c^{4/(d+4)} \tag{1.7}$$

as $c \to \infty$, with r an arbitrary but fixed positive constant.

An immediate consequence of this result is that as $d \to \infty$, less and less effort is spent making runs at individual search points θ_i, and correspondingly more effort on increasing the number of search points m. If we take $r = 1$ it is clear therefore that for large d we are better off not replicating runs at individual θ_i but should simply take $n = 1$. However some replication simplifies estimation of σ^2 by allowing calculation of this variance from the replicated observations at each given θ_i.

Once the observations (1.4) are obtained, our approach is to fit a statistical model to them.

To specify a statistical model for the observations (1.4) we note that W_i is simply the sum three terms: $(\mu + \overline{\eta})$ which is effectively a constant, X_i and ζ_i. Thus all we need to do is specify $F_X(\cdot)$ the distribution of X and $F_\zeta(\cdot)$ the distribution of ζ. The distribution of W is then the convolution of these two distributions plus the constant. For the situation where d is large we consider the case where we do not have to specify a definite value for d but can assume that a central limit theorem applies to the distribution of X so that it is asymptotically normally distributed. Moreover we shall only consider the situation where the errors are normally distributed. The distribution of W is then also normally distributed. Cheng [6] has discussed conditions under which this assumption of normality of W might be valid when $d \to \infty$, and we shall assume that this is the case here, analysing the behaviour of W under the assumption that the distribution of X_i is normal, i.e.

$$X_i \sim N\left(0, \omega^2\right), \tag{1.8}$$

where ω is unknown and has to be estimated.

Our statistical model of the observations (1.3) or (1.4) is completed by specifying the distribution of ε_{ij}, the random simulation induced error arising from the within-run stochastic variation. We shall simply assume that this is also normal, i.e.

$$\varepsilon \sim N\left(0, \sigma^2\right) \tag{1.9}$$

where σ is unknown but constant.

In summary, for the rest of the paper we make the following assumption.

Assumption A
(i) The RSO is for a problem where the dimension of each of the search points θ_i is large.
(ii) The *observed* performance measures take the form

$$Y_{ij} = \mu + X_i + \eta_j + \varepsilon_{ij}, \quad i = 1, 2, \ldots, m; j = 1, 2, \ldots, n. \tag{1.10}$$

with $X_i \sim N\left(0, \omega^2\right)$ and $\varepsilon_{ij} \sim N\left(0, \sigma^2\right)$ mutually independent so that (conditional on $\overline{\eta}$) W_i as defined in (1.4) takes the form

$$W_i = \mu + \overline{\eta} + X_i + \zeta_i \sim N\left(\mu + \overline{\eta},\ \psi^2\right) \tag{1.11}$$

where

$$\psi^2 = \omega^2 + n^{-1}\sigma^2. \tag{1.12}$$

It might appear strange that this Assumption does not involve δ, the minimum of $J(\theta)$ as given in (1.1). But this arises only in the limit as $d \rightarrow \infty$. A practical interpretation is that, as $d \rightarrow \infty$, the X_i, in tending to normality, have a lower limit, i.e. δ, that is increasingly unstable and unreliable to estimate. We are therefore better off in using (1.8) for the distribution of X_i, and rather than trying to estimate δ we should estimate a low quantile of (1.8) instead. We will consider adopting this approach later where we estimate

$$\delta_q = \mu + z_q\omega, \tag{1.13}$$

where z_q is the qth quantile of the standard normal distribution, with $q = 0.05$ say. Thus δ_q in (1.13) is estimated simply by estimating μ and ω.

1.3.2 *Estimating $X_{(1)}$*

As already discussed, the quantity of most interest in RSO is $X_{(1)}$, the unobserved actual performance achieved when $W_{(1)}$, as given in (1.6) is selected as being the best search point. The next best thing to obtaining $X_{(1)}$ itself is to estimate its distribution.

Under Assumption A, when X_i and ζ_i are both normally distributed and independent, we can calculate $F_{X_{(1)}}(\cdot)$ as follows.

As μ is a constant in (1.10) and $\overline{\eta}$ is effectively so, we need only focus on $Z_i = X_i + \zeta_i$ the random part of W_i, and consider the probability that $Z_{(1)}$ the smallest Z_i will occur at each given i and the way that this will occur. Thus suppose that $X_{(1)} = X_i$, for a given i. An elementary conditional argument shows that

$$\Pr\left(X_{(1)} = X_i \text{ and } X_i > x\right) = \int_{-\infty}^{\infty}\left\{\int_{-\infty}^{z-x} f_X(z-u)\, f_\zeta(u)[1-F_Z(z)]^{m-1} du\right\} dz.$$

Hence, as any of the i are equally likely to be selected, we have

$$\begin{aligned}\Pr\left(X_{(1)} < x\right) &= F_{X_{(1)}}(x) \\ &= 1 - m\int_{-\infty}^{\infty}\left\{\int_{-\infty}^{z-x} f_X(z-u)\, f_\zeta(u)[1-F_Z(z)]^{m-1} du\right\} dz,\end{aligned} \tag{1.14}$$

and

$$f_{X_{(1)}}(x) = m\int_{-\infty}^{\infty} f_X(x) f_\zeta(z-x)\,[1-F_Z(z)]^{m-1} dz. \tag{1.15}$$

Under Assumption A the distributions used in (1.14) and (1.15) are all normal, depending only on the variance parameters ω and $\sigma/\sqrt{n}$. Once they have been estimated, estimates of the CDF and PDF of $X_{(1)}$ can be calculated from (1.14) and (1.15) by numerical quadrature. In the next section we discuss how to estimate the parameters μ, ω and σ under Assumption A.

1.4 Fitting the Full Normal Model

1.4.1 Estimating μ, ω^2 and σ^2

We first consider a basic procedure for estimating the parameters. We suppose that the RSO observations take the form (1.3). We write Y_{ij} and X_i in lower case as a reminder that in the actual observations they are variate values.

We can estimate the x_i and η_j as fixed effects by minimizing the sum of squares

$$S = \sum_{i=1}^{m}\sum_{j=1}^{n}\left(y_{ij} - \mu - x_i - \eta_j\right)^2 \tag{1.16}$$

subject to

$$\sum_{i=1}^{m} x_i = \sum_{j=1}^{n} \eta_j = 0. \tag{1.17}$$

This gives the estimates

$$\widehat{\mu} = (nm)^{-1} \sum_{i=1}^{m} \sum_{j=1}^{n} y_{ij}, \tag{1.18}$$

$$\widehat{x}_i = n^{-1} \sum_{j=1}^{n} y_{ij} - \widehat{\mu}, \;\; i = 1, 2, \ldots, m, \tag{1.19}$$

$$\widehat{\eta}_j = m^{-1} \sum_{i=1}^{m} y_{ij} - \widehat{\mu}, \;\; j = 1, 2, \ldots, n. \tag{1.20}$$

The estimate for $Var\,[X_i] = \omega^2$ is then:

$$\widehat{\omega}^2 = m^{-1} \sum_{i=1}^{m} \widehat{x}_i^2, \tag{1.21}$$

and estimate of the variance of $Var\left[\varepsilon_{ij}\right] = \sigma^2$ is

$$\widehat{\sigma}^2 = (nm)^{-1} \sum_{i=1}^{m} \sum_{j=1}^{n} \left(y_{ij} - \widehat{\mu} - \widehat{x}_i - \widehat{\eta}_j\right)^2. \tag{1.22}$$

1.4.2 A Practical RSO Procedure

The basic RSO procedure with observations taking the form (1.4) is not very satisfactory as we want to have n as small as possible, i.e. to have $n = 1$. However we cannot then estimate σ and consequently will not be able to estimate the distribution of $X_{(1)}$ from (1.14) or (1.15). Our suggested practical procedure is to carry out the RSO in two steps.

Step 1: The purpose of this step is to obtain an estimate of σ^2. For a selected number, say $m = m_1$ of initial search points, carry out RSO with $n > 1$, say $n = n_1 = 5$. The parameter σ is then estimated from (1.22).

Step 2: Carry out the RSO proper, using m_2 search points, but now with $n = n_2 = 1$. The parameter ω is then estimated from Eqs. (1.18)–(1.21), with $m = m_2$ and $n = 1$.

1.5 A Fire Service Example

This example is taken from Cheng [3]. To save the reader having to access that paper for details, we summarize its main features here. The example is drawn from a very specific genuine application based on work done for the fire service emergency cover (FSEC) Section of UK Government Department of Communities and Local Government (DCLG).

1.5.1 Fire Service Emergency Cover

Regional Fire Brigades in the UK possess a very sophisticated tool for gathering and analysing incident data in a very comprehensive way. This information is used for planning and to provide operational statistics to the UK Government. It is realised by brigade management that the data could be used to inform day to day management decisions.

The specific question of interest was whether it would be possible to develop a simulation model that would run sufficiently fast to be used to evaluate risk in real time. Such a model might then be deployed as an operational tool to provide real-time advice to brigade officers in responding to actual incidents.

The speed at which such a model can be run is a determining factor of its practicality. In our case the discrete event simulation (DES) model, which was a very detailed one, was able to simulate a year's operation in about 3 s.

1.5.2 The 'Cover-Moves' Problem

An operational problem of particular interest is the *Cover-Moves Problem.* This occurs when a fire brigade responds to a large incident (one that needs a large, say 8 or more, number of fire appliances to attend). The incident controller then usually repositions a small number of vehicles not involved in the large incident in what are called *cover-moves*, to try to minimize risk in the remainder of the region. Here risk can be clearly defined. We shall take as our performance measure the expected fatality rate (as measured by the expected number of fatalities over a given period of time, under the conditions of the large incident). For simplicity in what follows, we refer to this as the *(observed) fatality count*.

The choice of a worthwhile cover-move combination (CMC) is an example of a problem in combinatorial optimization. It is not usually possible, certainly in real time, to identify the best solution. The real question is whether a worthwhile operational solution can be found.

We consider the kind of cover-moves solution achievable. In one example of a typical large incident, consideration was given to selecting 3 vehicles for cover-moves out of 16 available vehicles located in 11 stations. The 3 vehicles were to be sent to 3 out of the 6 stations that had supplied vehicles to attend the large incident. A simple combinatorial calculation shows that there are 25,800 distinct CMCs possible. In fact, the majority of these could be ruled out on operational grounds so that only 230 CMCs turned out in this instance to need serious consideration.

The strict (policy driven) operating requirement for the cover-moves problem is that a solution has to be found within *one minute* of the notification of occurrence of a large incident.

In our example, if simulations of a year's operation were used, then one could only make 20 runs in the one minute allowed. However if, say, each run simulated only two months' operation, then about 120 runs of the simulation model could be made. As the example is for discussion purposes only, we actually carried out simulation runs for all 230 CMCs each of 2 months' operation. This provides a benchmark to gauge how well our proposed real-time method would have worked out in this particular example. Figure 1.1 gives the observed fatality rates (i.e. the Y_i) for the 230 CMCs.

A run carried out for the situation when no large incident has occurred gave a fatalities count of 2.108, well below all the cases where the large incident has occurred, even with cover moves. A run where the large incident has occurred but no cover moves are made gave a fatality count of 2.278 which is lower than many of the fatality counts where a CMC was deployed. This shows that it is very possible for a CMC to be counter-productive.

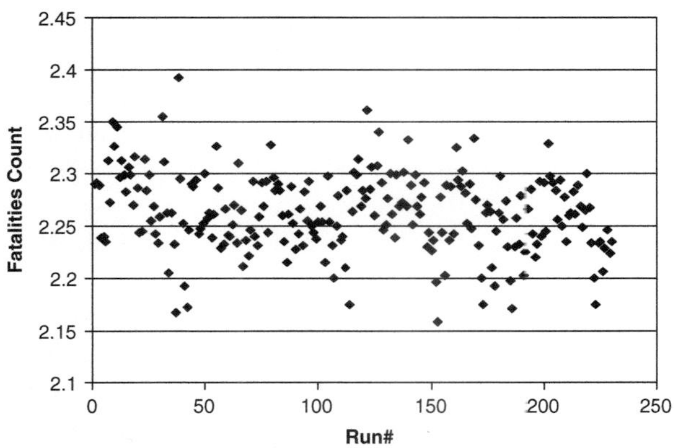

Fig. 1.1 Fatality count by run number for 230 CMCs

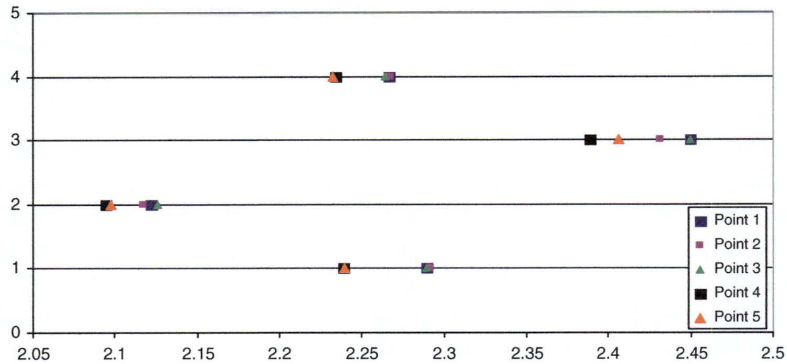

Fig. 1.2 Fatality counts obtained in the 20 simulation runs of Step 1 of the suggested RSO process

1.5.3 Real-Time Analysis of the Cover Moves Problem

We apply the method set out in Sect. 1.4.2 to analyse the cover moves problem.

In Step 1 of the RSO process we took $m_1 = 5$ and $n = 4$. Figure 1.2 shows the 20 observed values with the horizontal scale corresponding to the observed fatality counts. The five observations of each replicate are on the same horizontal line, with one line for each replicate. It will be seen that there is some significant variation in horizontal position of each group—this is due to the variation of η_j in (1.10), but that within each group the ranked order of the points remains very similar—thus the ranking is determined largely by X_i in (1.10), with the effect of ε_{ij} being much smaller in comparison.

These observations were used to estimate σ from Eq. (1.22) giving

$$\widehat{\sigma} = 0.00622.$$

For Step 2 of the RSO process we set $m_2 = 100$, $n = 1$. These observations correspond to the first 100 values depicted in Fig. 1.1. The lowest value is in this set is 2.168, the 37th value. Note that the first 100 observations happen not to be a particular good set of values compared with later CMCs, but of course in the time-critical situation where only 100 observations are made, we would not know this. Fitting the RSO model to these 100 observations gave the estimates

$$\widehat{\mu} = 2.267, \quad \widehat{\omega} = 0.0372.$$

Using these values allows us to calculate the distribution of $X_{(1)}$ from (1.14) or (1.15). Note that we are only using the Step 2 observations so that $Var\,[\zeta_i] = \sigma^2/n = \sigma^2$ in this case as $n = 1$. We have calculated the fitted PDF numerically from (1.15) using simple quadrature by Simpson's Rule with appropriately selected ranges of integration over which the integrand is not negligible. Equation (1.15) only shows how the distribution of $X_{(1)}$ depends on the X_i and ζ_i. These both have zero

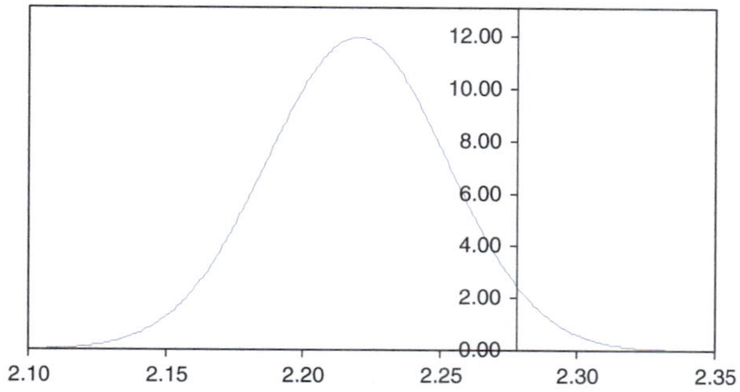

Fig. 1.3 Estimated distribution of $X_{(1)}$ the expected fatality count given by the cover move combination found by RSO under the one minute constraint within which the decision has to be made. The point where the y axis crosses the x-axis corresponds to the fatality count where the large incident has occurred, but no cover moves are deployed

Fig. 1.4 The EDF of the $m_2 = 100$ observations of Step 2 of the suggest RSO process, and the CDF of the fitted distribution. The value where the x-axis is crossed by the y axis has been set so that it corresponds to the fatality count where the large incident has occurred, but no cover moves are deployed

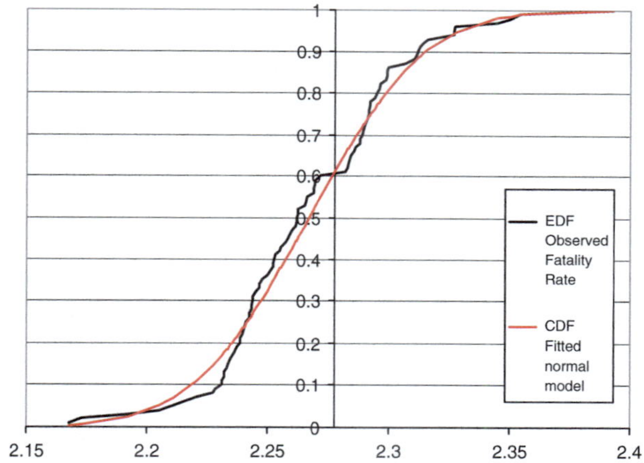

expectations. We therefore need to add the overall mean $\widehat{\mu} = 2.267$ to the argument of the PDF if this is to be the fatality rate. Figure 1.3 shows the behaviour of the density for the case $m_2 = 100$, corresponding to number of observations used in the Step 2 of the RSO process. The position where the depicted ordinate axis crosses the horizontal fatality count axis has been placed at $x = 2.278$, the value of the fatality count when cover moves are not deployed following despatch of appliances to the large incident. This thus corresponds to the breakeven fatality count with $X_{(1)}$ having to be less than this value to be effective. As one would wish, the bulk of the probability distribution of $X_{(1)}$ is significantly to the left of this value. However the small probability to the right of $x = 2.278$ shows that there is still a noticeable probability that the best value estimated by the RSO is less than effective.

Figure 1.4, shows the EDF of observed fatalities in the $m_2 = 100$ observations of Step 2 of the suggest RSO process together with the CDF of the fitted distribution. This latter is as given by Eqs. (1.11) and (1.12) with $\widehat{\mu} = 2.267$, $\widehat{\omega} = 0.0372$ and

$\widehat{\sigma} = 0.00622$. It has to be admitted that though the general fit is not unreasonable, the fit is poorest in the left hand tail and this is likely to have the most influence on the estimated distribution of $X_{(1)}$. However it seems likely that this lack of fit will not have much influence in estimating the probability that the chosen cover move will have *some* beneficial effect. This is clearly governed by those search points, for which there is some beneficial effect. As Fig. 1.4 shows, these make up almost exactly 60 % of the search points. The fitted CDF matches this proportion rather accurately at this x-value. We argue therefore that, whatever the true shape of the PDF of $X_{(1)}$, the value of the area under the PDF to the left of $x = 2.278$ in Fig. 1.4 will be close to that under the true PDF to the left of $x = 2.278$.

In the remainder of the chapter we consider the case where only a partial normal model can be used for the distribution of X.

1.6 The Partial Normal Model

We now consider the situation where we are able to approximate the distribution of X_i by the normal model, but only in its left tail. For simplicity we consider only the case where common random numbers are not used and all the runs in (1.3) are independent, so that

$$Y_{ij} = X_i + \varepsilon_{ij}, \quad i = 1, 2, \ldots, m; \; j = 1, 2, \ldots, n. \tag{1.23}$$

with the term η_j no longer needed. In (1.23) we have also changed the definition of X_i slightly so that the quantity μ appearing in (1.3) is now the mean of X, i.e. $E(X) = \mu$. The observed averaged observations are

$$W_i = n^{-1}\sum_{j=1}^{n} Y_{ij} = X_i + n^{-1}\sum_{j=1}^{n} \varepsilon_{ij} = X_i + \zeta_i, \quad i = 1, 2, \ldots, m. \tag{1.24}$$

We make the following assumption.

Assumption B
Let $W_1 < W_2 < \ldots W_m$ be the observed averaged observations given in (1.24), only now taken in ranked order. Given m, we assume ρ can be found with $0 < \rho < 1$ for which each of the averaged observations in the subsample

$$W_1 < W_2 < \ldots W_\nu \tag{1.25}$$

where

$$\nu = \lfloor m\rho \rfloor \tag{1.26}$$

takes the form

$$W_i = X_i + \zeta_i \tag{1.27}$$

with $X_i \sim N\left(\mu, \omega^2\right)$ and $\zeta_i \sim N\left(0, \sigma^2/n\right)$ and where they are mutually independent so that

$$W_i \sim N\left(\mu, \psi^2\right) \tag{1.28}$$

where, as in (1.12), $\psi^2 = \omega^2 + n^{-1}\sigma^2$.

In the next two section we show how to estimate the parameters μ, ω and σ under Assumption B.

1.6.1 Estimation of σ, μ and ω in the Partial Normal Model

We consider estimation of the parameters μ, ω and σ of the partial normal model given in Assumption B.

It is easiest to estimate σ first separately from μ and ω. As observations are replicated at each search point, an easy immediate, quite efficient, estimate of σ^2 is obtainable using

$$\widehat{\sigma}^2 = m^{-1}\sum_{i=1}^{m}(n-1)^{-1}\sum_{j=1}^{n}\left(X_{ij} - \overline{X}_i\right)^2 \tag{1.29}$$

where

$$\overline{X}_i = n^{-1}\sum_{j=1}^{n} X_{ij}.$$

Assuming that $\widehat{\sigma}$ is as given in (1.29) and using Assumption B, we shall apply the method of maximum likelihood to a *subsample* to estimate the other two parameters μ and ω. This type of method is used in estimating the value at risk of a financial portfolio (see [8], for example). From now on we shall assume that the W sample has been ordered so that $W_1 < W_2 < \cdots < W_m$ and set $\nu = \lfloor m\rho \rfloor$ as in (1.26). Clearly, as $m \to \infty$, W_ν tends in probability to the ρth quantile of the distribution (1.28). Thus we have to order $m^{-1/2}$, when m is large, that

$$\Phi\left(\left(W_\nu - \mu\right)/\psi\right) = \rho,$$

i.e.

$$\mu = W_\nu - z_\rho \psi \tag{1.30}$$

in probability, where z_ρ is the ρth quantile of the standard normal distribution and $\psi = \sqrt{\omega^2 + n^{-1}\widehat{\sigma}^2}$. Using this condition the loglikelihood is easily shown to be:

$$L\left(\mu, \omega \middle| \widehat{\sigma}\right) = -\frac{\nu}{2}\log\left(2\pi\right) - \nu\log\left(\psi\right) - \frac{1}{2\psi^2}\sum_{i=1}^{\nu}\left(W_i - W_\nu - \psi z_\rho\right)^2, \quad \psi \geq \widehat{\sigma}. \tag{1.31}$$

We can obtain the maximum likelihood (ML) estimate of ψ explicitly in this case:

$$\widehat{\psi} = \max\left\{ 2^{-1}\left(W_\nu - \overline{W}\right)\left\{\left[z_\rho^2 + 4\left(1 + s_W^2/\left(W_\nu - \overline{W}\right)^2\right)\right]^{1/2} - z_\rho\right\}, n^{-1/2}\widehat{\sigma}\right\}, \tag{1.32}$$

with the ML estimate of μ given by

$$\widehat{\mu} = W_\nu - z_p\widehat{\psi}. \tag{1.33}$$

The distribution of X thus has estimated CDF:

$$F_X\left(x \middle| \widehat{\mu}, \widehat{\omega}\right) = \Phi\left[\left(x - W_\nu + z_\rho\widehat{\psi}\right)/\widehat{\omega}\right], \tag{1.34}$$

where $\widehat{\omega} = \sqrt{\left(\widehat{\psi}^2 - n^{-1}\widehat{\sigma}^2\right)}$ provided $\hat{\psi} > \hat{\sigma}$. The case $\widehat{\psi} \leq n^{-1/2}\widehat{\sigma}$ is an indication that the variance of the error term (1.5) is so large that the effect of the variance of the performance measure is lost. In this case the results of the entire search are probably suspect and cannot be relied on.

There is an issue concerning the choice of the value of ρ. Making it too large might result in a poor fit because normality of the X_i cannot be guaranteed over the entire range of its distribution, but too small a choice would result in unnecessary loss of estimator efficiency and accuracy. We dealt with this simply by fitting the model over a range of ρ values, $\rho = 0.1, 0.2, \ldots, 0.9$ in our case, and then selecting a value where the estimates were reasonably stable.

1.6.2 Confidence Intervals for Quantities of Interest

In the numerical example to be presented in Sect. 1.7 we examine the distributional properties of three quantities of particular interest. The first two are:

(i) $\widehat{\delta}_q = \widehat{\mu} + z_q\widehat{\omega}$, the estimate of δ_q given in (1.13).
(ii) W_1, the smallest observed average performance measure appearing in (1.25).

We shall assess the effectiveness of $\widehat{\delta}_q$ and W_1 as estimators of δ_q and δ by examining their distributional properties using the *parametric bootstrap*. The method is described for example by Cheng [9]. The underlying idea is that if the assumptions concerning the distributions of X_i and ε_{ij} in the original observations (1.23) are correct then they will be well approximated by $F_X\left(\cdot\middle|\widehat{\mu},\widehat{\omega}\right)$ and $N\left(0,\widehat{\sigma}^2\right)$ respectively.

Here we have to make an approximation by using the full normal distribution $N\left(\widehat{\mu},\widehat{\omega}^2\right)$ to represent $F_X\left(\cdot\middle|\widehat{\mu},\widehat{\omega}\right)$ in the parametric bootstrapping. Strictly we need to rigorously justify this by showing that this will provide a reasonable approximation of the distributional behaviour of the bootstrapped version of the subsamples (1.25). This is yet to be established, but we argue that this will be the case when σ is small compared with ω as, in the limit, the sampled values of the X_i's appearing in (1.25) will be drawn from the normal part of the X distribution, so that the bootstrap subsamples will have the right distributional properties. We can therefore use these estimated normal distributions to carry out the bootstrap sampling to generate B parametric bootstrap (BS) replicates

$$\left\{Y_{ij}^*(k) = X_i^*(k) + \varepsilon_{ij}^*(k),\ i = 1,2,\ldots,m,\ j = 1,2..,n\right\},\ \ k = 1,2,\ldots,B \tag{1.35}$$

with $X_i^*(k) \sim N\left(\widehat{\mu},\widehat{\omega}^2\right)$ and $\varepsilon_{ij}^*(k) \sim N\left(0,\widehat{\sigma}^2\right)$, where an asterisk denotes a bootstrapped quantity. Each of the B BS replicates in (1.35) will, at least approximately, have subsamples corresponding to (1.25) with matching distributional properties. Thus t, where $t = \widehat{\delta}_q$ or $t = W_1$, which were calculated from the original observations (1.23) can also be calculated from each bootstrap replicate in (1.35), giving a sample of B bootstrap values of t: $\{t^*(k),\ \ k = 1,2,\ldots,B\}$. Under fairly general smoothness conditions, see Bickel and Freedman [10], the empirical distribution function (EDF) formed from this BS sample is a consistent estimate of the CDF of t. We can therefore use the BS sample to construct a CI for the unknown true δ_q or δ value being estimated.

In the numerical examples described in the next section the $\{t^*(k), k{=}1,2,\ldots,B\}$ sample is both skewed and biased. We used the following CI based on the conventional normal approximation CI as described by Davison and Hinkley [11, Section 5.2.1], but modified in a simple way to allow for this asymmetry in the $t^*(k)$ sample. Let $\{t^*(k), k = 1,2,\ldots,B\}$ represent the BS sample and let $\bar{t}^*$ be the BS sample mean obtained from the BS sample. Now assume that the sample is ordered and define B_1 as the subscript for which $t^*(k) \le \bar{t}^*$ for $k = 1,2,\ldots,B_1$ and $\bar{t}^* < t^*(k)$, for $k = B_1, B_1+1,\ldots,B$. Let

$$s_1^2 = \sum_{i=1}^{B_1}\left(t^*(k) - \bar{t}^*\right)^2/\left(B_1 - 1\right),\ \ s_2^2 = \sum_{i=B_1+1}^{B}\left(t^*(k) - \bar{t}^*\right)^2/\left(B - B_1 - 1\right).$$

The suggested 100 $(1 - p)$ % CI then has lower and upper limits

$$\left(t^{*L}(p),\ t^{*U}(p)\right) = \overline{t}^{*} \pm z_{p/2}s, \tag{1.36}$$

where $z_{p/2}$ is the upper $p/2$ quantile of the $N(0, 1)$ distribution and s is the larger of s_1 and s_2.

We consider one other quantity of particular practical interest:

(iii) $X_{(1)}$, the performance measure actually achieved when the search point corresponding to W_1 is selected as being the best. We write this as

$$W_1 = X_{(1)} + \zeta_1. \tag{1.37}$$

We have used a bracketed subscript in $X_{(1)}$ as a reminder that the actual performance measure corresponding to W_1 may not be the lowest actual performance measure that has been obtained amongst all the search points examined in the RSO.

The quantity $X_{(1)}$ is not observable in a real RSO. It can be estimated from the model but this is quite complicated. Instead we estimated it using the BS sample mean

$$\overline{X}^{*}_{(1)} = B^{-1}\sum_{k=1}^{B} X^{*}_{(1)}(k). \tag{1.38}$$

We can in this case also directly calculate a CI of the form (1.36), but with t^* now representing $X^{*}_{(1)}$, in exactly the same way as described for the cases $t^* = \widehat{\delta}^{*}$ and $t^* = W_1^*$. This is possible even in a real RSO where $X_{(1)}$ is not known, as the BS process generates all the individual $X_i^*(k)$ and $\varepsilon_{ij}^*(k)$ in (1.35) which are therefore all known.

The interesting issue arises here as to what is the unknown quantity that the interval (1.36) is the CI *for*, when $t^* = X^{*}_{(1)}$. It can of course be regarded as a CI for $E(X_{(1)})$, but it would be much more interesting to regard it, unconventionally, as a CI for the actual unknown $X_{(1)}$. the quantity of real interest, *even though this is random*. Though we do not give a justification here in detail it turns out that this is reasonable when the distribution of the BS observations in (1.35) tend to those of the original observations. We find that under suitable regularity conditions

$$\Pr\left(s\left(p,\widehat{\phi}_c\right) \le X_{(1)} \le t\left(p,\widehat{\phi}_c\right)\right) \to 1 - p \text{ with probability 1 as } c \to \infty, \tag{1.39}$$

where $\widehat{\phi}_c = (\widehat{\mu}_c, \widehat{\omega}_c, \widehat{\sigma}_c)$ are the estimates obtained from a RSO using c observations, and $s(p, \varphi)$ satisfies $F_{X_{(1)}}\left(s(p,\varphi)\,\middle|\,\varphi\right) = p/2$ and $t(p, \varphi)$ satisfies $F_{X_{(1)}}\left(t(p,\varphi)\,\middle|\,\varphi\right) = (1 - p/2)$. These latter are estimated from the BS CI (1.36) for $X_{(1)}$. Inversion of (1.39) in the usual way then gives a CI for $X_{(1)}$.

1.6.3 Goodness of Fit Test

An obvious concern is whether the fitted distribution of X_i, is correct or not. The Anderson–Darling (AD) statistic, A^2, goodness of fit test with its critical values calculated by parametric resampling can be used for this as discussed by Cheng [9]. The only change needed is that the AD statistic has to be modified to allow it to be applied to the subsample (1.25). In analogy to the standard AD statistic (see [12]) we define this as

$$A^2 = \nu \int_0^p \frac{\left(\widehat{F}_W - \tilde{F}_W\right)^2}{\widehat{F}_W\left(\rho - \widehat{F}_W\right)} d\widehat{F}_W \tag{1.40}$$

where $\widehat{F}_W = F_W\left(\cdot \middle| \widehat{\mu}, \widehat{\omega}, \widehat{\sigma}\right)$ is the fitted distribution and $\tilde{F}_W$ is the empirical distribution function (EDF) of the subsample (1.25). Written out explicitly we find that (1.40) is equivalent to

$$A^2 = -\rho\left\{\nu - 1 + (\nu - 1)^{-1} \sum_{i=1}^{\nu-1} (2i - 1)\left[\log\left(\widehat{F}_i\right) + \log\left(\rho - \widehat{F}_i\right)\right]\right\}, \tag{1.41}$$

where $\widehat{F}_i = F_W\left(W_i \cdot \middle| \widehat{\mu}, \widehat{\omega}, \widehat{\sigma}\right)$. This form is easier to use for numerical calculations than (1.40). Note that the summation in (1.41) does not include $\widehat{F}_\nu$ as the condition (1.30) requires $\widehat{F}_\nu = \rho$.

1.7 A Combinatorial Optimization Problem

A situation where our partial normal model of Sect. 1.6 might be appropriate occurs in combinatorial optimization. In such problems the set of solutions is usually discrete but typically has very large cardinality. Thus it seems reasonable to assume that the distribution of the objective function values obtained in a random search of points drawn from the solution set can adequately be approximated by a continuous distribution. The dimensionality in combinatorial problems is not usually considered. We argue however that if the dimension can be defined at all, it will typically be large. These considerations suggest that our statistical model given in Assumption B might be appropriate in such problems. We demonstrate this in this section by applying the method of the previous section to a travelling salesman problem (TSP) containing a stochastic element.

Table 1.1 gives the x,y coordinates of nine randomly generated points in the unit square. We define a tour as a path that starts and ends at a given point, visiting each other point just once. The TSP problem is to find the tour with the shortest

Table 1.1 The x, y coordinates of the nine points of the travelling salesman problem of Sect. 1.4

x, y	x, y	x, y
0.685, 0.991	0.195, 0.462	0.656, 0.664
0.083, 0.964	0.540, 0.360	0.054, 0.831
0.287, 0.111	0.673, 0.600	0.095, 0.206

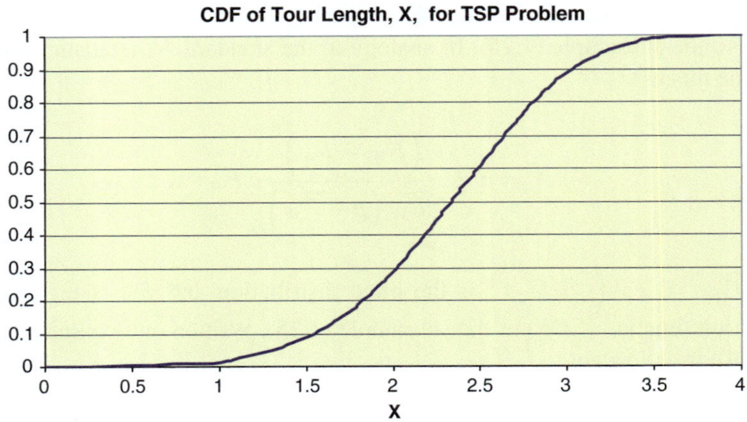

Fig. 1.5 The CDF of X_i the 20,160 tour lengths in the travelling salesman problem assuming all tours are equally likely to be selected. All tours are shifted by the amount of the shortest tour length, so that the shortest tour length corresponds to $\delta = 0$

total length, X, assuming the Euclidean distance is used for the distance from one point to the next on a tour. The length of each tour is the sum of nine distances, so that though a dimension is not usually associated with such a problem, it seems not unreasonable to regard each tour as associated with a point in 8-dimensional space, assuming the starting point to be fixed. The search space therefore comprises the $8!/2 = 20{,}160$ distinct points in this space corresponding to the distinct tours of the nine original points. The problem thus has a reasonable number of points in the search space, but sufficiently small to enable all tour lengths to be evaluated.

For simplicity of presentation we reduced all tour lengths by the amount of the shortest tour length, so that the minimum transformed tour length corresponds to $x_{\min} = 0$. If we select tours at random, each being equally likely, then we have the RSO problem where the distribution of the tour lengths has CDF depicted in Fig. 1.5. It will be seen that even in this relatively small example the left tail does have a shape one might associate with a normal tail, even if only superficially.

In our problem we assume tour lengths cannot be evaluated accurately and have added a standard normal error. Thus in our problem observed tour lengths are as in (1.3) with $\sigma = 1$.

Three metaexperiments were carried out, each with a different value of c: 100, 1,000 and 10,000, in order to encompass a representative range of c values that might be used in practice. Each metaexperiment was made up of 100 independent but otherwise identical experiments. In each experiment an RSO as described in

Sect. 1.3 was carried out using one of the c values. From (1.7) it is clear that with d large we should take m much larger n. We thus took $m = c/4$ and $n = 4$ to provide $3c/4$ degrees of freedom to estimate σ as described in Sect. 1.6.1.

The RSO produced a set of observations of the form (1.23), with, in each observation, X_i randomly selected from the 20,160 tours, all tours being equally likely to be selected, and with the ε_{ij} all standard normal variables. We then fitted the model of Assumption B. The three quantities of interest described in Sect. 1.6.2, namely. $\widehat{\delta}$, W_1 and $X_{(1)}$ were then calculated.

A set of parametric bootstrap versions of the RSO was then obtained, exactly as described in Sect. 1.6.2 to produce the three $100\,(1-p)\,\%$ CIs: $\left(\widehat{\delta}^{*L}(p),\ \widehat{\delta}^{*U}(p)\right)$, $(W_1^{*L}(p),\ W_1^{*U}(p))$, and $(X_{(1)}^{*L}(p),\ X_{(1)}^{*U}(p))$. These were used as CIs for $\delta_{0.05}$, so that $q = 0.05$ in Eq. (1.13), $x_{\min} = 0$ and $X_{(1)}$ respectively. We used 90 % CI's so that $p = 0.05$.

In a real RSO study none of these quantities are known. However in our experiments all are known, with $\gamma = 0$, $\delta_{0.05} = 1.303$, and with $X_{(1)}$ easily obtained from the observations (1.3). Thus in all three cases we can check if the CI covers the true value or not. The metaexperiment simply replicates the entire experiment just described a number of times, N say, to allow estimation of the true coverage by seeing how often each CI covers its true value.

We also carried out the goodness of fit test of Sect. 1.3.2 in each experiment of each metaexperiment, with the test returning the result either as 'reject' or 'not reject' the fitted statistical model, and with probability of not rejecting a correct model set at 90 %.

In all experiments the number of bootstraps, B was set at 100. The number of replicates, N, in a metaexperiment was also set at 100. Even though these are relatively low settings the results obtained provide a reasonably clear picture of the overall performance of the method over a range of conditions.

Table 1.2 summarizes the results obtained for the three metaexperiments carried out. The table gives, for each metaexperiment, ρ, the proportion of the main RSO sample used in fitting the model, and p_{GoF}, the proportion of the experiments for which the model was *not* rejected as a bad fit by the goodness of fit test. The rows M and SD are the sample mean and sample standard deviation of these samples, which therefore estimate the true behavior of each quantity. Each experiment also produced 100 BS samples of each quantity of interest giving a BS sample mean for each. The mean of these BS sample means, taken over the 100 experiments for each quantity, i.e. the grand mean for each quantity taken over all BS samples and all experiments in the metaexperiment, is given in row BM. The 100 BS values of each quantity in each experiment are also used to calculate a 90 % CI. The half-width was recorded in each experiment giving a sample of 100 half-widths. The sample mean of these half widths is recorded in the CI/2 row. The final row, PCI gives the proportion of the 100 experiments that the true value of the quantity of interest is covered by its CI.

The p_{GoF} values in Table 1.2 indicate that the model fit was satisfactory in the experiments.

Table 1.2 Results of 3 RSO metaexperiments for each of three values of c in the TSP example

	$c = 100$			$c = 1{,}000$			$c = 10{,}000$		
	m	ρ	p_{GoF}	m	ρ	p_{GoF}	m	ρ	p_{GoF}
	25	0.4	0.90	250	0.4	0.91	2,500	0.2	0.92
	$\widehat{\delta}_{0.05}$	W_1	$X_{(1)}$	$\widehat{\delta}_{0.05}$	W_1	$X_{(1)}$	$\widehat{\delta}_{0.05}$	W_1	$X_{(1)}$
M	1.140	0.726	1.286	1.330	0.178	1.022	1.318	−0.398	0.837
SD	0.422	0.396	0.417	0.120	0.306	0.404	0.036	0.251	0.388
BM	0.994	0.559	1.155	1.301	0.101	1.011	1.312	−0.446	0.660
CI/2	0.777	0.826	0.856	0.198	0.590	0.729	0.068	0.505	0.722
PCI	0.87	**0.61**	0.90	0.92	**0.99**	0.890	0.92	**0.74**	0.91

The table entries are as explained in the text

The sample means and sample standard deviations in rows M and SD behave generally as one would expect, showing improved accuracy as c increases.

Comparison of the bootstrap means of row BM with those in row M gives an indication of the general reliability of the bootstrap process. The BM values for $\widehat{\delta}$ and W_1 are not otherwise of particular interest, as the true values of these latter quantities, as given in the M row, are always observable in an RSO. The BM value, (1.38), for the quantity $X_{(1)}$ is however of more interest, as it is a point estimate of the true $X_{(1)}$ value, which will be unknown in a practical RSO. So it is of interest see how its mean value compares with its known true value in our experiments.

For each quantity of interest, the CI halfwidth in the CI/2 row is a direct measure of the spread in its BS sample. One would expect this to be roughly twice the sample SD value, which in most cases they are.

Perhaps of most interest in Table 1.2 are the PCI values, giving the observed coverages of the true values of each quantity. The nominal confidence level used in calculating the CIs is 90 %. The PCI values for $\widehat{\delta}_{0.05}$ and $X_{(1)}$ seem satisfactory. The PCI values for W_1 (highlighted in the table) show that W_1 is not a particular good estimator of the true minimum δ, over-estimating it when m is small and under-estimating it when m is large. This is what one might expect would happen. This indicates that our strategy of estimating $\delta_{0.05}$, a low quantile for $X_{(1)}$, is preferable.

1.8 Concluding Remarks

This paper has focused on the use of a full normal and a partial normal statistical model that allows a relatively easy analysis of the results obtained when one is attempting to improve system performance using random search optimization (RSO). RSO is very easy to implement, and indeed it is little different from the initial exploratory simulation runs carried out in developing a simulation model and in a preliminary evaluation of system performance.

If the simulation model runs fast enough and if it is to be used in improving system performance, then, in situations that involve real time adjustment of the system, the simulation model can be incorporated as a decision tool to assist in this process.

In the real time context, it may be unrealistic to expect true system optimization to be achievable. One should simply be satisfied with obtaining improved system performance. As a bottom line one would like some reassurance that the best way of running the real system found by RSO actually does lead to *some* improvement. This paper shows how to calculate a probability distribution which estimates how the unknown actual true system is likely to behave if it is run according to the best solution found by RSO. For the full normal model calculation can be done sufficiently fast to be incorporated in the real time decision making, so that an indication is available of how well the best solution found by RSO might actually perform.

It may be thought that the proposed normal models may be too narrowly applicable to be of general practical use. However as illustrated in the numerical examples, it may be sufficiently robust to at least give a clear indication of whether the RSO process has been worthwhile or not.

The use of bootstrapping enables the quality of estimates of quantities of interest to be gauged. In particular it enables estimation not only of $X_{(1)}$, the performance actually achieved when the search point corresponding to the best observed search point is selected as being the best, but also of quantile points, δ_q, as given in Eq. (1.13). The proportion of all possible solution points θ with objective function value less than (i.e. better than) δ_q is q. Thus comparison of the estimates of $X_{(1)}$ and δ_q gives an indication not only of the best value of the objective function obtained in the search, but also of the quality of this value.

References

1. Mousavi, A., Komashie, A., Tavakoli, S.: Simulation-based real-time performance monitoring (SIMMON): a platform for manufacturing and healthcare systems. In: Jain, S , Creasey, R.R., Himmelspach, J., White, K.P., Fu, M. (eds.) Proceedings of the 2011 Winter Simulation Conference, IEEE, Piscataway, pp. 600–611 (2011)
2. Huang, Y.-L., Suh, W., Alexopoulos, C., Fujimoto, R., Hunter, M.: Statistical issues in ad-hoc simulations. In: Jain, S., Creasey, R.R., Himmelspach, J., White, K.P., Fu, M. (eds.) Proceedings of the 2011 Winter Simulation Conference, IEEE, Piscataway, pp. 612–624 (2011)
3. Cheng, R.C.H.: Determining efficient simulation run lengths for real time decision making. In: Henderson, S.G., Biller, B., Hsieh, M.-H., Shortle, J., Tew, J.D., Barton, R.R. (eds.) Proceedings of the 2007 Winter Simulation Conference, IEEE, Piscataway, pp. 340–345 (2007)
4. Cheng, R.C.H.: Simulation assisted optimization by random search. In: Kotiadis, K., Currie, C.S.M., Robinson, S., Taylor, S.J.E. (eds.) Proceedings of the 2008 Operational Research Society Simulation Workshop (SW08), OR Society, pp. 79–85 (2008)

5. Cheng, R.C.H.: Random search in high dimensional stochastic optimization. In: Johansson, B., Jain, S., Montoya-Torres, J., Hugan, J., Yücesan, E. (eds.) Proceedings of the 2010 Winter Simulation Conference, IEEE, Piscataway, pp. 1012–1023 (2010)
6. Cheng, R.C.H.: Fitting statistical models of random search in simulation studies. ACM Trans. Model. Comput. Simul. **23**, 15 (2013)
7. Chia, Y.L., Glynn, P.W.: Optimal convergence rate for random search. In: Chen, C.-H., Henderson, S.G. (eds.) Proceedings of the 2007 INFORMS Simulation Society Workshop (2007)
8. Pickands, J.: Statistical inference using extreme order statistics. Ann. Stat. **3**, 119–131 (1975)
9. Cheng, R.C.H.: Validating and comparing simulation models using resampling. J. Simulat. **1**, 53–63 (2006)
10. Bickel, P.J., Freedman, D.A.: Some asymptotic theory for the bootstrap. Ann. Stat. **9**, 1196–1217 (1981)
11. Davison, A.C., Hinkley, D.V.: Bootstrap Methods and Their Application. Cambridge University Press, Cambridge (1997)
12. Anderson, T.W., Darling, D.A.: Asymptotic theory of certain 'goodness of fit' criteria based on stochastic processes. Ann. Math. Stat. **23**, 193–212 (1952)

Chapter 2
Metamodel-Based Robust Simulation-Optimization: An Overview

Gabriella Dellino, Jack P.C. Kleijnen, and Carlo Meloni

2.1 Introduction

The simulation-optimization process aims to identify the setting of input parameters leading to optimal system performance, evaluated through a simulation model of the system itself. The factors involved in the simulation model are often noisy and cannot be controlled or varied during the decision process, due to measurement errors or other implementation issues; moreover, some factors are determined by the environment, rather than by managers or decision makers. Therefore, the presumed optimal solution may turn out to be sub-optimal or even infeasible. Robust optimization tackles problems affected by uncertainty, providing solutions that are in some sense insensitive to perturbations in the model parameters.

G. Dellino (✉)
Istituto per le Applicazioni del Calcolo "Mauro Picone", CNR, Via Giovanni Amendola 122, 70126 - Bari, Italy
e-mail: g.dellino@ba.iac.cnr.it

J.P.C. Kleijnen
Department of Information Management/CentER, Tilburg School of Economics and Management, Tilburg University, Postbox 90153, 5000 LE Tilburg, The Netherlands
e-mail: kleijnen@uvt.nl

C. Meloni
Dipartimento di Ingegneria Elettrica e dell'Informazione, Politecnico di Bari, Via E. Orabona 4, 70125 Bari, Italy

Istituto per le Applicazioni del Calcolo "Mauro Picone", CNR, Via Giovanni Amendola 122, 70126 - Bari, Italy
e-mail: meloni@poliba.it

G. Dellino, C. Meloni (eds.), *Uncertainty Management in Simulation-Optimization of Complex Systems*, Operations Research/Computer Science Interfaces Series 59, DOI 10.1007/978-1-4899-7547-8_2

Several alternative methods have been proposed for achieving robustness in simulation-based optimization problems, adopting different experimental designs and/or metamodeling techniques. This chapter reviews the current state of the art on robust optimization approaches, focusing on simulated systems. First, we summarize—in Sect. 2.2—robust Mathematical Programming. Then, in Sect. 2.3, we discuss Taguchi's approach introduced in the 1970s and its extensions. Next, in Sect. 2.4, we consider methods to tackle robustness using metamodels, and Kriging in particular. The resulting methodology is illustrated in Sect. 2.5 through some variants of classic inventory models. Conclusions and future research directions are discussed in Sect. 2.6.

2.2 Robust Mathematical Programming Through Uncertainty Sets

The robust optimization methodology developed by [6] investigates different choices of uncertainty sets to model data uncertainty, in order to characterize the structure of the resulting robust counterparts of optimization problems. In particular, their research focuses on robust formulations for Linear Programming (LP), Mixed Integer Programming (MIP), Second Order Cone Programming (SOCP), and Semidefinite Programming (SDP) problems. For this family of problems a fundamental issue is related to the feasibility of the solutions with respect to the classical optima; in particular, the challenge is to guarantee that the constraints will be satisfied for any possible value of the parameters in a given uncertainty set. The computational complexity of the deterministic problem and its robust counterpart is also investigated, to ensure that the problem remains tractable.

Although this approach has a strong theoretical background, there are several practical problems to which it cannot be applied, for many reasons; see [11]. The main disadvantage is the need to model a real-world problem through a linear model with (at most) conic or quadratic constraints. Moreover, in order to satisfy all the assumptions under which the method is applicable, the approximate model might become very complex and difficult to manage. Finally, the methodology cannot be directly applied whenever the objective function is not defined through a mathematical expression but can only be evaluated through simulations.

Zhang [67] deals with some of the aforementioned cases, proposing a mathematical formulation extending Ben-Tal's approach to parameterized nonlinear programming, with both equality and inequality constraints; the inequality constraints are supposed to be strictly satisfiable and are referred to as *safety constraints*. Zhang points out that his approach is especially suitable for applications where meeting safety constraints is crucial. However, the formulation of the robust problem assumes that a reasonable estimate for the uncertain parameters is available, and the magnitude of the variations in the uncertain parameters is relatively small. He proved that his formulation reduces to Ben-Tal's formulation when the objective function and the inequality constraints are linear and there is no uncertainty in the equality constraints. Anyway, further research is needed to develop algorithms able to effectively solve the proposed formulation.

Mainly based on Ben-Tal's approach, Bertsimas proposes a formulation for stochastic and dynamic optimization problems using uncertainty sets, going beyond the stochastic programming approach which assumes full knowledge of the underlying probability distributions. Bertsimas and Sim [7] propose a robust optimization methodology—based on linear and mixed-integer programming—to find an optimal supply chain control strategy, assuming stochastic demand. Their approach incorporates demand randomness in a deterministic manner, without making any specific assumption on the demand distribution. First, a robust formulation is given for the simple uncapacitated single-station case; then, capacity constraints are introduced, both on the orders and on the inventory level; finally, the network case is considered. The numerical experiments showed that, if only the mean and the variance of the demand distribution are known, the robust policy often outperforms the nominal one, as well as those policies computed assuming full but erroneous knowledge of the demand distribution. The authors also prove that the nominal problem and its robust counterpart belong to the same complexity class, and that the robust formulation does not suffer from the curse of dimensionality. The method guarantees the robust solution to be feasible if less than a prespecified number of coefficients change; moreover, if the coefficient of variation affects a bigger number of factors, those authors provide a probabilistic guarantee that the solution will be feasible with high probability. The method has been applied by [8, 9].

In a recent paper, [10] propose an approach to solve robust optimization problems in which the objective function is not explicitly available, but is derived from simulation models. They implement an iterative local search method, moving along descent directions of the worst-case cost function. The first step of the proposed algorithm consists of exploring a (properly defined) neighborhood of the current point; then, a descent direction can be found by solving a SOCP problem. The robust local search is designed to terminate at a robust local minimum, which is a point where no improving directions are available for the algorithm.

2.3 Robust Optimization: Taguchi's Approach and Extensions

In the late 1970s, Genichi Taguchi, a Japanese textile engineer, introduced new ideas on quality improvement, resulting in an innovative parameter design approach for reducing variation in products and processes, see [61]. His methodology has been successfully applied in many important industries in the USA, such as Ford Motor Company and Xerox.

Taguchi identifies three stages in the design process: (1) *System Design* as a general approach to design a process that includes defining the system's objectives and goals; (2) *Parameter Design* which involves defining responses of interest and optimizing them w.r.t. their mean and variation; (3) *Tolerance Design* which deals with fine-tuning the variables that have been optimized in the previous stage by controlling the factors that affect them.

Notice that the last two stages may appear quite similar to each other, so it may be difficult to keep them distinct; see [11]. In fact, from a mathematical point of view, parameter and tolerance design differ only in the *granularity* by which design parameters are treated. On the other hand, from a practical point of view, it is important to distinguish between the two phases, because they can occur under very different constraints, e.g. design time versus operation time. Taguchi—focusing on Parameter Design—distinguishes between two different types of factors when designing a product or process:

- *control* or *decision* factors (which we denote by $d_j, j = 1, \ldots, n_d$) are under the control of the users; e.g., in inventory management, the order quantity may be controllable.
- *noise* or *environmental* factors (denoted by $e_k, k = 1, \ldots, n_e$) cannot be controlled while the process operates or the product is used; e.g. the demand rate in inventory problems.

Notice that, in practice, the controllability of a factor depends on the specific situation; e.g., in production or inventory management the decision makers may affect the demand rate through an advertising campaign.

Other authors distinguish between environmental uncertainty (e.g., demand uncertainty) and system uncertainty (e.g., yield uncertainty); see [46] and also [11]. Implementation errors may also be a source of uncertainty. These errors occur whenever recommended (optimal) values of control factors have to be realized in practice; see [60]. Continuous values are hard to realize in practice, because only limited accuracy is then possible; e.g., the optimal solution in the Economic Order Quantity model (EOQ) turns out to be the square root of some expression, but in practice only a discrete number of units could be ordered. Besides implementation errors, there are validation errors of the simulation model—compared with the real system—and the metamodel—compared with the simulation model; see [36].

Taguchi's basic idea in dealing with robust parameter design is to take account of the environmental (noise) factors in the experimental design and find the most insensitive, or robust, system configuration in the decision (controllable) factors with respect to the noise factors variation.

As far as the experimental strategy is concerned, Taguchi adopted crossed arrays, resulting from the product of two experimental designs; one design varies the decision factors **d** (obtaining the "inner array", as Taguchi calls it), and one design varies the environmental factors **e** (thus obtaining the "outer array"). Combining them together is equivalent to consider variations in the uncontrollable (environmental) factors at different locations in the space of the controllable factors. Taguchi further distinguishes between factors that have a *location* effect, changing the mean of the response or objective function, and factors that have a *dispersion* effect, since they affect the variance of the process. Therefore, in the optimization process, Taguchi takes into account the first two moments of the distribution of the objective function, and combines them using the signal-to-noise ratio (SNR). Taguchi suggests to consider three types of problems:

1. "Smaller the better": select the factor combination in the inner array that maximizes

$$SNR_S = -10 \log \sum_{i=1}^{n_0} \frac{w_i^2}{n_0} \tag{2.1}$$

where $w_i = w(\mathbf{d}, e_i)$ and n_0 is the number of runs in the outer array.
2. "Larger the better": select the inner array point that maximizes

$$SNR_L = -10 \log \frac{1}{n_0} \sum_{i=1}^{n_0} \frac{1}{w_i^2} \tag{2.2}$$

3. "Target is best". Here Taguchi proposes a two-step approach, suggesting two cases:

   (a) μ_w (mean of w) is not related to σ_w (standard deviation of w). In this case the steps are the following:

      i. Select some control factors that maximize

$$SNR_{T1} = -10 \log s^2 \tag{2.3}$$

      where s^2 is the sample variance of the outer array observations.
      ii. Select some other inner array factor (not varied before) to make

$$\overline{w} \approx \mathcal{T} \tag{2.4}$$

      where $\overline{w}$ is the average of the outer array observations and $\mathcal{T}$ is the target of the quality characteristic.

   (b) If σ_w is proportional to μ_w—a case likely to occur in practice—then

      i. Select some control factors to maximize

$$SNR_{T2} = -10 \log \frac{\overline{w}^2}{s^2} \tag{2.5}$$

      ii. Select some other control factors not varied before, to make

$$\overline{w} \approx \mathcal{T}.$$

      Because the standard deviation is assumed to be proportional to the mean, the controllable factors will change the mean but will not change the ratio $\overline{w}^2/s^2$ much.

2.3.1 Extensions to Taguchi's Methods

Some aspects of the Taguchian approach have been severely criticized; see [20, 47, 48]. The mostly debated issues were the following:

- A data set with no outer array variability and one with considerable outer array variability may result in the same SNR; therefore, SNR would be ineffective in Robust Parameter Design.
- No attention is paid to the computational costs required by the experimental design: in fact, using a crossed array design often requires a large number of runs, which can be prohibitive in some industrial processes.
- The method does not enable flexible modeling of the design variables, not taking into account the interactions either among decision factors or between decision and environmental factors. Standard ANOVA techniques can be used to identify the control factors that impact SNR [see 48, 53].
- Factors may have both location and dispersion effects, so the proposed two-step approach may be inadequate in practice. Moreover, the adoption of the SNR as performance characteristic appears to be too restrictive [51] and may confound the mean and variance contributions; keeping them separately, instead, can provide further insight into the process behavior.

Although based on Taguchi's view of modeling uncertainty in a design process, some authors [62] have suggested to directly model the response as a function of both decision and environmental factors, instead of using SNRs. Suppose we measure q performance indicators, $w_1, \ldots, w_q$; let $w_i(\mathbf{d}, \mathbf{e})$ denote the value of the ith performance indicator when control and noise factors assume values $(\mathbf{d}, \mathbf{e})$ and let $l[w_1(\mathbf{d}, \mathbf{e}), \ldots, w_q(\mathbf{d}, \mathbf{e})]$ denote the corresponding loss. A robust design approach will seek a combination of control factors that minimizes the expected loss, computed with respect to the random vector $\mathbf{e}$. If the distribution of $\mathbf{e}$ does not depend on $\mathbf{d}$, then the objective function is

$$L(\mathbf{d}) = \int l[w_1(\mathbf{d}, \mathbf{e}), \ldots, w_q(\mathbf{d}, \mathbf{e})]\, p(\mathbf{e})\, d\mathbf{e} \tag{2.6}$$

where $p(\mathbf{e})$ denotes the probability density function of $\mathbf{e}$. The question arises: how have statisticians sought to minimize (2.6)? A numerical optimizer would answer this question in the following manner:

1. A design is chosen that specifies the (d_j, e_j) at which the w_i have to be evaluated; this approach results in a single "combined" array, instead of inner and outer arrays.
2. The $w_i(d_j, e_j)$ are used to estimate cheap-to-compute surrogate models $\hat{y}_i$.
3. Optimization is carried out using the surrogate objective function

$$\hat{L}(\mathbf{d}) = \int l[\hat{y}_1(\mathbf{d}, \mathbf{e}), \ldots, \hat{y}_q(\mathbf{d}, \mathbf{e})]\, p(\mathbf{e})\, d\mathbf{e}. \tag{2.7}$$

A similar approach is suggested by [55], who proposes a robust methodology, starting from Taguchi's approach and combining it with metamodeling techniques. Focusing on discrete-event simulation models, she identifies some performance characteristic, denoted by $w(\mathbf{d})$, $\mathbf{d}$ being the vector of decision factors, and an associated target value $\mathcal{T}$. The goal would be to select the decision factors to keep the objective function on target, with zero variance. However, this would be an ideal situation—hard to realize in practice. Therefore, to find a trade-off between performance mean and variability, Sanchez proposes to use a quadratic loss function, defined as follows: assuming that no loss occurs when $w(\mathbf{d})$ achieves the target $\mathcal{T}$, the quadratic loss function can be written as

$$l(w(\mathbf{d})) = c[w(\mathbf{d}) - \mathcal{T}]^2 \tag{2.8}$$

where c is a scaling factor, accounting for possible units conversions. It follows from (2.8) that the expected loss associated with configuration $\mathbf{d}$ is

$$E[l(w(\mathbf{d}))] = c[\sigma^2 + (\mu - \mathcal{T})^2] \tag{2.9}$$

where μ and σ^2 denote the true mean and variance of the output function w.

As far as the robust design is concerned, Sanchez tries to characterize the system behavior as a function of the control factors only. First, an appropriate experimental design is planned, for both decision and environmental factors. Then, for every combination of decision factor configuration i and environmental factor configuration j, the sample average $\overline{w}_{ij}$ and sample variance s^2_{ij} are computed—after suitable truncation to remove initialization bias. Finally, summary measures across the environmental space for each decision factor configuration i are computed:

$$\overline{w}_{i\cdot} = \frac{1}{n_e} \sum_{j=1}^{n_e} \overline{w}_{ij} \tag{2.10}$$

$$\overline{V}_{i\cdot} = \frac{1}{n_e - 1} \sum_{j=1}^{n_e} (\overline{w}_{ij} - \overline{w}_{i\cdot})^2 + \frac{1}{n_e} \sum_{j=1}^{n_e} s^2_{ij} \tag{2.11}$$

where n_e is the number of combinations in the environmental design.

Two initial metamodels are then built, using regression polynomials: one for the performance mean, and one for the performance variability; for discrete-event simulation experiments, Sanchez recommends a design which allows for fitting at least a quadratic effect. Robust configurations are identified by combining information resulting from the mean and variance metamodels, using (2.9) where the true mean and variance are replaced by the estimate given in (2.10) and (2.11). If the configurations suggested by the robust design were not among those initially tested, further experimentation could be needed: in this case, however, computational time could be saved, by screening the decision factors involved in the experiment.

Al-Aomar [1] presents an iterative scheme to solve simulation-based optimization problems. His work considers a discrete-event simulation model; the (controllable) design parameters are $d_1, \ldots, d_n$, and its performances are evaluated through the metrics $w_1, \ldots, w_q$. Then, an overall utility function U is defined combining multiple performance measures into a single function. The general formulation of the system design problem can be defined as follows:

$$\begin{aligned} &\max\ U(w_1, \ldots, w_q) \\ &s.t.\ w_i = f_i(d_1, \ldots, d_n), \quad 1 \leq i \leq q \\ &d_j \in S, \quad 1 \leq j \leq n \end{aligned} \tag{2.12}$$

where S is the feasible space for the control variable $\mathbf{d}$. His methodology consists of four modules: (1) the Simulation Modeling (SM) module uses a discrete-event simulation model to evaluate the set of performance metrics w_i associated with each solution alternative $\mathbf{d}$, in terms of means and variances; (2) the Robustness Module (RM) transforms the mean and variance of each performance measure into a Signal-to-Noise Ratio—thus adopting a Taguchian approach; (3) the Entropy Method (EM) module builds the utility function U by linearly combining the performance criteria, through a proper choice of the weights, dynamically updated at each iteration; (4) the Genetic Algorithm (GA) module is utilized as a global optimizer, working on a set of possible solutions that are selected based on the overall utility function value at each point. A convergence test at the end of each step controls whether any stopping criterion is met (maximum number of generations reached or convergence rate achieved). For a detailed discussion we refer to [27].

Because of the criticism on SNRs, some authors like [48] suggest to build separate models for the mean and variance of the system performance, adopting the so-called Dual Response Surface approach. This methodology has some advantages:

- It provides an estimate of the mean and standard deviation at any location in the space of control design variables.
- Some insight can be gained regarding the roles of these variables in controlling process mean and variance.
- It could be easily integrated into process optimization based on a squared error loss criterion, $\hat{E}_{\mathbf{e}}(w - \mathcal{T})^2 = [\hat{E}_{\mathbf{e}}(w) - \mathcal{T}]^2 + \hat{\sigma}^2_{\mathbf{e}}(w)w$ or the maximization of an estimated quantile $\hat{E}_{\mathbf{e}}(w) - 2\hat{\sigma}_{\mathbf{e}}(w)$ in the Taguchian "larger the better" case, or the minimization of $\hat{E}_{\mathbf{e}}(w) + 2\hat{\sigma}_{\mathbf{e}}(w)$ in the Taguchian "smaller the better" case.
- It allows the use of constrained optimization; that is, choosing a target value of $\hat{\mu}_{\mathbf{e}}[w(\mathbf{d}, \mathbf{e})]$ or—better to say—a threshold T below which one cannot accept the solution. Therefore, the following problem has to be solved:

$$\min_{\mathbf{d}} \hat{\sigma}^2_{\mathbf{e}}[w(\mathbf{d}, \mathbf{e})] \quad s.t. \quad \hat{\mu}_{\mathbf{e}}[w(\mathbf{d}, \mathbf{e})] \leq T \tag{2.13}$$

Several values of T may be used to consider different user's alternatives.

The Dual Response Surface approach has been successfully applied to robust process optimization; see [20]. Quite often, in fact, the purpose is to reach a desired performance for the process that manufactures some products—e.g. by minimizing the cost of operation in a production process, or the variability of a quality characteristic, or by maximizing the throughput of the manufacturing process. Evidently, multiple—and sometimes conflicting—responses are usually considered in practical problems. However, due to noisy data and/or to uncertainty affecting some parameters of the model, achieving robust performances is of interest.

Miró-Quesada and del Castillo [45] point out that the classical Dual Response Surface approach takes into account only the uncertainty due to the noise factors; they identify an additional component due to the uncertainty in the parameter estimates. Therefore, they propose an extension of the Dual Response Surface approach, introducing the additional variance of the parameters estimates into an objective function that combines it with the noise factor variance. Optimizing such a function will achieve a process that is robust with respect to both noise factor variation and uncertainty in the parameter estimates. One such function is the variance of the predicted response, where the variance is now taken with respect to both the parameter estimates of the model and the noise factors.

Robustness is also a central issue in design optimization. Many engineering applications have to deal with the uncertainty which affects the components of the system under design; ignoring the source of uncertainty and assuming some parameters to be *exactly* known and constant might cause the designed system not to be adequate whenever the environmental setting changes.

Bates et al. [3] compare different methods to perform robust optimization, applying them to solve robust design optimization of a mechanical component: the objective is to achieve a given mean cycle time while minimizing the standard deviation of the cycle time. The authors discuss the following issues: the Taguchian approach, using a crossed-array design and maximizing the SNR; the Response Model analysis, involving both decision and environmental factors, and accounting for factor interactions; and the Dual Response Surface approach. They propose a framework called Stochastic Emulator Strategy, consisting of the following building blocks: (1) DoE, using an array that includes both design and noise factors; they prefer space-filling designs (such as LHS) or lattice designs rather than orthogonal arrays or fractional factorials, to achieve more uniform coverage of the input space. (2) Metamodel (or emulator, as they called it) fitting, to represent the relationship among all factors—disregarding whether they are decision or environmental factors—and the chosen response. (3) Metamodel prediction, to estimate the mechanical component cycle time for a given set of factor values and evaluate the effect of noise on the output by studying how it behaves when subjected to small changes in factor values. (4) Optimization process, minimizing the output variance with a target value for the mean cycle time.

Lee and Park [40] present a methodology—based on Kriging metamodels—to tackle robust optimization in deterministic simulation-based systems. They use simulated annealing to solve the optimization problem. The approach is basically the one proposed by Taguchi, employing mean and variance as statistics to study the insensitivity of the response to possible variations in the noise factors.

The use of Kriging as an approximation technique is justified because Kriging provides reliable approximation models of highly nonlinear functions, and this feature is even more useful in robust optimization than it is in classical optimization because in general the nonlinearity of the response variance could be higher than that of the mean. Kriging is also recommended by [32], who compare some metamodeling techniques and—based on the results of some tests performed on both mathematical functions and a more complex case study—they conclude that Kriging models provide higher accuracy than the other alternatives. However, [2] notice that regression modeling should not be quickly discarded for cases in which the number of runs is particularly low.

Lee and Park [40] aim at determining a design point **d** providing a target response value $\overline{\mu}_w$ with the smallest variation σ_w^2. Therefore they formulate the robust optimization problems as follows:

$$\min \quad \sigma_w^2 \tag{2.14}$$

$$s.t. \quad \mu_w \leq \overline{\mu}_w \tag{2.15}$$

Because the analytical computation of the mean and variance of a given response w is not always possible (too time expensive or too difficult), [40] approximate these two statistics by means of the first-order Taylor expansion:

$$\mu_w \approx w(\mathbf{d}, \mathbf{e})_{\bar{\mathbf{d}}, \bar{\mathbf{e}}} \tag{2.16}$$

$$\sigma_w \approx \sum_{i=1}^{n_d} \left(\frac{\partial w}{\partial d_i} \right)_{\bar{\mathbf{d}}}^2 \sigma_{d_i}^2 + \sum_{j=1}^{n_e} \left(\frac{\partial w}{\partial e_j} \right)_{\bar{\mathbf{e}}}^2 \sigma_{e_j}^2 \tag{2.17}$$

where $\bar{\mathbf{d}}$ and $\bar{\mathbf{e}}$ denote the mean vectors of the control and noise factors, and $\sigma_{d_i}^2$ and $\sigma_{e_j}^2$ represent the variance of the ith control variable and the jth noise variable. However, (2.16) and (2.17) are valid approximations only for monotonic functions, which is usually a property difficult to ascertain when working with black-box simulation models.

The following issues emerge from [40]:

- The authors fit one *single* metamodel over the control-by-noise factors space. They suggest this metamodel to be highly accurate, because it will be used to derive the approximation model for the variance.
- To derive a model for the mean of the response, they use the approximation provided by (2.16), applying it to the metamodel computed.
- To derive a model of the variance, they use Monte-Carlo simulations performed not on the simulation model but on the (inexpensive) metamodel obtained in the beginning.
- They point out that post-processing may be necessary because of the nonlinearity both of the mean response and (even more) of its variance, and the approximation

errors coming from fitting the metamodel of the variance based on the metamodel of the mean response function. The post-processing consists in solving the following optimization problem, restricting the search area to the neighborhood of the optimal solution found so far:

$$\min \quad \hat{\sigma}_w^2 = \sum_{i=1}^{n_d} \left(\frac{\partial \hat{y}}{\partial d_i} \right)^2 \sigma_{d_i}^2 + \sum_{j=1}^{n_e} \left(\frac{\partial \hat{y}}{\partial e_j} \right)^2 \sigma_{e_j}^2 , \tag{2.18}$$

$$s.t. \quad \hat{y}(\mathbf{d}, \mathbf{e})_{\bar{\mathbf{d}}, \bar{\mathbf{e}}} \leq \bar{\mu}_w \tag{2.19}$$

This post-processing would aim to further refine the robust optimum, but experimental results usually show rather small improvements.

- As a further research topic, they suggest to adopt two *distinct* metamodels, approximating the true response and the true variance. They suggest to adopt this approach for strongly nonlinear models, especially the variance model.

In our approach we keep the main Taguchian robustness concept that prescribes to optimize a specific performance measure, while minimizing its possible variations [22, 23]. However, instead of Taguchi's scalar loss function, we use Non-Linear Programming (see (2.20) below), in which one of these characteristics—namely, the mean of the primary simulation output $E(w)$—is the goal function to be minimized, while the other characteristics—namely, the standard deviation of the goal output s_w—must meet given constraints ([41] also minimize the mean while satisfying a constraint on the variance; they use a Bayesian approach):

$$\begin{aligned} &\min E(w) \\ &\text{s.t.} s_w \leq T . \end{aligned} \tag{2.20}$$

Because we assume costly simulations, we use a metamodel-assisted optimization; i.e., we replace $E(w)$ and s_w by their (Kriging) approximations. Next we change the threshold T in the constraint in (2.20), and estimate the Pareto-optimal efficiency frontier—briefly called the *Pareto frontier*—where we consider the mean and standard deviation as criteria between which finding a trade-off. This is a classical approach to solve optimization problems with multiple criteria; see [43]. For further discussion of robust optimization we also refer to [11, 31, 34, 51], and also the more recent [21, 24, 48, 64].

2.4 Robust Simulation-Optimization Using Kriging metamodels

To solve robust simulation-optimization problems, we propose the following two approaches—firstly presented in [23]—using Kriging metamodels:

1. Inspired by [22], we fit *two* Kriging metamodels; namely, one model for the mean and one for the standard deviation—both estimated from the *simulation*'s I/O data.
2. Inspired by [40], we fit a *single* Kriging metamodel to a relatively small number (say) n of combinations of the decision variables $\mathbf{d}$ and the environmental variables $\mathbf{e}$. Next we use this metamodel to compute the *Kriging predictions* for the simulation output w for $N \gg n$ combinations of $\mathbf{d}$ and $\mathbf{e}$ accounting for the distribution of $\mathbf{e}$.

In the first approach, which we refer to as One-Layer Kriging Metamodeling (1L-KM), we select the input combinations for the simulation model through a *crossed* (combined) design for the decision and environmental factors (as is also traditional in Taguchian design); i.e., we combine the (say) n_d combinations of the decision variables $\mathbf{d}$ with the n_e combinations of the environmental variables $\mathbf{e}$. These n_d combinations are *space-filling*, so we avoid extrapolation when using Kriging metamodels to obtain predictions; Kriging is known to give bad extrapolators, as observed by [63]. The n_e combinations are *sampled* from their input distribution; we use LHS for this sampling. Simulating these $n_d \times n_e$ combinations gives the outputs $w_{i,j}$ with $i = 1, \ldots, n_d$ and $j = 1, \ldots, n_e$. These I/O data enable the following estimators of the n_d conditional means and variances:

$$\overline{w_i} = \frac{\sum_{j=1}^{n_e} w_{i,j}}{n_e} \quad (i = 1, \ldots, n_d), \tag{2.21}$$

$$s_i^2 = \frac{\sum_{j=1}^{n_e} \left(w_{i,j} - \overline{w_i}\right)^2}{n_e - 1} \quad (i = 1, \ldots, n_d). \tag{2.22}$$

These two estimators are *unbiased* because they do not assume any metamodel; metamodels are only approximations so they may have lack of fit.

Note that in [22] a crossed design is used, even though RSM does not require such a design. An alternative for a crossed design is the split-plot design presented by [18] or Simultaneous Perturbation Stochastic Approximation (SPSA) recently described by [44]. Furthermore, the variability of the estimators is much smaller for the mean than it is for the variance; e.g., under the normality assumption $var(\overline{w}) = \sigma^2/n_e$ and $var(s^2) = 2(n_e - 1)\,\sigma^4/n_e^2$; this problem is also studied by [38].

In the second approach, referred to as Two-Layer Kriging Metamodeling (2L-KM) in [23], we select a relatively small number of input combinations for the simulation model (say) n, using a space-filling design for the $k + c$ input factors (k and c denote the number of decision and environmental factors, respectively); i.e., the environmental factors are not yet sampled from their distribution. Then, we use the I/O simulation data to fit a Kriging metamodel for the output w. Finally, for the larger design with N combinations, we use a space-filling design for the decision factors, but LHS for the environmental factors accounting for their distribution.

We do not simulate the N combinations of this large design but we compute the Kriging predictors for the output; then we derive the conditional means and standard deviations using equations analogue to (2.21) and (2.22); i.e., in the right-hand sides of (2.21) and (2.22) we replace n_e and n_d by N_e and N_d (the large-sample analogues of the small-sample n_e and n_d) and w by $\hat{y}$ where $\hat{y}$ denotes the Kriging predictor. These predictions are used to fit two Kriging metamodels for the mean and standard deviation of the output.

We shall further explain both approaches through some inventory examples in the next section. Our methodology assumes that the simulation model is expensive, in practice although we shall illustrate the two approaches through some inexpensive inventory simulation model.

Both approaches use their estimated Kriging metamodels for the mean and standard deviation to estimate the robust optimum that minimizes the mean while satisfying a constraint on the standard deviation, according to (2.20). Varying the value of the right-hand side for that constraint gives the estimated Pareto frontier.

This Pareto frontier is built on estimates of the mean and standard deviation of the output. Obviously, estimates are random, so we wish to quantify the variability in the estimated mean and standard deviation. To this aim, bootstrapping is a versatile statistical technique: see [26] and the many references in [35, pp. 84–87]. Whereas [22] apply parametric bootstrapping, [23] apply *nonparametric* or *distribution-free bootstrapping*; i.e., they resample—with replacement—the original simulation observations (which may follow any kind of distribution, not necessarily normal). Moreover, (both parametric and nonparametric) bootstrapping assumes that the original observations are Independently and Identically Distributed (IID). Because in our robust optimization procedure we cross the design for the decision variables and the environmental variables, the n_d observations on the output for a given combination of the environmental factors are not independent (this dependence may be compared with the dependence created by the use of Common Random Numbers in stochastic simulation, which is investigated by [16]). We therefore can resample the n_e *vectors* $\mathbf{w}_j$ $(j = 1, \ldots, n_e)$—with replacement. This resampling gives the n_e bootstrapped observations $\mathbf{w}_j^* = \left(w_{1,j}^*, \ldots, w_{nd,j}^*\right)$; the superscript "$*$" is the usual symbol for bootstrapped values. (Simar and Wilson [59] also use distribution-free bootstrapping, albeit in the context of Data Envelopment Analysis (DEA) instead of Pareto frontiers.) Analogously to (2.21) and (2.22) we estimate the n_d bootstrapped conditional means and variances:

$$\overline{w_i}^* = \frac{\sum_{j=1}^{n_e} w_{i,j}^*}{n_e} \quad (i = 1, \ldots, n_d), \tag{2.23}$$

$$s_i^{2*} = \frac{\sum_{j=1}^{n_e} \left(w_{i,j}^* - \overline{w_i}^*\right)^2}{n_e - 1} \quad (i = 1, \ldots, n_d). \tag{2.24}$$

We apply Kriging to the estimates computed through (2.23) and (2.24) respectively.

To reduce the sampling error when bootstrapping, we repeat this sampling (say) B times; B is called the bootstrap sample size. This sample size gives the B bootstrapped conditional averages and variances $\overline{w_{i;b}}^*$ and $s_{i;b}^{2*}$ ($b = 1, \ldots, B$); see (2.23) and (2.24). Next, we apply Kriging to $\overline{w_{i;b}}^*$ and $s_{i;b}^{2*}$. For each optimal solution $\widehat{\mathbf{d}^+}$ belonging to the "original" (i.e., non-bootstrapped) Pareto frontier we compute the predictions for the average and standard deviation of the output over the B bootstrapped metamodels, obtaining (say) $\overline{w_{i;b}}^{+*}$ and $s_{i;b}^{+*}$. The B bootstrap observations enable us to compute a *confidence region* for the mean and standard deviation of the output; i.e., we obtain simultaneous confidence intervals—called a confidence region—for these two outputs. These confidence intervals allow us to account for management's risk attitude associated with the threshold value. More specifically, we compute the following distribution-free bootstrapped confidence interval, see [26, pp. 170–174]:

$$\left[\hat{\overline{y}}^{+*}_{(\lfloor B(\alpha/2)/2 \rfloor)}, \hat{\overline{y}}^{+*}_{(\lceil B(1-(\alpha/2))/2 \rceil)}\right] \tag{2.25}$$

where $\hat{\overline{y}}^{+*}_{(\cdot)}$ denotes the bootstrapped mean output that the Kriging model predicts for the estimated Pareto-optimal decision variable $\widehat{\mathbf{d}^+}$, the subscript () denotes the order statistic (i.e., the B bootstrapped observations are sorted from smallest to largest), $\lfloor\,\rfloor$ denotes the floor function (which gives the integer part), $\lceil\,\rceil$ denotes the ceiling function (rounding upwards), $\alpha/2$ gives a two-sided confidence interval, Bonferroni's inequality implies that the type-I error rate for the interval per output is divided by the number of outputs (which is two; namely, the mean and standard deviation).

The following confidence interval for the standard deviation of the output is the analogue of (2.25):

$$\left[\hat{s}^{+*}_{(\lfloor B(\alpha/2)/2 \rfloor)}, \hat{s}^{+*}_{(\lceil B(1-(\alpha/2))/2 \rceil)}\right]. \tag{2.26}$$

We shall further detail our procedure through some inventory simulation-optimization examples, presented in the next section.

2.4.1 Kriging Metamodeling

The purpose of the section is to give a description of Kriging as used within our framework for robust simulation-optimization, where we still interpret the simulated system from the Taguchian viewpoint, while using Kriging as a metamodeling technique. We will describe the characteristics of the Kriging metamodeling technique adopting a notation which goes beyond the one characterizing our robust methodology. We also refer to [42, 54, 56] for a detailed exposition of both theory and implementation of Kriging.

A Kriging model is

$$y(\mathbf{x}) = f(\mathbf{x}) + Z(\mathbf{x}) , \tag{2.27}$$

where $f(\mathbf{x})$ is a function of the n-dimensional $\mathbf{x}$ that is a global model of the original function, and $Z(\mathbf{x})$ is a stochastic process with zero mean and non-zero variance that represents a local deviation from the global model. Usually, $f(\mathbf{x})$ is

$$f(\mathbf{x}) = \sum_{i=0}^{p} \beta_i \, f_i(\mathbf{x}) \tag{2.28}$$

where $f_i : \mathbb{R}^n \to \mathbb{R}$, $i = 0, \ldots, p$, are polynomial terms (typically of zero, first or second order). The coefficients β_i, $i = 1, \ldots, p$, are regression parameters. The $p + 1$ regression functions can be regarded as components of a vector

$$\mathbf{f}(\mathbf{x}) = \left[f_0(\mathbf{x}), \ldots, f_p(\mathbf{x}) \right]^T . \tag{2.29}$$

Suppose the design sites are $(\mathbf{x}_1, \ldots, \mathbf{x}_{N_s})$, where $\mathbf{x}_i \in \mathbb{R}^n$, $i = 1, \ldots, N_s$. Then we can compute the matrix $\mathbf{F}$ by evaluating the vector $\mathbf{f}(\mathbf{x})$ at the design sites, thus obtaining:

$$\mathbf{F} = \begin{bmatrix} \mathbf{f}^T(x_1) \\ \vdots \\ \mathbf{f}^T(x_{N_s}) \end{bmatrix} = \begin{bmatrix} f_0(\mathbf{x}_1), \ldots, & f_p(\mathbf{x}_{N_s}) \\ \vdots & \vdots \\ f_0(\mathbf{x}_1), \ldots, & f_p(\mathbf{x}_{N_s}) \end{bmatrix} . \tag{2.30}$$

The covariance of $Z(\mathbf{x})$ is:

$$Cov[Z(\mathbf{x}_j), Z(\mathbf{x}_k)] = \sigma^2 \mathbf{R}(\mathbf{x}_j, \mathbf{x}_k), \qquad j, k = 1, \ldots, N_s \tag{2.31}$$

where σ^2 is the so-called process variance and $\mathbf{R}$ is the correlation matrix with elements $R_{jk} = R_\theta(\mathbf{x}_j, \mathbf{x}_k)$, representing the correlation function between any two of the N_s samples $\mathbf{x}_j$ and $\mathbf{x}_k$, with unknown parameters θ. $\mathbf{R}$ is a symmetric matrix of dimension $N_s \times N_s$, with diagonal elements equal to 1. The form of the correlation function $R_\theta(\mathbf{x}_j, \mathbf{x}_k)$ can be chosen among a variety of functions proposed in the literature. Yet, the exponential family is used most frequently

$$R_{\theta,p}(\mathbf{x}_j, \mathbf{x}_k) = \prod_{i=1}^{n} exp\left(-\theta_i |x_{ji} - x_{ki}|^{p_i}\right) \tag{2.32}$$

where n is the dimension of the input variable. When $p_i = 2$, then (2.32) is called the Gaussian correlation function. The parameters p_i determine the smoothness of the correlation function; e.g., $p_i = 2$ implies an infinitely differentiable function.

The Kriging predictor can be written as a linear combination of the observed responses:

$$y(\mathbf{x}) = \mathbf{c}^T(\mathbf{x})\mathbf{y}_s\,, \tag{2.33}$$

where $\mathbf{y}_s$ is the vector of the response function evaluated at the N_s design sites, $\mathbf{y}_s = [y(\mathbf{x}_1), \ldots, y(\mathbf{x}_{N_s})]^T$. The weights $\mathbf{c}(\mathbf{x})$ are obtained by minimizing the Mean Squared Error (MSE), which is given by

$$MSE[y(\mathbf{x})] = E\left[\left(\mathbf{c}^T(\mathbf{x})\mathbf{y}_s - y(\mathbf{x})\right)^2\right]. \tag{2.34}$$

In order to keep the predictor unbiased, the following constraint has to be satisfied:

$$\mathbf{F}^T\mathbf{c}(\mathbf{x}) = \mathbf{f}(\mathbf{x})\,. \tag{2.35}$$

It can be proven that the MSE in (2.34) can be rewritten as

$$MSE[y(\mathbf{x})] = \sigma^2[1 + \mathbf{c}^T(\mathbf{x})\mathbf{R}\mathbf{c}(\mathbf{x}) - 2\mathbf{c}^T(\mathbf{x})\mathbf{r}(\mathbf{x})] \tag{2.36}$$

where $\mathbf{r}(\mathbf{x}) = [R(\mathbf{x}_1, \mathbf{x}), \ldots, R(\mathbf{x}_{N_s}, \mathbf{x})]^T$ is the vector of the correlations between $Z(\mathbf{x}_i)$ and $Z(\mathbf{x})$. Minimizing the MSE in (2.36) with respect to $\mathbf{c}(\mathbf{x})$ under the constraint (2.35) gives the Kriging predictor

$$\widehat{y(\mathbf{x})} = \hat{\mathbf{c}}^T(\mathbf{x})\mathbf{y}_s = \hat{\mathbf{r}}^T\hat{\mathbf{R}}^{-1}(\mathbf{y}_s - \mathbf{F}\hat{\boldsymbol{\beta}}) + \mathbf{f}^T\hat{\boldsymbol{\beta}}\,, \tag{2.37}$$

where

$$\hat{\boldsymbol{\beta}} = (\mathbf{F}^T\hat{\mathbf{R}}^{-1}\mathbf{F})^{-1}\mathbf{F}^T\hat{\mathbf{R}}^{-1}\mathbf{y}_s \tag{2.38}$$

follows from the Generalized Least-Squares (GLS) criterion or the Maximum Likelihood Estimation (MLE) criterion.

Assuming the stochastic process $Z(x)$ to be Gaussian, MLE maximizes a likelihood function using numerical optimization techniques to determine an estimate $\hat{\theta}$ [54]. The likelihood function depends on the coefficients $\boldsymbol{\beta}$ in the regression model, the process variance σ^2, and the correlation parameters $\boldsymbol{\theta}$. Given the correlation parameters θ and hence R, the MLE of $\boldsymbol{\beta}$ is given by (2.38), and the MLE of σ^2 is given by

$$\hat{\sigma}^2 = \frac{1}{N_s}(\mathbf{y}_s - \mathbf{F}\hat{\boldsymbol{\beta}})^T\mathbf{R}^{-1}(\mathbf{y}_s - \mathbf{F}\hat{\boldsymbol{\beta}})\,. \tag{2.39}$$

Therefore, the MLE of R follows from

$$\min_{\boldsymbol{\theta}} (\det\mathbf{R})^{1/N_s}\hat{\sigma}^2 \,; \tag{2.40}$$

this is a global nonlinear optimization problem, which requires a heuristic procedure for its solution.

In our own experiments we use so-called *ordinary Kriging*

$$y(\mathbf{x}) = \mu + Z(\mathbf{x}) \tag{2.41}$$

where $\mu = \beta_0$ and $f_0 \equiv 1$.

2.5 Inventory Simulation-Optimization Examples

To illustrate our methodology, we apply it to some inventory models starting from the well known EOQ inventory model for which [68, pp. 30–39] uses the following symbols and assumptions: (1) The demand is known and constant, say a units per time unit. (2) The order quantity is Q units. (3) Total costs consist of setup cost per order, K; cost per unit purchased or produced, c; and holding cost per inventory unit per time unit, h. Management's goal is to minimize the total costs per time unit, C, over an infinite time horizon.

It is easy to derive that this problem has the following *true I/O function*, which we shall use to check our simulation results:

$$C = \frac{aK}{Q} + ac + \frac{hQ}{2}\,. \tag{2.42}$$

This function implies that the EOQ is

$$Q_o = \sqrt{\frac{2aK}{h}}\,, \tag{2.43}$$

and the corresponding minimal cost is

$$C_o = C(Q_o) = \sqrt{2aKh} + ac\,. \tag{2.44}$$

In our example we use the parameter values of an example from the classic Operations Research textbook [30, pp. 936–937, 942–943]: $a = 8{,}000$, $K = 12{,}000$, $c = 10$, and $h = 0.3$. Substituting these values into (2.43) and (2.44) gives $Q_o = 25{,}298$ and $C_o = 87{,}589$.

To study robust simulation-optimization, we follow [22] and [23] and propose a variant of the classic EOQ model which assumes unknown demand rate and cost coefficients. The robustness of the EOQ model is also examined by [66], who uses other criteria and other methods than we do (he uses two minmax criteria and analytical methods instead of simulation). Further, [12] gives references to the literature on EOQ "in the presence of imprecision in the parameter estimates" (and then proceeds to sensitivity analysis, not robustness analysis).

2.5.1 Robust Optimization with Uncertain Demand Rate and Cost Coefficients

Inspired by [13], we extend the robust formulation of the simple inventory model proposed by [22] such that it accounts for fixed but uncertain cost parameters (holding and set-up costs), besides unknown (constant) demand rate. We assume that all the environmental factors follow normal distributions, with mean equal to the nominal value (the value when no uncertainty is assumed; namely, $\mu_a = 8,000$ for the demand rate, $\mu_h = 0.3$ for the holding cost, and $\mu_K = 12,000$ for the set-up cost); the standard deviation of each factor is equal to 10 % of the nominal value. This standard deviation can give negative values, so we resample until we get non-negative values only. We assume that the three factors are independent. We apply the two Kriging approaches sketched in Sect. 2.4.

2.5.1.1 1L-KM Approach: Kriging Models for Mean and Standard Deviation Estimated from Simulation I/O Data

We adopt a crossed design, combining a uniform space filling design of size $n_Q = 10$ for the decision factor Q within the range [15000, 45000] and a LHS design of size $n_\mathbf{e} = 120$ for the three-dimensional space of the environmental factors a, h, and K. This gives $n_Q \times n_\mathbf{e}$ input combinations, for which we run the simulation model obtaining cost values $C_{i,j}$ for $i = 1, \ldots, n_Q$ and $j = 1, \ldots, n_\mathbf{e}$.

Next we average over the environmental factors to derive a set of n_Q output values for both the mean and the standard deviation, using

$$\overline{C_i} = \frac{\sum_{j=1}^{n_\mathbf{e}} C_{i,j}}{n_\mathbf{e}} \quad (i = 1, \ldots, n_Q), \tag{2.45}$$

$$s_i = \left[\frac{\sum_{j=1}^{n_\mathbf{e}} \left(C_{i,j} - \overline{C_i}\right)^2}{n_\mathbf{e} - 1} \right]^{1/2} \quad (i = 1, \ldots, n_Q). \tag{2.46}$$

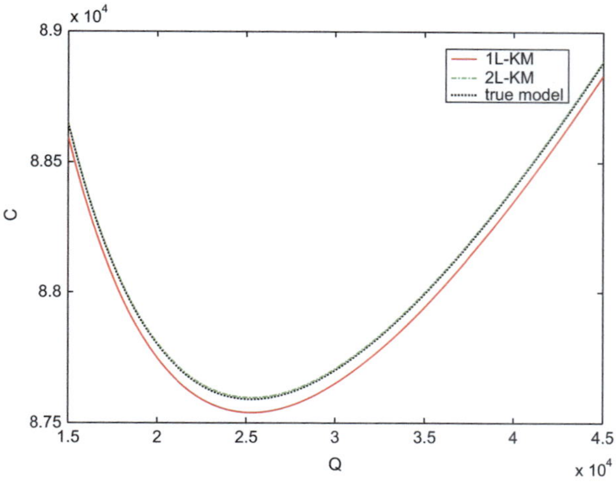

Fig. 2.1 Kriging metamodels for the expected total cost of the EOQ model with uncertain demand rate and cost coefficients, derived through 1L-KM (*solid curve*) and 2L-KM (*dashed curve*). The *dotted curve* represents the true model

The latter estimator is biased, because $E(\sqrt{s^2}) = E(s) \neq \sqrt{E(s^2)} = \sqrt{\sigma^2} = \sigma$; we ignore this bias.

Based on these I/O data, we fit one Kriging metamodel for each of the two outputs; see the solid curve in Figs. 2.1 and 2.2, which also displays the true cost function obtained from

$$E(C) = \left(\frac{\mu_K}{Q} + c\right)\mu_a + \frac{\mu_h Q}{2}, \tag{2.47}$$

and the true standard deviation computed through

$$\sigma_C = \sqrt{\sigma_a^2\left(c^2 + \frac{2c\mu_K}{Q} + \frac{\sigma_K^2 + \mu_K^2}{Q^2}\right) + \frac{\mu_a^2\sigma_K^2}{Q^2} + \frac{\sigma_h^2 Q^2}{4}}. \tag{2.48}$$

We use leave-one-out cross-validation to validate our two metamodels. Based on the relative prediction errors which are smaller than 1 %, we decide to accept both metamodels.

We let the threshold T vary in the interval [8200, 8600] (the same as for the EOQ model with uncertain demand rate only, proposed by [22]), which gives the estimated Pareto frontier in Fig. 2.3.

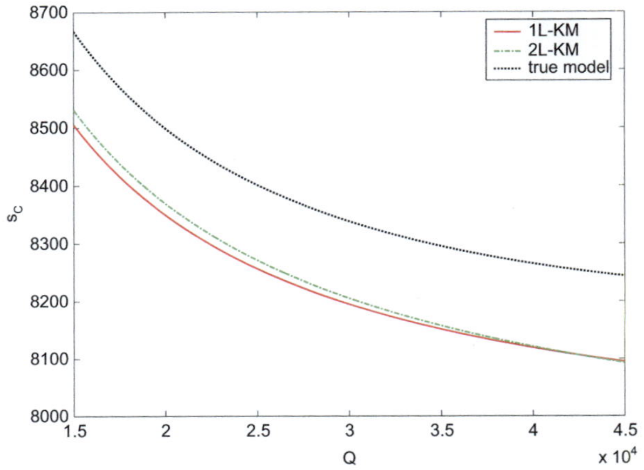

Fig. 2.2 Kriging metamodels for the expected standard deviation of cost of the EOQ model with uncertain demand rate and cost coefficients, derived through 1L-KM (*solid curve*) and 2L-KM (*dashed curve*). The *dotted curve* represents the true model

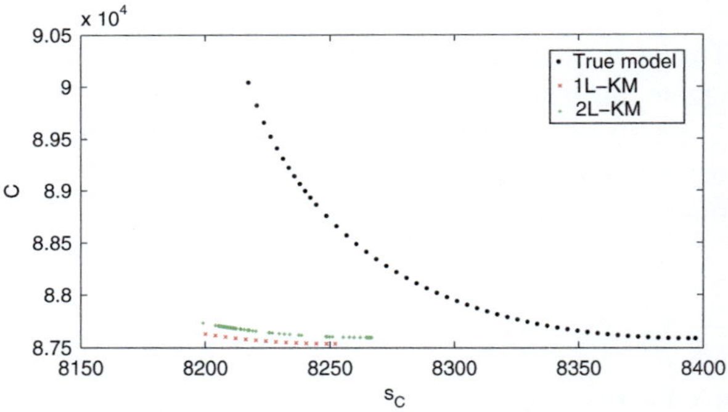

Fig. 2.3 Pareto frontiers for the EOQ model with uncertain demand rate and cost coefficients, derived through 1L-KM approach (*crosses*) and 2L-KM (*pluses*). True model is displayed through *dots*

2.5.1.2 2L-KM Approach: Kriging Models for Mean and Standard Deviation Estimated from Intermediate Kriging Predictions

Following the 2L-KM approach, we first build a LHS design for the four input factors, without distinguishing between decision and environmental factors. We choose a design of size $n = 1,200$, thus keeping the same sample size as in the 1L-KM approach.

We run the simulation model over these n input combinations, and collect the corresponding output values C_i $(i = 1, \ldots, n)$. Next, we fit a Kriging metamodel based on these n I/O combinations.

We produce a bigger DOE by crossing a uniform space filling design for the order quantity Q and a LHS design for the three environmental factors, accounting for their distribution; the overall design size is $N = N_Q \times N_{\mathbf{e}} = 30 \times 200 = 6,000$.

Notice that the bigger value for N does not imply a computationally expensive task, because we use this bigger design to compute Kriging predictions instead of running the simulation model.

We compute the Kriging predictions $\widehat{C_{i,j}}$ $(i = 1, \ldots, N_Q;\ j = 1, \ldots, N_e)$ for the latter N input combinations, using the Kriging metamodel estimated from the smaller experiment with the simulation model with n input combinations.

Next we compute the sample average of cost predictions and the sample standard deviation of cost, which are analogous to (2.45) and (2.46) but use a metamodel:

$$\widehat{C_i} = \frac{\sum_{j=1}^{N_e} \widehat{C_{i,j}}}{N_e} \quad (i = 1, \ldots, N_Q), \tag{2.49}$$

$$\widehat{\sigma_i} = \frac{\sum_{j=1}^{N_e} \left(\widehat{C_{i,j}} - \widehat{C_i}\right)^2}{N_e - 1} \quad (i = 1, \ldots, N_Q). \tag{2.50}$$

Then we derive two Kriging metamodels; namely, one for the expected cost, based on the N_Q estimated means resulting from (2.49), and one for the cost standard deviation, based on the N_Q estimated standard deviations resulting from (2.50); see again Figs. 2.1 and 2.2.

We validate these metamodels through leave-one-out cross-validation. Both metamodels give small relative prediction errors; namely, around 10^{-6}. So we accept these two Kriging metamodels as adequate approximations.

Finally, we take 100 equally spaced values of the threshold T in the interval $[8200, 8600]$, and collect the corresponding optimal solutions to estimate the Pareto frontier; see again Fig. 2.3.

2.5.1.3 Bootstrapped Confidence Regions

As we discussed in Sect. 2.4, we estimated the Pareto frontier through *random* simulation outputs $C_{i,j}$ (whether we use the 1L-KM or the 2L-KM approach), as a consequence of the uncertainty in the demand rate and cost coefficients. Therefore, it becomes important to perform further analyses of the statistical variation of this frontier, in order to understand the performance of the two approaches proposed. To estimate this variability, we use *distribution-free bootstrapping* described through (2.23) and (2.24) to derive the bootstrapped output data, $\overline{C_b}^*$ and s_b^* $(b = 1, \ldots, B)$. We use them to fit B pairs of bootstrapped Kriging metamodels.

Results for 1L-KM are given in Fig. 2.4, where the vertical line will be explained below. This figure shows that the bootstrapped curves envelop both the original curve and the true curve. In particular, focussing on the original (non-bootstrapped) Pareto frontier, we study the variability of the optimal solutions $\widehat{Q^+}$ using the

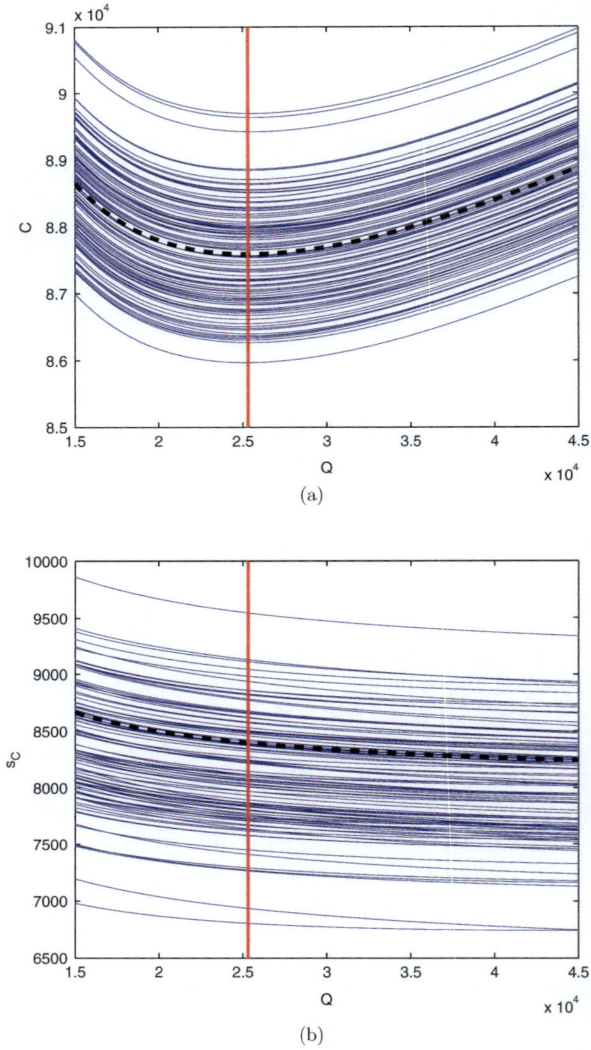

Fig. 2.4 (**a**) Bootstrapped estimated mean costs, original Kriging metamodel in 1L-KM, and true mean cost (*dashed curve*); (**b**) Bootstrapped estimated standard deviations of cost, original Kriging metamodel in 1L-KM, and true standard deviation (*dashed curve*)

bootstrapped pairs of metamodels. Such analysis considers the implications of a decision (in terms of $\widehat{Q^+}$) based on this Pareto frontier, due to uncertainty. In fact, given the original Pareto frontier, management selects their preferred combination of the mean and standard deviation of the inventory cost; e.g., $\hat{\overline{C}} = 87,538.28$ and $\hat{s} = 8,251.94$. Making the standard deviation not exceed its threshold (namely, $T = 8,600$) implies a specific order quantity; namely, $\widehat{Q^+} = 25,291.39$; see Fig. 2.2. Actually, this order quantity may give a mean and a standard deviation that differ from the "original" values in Fig. 2.4; see the vertical lines in Fig. 2.4, parts (a) and (b), at $Q = \widehat{Q^+} = 25,291.39$.

The solution $\widehat{Q^+}$ selected by the management is subject to variability, which we need to take into account when using the Pareto frontier as a "decision-making tool"; we adopt bootstrapping to study this variability. So this estimated Pareto-optimal order quantity $\widehat{Q^+}$ corresponds with B bootstrapped values for the mean and standard deviation respectively. From these B values, we estimate a *confidence region* for the mean and standard deviation of the cost, given the optimal order quantity $\widehat{Q^+}$, applying (2.25) and (2.26). The rectangular *confidence regions* for two points on the original estimated Pareto curve are displayed in Fig. 2.5. Part (a) corresponds with the relatively small threshold value $T = 8,250$ so $\widehat{Q^+} = 25,531.91$ for the 1L-KM approach and $\widehat{Q^+} = 29,943.98$ for the 2L-KM approach; part (b) corresponds with the larger threshold value $T = 8,600$ so we obtain the smaller $\widehat{Q^+} = 25,291.39$ for 1L-KM and $\widehat{Q^+} = 24,001.84$ for 2L-KM. These two threshold values may reflect *risk-averse* and *risk-seeking* management. Both Kriging approaches give confidence regions that cover the true solution point, although the confidence region associated with 2L-KM is smaller.

The confidence interval for the standard deviation shows that the original estimated Pareto-optimal order quantity may still give a standard deviation that violates the threshold due to the metamodels' variability (see Fig. 2.4b). In fact, we could also use the confidence region derived to estimate the degree of infeasibility of a solution (i.e., the probability that an optimal solution obtained for a given T becomes infeasible due to uncertainty) as the fraction of the overall area which is beyond (i.e., to the right of) the threshold value T used in the optimization problem. Confronted with this possibility, management may prefer to implement a solution providing a relatively small probability of becoming infeasible (estimated through the confidence region), accepting higher costs; e.g., management may switch from the relatively small threshold (and corresponding high Q) in Fig. 2.5a to the higher threshold (and smaller Q) in Fig. 2.5b. The formalization of the problem of choosing among random outputs is beyond this article; a classic reference is [33]. We also refer to Sect. 2.6, which covers future research issues.

2.6 Conclusions and Future Research

Robust optimization of simulated systems may use *Taguchi*'s worldview, which distinguishes between decision variables that may be optimized and environmental variables that remain uncertain but should be taken into account when optimizing. Taguchi's statistical techniques, however, may be replaced by *Kriging* metamodels (instead of low-order polynomials) and their space-filling designs such as LHS (instead of Taguchian or RSM designs). We considered two Kriging-based methods; namely, the 1L-KM approach that fits one Kriging metamodel for the mean and one for the standard deviation estimated from simulation data, and the 2L-KM approach that fits a single Kriging metamodel to a relatively small simulation sample and

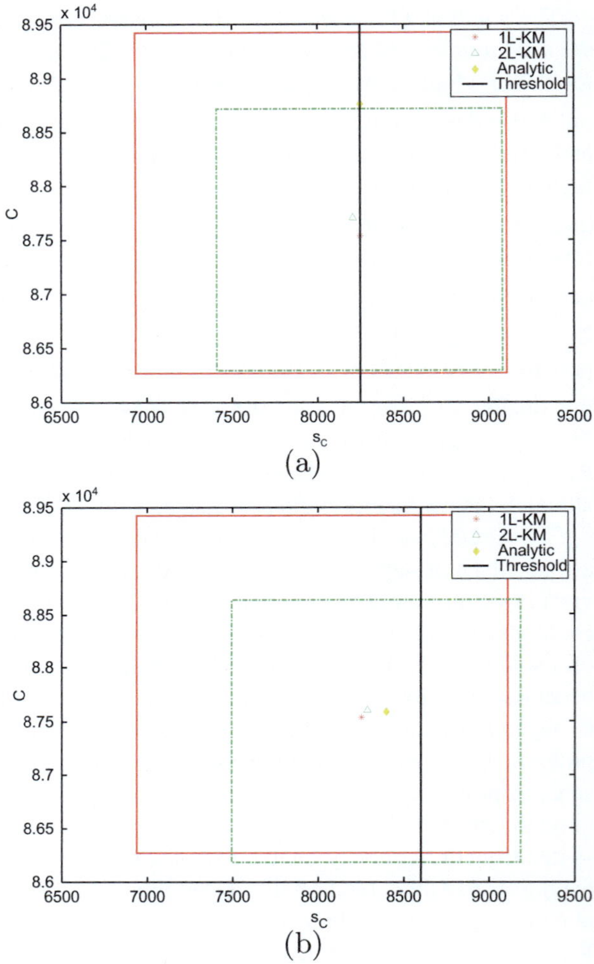

Fig. 2.5 Confidence regions for σ_C (on x-axis) and $E(C)$ (on y-axis) based on bootstrapped Kriging in 1L-KM (*solid rectangle*) and 2L-KM (*dash-dotted rectangle*) at (**a**) $T = 8,250$ and (**b**) $T = 8,600$ (see the *vertical line*). "$*$" and "Δ" denote the "true" solutions based on (2.47) and (2.48) in 1L-KM and 2L-KM respectively; namely, (**a**) ($\hat{\bar{C}}_{1L-KM} = 87,538.62$, $\hat{s}_{1L-KM} = 8,248.49$) at $\widehat{Q^+}_{1L-KM} = 25,531.91$, and ($\hat{\bar{C}}_{2L-KM} = 87,703.95$, $\hat{s}_{2L-KM} = 8,205.61$) at $\widehat{Q^+}_{2L-KM} = 29,943.98$, (**b**) ($\hat{\bar{C}}_{1L-KM} = 87,538.28$, $\hat{s}_{1L-KM} = 8,251.94$) at $\widehat{Q^+}_{1L-KM} = 25,291.39$, and ($\hat{\bar{C}}_{2L-KM} = 87,605.84$, $\hat{s}_{2L-KM} = 8,287.48$) at $\widehat{Q^+}_{2L-KM} = 24,001.84$

uses this metamodel to compute Kriging predictions for a larger sample. In the inventory examples, 2L-KM gives more accurate predictions than 1L-KM, given the same computational cost measured by the number of expensive simulation runs. Moreover, we point out that the only way to improve the metamodels' accuracy for 1L-KM is to run additional expensive simulations, thus increasing the computational cost of this approach. On the contrary, we can arbitrarily increase the accuracy of the metamodels derived through 2L-KM with negligible costs, because we do not need to use simulations anymore; however, this is possible only if the metamodel obtained in the first layer is sufficiently accurate to provide "reliable" predictions.

In other words, the high accuracy in the metamodel of total inventory cost obtained in the first layer of the 2L-KM approach implies that predictions computed from this metamodel can be treated as if they were simulated data. In fact, from this point on, the two approaches perform the same computations. Therefore, the 2L-KM approach can provide better results than the 1L-KM approach, at the same computational costs.

The whole Kriging-based methodology for robust optimization may be further enhanced by *distribution-free bootstrapping*, which quantifies the variability of the estimated robust optimization results so it may help management to make the final compromise decision [21]. The confidence regions derived through bootstrapping for both approaches confirm that the 2L-KM approach performs better than the 1L-KM approach in the considered inventory examples.

Future research may address the following issues. Instead of minimizing the mean under a variance constraint, we may minimize a specific quantile of the simulation output (see [4, 5, 37]), or minimize the Conditional Value at Risk (CVaR) (see [17, 19, 28] and [50]); the mean-variance trade-off is also criticized by [65]. Besides CVaR, other risk measures are surveyed by [58], including the "expected shortfall at level p", which is popular in the actuarial literature. Our Kriging-based methods may be compared with alternative approaches, either based on different metamodeling techniques (e.g., the so-called Universal Kriging discussed in the Kriging literature and applied in classic and robust optimization in engineering, RSM (low-order polynomial linear-regression) models proposed by [22] for robust optimization, and Generalized Linear Models proposed by [39]) or adopting different optimization solvers (e.g., Evolutionary Algorithms proposed by [14] for robust optimization of noisy systems, and by [31] for robust optimization with a multi-objective formulation). Investigating the performance of alternative DOEs might also be of interest; see [18]. Based on the promising results obtained from the bootstrap procedure, we plan to further investigate and refine this analysis. Further research directions also include (1) to adjust the considered methodology to accommodate *random* simulation models, which imply aleatory uncertainty besides epistemic uncertainty (these two types of uncertainty are discussed by [25, 29]); (2) to apply this methodology to complex *supply chain* models (e.g., see [15, 49, 52, 57]).

References

1. Al-Aomar, R.: A robust simulation-based multicriteria optimization methodology. In: Yücesan, E., Snowdon, C.-H., Charnes, J.M. (eds.) Proceedings of the Winter Simulation Conference, pp. 1931–1939 (2002)
2. Allen, T.T., Bernshteyn, M.A., Kabiri-Bamoradian, K.: Constructing meta-models for computer experiments. J. Qual. Technol. **35**, 264–274 (2003)
3. Bates, R.A., Kenett, R.S., Steinberg, D.M., Wynn, H.P.: Achieving robust design from computer simulations. Qual. Tech. Quant. Manag. **3**, 161–177 (2006)
4. Batur, D., Choobineh, F.: A quantile-based approach to system selection. Eur. J. Oper. Res. **202**, 764–772 (2010)
5. Bekki, J.M., Fowler, J.W., Mackulak, G.T., Kulahci, M.: Simulation-based cycle-time quantile estimation in manufacturing settings employing non-FIFO dispatching policies. J. Simul. **3**, 69–83 (2009)

6. Ben-Tal, A., Nemirovski, A.: Selected topics in robust convex optimization. Math. Program. **112**, 125–158 (2008)
7. Bertsimas, D., Sim, M.: The price of robustness. Oper. Res. **52**, 35–53 (2004)
8. Bertsimas, D., Thiele, A.: A robust optimization approach to supply chain management. Integer Programming and Combinatorial Optimization. Lecture Notes in Computer Science, vol. 3064, pp. 86–100. Springer, Heidelberg (2004)
9. Bertsimas, D., Thiele, A.: A robust optimization approach to inventory theory. Oper. Res. **54**, 150–168 (2006)
10. Bertsimas, D., Nohadani, O., Teo, K.M.: Robust optimization for unconstrained simulation-based problems. Oper. Res. **58**, 161–178 (2010)
11. Beyer, H., Sendhoff, B.: Robust optimization—a comprehensive survey. Comput. Methods Appl. Mech. Eng. **196**, 3190–3218 (2007)
12. Borgonovo, E.: Sensitivity analysis with finite changes: an application to modified EOQ models. Eur. J. Oper. Res. **200**, 127–138 (2010)
13. Borgonovo, E., Peccati, L.: Global sensitivity analysis in inventory management. Int. J. Prod. Econ. **108**, 302–313 (2007)
14. Branke, J., Schmidt, C., Schmeck, H.: Efficient fitness estimation in noisy environments. In: Proc. of Genetic and Evolutionary Computation, pp. 243–250 (2001)
15. Cannella, S., Ciancimino, E.: Up-to-date supply chain management: The coordinated (S, R) order-up-to. In: Dangelmaier, W., et al. (eds.) Advanced Manufacturing and Sustainable Logistics: 8th International Heinz Nixdorf Symposium, pp. 175–185. Springer, Berlin (2010)
16. Chen, X., Ankenman, B., Nelson, B.L.: The effects of common random numbers on stochastic Kriging metamodels. ACM Transactions on Modeling and Computer Simulation 22, 2, Article 7 (2012)
17. Chen, Y., Xu, M., Zhang, Z.G.: A risk-averse newsvendor model under CVaR criterion. Oper. Res. **57**, 1040–1044 (2009)
18. Dehlendorff, C., Kulahci, M., Andersen, K.: Designing simulation experiments with controllable and uncontrollable factors for applications in health care. J. R. Stat. Soc. Ser. C Appl. Stat. **60**, 31–49 (2011)
19. Dehlendorff, C., Kulahci, M., Merser, S., Andersen, K.: Conditional value at risk as a measure for waiting time in simulations of hospital units. Qual. Technol. Quant. Manag. **7**, 321–336 (2010)
20. Del Castillo, E.: Process Optimization: A Statistical Approach. Springer, New York (2007)
21. Dellino, G., Meloni, C.: Quantitative methods to analyze simulation metamodels variability. In: R.M. Spitaleri (ed.) Proceedings of the 11th Meeting on Applied Scientific Computing and Tools. IMACS Series in Computational and Applied Mathematics, vol. 17, pp. 91–100 (2013)
22. Dellino, G., Kleijnen, J.P.C., Meloni, C.: Robust optimization in simulation: Taguchi and response surface methodology. Int. J. Prod. Econ. **125**, 52–59 (2010)
23. Dellino, G., Kleijnen, J.P.C., Meloni, C.: Robust optimization in simulation: Taguchi and Krige combined. INFORMS J. Comput. **24**(3), 471–484 (2012)
24. Dengiz, B.: Redesign of PCB production line with simulation and Taguchi design. In: Rossetti, M.D., Hill, R.R., Johansson, B., Dunkin, A., Ingalls, G. (eds.) Proceedings of the 2009 Winter Simulation Conference, pp. 2197–2204 (2009)
25. De Rocquigny, E., Devictor, N., Tarantola, S.: Uncertainty settings and natures of uncertainty. In: De Rocquigny, E., Devictor, N., Tarantola, S. (eds.) Uncertainty in Industrial Practice. Wiley, Chichester (2008)
26. Efron, B., Tibshirani, R.J.: An Introduction to the Bootstrap. Chapman & Hall, New York (1993)
27. El-Haik, B., Al-Aomar, R.: Simulation-Based Lean Six-Sigma and Design for Six-Sigma. Wiley, New York (2006)
28. García-González, J., Parrilla, E., Mateo, A.: Risk-averse profit-based optimal scheduling of a hydro-chain in the day-ahead electricity market. Eur. J. Oper. Res. **181**, 1354–1369 (2007)
29. Helton, J.C.: Conceptual and computational basis for the quantification of margins and uncertainty. SANDIA Report SAND2009-3055 (2009)

30. Hillier, F.S., Lieberman, G.J.: Introduction to Operations Research, 7th edn. McGraw Hill, Boston (2001)
31. Jin, Y., Sendhoff, B.: Trade-off between performance and robustness: an evolutionary multiobjective approach. In: Fonseca, C.M., Fleming, P.J., Zitzler, E., Deb, K., Thiele, L. (eds.) Evolutionary Multi-Criterion Optimization. LNCS, vol. 2632, pp. 237–252. Springer, Heidelberg (2003)
32. Jin, R., Du, X., Chen, W.: The use of metamodeling techniques for optimization under uncertainty. Struct. Multidiscip. Optim. **25**, 99–116 (2003)
33. Keeney, R.L., Raiffa, H.: Decisions with Multiple Objectives: Preferences and Value Tradeoffs. Wiley, New York (1976)
34. Kenett, R., Steinberg, D.: New frontiers in design of experiments. Qual. Progr. **39**(8), 61–65 (2006)
35. Kleijnen, J.P.C.: Design and Analysis of Simulation Experiments. Springer, New York (2008)
36. Kleijnen, J.P.C., Sargent, R.G.: A methodology for the fitting and validation of metamodels in simulation. Eur. J. Oper. Res. **120**, 14–29 (2000)
37. Kleijnen, J.P.C., Pierreval, H., Zhang, J.: Methodology for determining the acceptability of given designs in uncertain environments. Eur. J. Oper. Res. **209**, 176–183 (2011)
38. Koch, P.K., Mavris, D., Allen, J.K., Mistree, F.: Modeling noise in approximation-based robust design: a comparison and critical discussion. In: ASME Design Engineering Technical Conferences, Atlanta (1998)
39. Lee, Y., Nelder, J.A.: Robust design. J. Qual. Technol. **35**, 2–12 (2003)
40. Lee, K.H., Park, G.J.: A global robust optimization using Kriging based approximation model. J. Jpn. Soc. Mech. Eng. **49**, 779–788 (2006)
41. Lehman, J.S., Santner, T.J., Notz, W.I.: Designing computer experiments to determine robust control variables. Stat. Sin. **14**, 571–590 (2004)
42. Lophaven, S.N., Nielsen, H.B., Søndergaard, J.: DACE: a MATLAB Kriging toolbox (version 2.0). Technical Report IMM-TR-2002-12, Technical University of Denmark, Lyngby (2002)
43. Miettinen, K.M.: Nonlinear Multiobjective Optimization. Kluwer Academic, Boston (1999)
44. Miranda, A.K., del Castillo, E.: Robust parameter design optimization of simulation experiments using stochastic perturbation methods. J. Oper. Res. Soc. **62**, 198–205 (2011)
45. Miró-Quesada, G., del Castillo, E.: Two approached for improving the dual response method in robust parameter design. J. Qual. Technol. **36**, 154–168 (2004)
46. Mula, J., Poler, R., García-Sabater, J.P., Lario, F.C.: Models for production planning under uncertainty : a review. Int. J. Prod. Econ. **103**, 271–285 (2006)
47. Myers, R.H., Khuri, A.I., Vining, G.: Response surface alternatives to the Taguchi robust parameter design approach. Am. Stat. **46**, 131–139 (1992)
48. Myers, R.H., Montgomery, D.C., Anderson-Cook, C.M.: Response Surface Methodology: Process and Product Optimization Using Designed Experiments, 3rd edn. Wiley, New York (2009)
49. Narasimhan, R., Talluri, S. (eds.): Special issue: perspectives on risk management in supply chains. J. Oper. Manag. **27**, 114–118 (2009)
50. Natarajan, K., Pachamanova, D., Sim, M.: Constructing risk measures from uncertainty sets. Oper. Res. **57**, 1129–1141 (2009)
51. Park, G.-J., Lee, T.-H., Lee, K.H., Hwang, K.-H.: Robust design: an overview. AIAA J. **44**, 181–191 (2006)
52. Rao, S., Goldsby, T.J.: Supply chain risks: a review and typology. Int. J. Log. Manag. **20**, 97–123 (2009)
53. Robinson, T.J., Borror, C.M., Myers, R.H.: Robust parameter design: a review. Qual. Reliab. Eng. Int. J. **20**, 81–101 (2004)
54. Sacks, J., Welch, W.J., Mitchell, T.J., Wynn, H.P.: Design and analysis of computer experiments. Stat. Sci. **4**, 409–435 (1989)
55. Sanchez, S.M.: Robust design: seeking the best of all possible worlds. In: Joines, J.A., Barton, R.R., Kang, K., Fishwick, P.A. (eds.) Proceedings of the Winter Simulation Conference, pp. 69–76 (2000)

56. Santner, T.J., Williams, B.J., Notz, W.I.: The Design and Analysis of Computer Experiments. Springer, New York (2003)
57. Shukla, S.K., Tiwari, M.K., Wan, H.-D., Shankar, R.: Optimization of the supply chain network: simulation, Taguchi, and psychoclonal algorithm embedded approach. Comput. Ind. Eng. **58**, 29–39 (2010)
58. Sordo, M.A.: Comparing tail variabilities of risks by means of the excess wealth order. Insur. Math. Econ. **45**, 466–469 (2009)
59. Simar, L., Wilson, P.W.: Sensitivity analysis of efficiency scores: how to bootstrap in nonparametric frontier models. Manag. Sci. **44**, 49–61 (1998)
60. Stinstra, E., den Hertog, D.: Robust optimization using computer experiments. Eur. J. Oper. Res. **191**, 816–837 (2008)
61. Taguchi, G.: System of Experimental Designs, vols. 1 and 2. UNIPUB/ Krauss International, White Plains (1987)
62. Trosset, M.W.: Taguchi and Robust Optimization, Dept. of Computational and Applied Mathematics, Rice University, Technical Report 96–31, Houston (1997)
63. Van Beers, W.C.M., Kleijnen, J.P.C.: Kriging interpolation in simulation: a survey. In: Ingalls, R.G., Rossetti, M.D., Smith, J.S., Peters, B.A. (eds.) Proc. of the 2004 Winter Simulation Conference, pp. 113–121 (2004)
64. Wu. J., Li, J., Wang, S., Cheng, T.C.E.: A note on mean-variance analysis of the newsvendor model with stockout cost. Omega **37**, 724–730 (2009)
65. Yin, Y., Madanat, S.M., Lu, X.-Y.: Robust improvement schemes for road networks under demand uncertainty. Eur. J. Oper. Res. **198**, 470–479 (2009)
66. Yu, G.: Robust economic order quantity models. Eur. J. Oper. Res. **100**, 482–493 (1997)
67. Zhang, Y.: General Robust-Optimization Formulation for Nonlinear Programming, Dept. of Computational and Applied Mathematics, Rice University, Technical Report 04-13, Houston (2004)
68. Zipkin, P.H.: Foundations of Inventory Management. McGraw-Hill, New York (2000)

Chapter 3
Simulation-Based Modelling of a Stochastic Equilibrium

Leonidas Sakalauskas

3.1 Introduction

Phenomena of the stochastic equilibrium arise in many fields of economy and finance usually analyzed as the stochastic Nash and/or Stakelberg equilibrium. Multiple decisions making is often related with a competition of several decision makers/players seeking their's own interests. Very often these players are non-cooperative and their decisions intervene with each other, which calls forth the problem of finding the Nash equilibrium. Over the past few decades, various stochastic Nash equilibrium models have been proposed to study specific practical decision making problems, that involve random data as well as multiple decision makers, who are in a competitive relationship (see, [11, 15, 16, 30–32], etc.).

A large range of equilibrium problems in economy and engineering are also covered by two-level models of decision-reactions, where a particular interest is paid to the order of play. These models, usually known as bi-level programs or Stakelberg games, present themselves as the parametric optimization problems, aimed at obtaining values at the parameters, so that the optimal solution to a related problem has a desired property. These problems admit a number of important applications, where the *leader*, who maximizes (minimizes) the overall objective at the upper level, is selecting the control variables based on the reaction of a *follower* at the lower level, who, in its turn, is optimizing individually his utility (see, [5, 7, 9, 12, 17], etc.). It is of interest, that many classical problems, such as the minimax problem, hierarchical optimization, etc., can be presented as bilevel programs.

L. Sakalauskas (✉)
Institute of Mathematics and Informatics, Vilnius University,
Akademijos 4, LT-08663 Vilnius, Lithuania
e-mail: sakal@ktl.mii.lt

G. Dellino, C. Meloni (eds.), *Uncertainty Management in Simulation-Optimization of Complex Systems*, Operations Research/Computer Science Interfaces Series 59,
DOI 10.1007/978-1-4899-7547-8_3

An important property of the stochastic equilibrium is the uncertainty of environment, in which the players have to play. In some cases, uncertainties are due to measurement errors, and in other cases, the errors come from inaccurate predictions of the future state of the system to be modelled. Regardless of the source of the uncertainty and neglecting the possible variation in the optimization, the model can result in costly errors, if the model results are applied in practice.

Usually the uncertainty of players' environment is modelled by some probability distribution. In stochastic programming it is a common to use sampling approximations when the probability distribution of the uncertain parameters is known. The aim here is to model an entire uncertain parameter space as closely as possible by a sufficient number of samples aimed to improve the probabilistic objective function value at each iteration. In sampling based methods, that is achieved by model simulations for a given number of samples and the subsequent computation of the probabilistic functions (e.g., expected value of the objective function or probabilities of some events). Two most often used approaches of such kind are the sampling based decomposition ([3, 18, 21, 25, 27, 33], etc.) and the sequential stochastic search ([2, 6, 10, 22, 23], etc.). Since the amount of simulated samples can achieve a significant volume, the key feature is to decrease the number of scenarios needed to obtain the reliable statistical estimate of the probabilistic function to be optimized.

This paper surveys the simulation-based search for the stochastic equilibrium with admissible accuracy by using a reasonable amount of simulated samples. The paper rests as follows: the next section contains the basic definitions of objectives and constraints functions as well as a system of Monte-Carlo estimates, to be applied in the estimation of functions and iterative stochastic search, Sect. 3.3 presents an application of simulation-based approach to stochastic nonlinear Nash equilibrium problems with an example of modelling the electricity market, and the last two sections focus on solving certain stochastic nonlinear bilevel problems by the simulation-based approach. Since the bi-level stochastic programming distinguishes itself by the variety of possible programs, we confined ourselves by stochastic programming with importance sampling and stochastic programming with *CVaR* considered in the bi-level framework. Namely, the importance sampling approach to nonlinear stochastic programming is developed and presented in Sect. 3.4 as well as optimization with *CVaR* in the objective and constraints are considered in Sect. 3.5, both presenting numerical examples.

3.2 Assumptions and Notations

Let us consider m players whose strategies are expressed by the set of m vectors

$$x = (x_1, x_2, \dots, x_m), \quad x_j \in D_j \subset \Re^{n_j}, \qquad n = \sum_{j=1}^{m} n_j, \quad 1 \leqslant j \leqslant m. \quad (3.1)$$

Assume the players to be acting in a random environment, defined by the probability space (Ω, Σ, P_x), where the measure P_x is absolutely continuous and depends on the set of strategies in general, i.e., it is defined by the parameterized probability density $p : D \times \Omega \to \Re_+$, where $D = D_1 \otimes D_2 \otimes \cdots \otimes D_m \subset \Re^n$ is the set of feasible strategies. Of course, the objective of the j-th player depends on his strategy and that of other players as well, taking into account random scenarios $\zeta \in \Omega$:

$$f_j : D \times \Omega \to \Re, \quad 1 \leqslant j \leqslant m. \tag{3.2}$$

Assume hereinafter, the random objective functions to be Lipshitzian and convex. Then the efficiency of the strategy of the j-th player is characterized by its probabilistic objective function:

$$F_j(x_1, x_2, \ldots, x_m) = Ef_j(x_1, x_2, \ldots, x_m, \zeta), \quad 1 \leqslant j \leqslant m, \tag{3.3}$$

where E is a symbol of mathematical expectation.

The concept of a stochastic gradient is the key to explore the differentiability of a probabilistic objective function. Hence, the random vector $g_j : \Re^n \times \Omega$ is called as a stochastic gradient of the smoothly differentiable function $F_j(x), x \in \Re^n$, if

$$\nabla_x F_j(x) = Eg_j(x, \zeta), \tag{3.4}$$

(see, [1], etc.).

Note, that subgradients $\partial f_i(x, \zeta)$ of the functions $f_i(x, \zeta)$, $i = 0, 1, \ldots, m$, are available for each scenario ζ due to the Lipshitz property [1]. Since the uncertainty is described by an absolutely continuous measure, expectations in the formulas above are smoothly differentiable functions (see [1, 20]). If in addition the probability density p obeys the Lipshitz property, then the probabilistic objective functions are smoothly twice differentiable [1]. Consequently, at first, the probabilistic objective functions of players and their gradients can be treated as smoothly differentiable under rather wide conditions and, second, they and their gradients are presented by expectations in some probabilistic space ([22, 25], etc.).

The stochastic two-stage linear objective functions are of interest due to their wide applicability:

$$\begin{aligned} & F_j(x) = \sum_{i=1}^{m} c_j^i \cdot x_i + E\{q_j \cdot y_j\} \to \min_{x_j}, \\ \text{s.t. :} \quad & \sum_{i=1}^{m} A_i \cdot x_i = b_j, \quad x_i \in \Re_+^{n_i}, \\ & y_j = \arg\min_y \left[v_j \cdot y \,\middle|\, W_j \cdot y + \sum_{i=1}^{m} T_j^i \cdot x_i \leqslant h_j,\ y \in R_+^{l_j} \right], \end{aligned} \tag{3.5}$$

where the recourse at second stage is assumed to be complete, the solution in this stage is a singleton, $A_j \in \Re^{n_j \times s_j}$, $b_j \in \Re^{s_j}$, $c_j^i \in \Re_+^{n_i}$, and some vectors $q_j \in \Re_+^{l_j}$, $v_j \in \Re_+^{l_j}$, $h_j \in \Re_+^{r_j}$, and/or matrices $W_j \in \Re^{r_j \times l_j}$, $T_j^i \in \Re^{r_j \times n_i}$, $1 \leqslant i, j \leqslant m$, can be random. The measure P_x is usually presented by a distribution of random vectors and matrices $\zeta = (q_j, v_j, h_j, W_j, T_j,\ 1 \leqslant j \leqslant m)$.

Stochastic two-stage linear objective functions found many applications in finance, business and market modelling. For instance, the constraints $W_j \cdot y + \sum_{i=1}^{m} T_j^i \cdot x^i \leqslant h_j$ in the model can describe future demands for the corresponding resources and services, depending on random factors h_j, the values of which remain uncertain when making decision at the first stage, etc.

A feasible set of strategies of the j-th player is $D_j = \{x_j \mid \sum_{i=1}^{m} A_j^i \cdot x_i = b_j,\ x_j \in R_+^{n_i}\}$, $1 \leqslant j \leqslant m$, whose strategy depends on the second stage linear problem as well:

$$\min_{\substack{W_j \cdot y + \sum_{i=1}^{m} T_j^i \cdot x_i \leqslant h_j \\ y \in R_+^{l_j}}} v_j \cdot y, \tag{3.6}$$

under a random scenario, distributed according to the measure P_x. Thus, according to the given scenario, a random objective function of this player is as follows:

$$f_j(x, \zeta) = \sum_{i=1}^{m} c_j^i \cdot x_i + q_j \cdot y_j, \tag{3.7}$$

where y_j is the solution of linear problem (3.6), $1 \leqslant j \leqslant m$. Note, that if the coefficients of variables y of the second stage are coincident at the first and second levels, i.e., $q \equiv v$, then the objective function (3.5) corresponds to that of standard two-stage stochastic linear problem.

Let us consider the gradient of stochastic two-stage linear function (3.5). Indeed, it is well known that the sensitivity matrix of the solution of the LP problem against the constraint vector is coincident with the inverse of the basic simplex matrix (see, e.g., [29]). Hence, the subgradient of a random linear objective function of the j-th player (3.7) is defined by means of the basic simplex matrix $W_{b,j}$, obtained at the last step of simplex procedure, in the following way:

$$q_j \cdot \partial y_j = -q_j \cdot W_{b,j}^{-1} \cdot T_j^j, \quad 1 \leqslant j \leqslant m. \tag{3.8}$$

Therefore the stochastic gradient of objective function (3.5) is as follows:

$$\partial_{x_j} f_j = c_j^j - q_j \cdot W_{b,j}^{-1} \cdot T_j^j. \tag{3.9}$$

Next, the properties of mathematical expectations imply the following expression of a gradient of the function $F_j(x)$ (see, [22, 23, 33]):

$$\nabla_{x_j} F_j(x) = E\left(c_j^j - q_j \cdot W_{b,j}^{-1} \cdot T_j^j\right). \tag{3.10}$$

Note, that if $q \equiv v$, then the stochastic gradient is given by the well known expression:

$$g_j(x_j, \zeta) \equiv \partial_{x_j} f_j = c_j - T_j^j \cdot u_j^*, \tag{3.11}$$

where u_j^* is the solution of the dual linear problem:

$$\left(h_j - \sum_{i=1}^{m} T_j^i \cdot x_i\right)^T \cdot u_j^* = \max_u \left[\left(h_j - \sum_{i=1}^{m} T_j^i \cdot x_i\right) \Big| \, u \cdot W_j^T + q_j \geqslant 0, \; u \in R_+^{n_j}\right].$$

Now, whenever the objective functions and their gradients are expressed both as expectations in a certain probabilistic space, the sampling approximations can be applied with a view to establish the equilibrium with an admissible accuracy. Let us define Monte-Carlo estimators to approximate the probabilistic objective functions and their gradients as well. Assume, for simplicity, only the right-hand side vectors h at the second stage of objective function (3.5) to be random.

Next, assume to be possible to simulate the Monte-Carlo samples of a certain size N for any feasible solution $x \in \Re^n$:

$$H = \left(h^1, h^2, \ldots, h^N\right), \tag{3.12}$$

where h^j, $1 \leqslant j \leqslant N$, are independent random vectors, identically distributed with the density $p(x, h)$, and afterwards, to compute the samples of objective functions η_j^k, as well as the samples of their stochastic gradients g_j^k, where $\eta_j^k = f_j(x, h^k)$, $g_j^k = g_j(x, h^k)$, $1 \leqslant j \leqslant m$, $1 \leqslant k \leqslant N$. The following sampling estimators are computed using these samples:

$$\tilde{F}_j(x) = \frac{1}{N} \sum_{k=1}^{N} \eta_j^k, \tag{3.13}$$

$$\tilde{G}_j(x) = \frac{1}{N} \sum_{k=1}^{N} g_j^k, \tag{3.14}$$

$1 \leqslant j \leqslant m$. Assume, the second moments of random objective functions to be existing. Then the sampling variances of objective functions are computed, too:

$$D_j^2(x) = \frac{1}{N} \sum_{k=1}^{N} \left(\eta_j^k - F_j(x)\right)^2, \tag{3.15}$$

that help us to estimate the confidence intervals of estimates (3.13). Let us join the samples of the stochastic gradient of players to one sample: $g^k = (g_1^k, g_2^k, \ldots, g_m^k)$,

$1 \leqslant k \leqslant N$, $1 \leqslant j \leqslant m$, as well as estimators of gradients to one vector: $\tilde{G} = (\tilde{G}_1, \tilde{G}_2, \ldots, \tilde{G}_m)$, $G_j = G_j(x)$, $1 \leqslant j \leqslant m$. Now, let us introduce the sampling covariance matrix of stochastic gradients:

$$Q(x) = \frac{1}{N} \sum_{k=1}^{N} \left(g^k - G(x)\right) \cdot \left(g^k - G(x)\right)^T, \tag{3.16}$$

further will be applied that to normalize the stochastic gradient.

3.3 Search for the Stochastic Nash Equilibrium

Let us consider the problem of stochastic equilibrium of m players, who are in a competitive relationship:

$$F_j(x_1, x_2, \ldots, x_m) = Ef(x_1, x_2, \ldots, x_m, \zeta) \to \min_{x_j \in D_j \subset \Re^{n_j}} \tag{3.17}$$

where objective functions of players obey the conditions and assumptions given above.

If the objective functions are smoothly differentiable, their gradients $G_j : \Re^n \to \Re^{n_j}$, i.e., $G_j(x_1, x_2, \ldots, x_m) = \frac{\partial F_j(x_1, x_2, \ldots, x_m)}{\partial x_j}$, $1 \leqslant j \leqslant m$, are available. It is well-known, that the solution $x^+ = (x_1^+, x_2^+, \ldots, x_m^+)$ of problem (3.17) has to satisfy the "fixed point" conditions [26]:

$$G_j(x_1^+, x_2^+, \ldots, x_m^+) = 0, \quad 1 \leqslant j \leqslant m. \tag{3.18}$$

Let some initial set of strategies be given $x^0 \in D \subset R^n$, the initial Monte-Carlo sample (3.12) of some initial size *N0* be simulated and the relative estimates (3.13)–(3.16) be computed. The simulation based iterative approach to search for the equilibrium point in (3.17) is as follows:

$$x_j^{t+1} = x_j^t - \rho_j \cdot \tilde{G}_j(x^t), \tag{3.19}$$

where $\rho_j > 0$ are certain step-length multipliers, $\tilde{G}_j(x^t)$ is the sampling estimator of gradient (3.14), $1 \leqslant j \leqslant m$.

Certainly, the sequence of sets of the strategies, constructed by means of procedure (3.19) is inherently random and tends only to approximation of the solution. The accuracy of this approximation depends mainly on the Monte-Carlo sample size. Sometimes this size is chosen rather large, in order to ensure the admissible accuracy at all iterations. However, there is no necessity to compute Monte-Carlo estimators with a high accuracy at the beginning of search, when it is enough only to establish an approximate direction to the solution of the equilibrium problem. Hence, the first samples can be taken small, afterwards increasing their size with a view to simulate large samples only at the moment of decision making on solution finding ([22, 23]). This approach is implemented taking the sample size inversely proportional to the square of the stochastic gradient norm in the appropriate metric, as in the following rule:

$$N^{t+1} = \left[\frac{n \cdot Fish(\gamma, n, N^t - n)}{\rho \cdot (\tilde{G}(x^t)^T \cdot (Q(x^t))^{-1} \cdot (\tilde{G}(x^t)} \right] + n, \tag{3.20}$$

where $Fish(\gamma, n, N^t - n)$ is the quantile of Fisher distribution with $(n, N^t - n)$ degrees of freedom, γ is the significance. In order to avoid large fluctuations in the sample size, some minimal and maximal bounds on sample sizes are helpful: $N_{\min} \approx 20 \ldots 50$, and $N_{\max} \approx 1000 \ldots 5000$.

The decision on finding the equilibrium point with an admissible accuracy should be checked for each iteration. Since only Monte-Carlo estimators of objective functions and their gradients are available, only statistical hypotheses on optimality of approximation achieved should be tested. Henceforth, let us consider approximation (3.19) obtained to be sufficient to approximate the solution of problem (3.17), whenever, firstly, the statistical hypothesis about the equality of the gradient to zero (3.18) is not rejected, and, secondly, the confidence intervals of estimates of the objective functions are of the appropriate length. In order to develop the corresponding statistical criteria to test the latter hypotheses, note that, according to CLT, the probability distributions of estimates (3.13) and (3.14) are Gaussian in asymptotics, when the sample size increases. Thus, hypothesis (3.18) on a multiple equality of gradients to zero can be tested by means of multivariate Hotelling T^2-statistics:

$$T_t^2 \equiv \left(N^t - n\right) \cdot \left(\tilde{G}(x^t)\right)^T \cdot \left(Q(x^t)\right)^{-1} \cdot \left(\tilde{G}(x^t)\right)/n \leqslant Fish\left(\mu, n, N^t - n\right). \tag{3.21}$$

Next, one can apply the asymptotic normality again, and decide that confidence intervals are smaller than a certain prescribed value ε with probability β, if: T_t^2/F_μ

$$\eta_\beta \cdot \tilde{D}_j\left(x^t\right)/\sqrt{N^t} \leqslant \varepsilon, \quad 1 \leqslant j \leqslant m, \tag{3.22}$$

where η_β is a β—quantile of the standard normal distribution.

If at least one condition from (3.21) and (3.22) is not valid, then procedure (3.19) is repeated by simulating new samples (3.12) and computing estimates (3.13)–(3.16) at the point x_j^{t+1} and taking the sample size according to (3.20). However, if both criteria (3.21), (3.22) are satisfied then there no reasons to reject the optimality hypothesis, which makes a basis to terminate the search for equilibrium and decide about finding it with an admissible accuracy. The search process should converge a.s. to equilibrium under certain conditions on the convexity and smoothness of the objective functions of players (see, [22, 23]). Thus, the equilibrium is established with an admissible accuracy and search terminates after a random but finite number of simulated samples.

Example 1 (Stochastic Nash equilibrium of electricity market). Let us consider an electricity spot market with M generators, which compete with one another in dispatching electricity. Assume, the inverse demand function to be $p(Q, \zeta(\omega))$, where $p(Q, \zeta(\omega))$ is the market price, Q is the total electricity supply to the market and $\zeta : \Omega \to \Re$ is a random variable, which describes the uncertainty of demand (see, more details in [33]). Each i-th generator chooses the quantity of electricity q_i to be produced and supplied for dispatch, $1 \leqslant i \leqslant M$. Then the expected profit of ith generator is

$$R_i(q_i, Q_{i-1}) = E\left[q_i p(Q, \zeta) - C_i(q_i) + H_i\big(p(Q, \zeta)\big)\right], \tag{3.23}$$

where $Q_{i-1} = Q - q_i$ stands for the bids offered to the market by all competitors of the ith generator, $C_i(q_i)$ denotes the cost of producing the quantity q_i of electricity by the ith's generator, $H_i(p(Q, \zeta))$ denotes the payments related to contracts, which generators sign with retailers before entering the spot market, $1 \leqslant i \leqslant M$. The contracts are used to hedge risks arising due to uncertainty in market demand. By selling a call option at a strike price f, the i-th generator pays $w_i \cdot (p - f)$ to the contract holder, if $p > f$, but no payment is made, if $p \leqslant f$, where w_i is the quantity signed by the generator on contract at the strike price f, i.e.:

$$H_i\big(p(Q, \zeta)\big) = -w_i \max\big(p(Q, \zeta) - f, 0\big). \tag{3.24}$$

The decision making problem of the i-th generator is to choose an optimal quantity q_i such that its expected profit were maximized. Hence, assuming every generator to be maximizing its profit, the competition of generators in the electricity market is presented as a stochastic Nash equilibrium problem:

$$-E\big(q_i p(Q, \xi) - C_i(q_i) - w_i \max\big(p(Q, \xi) - f, 0\big)\big) \to \min_{0 \leqslant q_i \leqslant q_{i,\max}}, \tag{3.25}$$

where $q_{i,\max}$ is the maximal generation capacity of the i-th generator, $1 \leqslant i \leqslant M$.

Let us consider, for example, the competition of $M = 3$ generators with an inverse demand function $p(q, \zeta) = \alpha \cdot \zeta + \alpha_0 - q$, $\alpha = 20$, $\alpha_0 = 30$, the strike price is $f = 22$, ζ is random with an uniform distribution on [0, 1]. The quantities of call options and cost functions for the three generators are presented in Table 3.1.

Table 3.1 Call options and cost functions

Generator	w_i	$C_i(q_i)$
1	10	$q_1^2 + 2q_1$
2	8	$2q_2^2 + 2q_2$
3	0	$2q_3^2 + 3q_3$

Table 3.2 Exact and computed equilibrium

t	q_1	q_2	q_3	Q	$\mathrm{E}[p(Q,\xi)]$	R_1	R_2	R_3	N^t	T_t^2/F_μ
1	10	10	10	30	10.274	−17.26	−117.26	−127.26	2	6.4 × 103
2	7.827	5.827	5.727	19.382	20.708	65.91	25.69	35.81	9	70.263
3	7.784	5.132	4.634	17.550	22.324	70.64	30.05	46.60	204	2.474
4	7.983	5.000	4.250	17.233	22.547	72.65	30.62	46.95	2,233	1.004
5	8.151	4.961	4.079	17.191	22.959	74.33	30.70	48.14	926	0.999
6	8.358	5.022	4.036	17.416	22.505	73.38	30.02	46.14	4,085	1.002
7	8.440	4.992	3.968	17.401	22.793	74.58	30.21	47.05	10,316	0.970
8	8.532	5.011	3.963	17.506	22.540	74.79	30.58	46.03	3,656	1.000
9	8.552	4.980	3.936	17.468	22.384	74.37	30.46	45.31	2,538	1.000
10	8.544	4.944	3.906	17.394	22.609	74.93	30.48	46.08	39,748	0.252
Analytical solution										
q^*	8.642	4.980	3.923	17.547	21.687	75.70	30.70	46.50		

The task considered has been solved starting from the set of strategies $q = (10, 10, 10)$, afterwards simulating the Monte-Carlo samples, choosing the strategies (q_1, q_2, q_3) in a sequential way according to (3.19) and adopting the sample size N^t according to (3.20). The results of computer simulation are presented in Table 3.2, where an analytically obtained solution of the problem is given for comparison and for brevity of notation denoted: $F_\mu = Fish(\mu, n, N^t - n)$. The results presented enable us to conclude that only a few samples have to be simulated in order to obtain the set of equilibrium strategies.

3.4 Importance Sampling by Bilevel Stochastic Programming

A lot of equilibrium problems are solved as bilevel optimization problems:

$$\begin{aligned} F(x, y) &= Ef(x, y, \zeta) \to \min_{x \in D \subset \Re^n}, \\ \Psi(x, y) &= E\varphi(x, y, \zeta) \to \min_{y \in B \subset \Re^m}, \end{aligned} \tag{3.26}$$

where using the terminology of bi-level programming the first problem is called the *leader* problem and the next one is called the *follower* problem ([5]). Assume that the objective functions in (3.26) obey the conditions and assumptions of Sect. 3.2.

In order to show the technique of sequential bi-level stochastic programming, let us consider as an example an application of importance sampling to stochastic programming. Importance sampling is a variance reduction technique that can be used to decrease the number of simulated scenarios in the sampling approximation of stochastic programming. The idea behind importance sampling is that certain values of the input random variables in a simulation make a greater impact on the parameter being estimated than others [4, 8, 13]. If these "important" values are emphasized by sampling more frequently, then the estimator variance can be reduced. Hence, the basic methodology in importance sampling is to choose a distribution such that "encourages" the important values. The fundamental issue in implementing the importance sampling simulation is the choice of a new distribution which encourages the important regions of input variables. Hence, the choice of the importance sampling distribution is considered as the follower problem to the main optimization solved as a leader problem.

Thus, let that the problem to be solved is the optimization of expectation:

$$F(x) = Ef(x, \zeta) \to \min_{x \in D \subset \Re^n}. \tag{3.27}$$

Under the assumptions made let us write down the objective function of the problem considered as a multivariate integral:

$$F(x) \equiv \int_\Omega f(x,s)p(x,s)\,ds. \tag{3.28}$$

Now, we apply the measure change approach by introducing a new density $\varphi : \Re^m \times \Omega \to \Re_+$, depending on certain parameters $y \in \Re^m$, the choice of which is discussed below. Thus, the objective function (3.28) becomes an expectation with respect to this new random vector:

$$F(x) \equiv \int_\Omega \left(f(x,s)\cdot q(x,y,s)\right)\cdot \varphi(y,s)\,ds, \tag{3.29}$$

where $q(x,y,s) = \frac{p(x,s)}{\varphi(y,s)}$, and, besides, it is assumed that $\varphi(y,s) > 0$ for any $s \in \Omega$. The second moment of the random function under integration in expectation (3.29) is as follows:

$$D(x,y) = \int_\Omega \left(f(x,s)\cdot q(x,y,s)\right)^2 \cdot \varphi(y,s)\,ds = \int_\Omega \frac{(f(x,s)\cdot p(x,s))^2}{\varphi(y,s)}\,ds. \tag{3.30}$$

Thus, the variance of the random function under integration in (3.29), which is obviously $D(x,y) - F(x)^2$, decreases, if the second moment (3.30) decreased. Hence, by changing the variable y in (3.30) in an appropriate way it is possible to reduce the variance and so the idea is to apply optimization in such a case. To this end the bi-level stochastic optimization problem has to be solved:

$$F(x) \equiv \int_\Omega f(x,s)\cdot q(x,y,s)\cdot \varphi(y,s)\,ds \to \min_{x \in D \subset \Re^n}, \tag{3.31}$$

$$D(x,y) \equiv \int_\Omega \left(f(x,s)\cdot q(x,y,s)\right)^2 \cdot \varphi(y,s)\,ds \to \min_y, \tag{3.32}$$

where the first one is the leader problem and the second one is the follower problem.

Let us apply the approach considered in solving the two stage stochastic linear problem with objective function (3.5):

$$F(x) = c \cdot x + E\{\min_{y} \left[q \cdot z \,\middle|\, W \cdot z + T \cdot x \leqslant h,\ z \in R_{+}^{m} \right]\} \to \min, \qquad Ax = b, \quad x \in \Re_{+}^{n}, \tag{3.33}$$

where matrices W, T, A, and vectors c, q, h, b are of appropriate size, $c = q$, the vector h is multi-normal random $N(\mu, \Sigma)$, μ is the mean vector, and Σ is the covariance matrix. Denote the density function of a normally distributed vector $N(y, \Sigma)$ by $p(\cdot, y) : \Re^{m} \to \Re_{+}$, and apply this density to change of a measure, by changing the mean vector y in order to decrease the variance (3.32). Thus, denote

$$f(x,h) = \min_{\substack{W \cdot z + T \cdot x \leqslant h \\ z \in R_{+}^{m}}} q \cdot z. \tag{3.34}$$

Now, after simple manipulations one can get sure that:

$$F(x) \equiv \int_{\Omega} f(x,h) \cdot q(y,h) \cdot p(h,y)\, dh, \tag{3.35}$$

where

$$q(y,h) = \frac{p(h,\mu)}{p(h,y)} = \exp\left(-(\mu - y)^{T} \cdot \Sigma^{-1} \cdot (\mu + y - 2h) \right). \tag{3.36}$$

Consequently:

$$D(x,y) = \int_{\Omega} \frac{(f(x,h) \cdot p(h,\mu))^{2}}{p(h,y)}\, dh. \tag{3.37}$$

It is easy to make sure that the gradient of variance (3.37) with respect to the parameter vector y is as follows:

$$B(x,y) \equiv \frac{\partial D(x,y)}{\partial y} = \int_{\Omega} (y - h) \cdot \Sigma^{-1} \cdot b(x,y,h) \cdot p(h,y)\, dh, \tag{3.38}$$

where

$$b(x,y,h) = \left(f(x,h) \cdot q(y,\mu) \right)^{2}. \tag{3.39}$$

Note, that the gradient of the objective function in (3.33) with respect to the variable x is presented by means of (3.11) as a mathematical expectation of the vector function $g(x,y)$. Now, since objective functions $F(x)$, $D(x,y)$ and their gradients are presented as expectations, the Monte-Carlo simulation-based approach becomes a tool way to solve bi-level problem (3.31) and (3.32).

Let us define Monte-Carlo estimators and the iterative procedure to solve the stochastic programming problem (3.33) by importance sampling using (3.31) and (3.32). Assume the random sample (3.12), distributed with respect to the density $p(\cdot, \cdot)$, to be simulated as well as the corresponding Monte-Carlo estimates (3.13) of the objective function (3.33) and the variance (3.37), i.e., $\tilde{F}(x, y)$ and $\tilde{D}(x, y)$, to be computed. Besides, the corresponding estimates (3.14) of gradients $\tilde{G}(x, y)$ and $\tilde{B}(x, y) = \frac{1}{N}\sum_{j=1}^{N}(h^j - y) \cdot \Sigma^{-1} \cdot b(x, y, h^j)$ are computed with respect to expectations in (3.10) and (3.38) as well. The sampling covariance matrix (3.16) of a sample of the stochastic gradient of the objective function is also computed for a further normalization of stochastic gradient.

Let us develop a simulation-based importance sampling approach for solving a two-stage stochastic linear problem by the method of ε-projection of the stochastic gradient [23, 24]. Suppose that initial approximations $x^0 \in D \subset \Re^n$, $y^0 = \mu$, are given, a certain initial sample size N^0 is chosen and the random sequence $\{x^t, y^t, N^t\}_{t=0}^{\infty}$ is defined according to

$$x^{t+1} = x^t - \rho \cdot \tilde{G}_\varepsilon(x^t, y^t), \tag{3.40}$$

$$y^{t+1} = y^t - \alpha \cdot \tilde{B}(x^t, y^t), \tag{3.41}$$

$$N^{t+1} = \frac{1}{b^t} \cdot N^t, \tag{3.42}$$

where $\tilde{G}_\varepsilon(x^t, y^t)$ is the ε-projection of the stochastic gradient to a feasible set (see definition in [23, 24]), $\rho > 0$, $\alpha > 0$, $b^t > 0$ are some parameters of the method.

It can be proved by the martingale approach that, under an appropriate choice of parameters of the method, the sequence (3.40) and (3.41) converges a.s. to the solution of problem (3.31), (3.32), meanwhile, the sample size, chosen according to (3.42), is infinitely increased (see, [22, 23]). Note that the choice of Monte-Carlo sample size according to (3.42), where the sample size is selected inversely proportional to the square of the stochastic gradient similarly as in (3.20), allows us to solve the problem by simulating a reasonable volume of random samples.

Also, the necessary optimality condition means that the gradient of the objective function is equal to zero in the optimum. Hence, the optimization is terminated when the gradient of the leader problem becomes smaller than some admissible value. Indeed, the iterative process can be stopped, when testing the statistical hypothesis on the equality of the gradient of the objective function to zero is not rejected, and, besides, the confidence interval of estimator of objective function becomes of the proper length. Since the sample size increases during optimization, the distribution of the Monte-Carlo estimators is approximated by the normal law, which enables us to construct statistical termination rules similar to (3.21) and (3.22) (see, [23, 24]).

Example 2. The developed importance sampling approach has been explored by computer simulation, when solving the two-stage stochastic linear optimisation test problem taken from the database at http://www.math.bme.hu/~deak/twostage/

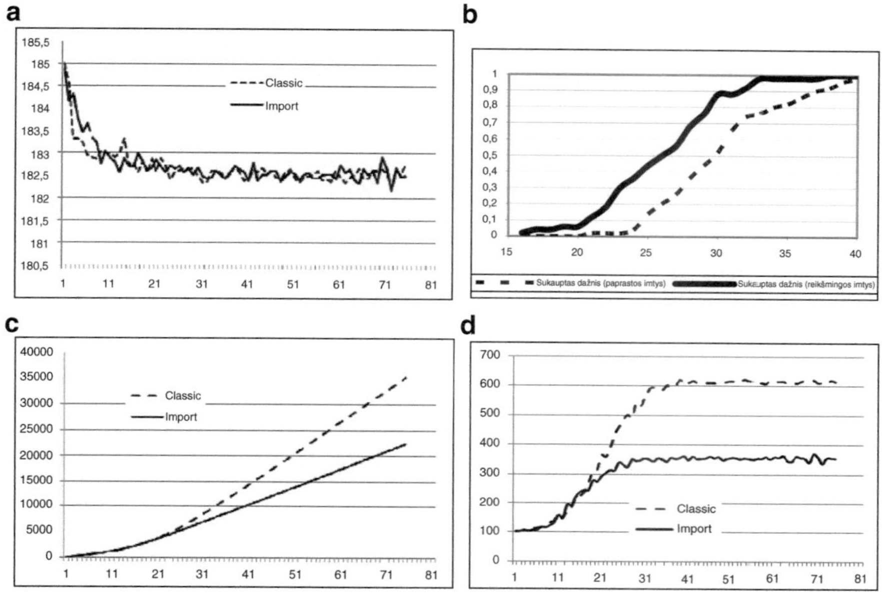

Fig. 3.1 Average results: (**a**) objective function value: (**b**) frequency of termination; (**c**) total size of Monte-Carlo samples; (**d**) Monte-Carlo sample size

11/20x20.1 (see, also [24]). The dimensions of the task are as follows: the first stage has 10 rows and 20 variables; the second stage has 20 rows and 30 variables. The estimate of the optimal value of the objective function given in the database is 182.94234 ± 0.066.

The example has been tested 100 times by the approach develcped with the following parameters: $\rho = 0.0005$, $\alpha = 0.1$, b^t was chosen in the way described in [24]. The number of iterations has been checked when the termination conditions were satisfied the first time (the statistical hypothesis of gradient equality to zero was not rejected with the probability $1 - \mu = 0, 95$, and the confidence interval of the objective function estimate didn't exceeded the admissible value $\varepsilon = 2$).

The averaged dependencies of the objective function value on the number of iterations are depicted in Fig. 3.1a, obtained by the stochastic sequential optimisation with the importance sampling (*Import*) and without (*Classic*). In Fig. 3.1a one can see the convergence of the approach considered in both cases. The dependence of frequency of termination is presented in Fig. 3.1b, which illustrates the decrease in the number of iterations under termination using the importance sampling. The total size of Monte-Carlo samples applied in the optimization and the Monte-Carlo sample size in each current iteration are depicted in Fig. 3.1c, d, which show that the importance sampling enables us to decrease the amount of samples required for optimisation about twice.

Thus, the results obtained enable us to conclude that the importance sampling enables us to decrease the number of iterations needed to achieve the termination conditions as well as to decrease the Monte-Carlo sample size at each iteration.

3.5 Stochastic Programming with *CVaR*

An operationally convenient definition of *CVaR* is given by Rockafellar and Uryasev [19]:

$$CVaR_\alpha(x) = \min_{u \in \Re}\left(u + \frac{1}{1-\alpha}E\left[f(x,\zeta) - u\right]^+\right) \tag{3.43}$$

where $[t]^+ = \max(0,t)$, $0 < \alpha < 1$ is a probability of risk, $f : D \times \Omega \to \Re$ is a random objective function.

The level of risk-aversion is expressed as a weighted sum with the weight θ on the function to be optimized and with the weight $(1-\theta)$ on the risk measure, where $0 \leqslant \theta \leqslant 1$. Let us consider the risk-aversion level optimization problem with multiple *CVaR* constraints:

$$\begin{aligned} F_0(x) &= \theta \cdot E\left[f_0(x,\zeta)\right] + (1-\theta)\cdot CVaR_{\alpha_0}\left[f_0(x,\zeta)\right] \to \min_x \\ F_i(x) &= CVaR_{\alpha_i}\left[f_i(x,\zeta)\right] \leqslant \eta_i, \quad i = 1,2,\ldots,m, \end{aligned} \tag{3.44}$$

where the conditional value at risk follows by definition (3.43), $0 < \alpha_i < 1$, $i = 0,1,2,\ldots,m$, objective functions f and probability density p obey assumptions described in Sect. 3.2.

Thus, problem (3.44) is written down in a framework of bi-level stochastic optimisation:

$$\begin{aligned} F_0(x) = \theta \cdot \int_{R^l} f_0(x,z)\cdot p(x,z)\,dz + (1-\theta) \\ \cdot\left(u_0 + \frac{1}{\alpha_0}\cdot\int_{R^l}\left(f_0(x,z) - u_0\right)^+ \cdot p(x.z)\,dz\right) \to \min_{x,u_0} \end{aligned} \tag{3.45}$$

$$F_i(x) = \min_{u_i \in \Re}\left(u_i + \frac{1}{\alpha_i}\cdot\int_{R^l}\left(f_i(x,z) - u_i\right)^+ \cdot p(x,z)\,dz\right) \leqslant \eta_i, \quad i = 1,2,\ldots,m.$$

Note, that the standard Lagrangian of problem (3.45) is $F_0(x) + \sum_{i=1}^m \lambda_i \cdot F_i(x)$, to compute which one has to solve the problem (3.43) on the second level. Let us introduce the extended Lagrange function (LF):

$$L(x,\lambda,u) \equiv El(x,\lambda,u,\zeta) = \theta \cdot \int_{R^l} f_0(x,z) \cdot p(x,z)\,dz$$
$$+ \sum_{i=0}^{m} \lambda_i \cdot \left(u_i - \eta_i + \frac{1}{\alpha_i} \cdot \int_{R^n} \left(f_i(x,z) - u_i\right)^+ \cdot p(x,z)\,dz \right), \quad (3.46)$$

as well as extended constraint functions (CF)

$$L_i(x,u) \equiv El(x,u,\zeta) = u_i - \eta_i + \frac{1}{\alpha_i} \cdot \int_{R^n} \left(f_i(x,z) - u_i\right)^+ \cdot p(x,z)\,dz, \quad (3.47)$$

that may be treated as expectations of the stochastic Lagrange function

$$l(x,\lambda,u,\zeta) = \theta \cdot f_0(x,\zeta) + \sum_{i=0}^{m} \lambda_i \cdot \left(u_i - \eta_i + \frac{(f_i(x,\zeta) - u_i)^+}{\alpha_i} \right), \quad (3.48)$$

and of random constraint functions, respectively,

$$l_i(x,u,\zeta) = u_i - \eta_i + \frac{(f_i(x,\zeta) - u_i)^+}{\alpha_i}, \quad (3.49)$$

where $\lambda = (\lambda_0, \lambda_1, \ldots, \lambda_m)$, $\lambda_i \geqslant 0$, $i = 1,2,\ldots,m$, $\lambda_0 = 1 - \theta$, $\eta_0 = 0$, $u = (u_0, u_1, \ldots, u_m)$.

Note, that the functions $l(x,\lambda,u,\zeta)$ and $l_i(x,u,\zeta)$, $i = 1,2,\ldots,m$, are Lipschitzian with respect to x and u, and therefore their subgradients are available, which can be taken as stochastic gradients. Following the remarks about differentiability of objective functions in Sect. 3.2, the extended Lagrange function $L(x,\lambda,u)$ and constraint functions $L_i(x,u)$ are smoothly differentiable and allow their expression by expectations. Hence, denote the gradient of LF as $G(x,\lambda,u) = Eg(x,\lambda,u,\zeta)$ and that of CF as $G_i(x,u) = Eg_i(x,u,\zeta)$, $i = 1,2,\ldots,m$.

Let $x^* \in R^n$ be now the solution of SP problem (3.44). By virtue of the Karush–Kuhn–Tucker theorem and rules of *CVaR* differentiation [19] the values $\lambda_i^* \geqslant 0$, $u_i^* \geqslant 0$, $i = 0,1,\ldots,m$, exist such that

$$\begin{aligned} &G(x,\lambda,u) \equiv \nabla F_0(x^*) + \sum_{i=0}^{m} \lambda_i^+ \cdot G_i(x,u) = 0, \\ &\lambda_i^* \cdot \left(L_i(x,u) - \eta_i\right) = 0, \quad i = 1,2,\ldots,m, \\ &\Pr\left(f_i(x^*,\zeta) \geqslant u_i^*\right) = \alpha_i, \quad i = 0,1,\ldots,m. \end{aligned} \quad (3.50)$$

If the random objective functions $f_i(x^*,\zeta)$, $i = 0,1,\ldots,m$, are linear, one may transform the given problem to a large linear programming (LP) problem and solve it by the Sample Average Approximation (SAA) approach. However, the attained LP problem may be very large and so to solve it, one may require huge computing resources. On the other hand, it is not clear how to solve the problem, where some of the functions $f_i(x^*, \zeta), i = 0, 1, \ldots, m$, are nonlinear. Therefore the simulation-based approach is of interest by using sequences of Monte Carlo samples.

Assume, random sample (3.12) to be simulated and the corresponding samples of functions $l(x, \lambda, u, \zeta)$ and $l_i(x, u, \zeta)$, as well as the stochastic gradients $g(x, \lambda, u, \zeta)$ and $g_i(x, u, \zeta), i = 1, 2, \ldots, m$, be computed. Thus, one can compute the Monte-Carlo estimates $L(x, \lambda, u)$, $L_i(x, u)$, $\tilde{G}(x, \lambda, u)$ and $G_i(x, u)$, $i = 1, 2, \ldots, m$ of LF, CF and their gradients. Denote the corresponding sampling variances of stochastic constraint functions by $\tilde{D}_i^2(x, u)$, $i = 1, 2, \ldots, m$, and the sampling covariance matrix of the stochastic gradient of LF by $Q(x, \lambda, u)$ [see (3.15) and (3.16)]. Besides, denote the ratios

$$\mathrm{Pr}_i = \frac{N_i}{N}, \tag{3.51}$$

where N_i are the frequencies of events $\{u_i\colon F_i(x, z^j) \geqslant u_i\}$, that occurred in the Monte-Carlo sample (3.12), $i = 0, 1, \ldots, m$.

In order to find the solution to problem (3.44), we apply the Monte-Carlo estimators introduced. Note, that the steepest descent method of stochastic nonlinear optimization by Monte-Carlo series has been developed in [22], however, the steepest descent algorithm slowly converges for functions with poorly defined Hessian. Therefore, let us consider the Stochastic Variable Metric (SVM) method, which helps us fasten the convergence (see [28]). Thus, assume that the initial point $x^0 \in \Re^n$ and vectors $\lambda^0, u^0 \in \Re^m_+$ to be given as well as random sample (3.12) of a certain initial size N^0 to be generated at this point, and the corresponding Monte-Carlo estimates (3.13)–(3.16) to be computed. Thus, the following stochastic procedure of SVM is applicable:

$$x^{t+1} = x^t - \left(Q^t\right)^{-1} \cdot \tilde{G}\left(x^t, \lambda^t, u^t\right),$$

$$\lambda_i^{t+1} = \max\left[0, \lambda_i^t + \gamma_i\left(\tilde{L}_i(x^t) + \mu_\beta \cdot \tilde{D}_i(x^t)\right)\right], \quad i = 1, 2, \ldots, m, \tag{3.52}$$

$$u_i^{t+1} = u_i^t + \pi_i \cdot \left(\frac{\mathrm{Pr}_i}{\alpha_i} - 1\right), \quad i = 0, 1, \ldots, m$$

where $\gamma_i > 0$, $\pi_i > 0$ are normalizing multipliers, μ_β is the β-quantile of the standard normal distribution, and the stochastic gradient covariance matrix Q is applied to change a variable metric. Note that, in order to ensure the validity of constraints with an admissible confidence β, when Lagrange multipliers λ are computed, the upper bound is applied here on constraints, where μ_β is the quantile of the standard normal distribution.

Since Monte-Carlo estimates applied here are random, in general, the sample size regulation similar to (3.20), is also used, taking the sample size inversely proportional to the square norm of the gradient estimate of LF. Termination of algorithms is also performed in the statistical way, testing the statistical hypothesis of equality of the LF gradient to zero and validity of *CVaR* and *VaR* constraints in (3.50). Hence, the algorithm can be terminated, if the hypothesis on the equality of the LF gradient to zero is not rejected according to the criteria similar to (3.20), the constraint conditions vanish with a given probability β_i:

$$\tilde{f_i}(x^t) + \mu_{\beta_i} \cdot \tilde{D}_{f_i}(x^t) \leqslant 0, \quad i = 1, 2, \ldots, m, \tag{3.53}$$

the estimated lengths of the confidence interval of the objective function and that of the constraints do not exceed the given accuracy ε_i:

$$2\eta_{\beta_i} \cdot D_{F_i}/\sqrt{N} \leqslant \varepsilon_i, \quad i = 0, 1, \ldots, m, \tag{3.54}$$

η_{β_i} is the β_i-quantile of the standard normal distribution, and parameters u are properly chosen when estimating *CVaR*:

$$|\Pr_i - \alpha_i| \leqslant \eta_{\tau_i} \cdot \sqrt{\frac{\Pr_i \cdot (1 - \Pr_i)}{N}}, \quad i = 1, 2, \ldots, m. \tag{3.55}$$

If these conditions are valid, there is a basis to terminate the optimization and make a decision on the optimum finding with a permissible accuracy. If only one of these conditions is not satisfied, then the next sample should be generated and the optimization be continued.

Example 3. The sequential simulation-based approach for stochastic programming with *CVaR* has been tested by the Monte-Carlo method by simulating the piecewise-linear test functions:

$$f_i(x, \zeta) = \max_{1 \leqslant k \leqslant k_n} \left(a_{0,k} + \sum_{j=1}^{n} a_{j,k} \cdot (x_j + \zeta_j) \right), \quad 0 \leqslant i \leqslant m, \tag{3.56}$$

where the coefficients $a_{j,k}$ were chosen random. For each number of variables $n = 2, 5, 10, 20, 50, 100$, the sample from $M = 100$ sets of normally distributed coefficients $a_{j,k}$ has been simulated with the following values: $a_{0,0} = \vartheta$, $a_{1,0} = 1 + 3 \cdot \vartheta$, $a_{i,k} = a'_{i,k} - \frac{1}{k_n} \cdot \sum_{k1=1}^{k_n} a'_{i,k1}$, $a'_{0,k} = 2\vartheta$, $a'_{1,k} = \vartheta$, $1 \leqslant k \leqslant k_k$, $m = 0, 1$, where ϑ is a standard normal. Details of the test problem are given in Table 3.3.

Table 3.3 Data of the test problem

n	u_0	u_1	η_1	ε	k_n	min, *it*	max, *it*	aver., *it*
2	3.34	3.46	4.5	0.015	5	8	16	9.4
5	4.93	6.82	7	0.1	11	8	22	12.5
10	8.33	8.63	9	0.1	21	6	14	7.7
20	12.42	9.59	11.5	0.075	31	14	53	26.6
50	20.84	14.01	15	0.1	76	44	88	59.9

The confidence levels of *CVaR* have been taken $\alpha_0, \alpha_1 = 0,1$, the value of η_1 in *CVaR* constraint is given in Table 3.3. Termination conditions in (3.20), (3.54) and (3.55) have been tested with probability 0.95.

Next, the Expected Value solution (EVS) of the problem (3.45) has been obtained [14] for respective test functions (3.56), where the variables ζ_k were distributed normally $N(0; 0,5)$. EVS of *CVaR* threshold variables u_0 and u_1 are given in Table 3.3, which have been taken as initial approximations to the method defined by (3.54) and (3.55).

The results of optimization by this method are given in Table 3.3 as well as depicted in Fig. 3.2a–f, where the left column of pictures presents the results for $n = 2$ and, the right column shows the same for $n = 50$. The averaged dependencies of the objective function value as well as the probabilities of *CVaR* on the number of iterations are given in Fig. 3.2a–c, illustrating the convergence of the approach

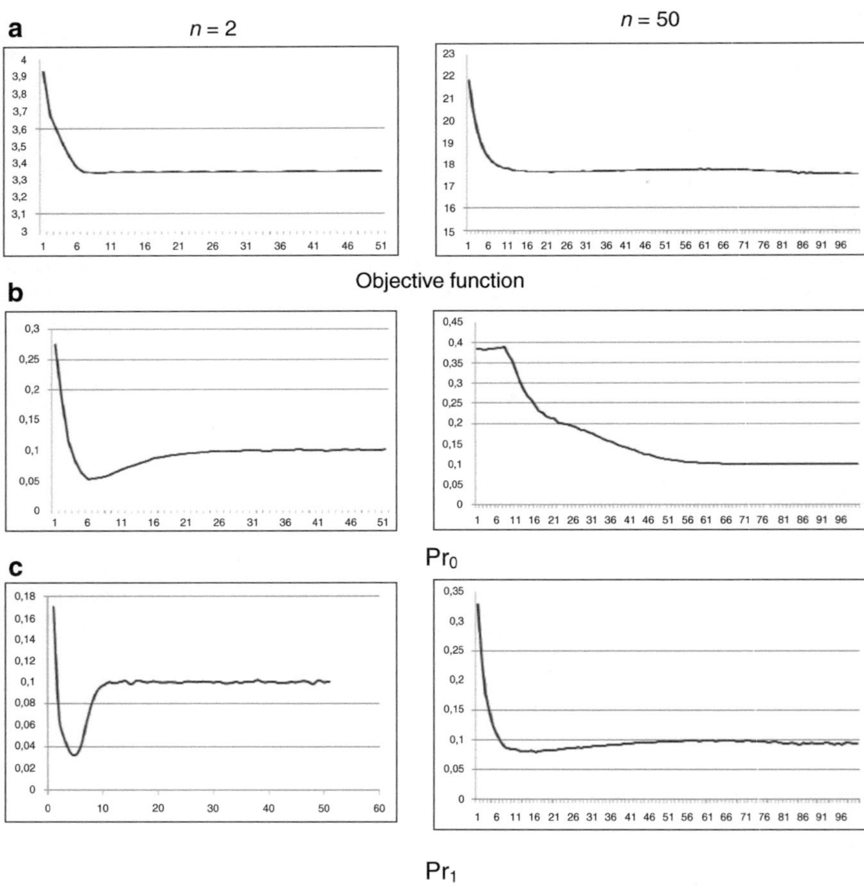

Fig. 3.2 Averaged results of simulation: (**a**) objective function value; (**b**) frequency Pr_0; (**c**) frequency Pr_1; (**d**) frequency of termination; (**e**) ratio of Hotelling criteria (3.20) with 0.95-quantile of Fisher distribution; (**f**) Monte-Carlo sample size at iteration. The results for $n = 2$ are presented in the *left column* and, that for $n = 50$ is presented in the *right column*

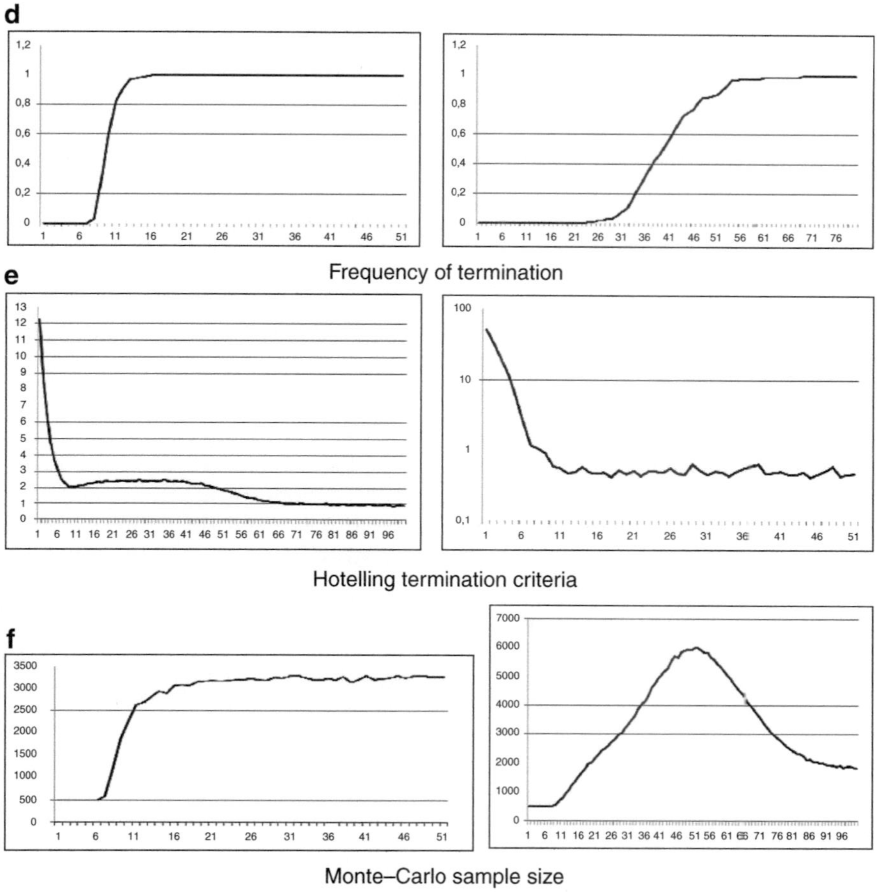

Fig. 3.2 (continued)

developed. All the test problems in samples have been solved with admissible accuracy, i.e., terminated according to criteria (3.20), (3.54) and (3.55) after a certain number of iterations. The maximal, minimal, and averaged number of iterations needed for termination of the test functions, depending on number of variables n and an admissible length of the confidence interval ε are shown in Table 3.3. The frequency of termination under a the number of iterations is presented in Fig. 3.2d. The change of the ratio of Hotelling criteria with the corresponding quantile of Fisher distribution depending on the number of iterations is given in Fig. 3.2e, which shows how this ratio tends to the critical termination value 1. The averaged number of Monte-Carlo sample size at each iteration is given in Fig. 3.2f, which shows the adaptation of this sample during the optimization process. Thus, the results of Monte-Carlo simulation are illustrating the convergence of this approach and ability to solve the stochastic programming problems, when *CVaR* is included in objective and constraints, with admissible accuracy treated in a statistical manner.

3.6 Discussion and Conclusions

The sequential simulation-based approach has been developed to solve the stochastic equilibrium problems by finite sequences of Monte-Carlo samples. The approach is grounded on the stochastic termination procedure and the rule for iterative regulation of the size of Monte-Carlo samples. Also, the approach enables us to take into account the stochastic model risk.

The regulation of sample size, if the size is taken inversely proportional to the square of the gradient norm of the Monte-Carlo estimate, allows us to solve stochastic equilibrium problems rationally from the computational viewpoint and guarantees the convergence. Besides, the proposed stopping procedure allows us to test the optimality hypothesis and to evaluate the confidence intervals of the objective and constraint functions in a statistical way. The numerical study and the practice example corroborate theoretical conclusions. Although it was confined itself to the stochastic Nash equilibrium, the stochastic two-stage programming with importance sampling and stochastic programming with *CvaR*, one can conclude that the method can be applied to a variety of other stochastic programming problems, too.

References

1. Bartkute, V., Sakalauskas, L.: Simultaneous perturbation stochastic approximation for nonsmooth functions. Eur. J. Oper. Res. **181**(3), 1174–1188 (2007). ISSN: 0377–2217
2. Bayraksan, G., Morton, D.P.: A sequential sampling procedure for stochastic programming. Oper. Res. **59**(4), 898–913 (2011)
3. Birge, J.R., Louveaux, F.: Introduction to Stochastic Programming. Springer Series in Operations Research. Springer, New York (2010)
4. Bucklew, J.A.: Introduction to Rare Event Simulation. Springer, New York (2004)
5. Bard, J.F.: Practical Bilevel Optimization. Nonconvex Optimization and Its Applications, vol. 30. Kluwer Academic, Dordrecht (1988)
6. Cairoli, R., Dalang, R.C.: Sequential Stochastic Optimization. Wiley Series in Probability and Statistics. Wiley, New York (1996)
7. Carrión, M., Arroyo, J.M., Conejo, A.J.: A bilevel stochastic programming approach for retailer futures market trading. IEEE Trans. Power Syst. **24**(3), 1446–1456 (2009)
8. Changhe, Y.C., Druzdzel, M.J.: Importance sampling algorithms for bayesian networks: principles and performance. Math. Comput. Model. **43**(9–10), 1189–1207 (2006)
9. Colson, B., Marcotte, P., Savard, G.: An overview of bilevel optimization. Ann. Oper. Res. **153**(1), 235–256 (2007)
10. Dempster, M.A.H.: Sequential importance sampling algorithms for dynamic stochastic programming. Trans. St. Petersburg Steklov Math. Inst. **312**, 94–129 (2004)

11. Henrion, R., Römisch, W.: On M-stationary point for a stochastic equilibrium problem under equilibrium constraints in electricity spot market modeling. Appl. Math. **52**, 473–494 (2007)
12. Kosuch, S., Le Bodic, P., Leung, J., Lisser, A.: On a stochastic bilevel programming problem. Networks **59**(1), 107–116 (2012)
13. Kurtz, N., Song, J.: Cross-entropy-based adaptive importance sampling using Gaussian mixture. Struct. Saf. **42**, 35–44 (2013)
14. Maggioni, G., Wallace, S.: Analyzing the quality of the expected value solution in stochastic programming. Ann. Oper. Res. **200**(1), 37–54 (2012)
15. Mockus, J.: On simulation of the Nash equilibrium in the stock exchange contest. Informatica **23**(1), 77–104 (2012)
16. Ngo, M.H., Krishnamurthy, V.: Game theoretic cross-layer transmission policies in multipacket reception wireless networks. IEEE Trans. Signal Process. **55**, 1911–1926 (2007)
17. Patriksson, M., Wynster, L.: Stochastic nonlinear bilevel programming. Comput. Chem. Eng. **28**, 767–773 (2004)
18. Ponce-Ortega, J.M., Rico-Ramirez, V., Hernandez-Castro, S., Diwekar, U.M.: Improving convergence of the stochastic decomposition algorithm by using an efficient sampling technique. Comput. Chem. Eng. **28**(5), 767–773 (2004)
19. Rockafellar, R.T., Uryasev, S.: Optimization of conditional value-at-risk. J. Risk **2**, 21–41 (2000)
20. Rubinstein, R.Y., Melamed, B.: Modern Simulation and Modeling. Wiley Series in Probability and Statistics: Applied Probability and Statistics. Wiley, New York (1998)
21. Ruszczynski, A.: Decomposition methods. In: Ruszczynski, A., Shapiro, A. (eds.) Handbook in Operations Research and Management Science, vol. 10, pp. 141–212. Elsevier Science, Amsterdam (2003)
22. Sakalauskas, L.: Nonlinear stochastic programming by Monte-Carlo estimators. Eur. J. Oper. Res. **137**, 558–573 (2002)
23. Sakalauskas, L.: Nonlinear stochastic optimization by Monte-Carlo estimators. Informatica **15**(2), 271–282 (2004)
24. Sakalauskas, L., Žilinskas, K.: Epsilon-projection method for two-stage SLP. Lith. Math. J. **48/49**, 320–326 (2008)
25. Shapiro, A.: Stochastic programming with equilibrium constraints. J. Optim. Theory Appl. **128**(1), 223–243 (2006)
26. Shoham, Y., Leyton-Brown, K.: Multiagent Systems: Algorithmic, Game-Theoretic, and Logical Foundations. Cambridge University Press, New York (2009)
27. Sutiene, K., Makackas, D., Pranevicius, H.: Multistage K-Means clustering for scenario tree construction. Informatica **21**(1), 123–138 (2010)
28. Uryasev, S.: A stochastic quasi-gradient algorithm with variable metric. Ann. Oper. Res. **39**, 251–267 (1992)
29. Vanderbei, R.J.: Linear Programming: Foundations and Extensions. International Series in Operations Research & Management Science. Springer, Berlin (2008)
30. Vorobeychik, Y., Wellman, M.P.: Stochastic search methods for Nash equilibrium approximation in simulation-based games. In: Padgham, L., Parkes, D.C., Müller, J., Parsons, S. (eds.) Proceedings of 7th International Conference on Autonomous Agents and Multiagent Systems (AAMAS 2008), pp. 1055–1062, 2008
31. Waitling, D.: User equilibrium traffic network assignment with stochastic travel times and late arrival penalty. Eur. J. Oper. Res. **175**, 1539–1556 (2006)
32. Wei, J.-Y, Smeers, Y.: Spatial oligopolistic electricity models with Cournot generators and regulated transmission prices. Oper. Res. **47**, 102–112 (1999)
33. Xu, H., Zhang, D.: Stochastic Nash equilibrium problems: sample average approximation and applications. Comput. Optim. Appl. **55**(3), 597–645 (2013)

Part II
Uncertainty Management Approaches

Chapter 4
Uncertainty Management Using Sequential Parameter Optimization

Thomas Bartz-Beielstein, Christian Jung, and Martin Zaefferer

4.1 Introduction

Sequential Parameter Optimization (SPO) is a meta-model based search heuristic that combines classical and modern statistical techniques. It was originally developed for the analysis of search heuristics such as simulated annealing, particle swarm optimization and evolutionary algorithms [6]. Here, SPO itself will be used as a search heuristic, i.e., SPO is applied to the objective function directly. An introduction to the state-of-the-art R implementation of SPO, the so-called *sequential parameter optimization toolbox* (SPOT), is presented in [5].

Meta models, also called surrogate models, simplify the simulation optimization, because the run times are generally much shorter than the original function evaluations (simulation runs) [2, 25]. Cost-intensive optimization problems in engineering have often less costly, less accurate representations which can be evaluated. That means, two functions of different fidelity are available for the optimization process, the fine function (expensive, time-consuming, accurate) and the coarse function. Intermediate fidelity levels can be available, too. In the remainder of this chapter, M_e denotes the expensive model, e.g., computationally expensive simulations or real-world experiments such as crash test. The simplified (cheap) meta model will be denoted as M_c. The combination of information from M_c and M_e models will be referred to as *multi-fidelity analysis* [24]. An interesting aspect is the computational budget (number of function evaluations) that is spent for selecting new design points and the relationship between evaluations of the cheap and the expensive model.

T. Bartz-Beielstein (✉) • C. Jung • M. Zaefferer
Fachhochschule Köln, Faculty of Computer Science and Engineering Science, Steinmüllerallee 1, 51643 Gummersbach, Germany
e-mail: thomas.bartz-beielstein@fh-koeln.de; christian.jung@fh-koeln.de; martin.zaefferer@fh-koeln.de, http://www.spotseven.de

G. Dellino, C. Meloni (eds.), *Uncertainty Management in Simulation-Optimization of Complex Systems*, Operations Research/Computer Science Interfaces Series 59,
DOI 10.1007/978-1-4899-7547-8_4

A powerful multi-fidelity technique is co-Kriging [17], which exploits correlation between the different fidelity levels to improve the meta model of the highest fidelity function.

Uncertainty may arise in many real-world optimization settings, e.g., from noisy sensors, imperfect models, or the inherently stochastic nature of the simulated system. Therefore, uncertainty-handling techniques are necessary [1, 21]. An elementary approach to cope with uncertainty is to increase the number of function evaluations. SPOT integrates *sharpening* as a simple method, which guarantees a fair comparison of the obtain solutions. Lasarczyk [27] and Bartz-Beielstein et al. [3, 8] analyzed the integration of a more sophisticated control-theoretic simulation technique called *optimal computing budget allocation* (OCBA) into SPOT. The OCBA approach can intelligently determine the most efficient replication numbers [12]. The goal is to obtain the highest decision quality using a fixed computing budget or to attain a desired simulation decision quality using a minimum computing budget. This SPOT-OCBA variant is compared to SPOT's standard technique of increasing the number of repeats.

Since Forrester et al. [17] describe co-Kriging for deterministic settings, it is of great interest to extend this analysis to noisy environments. Currently, there are only a few publications available, which analyze co-Kriging under uncertainty. For example, Wankhede et al. [40] compare a co-Kriging based optimization strategy with a standard Kriging based optimization strategy for the design of a 2D combustor.

These considerations motivated the central question of this publication:

> Are results from optimization runs under uncertainty, which are based on a large quantity of cheap data and a small quantity of expensive data, better than results from runs which are based on a small quantity of expensive data?

This question motivated the following experimental setup. Two classes of meta models, which have been proven useful in the SPOT framework, i.e., (1) tree-based models such as random forest [9, 10, 28] and (2) stochastic process models (Gaussian processes, Kriging) [29, 34, 35], will be used. A comparison of the rather simple tree-based techniques with sophisticated Kriging and co-Kriging techniques is of great interest. To enable a fair comparison, a sweeping method based on *Latin hypercube sampling* (LHS) is added to our experimental portfolio [30]. Summarizing, the following portfolio is used: (1) simple sweep of the search space by Latin hypercube sampling, (2) random forest, (3) Kriging, and (4) Co-kriging models. This setup allows the investigation of the following research questions:

Question 1. Does co-Kriging perform well under the presence of noise, in combination with uncertainty handling techniques like OCBA?

Question 2. How do random-forest based meta models perform in comparison to Kriging-based meta models?

Results from this study are applicable to other meta-model search heuristics such as *sequential kriging optimization* [19].

This chapter, which describes uncertainty-handling techniques for meta-model based search heuristics in combination with multi-fidelity analysis, is structured as follows. Section 4.2 introduces SPOT and the meta models such as random forest, Kriging and co-Kriging, used in this study. Uncertainty-handling techniques are described in Sect. 4.3. The experimental setup, e.g., objective function and run length, number of repeats etc. and results are presented in Sect. 4.4. A real-world example is described in Sect. 4.5. Finally, the chapter concludes with a Summary in Sect. 4.6.

4.2 SPO Variants

4.2.1 SPOT in a Nutshell

SPOT uses the available budget (e.g., simulator runs, number of function evaluations) sequentially, i.e., it uses information from the exploration of the search space to guide the search by building one or several meta models. Predictions from meta models are used to select new design points. Meta models are refined to improve knowledge about the search space. SPOT provides tools to cope with noise, which typically occurs when real-world applications, e.g., stochastic simulations, are run. It guarantees comparable confidence for search points. Users can collect information to learn from this optimization process, e.g., by applying *exploratory data analysis* (EDA) [11, 39]. Last, but not least, SPOT provides mechanisms both for interactive and automated tuning [4, 7]. An R version of this toolbox for interactive and automatic optimization of algorithms can be downloaded from CRAN.[1] Programs and files from this study can be requested from the author.

As can be seen from Algorithm 1, SPOT requires a mechanism to generate an initial design. Additionally, SPOT generates new design points during the sequential step. *Latin hypercube sampling* was chosen as the generator of design points during the initial and sequential SPOT steps. LHS was chosen, because it is easy to implement and understand. Many design point generators are available in R, see, e.g., the *CRAN Task View: Design of Experiments (DoE) & Analysis of Experimental Data*.[2]

There is a strong interaction between design generators and meta models, because the optimality of a design point depends on the meta model [32, 35]. This paper modifies SPOT's meta models, while design generators remain unchanged. The impact of the variation of the design generators on the algorithm's performance will be subject of a forthcoming paper.

[1] http://cran.r-project.org/web/packages/SPOT/index.html.

[2] http://cran.r-project.org/web/views/ExperimentalDesign.html.

Table 4.1 SPOT meta models used in this study

Type	Name of the SPOT plugin	Abbreviation
Kriging (Gaussian processes)	spotPredictForrester	KR
Co-Kriging (multi-output Gaussian processes)	spotPredictCoForrester	CK
Random forest	spotPredictRandomForest	RF

4.2.2 Meta Models Used During SPOT Runs

SPOT processes data sequentially, i.e., starting from a small initial design, further design points are generated using a meta model. Many meta models are available in R. Similar as for the design generators the user has the option of choosing between state-of-the-art meta models for tuning his algorithm or writing his own meta model and use it as a plugin for SPOT. The default SPOT installation contains several meta models. The R implementation of `randomForest` was chosen as SPOT's default one. This is quite robust and can handle categorical and numerical values needing only a comparably small amount of computational resources. Table 4.1 summarizes meta models used for experiments described in this document.

4.2.2.1 Random Forest-Based Parameter Tuning

The *random forest* (RF) method from the R package `randomForest` implements Breiman's algorithm, which is based on Breiman and Cutler's original Fortran code, for classification and regression [9]. It is implemented as a SPOT plugin, which can be selected via setting the command `seq.predictionModel.func` according to Table 4.1 in SPOT's configuration file. A detailed description of the SPOT configuration is given in [5].

4.2.2.2 Kriging-Based SPO

Kriging is one of the most promising surrogate models for optimization problems [26, 29]. It provides a very flexible and efficient way to model continuous landscapes, providing a good predictive quality for finding solutions of increased optimality in the design space. Kriging provides a way to estimate the local uncertainty of the model. For deterministic problems the uncertainty is zero at observed locations, and will increase with rising distance to such locations as well as increased curvature of the model. This variance estimate allows for an efficient way to balance between exploitation and exploration during the optimization process. Jones et al. introduced this method as *efficient global optimization* (EGO) [22]. Forrester et al. [17] also utilize variance estimates as a penalty for imputation of failed target function evaluations.

Several Kriging implementations are available in R, provided by packages like `mlegp`, `DiceKriging`, `kernlab` or `fields` [15, 18, 23, 33]. `SPOT` includes examples of interfacing with several different implementations. Most notably, the SPOT package itself provides two implementations, which are a DACE (Design and Analysis of Computer Experiments) based implementation [29] and an implementation based on Code by Forrester et al. [17]. They were chosen to be reimplemented in the SPOT R-Version, as they were also used in the earlier SPOT matlab version. Both are numerically robust and show good performance. While the former provides a flexible interface to choose different Kernels or polynomial functions, the latter includes a co-Kriging implementation. Co-Kriging will be introduced below. In this article, the Kriging implementation based on Forrester et al. [17] is used.

4.2.2.3 Co-Kriging

For many real world engineering problems, the target function can be evaluated at different levels of fidelity or granularity. For instance, a CFD simulation might provide a very time consuming but accurate way to estimate the quality of a solution.The same solution could be evaluated based on simplified analytical equations, leading to a cheaper but less accurate estimate. Combining these different levels of fidelity in a model-based optimization process is referred to as *multi-fidelity optimization*. Kennedy and O'Hagan [24] explore ways in which models with different fidelities can be used to make inference about the output from the most expensive, complex or fine-grained model.

One possible approach to multi-fidelity optimization is *co-Kriging*. Co-Kriging can be defined as a variant of kriging, which uses information from an additional, highly correlated variable together with the primary variable to improve estimates of the function values. Forrester et al. [16] introduce co-Kriging together with a simple test function and a real-world example. They show, how co-Kriging can employ the lower fidelity function to improve the model of the higher fidelity function. The simple test-function introduced by Forrester et al. [16] will be used in a slightly changed way for the experiments described in Sect. 4.4.

It has to be noted, that in this study, co-Kriging requires the design points evaluated on the fine target function to be nested into the larger design of the coarse target function. In SPOT it is ensured that the designs of the different fidelity levels are still space-filling. The creation of the lower levels design is therefore always based on the upper levels design.

4.2.2.4 Kriging/Co-Kriging and Noise

A standard Kriging model would not be perfectly suitable for a noisy problem, because Kriging is a strictly interpolating approach. That means, the predicted mean values exactly match with the known observations. However, a regularization constant can be introduced (also called nugget effect) to transform the model to a regressing one, where prediction and observation can deviate from each other. If *expected improvement* (EI) [22] is used, this will lead to non-zero variance estimates at already evaluated design points. This may deteriorate the explorative properties of EGO. However, a reinterpolating approach can be used to deal with this problem, both for Kriging [17] and co-Kriging [16].

Besides this, repeated evaluation of design points has to be considered for the coarse function. The uncertainty handling methods in SPOT, namely OCBA and sharpening, are introduced in Sect. 4.3. They are methods to select design points for re-evaluation, which are based on quality and/or variance. Sharpening and OCBA are not directly applicable to the coarse function design from the M_c model. The coarse function optimum can be completely meaningless for the true function, which means that the quality value becomes rather meaningless. A suitable method should therefore either focus on a good global fit of the coarse function (e.g. even spread of repeats). This should be especially well applicable when the function is indeed very cheap to evaluate. Or the coarse function budget should focus on the area of interest, as identified by fine function evaluations. In this study, a larger number of repeats is evenly spread over the whole design space. Still, points of the fine function design, which are nested in the coarse function design and chosen for repetition, will also be re-evaluated on the coarse function.

4.3 Uncertainty Handling Techniques

4.3.1 Sharpening

In the presence of noise, averaging over several function evaluations may help to manage uncertainty and to improve confidence. In the context of evolutionary algorithms, Stagge [36] demonstrated that a reduction of noise is not necessary for every single point in the search space but only for the best ones. The decision which ones are the best is facilitated by averaging but possibly a small number of evaluations is enough for that decision. Stagge [36] experimentally demonstrated that this idea can reduce the number of function evaluations significantly.

SPOT provides tools for managing uncertainty and improving the confidence during the search. First approaches increased the number of repeats. An early SPOT implementation proceeded as follows [6]:

> At each step, two new designs are generated and the best is re-evaluated. This is similar to the selection procedure in $(1 + 2)$-Evolution Strategies. The number of repeat runs, k, of the algorithm designs is increased (doubled), if a design has performed best twice or more. A starting value of $k = 2$ was chosen.

A slightly modified approach, which will be referred to as *sharpening* (SHRP), is implemented in more recent SPOT versions. Sharpening consists of two phases, (i) the model construction and (ii) sequential improvement. Phase (i) determines a population of initial designs in algorithm parameter space and runs the algorithm k times for each design. Phase (ii) consists of a loop with the following components: By means of the obtained data, the model is built or updated, respectively. Then, a possibly large set of design points is generated and their predicted utility computed by sampling the model. A small set of the seemingly best design points is selected and the algorithm is run $k+1$ times for each of these. The algorithm is also run once for the current best design point and k is increased by one. Note, other update rules for the number of repeats, k, are possible. The new design points are added to the population and the loop starts over if the termination criterion is not reached (usually a preset budget is granted to the process). In consequence, this means that the number of repeats is always increased by one if the current best design point stays at the top of the list or a newly generated one gets there. Due to nondeterministic responses of the algorithm, it may however happen that neither of these is found at the top of the list after finishing the loop. In this case, k may effectively shrink as performance comparisons have to be fair and thus shall be based on the same number of repeats.

4.3.2 Optimal Computing Budget Allocation

The sharpening approaches from Sect. 4.3.1 do not use any information about the uncertainty (variance). Here come techniques such as *optimal computing budget allocation* (OCBA) into play [13, 14, 20]. OCBA was developed to ensure a high *probability of correct selection* (PCS). To maximize PCS, a larger portion of the available budget is allocated to those designs that are critical to the process of identifying the best candidates. OCBA uses sample means and variances in the budget allocation procedure in order to maximize PCS.

OCBA's central idea can be explained as follows. Consider a number of simulation replications, say T, which can be allocated to m competing design points with means $\overline{Y}_1, \overline{Y}_2, \ldots, \overline{Y}_m$ and finite variances $\sigma_1^2, \sigma_2^2, \ldots, \sigma_m^2$, respectively. The *approximate probability of correct selection* can be asymptotically maximized when

$$\begin{aligned} \frac{N_i}{N_j} &= \left(\frac{\sigma_i/\delta_{b,i}}{\sigma_j/\delta_{b,j}}\right)^2, \quad i, j \in \{1,2,\ldots,m\}, \text{ and } i \neq j \neq b, \\ N_b &= \sigma_b \sqrt{\sum_{i=1, i\neq b} \frac{N_i^2}{\sigma_i^2}}, \end{aligned} \tag{4.1}$$

where N_i is the number of replications allocated to design i, and $\delta_{b,j} = \overline{Y}_b - \overline{Y}_i$ denotes the difference of the i-th and b-th mean with $\overline{Y}_b \leq \min_{i\neq b} \overline{Y}_i$. As can be seen from (4.1), the allocated computing budget is proportional to variance and inversely proportional to the difference from the best design. Chen and Lee present a comprehensive coverage of the OCBA methodology [12].

Table 4.2 SPOT setup

SPOT setup parameter	Value
`auto.loop.nevals`	100
`init.design.size`	10
`init.design.repeats`	2
`init.design.func`	"spotCreateDesignLhd"
`init.design.retries`	100
`spot.ocba`	True | False
`seq.ocba.budget`	3
`seq.design.size`	200
`seq.design.oldBest.size`	3
`seq.design.new.size`	3
`seq.design.func`	"spotCreateDesignLhd"

Lasarczyk was the first who combined SPOT and OCBA [27]. The OCBA implementation in this study is based on Lasarczyk's work. SPOT with OCBA is shown in Algorithm 1. New design points which were proposed by the meta model are evaluated several times, e.g., twice. This value can be modified using the `init.design.repeats` variable in SPOT's config file. During each SPOT step, a certain budget (here: `spot.ocba` = 3, as can be seen from Table 4.2) is allocated to the candidate solutions to ensure a high PCS for the best design point.

4.4 Experiments

4.4.1 Objective Function

To demonstrate the effectiveness of different approaches the one-variable test-function, that Forrester et al. [17] introduced, is investigated in the experiments. Although this function is rather simple, it allows a comparison with previous results and is therefore well suited to demonstrate the applicability of specific approaches, especially to find answers for Questions 1 and 2 as stated in Sect. 4.1. The expensive function, which is associated with the fine model M_e, is defined as

$$f_e(x) = (6x-2)^2 \times \sin(12x-4),$$

and the cheap function associated with M_c as

$$f_c(x) = 0.5 f_e(x) + 10x - 10.$$

The optimization is performed on the unit interval between zero and one. For the purpose of the experiments, noise is added to both functions. The noise term is additive, normally distributed with zero mean and standard deviation one.

Algorithm 1: SPOT-OCBA.
t_0 = `init.design.repeats`, t = `seq.ocba.budget`,
l = `seq.design.size`, d = `seq.design.new.size`

```
// phase 1, building the model:
```
let F be the tuned algorithm;
```
// design considerations necessary:
```
generate an initial population $X = \{\bar{x}^1, \ldots, \bar{x}^m\}$ of m parameter vectors;
let t_0 be the initial number of tests for determining estimated function values;
foreach $\bar{x} \in X$ **do**
  evaluate F with $\bar{x}$ t_0 times to determine the estimated function value $\hat{y}$ of $\bar{x}$;
end
```
// phase 2, using and improving the model:
```
while *termination criterion not true* **do**
  `// OCBA:`
  let $B \subseteq X$ denote the subset of candidate solutions with best estimated function value $\hat{y}$;
  let t denote the OCBA budget;
  distribute t among B, i.e., generate OCBA distribution $\mathcal{O}$;
  `// model considerations necessary:`
  build meta model f based on X and $\{\hat{y}^1, \ldots, \hat{y}^{|X|}\}$;
  `// design considerations necessary:`
  generate a set X' of l new parameter vectors by random sampling;
  foreach $\bar{x} \in X'$ **do**
    calculate $f(\bar{x})$ to determine the estimated function value $f(\bar{x})$ of $\bar{x}$;
  end
  select set X'' of d parameter vectors from X' with best predicted utility ($d \ll l$);
  evaluate F with B following the OCBA distribution $\mathcal{O}$; `// (improve confidence)`
  evaluate F t_0 times with each $\bar{x} \in X''$ to determine the estimated function values $\hat{y}$;
  extend the population by $X = X \cup X''$;
end

In Fig. 4.1, the functions are depicted with and without a noise sample. The deterministic term, without noise, will only be used to evaluate the quality of the best found solution. The optimum of the deterministic fine function is at $x_{\text{opt}} \approx 0.76$, the related function value reads $f_e(x_{\text{opt}}) \approx -6.02$.

4.4.2 Pre-experimental Planning

To compare the different modeling approaches based on their performance on the above described test function, the following problem setup is used. Two function evaluation budgets are tested, the first with $n = 20$ and the second with $n = 50$ evaluations, respectively. For the former case, the initial design size will be chosen with five points, for the latter case ten points. In both cases, points from the initial design are evaluated twice. This setup splits the available budget between initial

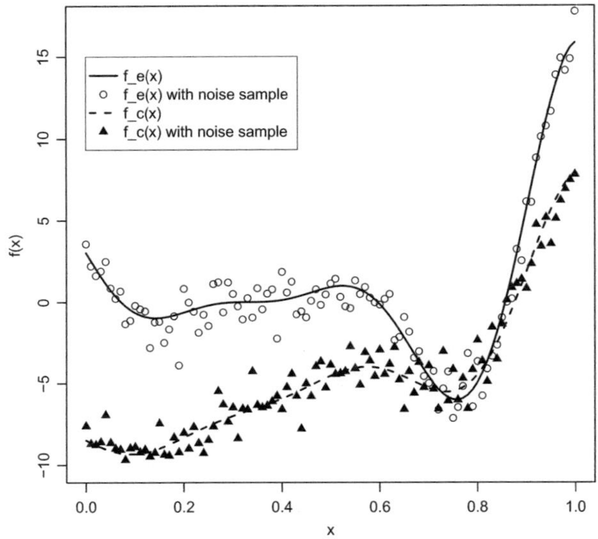

Fig. 4.1 The one variable test-functions for multi-fidelity optimization, with and without noise. The *solid line* denotes f_e, whereas a *dashed line* is used to illustrate the cheap function f_c

design and sequential design points in such a manner that not more than 50 % of the budget is used for the initial design.

Six different combinations are tested, with respect to the models random forest, Kriging and co-Kriging as well as the uncertainty handling techniques sharpening and OCBA. To enable a fair comparison with random forest, no EI criterion is used, leading to a pure model-exploitation situation. While it would be possible to get a variance estimate (and thus EI) from a random-forest model by integrating results from individual trees, this variance estimate would have different properties than the Kriging one. All other important, non-default settings are identical for each of the experimental runs. The settings are summarized in Table 4.3. Each experimental run is repeated 50 times to produce statistically sound results.

As a reference for the comparison with the model-based approaches (RF and Kriging), a sweep of the search space was performed: the whole budget was used to evaluate randomly generated design points, and each design point is evaluated twice. A space-filling design (Latin hypercube sampling) was used to cover the search space. All approaches that perform worse than this basic sampling approach should be disregarded.

4.4.3 Results: Random Forest

Figure 4.2 presents a boxplot all experimental results. The statistical properties of the results with random forest are summarized in Table 4.4. Random forest does not perform well in case of the 20 function evaluations budget. It does not manage

Table 4.3 SPOT configuration for the experimental runs

Parameter	Value
Surrogate model	Random forest or Kriging or co-Kriging
Surrogate optimization	
Algorithm	Bounded Nelder-Mead
Restarts	True
Budget	1,000
Design and repeats	
Initial design size	5 or 10
Initial evaluations per point	2
Max. evaluations per design point	10
New points evaluated per step	1
Old points reevaluated per step	3
Use OCBA	True or false
Size of coarse function design	20
Coarse function evaluations per point	5

to outperform the basic LHS approach, regardless of the insignificant influence of OCBA and sharpening. However, if more evaluations ($n = 50$) are used, RF with sharpening performs quite good. It is at least competitive, even though it seems to produce a slightly larger number of outliers than the Kriging based models do. RF with OCBA, however, is still not better than the LHS. Unlike the 20 function evaluation budget, OCBA and sharpening differ significantly in the long run.

Figure 4.3 shows one example of how the RF model looks like, after a completed long optimization run with $n = 50$ function evaluations. As can be seen, the global structure is represented in a very rough way. It can be observed that the RF models behavior is not linked to the chosen uncertainty handling technique. This is despite the significant difference between the overall optimization performance. This can be explained by the main dependence of the global structure on the initial design, which is identical for both. The advantage of sharpening is therefore not linked to an actual improvement of the model, but rather to an improved identification of optimal points in the evaluated solutions. Sharpening focuses the budget only one the best of the known solutions, being more exploitative. OCBA allow the selection of even slightly less optimal points for repetition, which results in a more explorative and less exploitive behavior. It seems like the RF models structure works better with the exploitive approach.

4.4.4 Kriging

In case of the short optimization runs with a budget of $n = 20$ function evaluations, Kriging (KR) performs very similar to RF, also not outperforming LHS, regardless of the chosen uncertainty handling technique. For the longer runs with $n = 50$

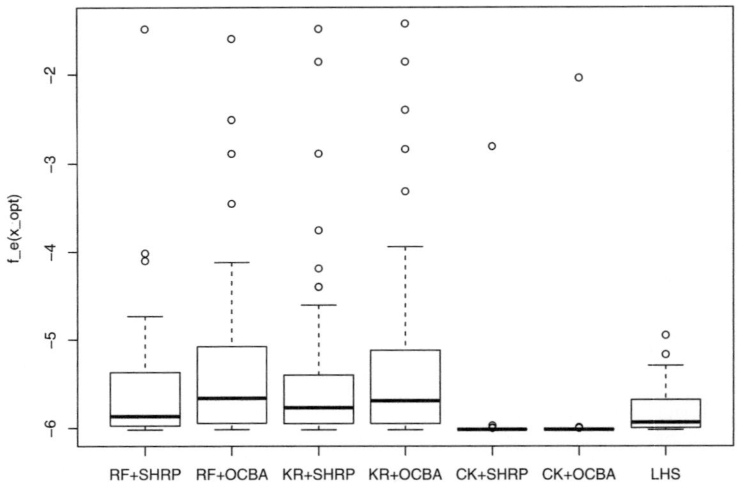

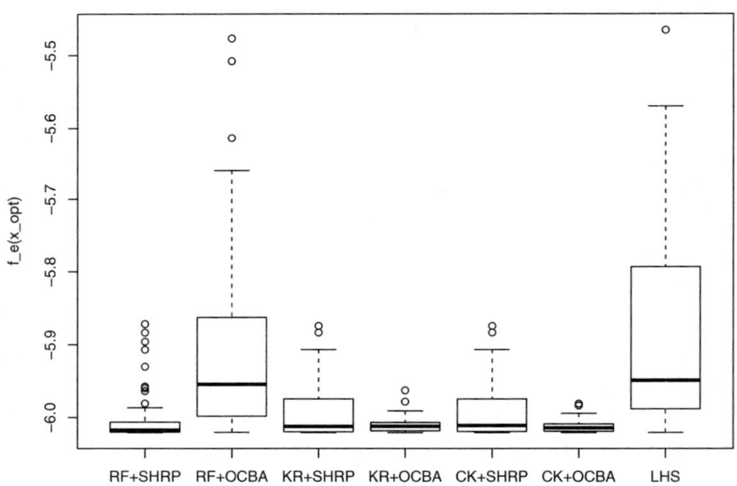

Fig. 4.2 Boxplot of optimization results with 20 function evaluation budget (*upper graph*) and 50 evaluations (*lower graph*). Depicted are the true deterministic fine function values of the best points as identified by the optimization process, $f_e(x_{\text{opt}})$

evaluations, however, Kriging shows a different behavior. While KR with SHRP performs slightly worse, KR with OCBA produces good results, with less outliers than RF with SHRP but showing otherwise very similar behavior. It can be seen that the trend towards OCBA is rather small, but at least, OCBA does not degrade performance with KR, as seen with RF. The statistical properties of the results with Kriging are summarized in Table 4.5. The earlier examples of final model shape seen for RF in Fig. 4.3 can also be compared to the respective graphs for KR in Fig. 4.4. It can be clearly seen that the KR model approximates the true global

Table 4.4 Statistical properties of the results with random forest

	RF + SHRP (S)	RF + OCBA (S)	RF + SHRP (L)	RF + OCBA (L)
Minimum	−6.021	−6.016	−6.021	−6.020
First quartile	−5.947	−5.944	−6.020	−5.994
Median	−5.867	−5.663	−6.017	−5.955
Mean	−5.536	−5.324	−6.000	−5.905
Third quartile	−5.393	−5.091	−6.007	−5.864
Maximum	−1.490	−1.600	−5.871	−5.477

(*S*) indicates short runs, i.e., $n = 20$ and (*L*) indicates long runs with a budget of $n = 50$ function evaluations

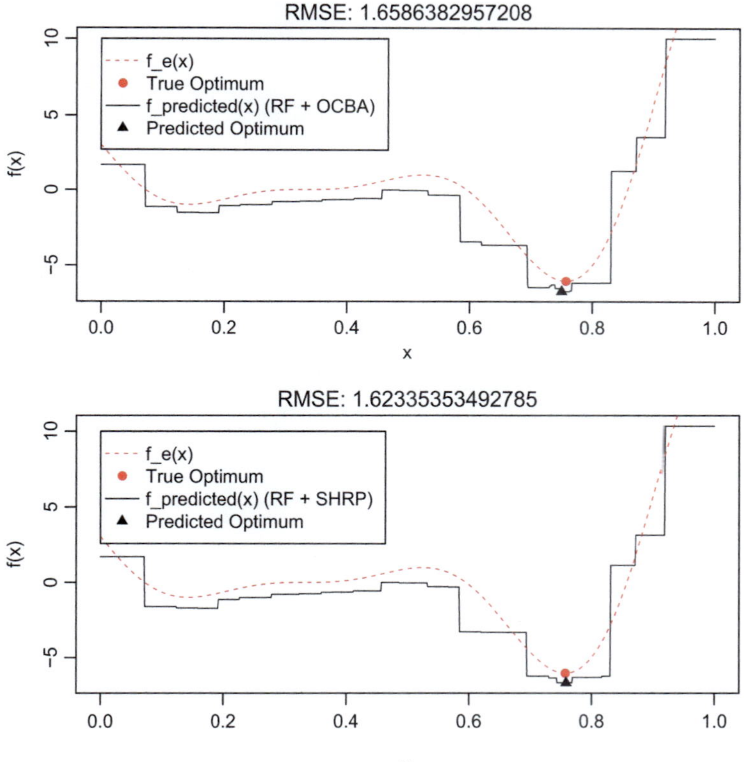

Fig. 4.3 The prediction of the final model after an optimization run with 50 evaluations with random forest and OCBA (*upper graph*) or sharpening (*lower graph*)

shape much better, which is no surprise, as the problem is a continuous one which can hardly be modeled in much detail by the discontinuous RF approach. When an exact representation of the global landscape would be desired, KR would be clearly preferred over RF.

Table 4.5 Statistical properties of the results with Kriging

	KR+SHRP (S)	KR+OCBA (S)	KR+SHRP (L)	KR+OCBA (L)
Minimum	−6.021	−6.021	−6.021	−6.021
First quartile	−5.949	−5.948	−6.020	−6.018
Median	−5.770	−5.692	−6.012	−6.012
Mean	−5.393	−5.242	−5.993	−6.011
Third quartile	−5.409	−5.152	−5.976	−6.007
Maximum	−1.490	−1.431	−5.874	−5.963

(*S*) indicates short runs, (*L*) indicates long runs

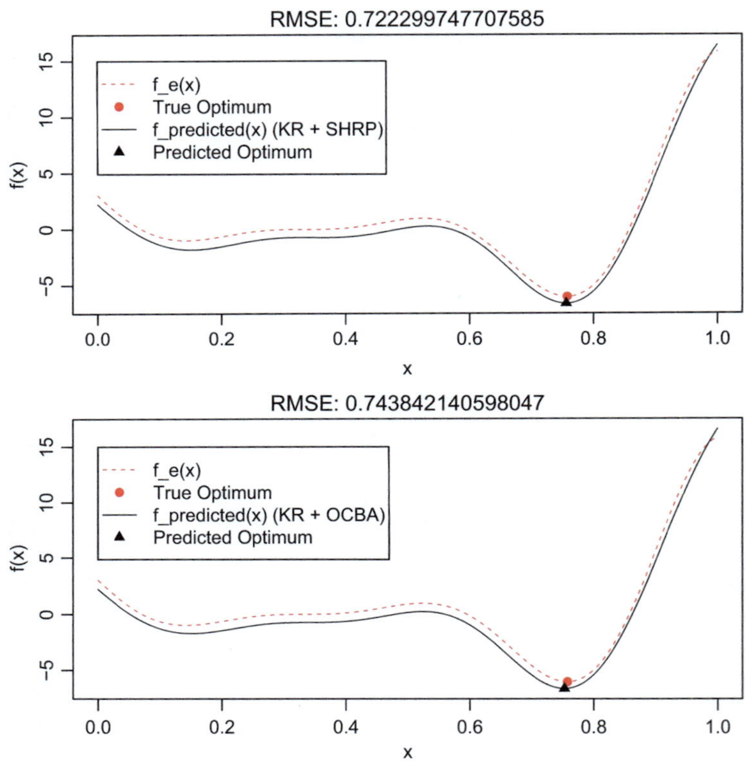

Fig. 4.4 The prediction of the final model after an optimization run with 50 evaluations with Kriging and OCBA (*upper graph*) or sharpening (*lower graph*)

4.4.5 Co-Kriging

The most striking advantage of co-Kriging (CK) in this experiment can be observed for the short optimization runs. It outperforms all other approaches significantly. Still, it shares the feature that uncertainty handling techniques do not impact the performance for short runs. For the longer runs, CK is on par with the other methods, thus being over-all the most recommendable method in this situation and

Table 4.6 Statistical properties of the results with co-Kriging

	CK+SHRP (S)	CK+OCBA (S)	CK+SHRP (L)	CK+OCBA (L)
Minimum	−6.021	−6.021	−6.021	−6.021
First quartile	−6.020	−6.020	−6.019	−6.019
Median	−6.017	−6.017	−6.011	−6.014
Mean	−5.951	−5.936	−5.993	−6.012
Third quartile	−6.014	−6.014	−5.976	−6.009
Maximum	−2.807	−2.041	−5.874	−5.981

(*S*) indicates short runs, (*L*) indicates long runs

the only one to steadily outperform the LHS approach. The lack of improvement for the longer runs is probably due to the fact that the simple Kriging model can already model this very simple test-function sufficiently well. Exploiting additional information from the coarse function can not yield further progress in this setting. The statistical properties of the results with co-Kriging are summarized in Table 4.6. This is supported by the very similar shape of the Kriging models in Fig. 4.4 and the co-Kriging models Fig. 4.5, although the RMSE is improved for the co-Kriging Models. The improved RMSE can be observed for most experiments, but does not lead to improved optimization performance.

In a real-world use case, one would of course have to consider that CK needs increased effort. This additional effort includes the evaluations of the coarse (supposedly cheap) target function, as well as the more complex model building and prediction. Thus, it's usefulness would depend on the difference in time consumption for the coarse and fine function, as well as the time consumption of the model building for the given design space dimensionality and number of observations.

4.4.6 Discussion of the Experimental Results

The experiments described are of course only related to a single one-dimensional test-function. This has several implications. Firstly, things might look different for different functions of various dimensionality. Secondly, real-world problems present a large array of additional challenges not considered here, for instance the handling of failed target function evaluations. Still, the results do show that co-Kriging can help to improve the optimization performance in the presence of noise. This gives a preliminary answer to *Question 1*. Although this result is rather vague, it could be shown that co-Kriging is beneficial even in optimization under uncertainty.

Another important lesson to be learned from these experiments is that there can be no general recommendation towards a single uncertainty handling method. This clearly depends on the available budget as well as the choice of optimization process parameters, e.g., the chosen meta model. Problem features like the type of noise will also have an effect, but are not considered here. Therefore, no simple answer can be given to *Question 2*.

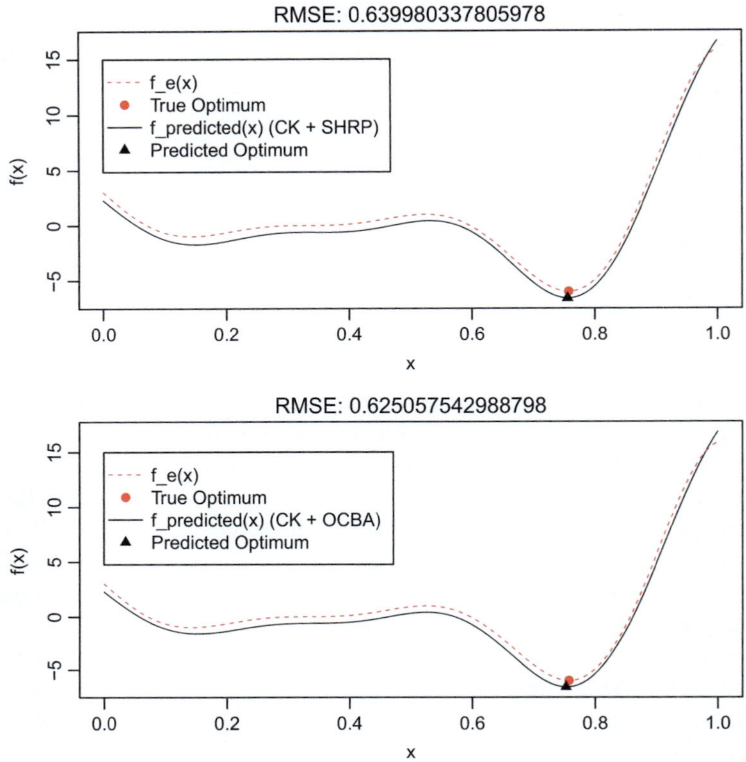

Fig. 4.5 The prediction of the final model after an optimization run with 50 evaluations with co-Kriging and OCBA (*upper graph*) or sharpening (*lower graph*)

OCBA and SHRP do have different influences on the optimization process behavior, promoting either exploration or exploitation. A similar effect to OCBA could be assumed when expected improvement comes into play because it is a method to balance towards exploration as well. The difference here is of course, that OCBA explores the number of samples for each known location in the design space, while EI explores regions not yet well represented by the learned meta model.

4.5 Real-World Example: Heavy Width Reduction of Steel Slabs

4.5.1 The Hot Steel Rolling Process

One important quality parameter in the complex process of hot steel rolling is the prediction and optimization of the width for plates and strips. Rectangular steel

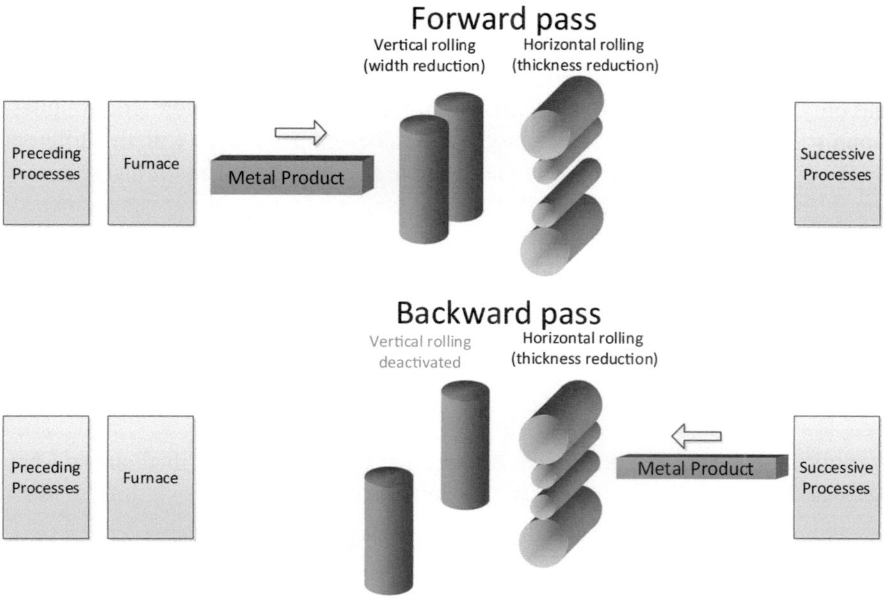

Fig. 4.6 Illustration of a rolling process step in several passes. The entry side is on the left. Measurements are available on the right after each forward pass, whereas no measurements can be obtained on the left. The rolling process consists of several, e.g., $N = 7$ forward and backward passes

slabs, which are used for the manufacture of all flat steel products such as coils, are hot rolled. Width reduction has become increasingly important in the production of hot steel strips.

The rolling process is divided into several passes. Each pass can consist of a thickness (horizontal rolling) and a width reduction (vertical rolling). The width reduction is only performed in forward passes and the vertical rolling process has no effect in the backwards direction. This situation is depicted in Fig. 4.6.

In general the vertical rolling process is performed before the horizontal rolling process. During this vertical rolling process a so called dogbone shape is added to the product which will then again be flattened in the horizontal rolling process. The dogbone shape cannot be measured because it only occurs between the vertical and horizontal stands of the steel mill and there are no measurement systems available which are working properly in this environment. Contrary to the plate and strip thickness the width after each pass cannot be set directly and an accurate model is needed to obtain a proper width shape of the product. Each deformation step without any width reduction results in an increased product width. The number of passes in reversing mills, say N, has always to be odd because normally the product is transferred to further processes away from the furnace. This leads to $(N + 1)/2$ forwards passes and $(N - 1)/2$ backwards passes. Usually, the reversing mills are equipped only with one width gauge at the exit side of the stand so there are only measurements after each forward pass. Due to the fact that the width cannot be measured at the entry side, a hidden state problem occurs. The dogbone shape, which results after the width reduction process, is hard to describe analytically. This has only been done for a few standard steel grades within narrow geometric confines. Sophisticated time-consuming methods have to be applied to cope with the different working points. The occurrence of the dogbone will result in an additional spread in the following process of horizontal rolling. Assuming that the incoming geometries of the product before the first deformation process are known then there are two successional processes which modify the product width.

4.5.2 Modeling

Various models can be constructed to represent the process described above. They are based on the following input parameters:

- product attributes such as geometry (thickness, width), material components (chemical decomposition), and thermo-mechanical properties
- process parameters such as roll gap settings, velocity, and cooling.

The output parameter is the width of the product.

To model the complete physical process every deformation step should be modeled separately, including a model of the dogbone shape. However, this is not possible, because measurements are not available between the vertical and horizontal rolling step. Therefore, the following two models will be considered further:

1. a model, which describes each pass with its input and output parameters, ignoring the dogbone shape
2. a model, which neglects the hidden state after the backwards pass.

These two models can be built based on different approaches:

1. using a data-driven approach, which processes real-world data, or alternatively
2. using an analytical model, for example as presented in [31, 37, 38].

This classification allows the generation of four different models. Subject of our current research is the implementation of models using different levels of fidelity. Two models will be considered further. The first, high-fidelity model M_e will be called the *data-driven model*. It uses data from the real-world process to generate a Kriging model. The second, coarse or lower fidelity model, say M_c, describes the input-output relationship using the simple analytical formula. The second model will be referred to as the *analytical model*. Co-Kriging could additionally exploit information from the lower fidelity analytical model. Note, that for all data-driven models, expensive data pre-processing is necessary.

4.6 Summary

This article illustrates that co-Kriging can work under the presence of noise in the coarse and fine target function, and can be combined with the uncertainty handling techniques included in SPOT. Starting point of our experimental analysis was the co-Kriging test function, which was introduced by Forrester et al. [17]. We demonstrated that co-Kriging can be beneficial in uncertain environments. Unsurprisingly, no general recommendations for uncertainty handling techniques can be given. Each experimental setup has different requirements. Modifications of the computational budget, e.g., increasing the number of function evaluations from $n = 20$ to $n = 50$ leads to different results. As a rule of thumb, we can state that complex models such as Kriging require larger computational budgets than simple models such as random forest. However, this difference vanishes if information from cheap and expensive models can be combined. Co-Kriging seems to be a promising approach for costly real-world optimization problems.

The hot steel rolling process was introduced as an important real-world optimization problem. This problem is subject of our current research. A modeling approach, which combines information from a simple mathematical model with information from an expensive data-driven Kriging model was presented. This is only one significant real-world problem where multi-fidelity models are of great importance, which can be adapted to other areas.

References

1. Arnold, D.V., Beyer, H.-G.: A comparison of evolution strategies with other direct search methods in the presence of noise. Comput. Optim. Appl. **24**(1), 135–159 (2003)
2. Barton, R.R., Meckesheimer, M.: Metamodel-based simulation optimization. In: Henderson, S.G., Nelson, B.L. (eds.) Simulation. Handbooks in Operations Research and Management Science, vol. 13, pp. 535–574. Elsevier, Amsterdam (2006)
3. Bartz-Beielstein, T., Friese, M.: Sequential parameter optimization and optimal computational budget allocation for noisy optimization problems. CIOP Technical Report 02/11, Research Center CIOP (Computational Intelligence, Optimization andData Mining), Cologne University of Applied Science, Faculty of Computer Science and Engineering Science, Jan 2011
4. Bartz-Beielstein, T., Preuss, M.: The future of experimental research. In: Bartz-Beielstein, T., Chiarandini, M., Paquete, L., Preuss, M. (eds.) Experimental Methods for the Analysis of Optimization Algorithms, pp. 17–46. Springer, Berlin/Heidelberg/New York (2010)
5. Bartz-Beielstein, T., Zaefferer, M.: A gentle introduction to sequential parameter optimization. Technical Report TR 01/2012, CIplus, 2012
6. Bartz-Beielstein, T., Parsopoulos, K.E., Vrahatis, M.N.: Design and analysis of optimization algorithms using computational statistics. Appl. Numer. Anal. Comput. Math. (ANACM), **1**(2), 413–433 (2004)
7. Bartz-Beielstein, T., Lasarczyk, C., Preuss, M.: The sequential parameter optimization toolbox. In: Bartz-Beielstein, T., Chiarandini, M., Paquete, L., Preuss, M. (eds.) Experimental Methods for the Analysis of Optimization Algorithms, pp. 337–360. Springer, Berlin/Heidelberg/New York (2010)

8. Bartz-Beielstein, T., Friese, M., Zaefferer, M., Naujoks, B., Flasch, O., Konen, W., Koch,P.: Noisy optimization with sequential parameter optimization and optimal computational budget allocation. In: Proceedings of the 13th Annual Conference Companion on Genetic and Evolutionary Computation, GECCO '11, pp. 119–120. ACM, New York, NY (2011)
9. Breiman, L.: Random forests. Mach. Learn. **45**(1), 5–32 (2001)
10. Breiman, L., Friedman, J.H., Olshen, R.A., Stone, C.J.: Classification and Regression Trees. Wadsworth, Monterey, CA (1984)
11. Chambers, J., Cleveland, W., Kleiner, B., Tukey, P.: Graphical Methods for Data Analysis. Wadsworth, Belmont, CA (1983)
12. Chen, C.-H., Lee, L.H.: Stochastic Simulation Optimization. World Scientific, Singapore (2011)
13. Chen, H.C., Chen, C.H., Dai, L., Yücesan, E.: New development of optimal computing budget allocation for discrete event simulation. In: Andradóttir, S., Healy, K.J., Withers, D.H., Nelson, B.L. (eds.) Proceedings of the 1997 Winter Simulation Conference, pp. 334–341. IEEE Computer Society, Piscataway, NJ (1997)
14. Chen, J., Chen, C., Kelton, D.: Optimal computing budget allocation of indifference-zone-selection procedures. Technical Report, 2003. Working Paper. http://www.cba.uc.edu/faculty/keltonwd. Accessed 6 Jan 2005
15. Dancik, G.M., Dorman, K.S.: mlegp: statistical analysis for computer models of biological systems using R. Bioinformatics **24**(17), 1966–1967 (2008)
16. Forrester, A., Sóbester, A., Keane, A.: Multi-fidelity optimization via surrogate modelling. Proc. Roy. Soc. A Math. Phys. Eng. Sci. **463**(2088), 3251–3269 (2007)
17. Forrester, A., Sobester, A., Keane, A.: Engineering Design via Surrogate Modelling. Wiley, New York (2008)
18. Furrer, R., Nychka, D., Sain, S.: Fields: tools for spatial data. R package version 6.3 (2010)
19. Huang, D., Allen, T.T., Notz, W.I., Zeng, N.: Global optimization of stochastic black-box systems via sequential kriging meta-models. J. Glob. Optim. **34**(3), 441–466 (2006)
20. Jin, Y.: A comprehensive survey of fitness approximation in evolutionary computation. Soft. Comput. **9**(1), 3–12 (2005)
21. Jin, Y., Branke, J.: Evolutionary optimization in uncertain environments—a survey. IEEE Trans. Evol. Comput. **9**(3), 303–317 (2005)
22. Jones, D., Schonlau, M., Welch, W.: Efficient global optimization of expensive black-box functions. J. Glob. Optim. **13**, 455–492 (1998)
23. Karatzoglou, A., Smola, A., Hornik, K., Zeileis, A.: kernlab – an S4 package for kernel methods in R. J. Stat. Softw. **11**(9), 1–20 (2004)
24. Kennedy, M.C., O'Hagan, A.: Predicting the output from a complex computer code when fast approximations are available. Biometrika **87**(1), 1–13 (2000)
25. Kleijnen, J.P.C.: Design and Analysis of Simulation Experiments. Springer, New York, NY (2008)
26. Krige, D.G.: A statistical approach to some basic mine valuation problems on the witwatersrand. J. Chem. Metall. Min. Soc. S. Afr. **52**(6), 119–139 (1951)
27. Lasarczyk, C.W.G.: Genetische programmierung einer algorithmischen chemie. Ph.D. thesis, Technische Universität Dortmund (2007)
28. Liaw, A., Wiener, M.: Classification and regression by randomforest. R News **2**(3), 18–22 (2002)
29. Lophaven, S., Nielsen, H., Søndergaard, J.: DACE—a matlab kriging toolbox. Technical Report IMM-REP-2002-12, Informatics and Mathematical Modelling, Technical University of Denmark, Copenhagen, Denmark (2002)
30. McKay, M.D., Beckman, R.J., Conover, W.J.: A comparison of three methods for selecting values of input variables in the analysis of output from a computer code. Technometrics **21**(2), 239–245 (1979)
31. Okada, M., Ariizumi, T., Noma, Y., Yamazaki, Y.: On the behavior of edge rolling in hot strip mills. In: International Conference on Steel Rolling, vol. 1, pp. 275–286 (1980)
32. Pukelsheim, F.: Optimal Design of Experiments. Wiley, New York, NY (1993)

33. Roustant, O., Ginsbourger, D., Deville, Y.: Dicekriging, diceoptim: two r packages for the analysis of computer experiments by kriging-based metamodeling and optimization. J. Stat. Softw. **51**, 1–55 (2010)
34. Sacks, J., Welch, W.J., Mitchell, T.J., Wynn, H.P.: Design and analysis of computer experiments. Stat. Sci. **4**(4), 409–435 (1989)
35. Santner, T.J., Williams, B.J., Notz, W.I.: The Design and Analysis of Computer Experiments. Springer, Berlin/Heidelberg/New York (2003)
36. Stagge, P.: Averaging efficiently in the presence of noise. In: Eiben, A. (ed.) Parallel Problem Solving from Nature, PPSN V, pp. 188–197. Springer, Berlin/Heidelberg/New York (1998)
37. Takei, H., Onishi, Y., Yamasaki, Y., Takekoshi, A., Yamamoto, M., Okado,M.: Automatic width control of rougher in hot strip mill. Nippon Kokan Technical Report 34, Computer Systems Development Department Fukuyama Works (1982)
38. Takeuchi, M., Hoshiya, M., Watanabe, K., Hirata, O., Kikuma, T., Sadahiro, S.: Heavy width reduction rolling of slabs. Nippon Steel Technical Report. Overseas, No. 21, pp. 235–246 (1983)
39. Tukey, J.: The philosophy of multiple comparisons. Stat. Sci. **6**, 100–116 (1991)
40. Wankhede, M.J., Bressloff, N.W., Keane, A.J.: Combustor design optimization using co-kriging of steady and unsteady turbulent combustion. J. Eng. Gas Turbines Power **133**(12), 121504 (2011)

Chapter 5
A Review on Global Sensitivity Analysis Methods

Bertrand Iooss and Paul Lemaître

5.1 Introduction

While building and using numerical simulation models, Sensitivity Analysis (SA) methods are invaluable tools. They allow to study how the uncertainty in the output of a model can be apportioned to different sources of uncertainty in the model input (Saltelli et al. [77]). It may be used to determine the most contributing input variables to an output behavior as the non-influential inputs, or ascertain some interaction effects within the model. The objectives of SA are numerous; one can mention model verification and understanding, model simplifying and factor prioritization. Finally, the SA is an aid in the validation of a computer code, guidance research efforts, or the justification in terms of system design safety.

There are many application examples, for instance Makowski et al. [58] analyze, for a crop model prediction, the contribution of 13 genetic parameters on the variance of two outputs. Another example is given in the work of Lefebvre et al. [52] where the aim of SA is to determine the most influential input among a large number (around 30), for an aircraft infrared signature simulation model. In nuclear engineering field, Auder et al. [2] study the influential inputs on thermohydraulical phenomena occurring during an accidental scenario, while Iooss et al. [37] and Volkova et al. [92] consider the environmental assessment of industrial facilities.

B. Iooss (✉)
EDF R&D, 6 Quai Watier - 78401 Chatou, France

Institut de Mathématiques de Toulouse, 118 route de Narbonne - 31062 Toulouse, France
e-mail: bertrand.iooss@edf.fr

P. Lemaître
EDF R&D, 6 Quai Watier - 78401 Chatou, France

INRIA Sud-Ouest, 351 cours de la libération - 33405 Talence, France

G. Dellino, C. Meloni (eds.), *Uncertainty Management in Simulation-Optimization of Complex Systems*, Operations Research/Computer Science Interfaces Series 59,
DOI 10.1007/978-1-4899-7547-8_5

The first historical approach to SA is known as the local approach. The impact of small input perturbations on the model output is studied. These small perturbations occur around nominal values (the mean of a random variable for instance). This deterministic approach consists in calculating or estimating the partial derivatives of the model at a specific point. The use of adjoint-based methods allows to process models with a large number of input variables. Such approaches are commonly used in solving large environmental systems as in climate modeling, oceanography, hydrology, etc. (Cacuci [9], Castaings et al. [13]).

From the late 1980s, to overcome the limitations of local methods (linearity and normality assumptions, local variations), a new class of methods has been developed in a statistical framework. In contrast to local sensitivity analysis, it is referred to as "global sensitivity analysis" because it considers the whole variation range of the inputs (Saltelli et al. [77]). Numerical model users and modelers have shown large interests in these tools which take full advantages of the advent on computing materials and numerical methods (see Helton [30], de Rocquigny et al. [19] and Faivre et al. [23] for industrial and environmental applications). Saltelli et al. [78] and Pappenberger et al. [67] emphasized the need to specify clearly the objectives of a study before making a SA. These objectives may include:

- identify and prioritize the most influential inputs,
- identify non-influential inputs in order to fix them to nominal values,
- map the output behavior in function of the inputs by focusing on a specific domain of inputs if necessary,
- calibrate some model inputs using some available information (real output observations, constraints, etc.).

With respect to such objectives, first syntheses on the subject of SA were developed (Kleijnen [43], Frey and Patil [25], Helton et al. [32], Badea and Bolado [4], de Rocquigny et al. [19], Pappenberger et al. [67]). Unfortunately, between heuristics, graphical tools, design of experiments theory, Monte Carlo techniques, statistical learning methods, etc., beginners and non-specialist users can be found quickly lost on the choice of the most suitable methods for their problem. The aim of this chapter is to provide an educational synthesis of SA methods inside an applicative methodological framework.

The model input vector is denoted $\mathbf{X} = (X_1, \dots, X_d) \in \mathbb{R}^d$. For the sake of simplicity, we restrict the study to a scalar output $Y \in \mathbb{R}$ of the computer code (also called "model") $f(\cdot)$:

$$Y = f(\mathbf{X}) . \tag{5.1}$$

In the probabilistic setting, $\mathbf{X}$ is a random vector defined by a probability distribution and Y is a random variable. In the following, the inputs X_i $(i = 1 \dots d)$ are assumed to be independent. More advanced works, listed in the last section, take into account the dependence between components of $\mathbf{X}$ (see Kurowicka and Cooke [48] for an introduction to this issue). Finally, this review focuses on the SA with respect to the global variability of the model output, usually measured by its variance.

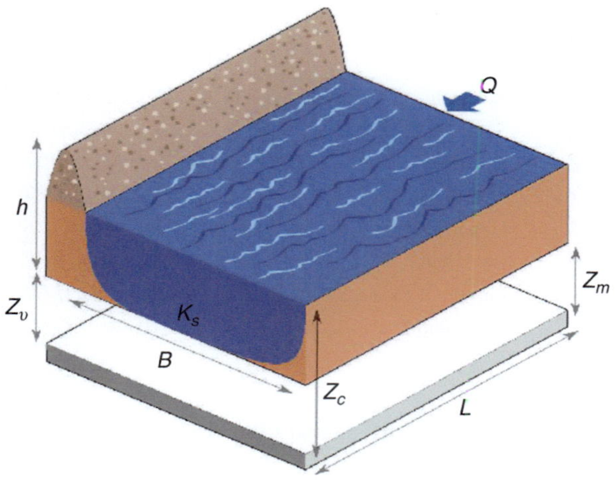

Fig. 5.1 The flood example: simplified model of a river

All along this chapter, we illustrate our discussion with a simple application model that simulates the height of a river and compares it to the height of a dyke that protects industrial facilities (Fig. 5.1). When the river height exceeds the one of the dyke, flooding occurs. This academic model is used as a pedagogical example in de Rocquigny [18] and Iooss [35]. The model is based on a crude simplification of the 1D hydro-dynamical equations of SaintVenant under the assumptions of uniform and constant flowrate and large rectangular sections. It consists of an equation that involves the characteristics of the river stretch:

$$S = Z_v + H - H_d - C_b \quad \text{with} \quad H = \left(\frac{Q}{BK_s\sqrt{\frac{Z_m - Z_v}{L}}} \right)^{0.6}, \tag{5.2}$$

where S is the maximal annual overflow (in meters), H is the maximal annual height of the river (in meters) and the other variables ($d = 8$ inputs) are defined in Table 5.1 with their probability distribution. Among the input variables of the model, H_d is a design parameter. Its variation range corresponds to a design domain. The randomness of the other variables is due to their spatio-temporal variability, our ignorance of their true value or some inaccuracies of their estimation. We suppose that the input variables are independent.

We also consider another model output: the associated cost (in million euros) of the dyke,

$$C_p = 1\!\!1_{S>0} + \left[0.2 + 0.8\left(1 - \exp^{-\frac{1000}{S^4}}\right)\right] 1\!\!1_{S\leq 0} + \frac{1}{20}\left(H_d 1\!\!1_{H_d>8} + 8 1\!\!1_{H_d\leq 8}\right), \tag{5.3}$$

with $1\!\!1_A(x)$ the indicator function which is equal to 1 for $x \in A$ and 0 otherwise. In this equation, the first term represents the cost due to a flooding ($S > 0$) which

Table 5.1 Input variables of the flood model and their probability distributions

Input	Description	Unit	Probability distribution
Q	Maximal annual flowrate	m^3/s	Truncated gumbel $\mathcal{G}(1013, 558)$ on $[500, 3000]$
K_s	Strickler coefficient	–	Truncated normal $\mathcal{N}(30, 8)$ on $[15, +\infty[$
Z_v	River downstream level	m	Triangular $\mathcal{T}(49, 50, 51)$
Z_m	River upstream level	m	Triangular $\mathcal{T}(54, 55, 56)$
H_d	Dyke height	m	Uniform $\mathcal{U}[7, 9]$
C_b	Bank level	m	Triangular $\mathcal{T}(55, 55.5, 56)$
L	Length of the river stretch	m	Triangular $\mathcal{T}(4990, 5000, 5010)$
B	River width	m	Triangular $\mathcal{T}(295, 300, 305)$

is 1 million euros, the second term corresponds to the cost of the dyke maintenance ($S \leq 0$) and the third term is the investment cost related to the construction of the dyke. The latter cost is constant for a height of dyke less than 8 m and is growing proportionally with respect to the dyke height otherwise.

The following section discusses the so-called screening methods, which are qualitative methods for studying sensitivities on models containing several tens of input variables. The most used quantitative measures of influence are described in the third section. The fourth section deals with more advanced tools, which aim to provide a subtle exploration of the model output behavior. Finally, a conclusion provides a classification of these methods and a flowchart for practitioners. It also discusses some open problems in SA.

5.2 Screening Techniques

Screening methods are based on a discretization of the inputs in levels, allowing a fast exploration of the code behaviour. These methods are adapted to a large number of inputs; practice has often shown that only a small number of inputs are influential. The aim of this type of method is to identify the non-influential inputs with a small number of model calls while making realistic hypotheses on the model complexity. The model is therefore simplified before using other SA methods, more subtle but more costly.

The most engineering-used screening method is based on the so-called "One At a Time" (OAT) design, where each input is varied while fixing the others (see Saltelli and Annoni [74] for a critique of this basic method). In this section, the choice has been made to present the Morris method [65], which is the most complete and most costly one. However, when the number of experiments has to be smaller than the number of inputs, one can quote the usefulness of the supersaturated design (Lin [56]), the screening by groups (Dean and Lewis [20]) and the sequential bifurcation method (Bettonvil and Kleijnen [5]). When the number of experiments is of the same order than the number of inputs, the classical theory of experimental design applies (Montgomery [64]) for example with the so-called factorial fractional design.

The method of Morris allows to classify the inputs in three groups: inputs having negligible effects, inputs having large linear effects without interactions and inputs having large non-linear and/or interaction effects. The method consists in discretizing the input space for each variable, then performing a given number of OAT design. Such designs of experiments are randomly chosen in the input space, and the variation direction is also random. The repetition of these steps allows the estimation of elementary effects for each input. From these effects, sensitivity indices are derived.

Let us denote r the number of OAT designs (Saltelli et al. [78] propose to set parameter r between 4 and 10). Let us discretize the input space in a d-dimensional grid with n levels by input. Let us denote $E_j^{(i)}$ the elementary effect of the jth variable obtained at the ith repetition, defined as:

$$E_j^{(i)} = \frac{f(\mathbf{X}^{(i)} + \Delta e_j) - f(\mathbf{X}^{(i)})}{\Delta} \tag{5.4}$$

where Δ is a predetermined multiple of $\frac{1}{(n-1)}$ and e_j a vector of the canonical base. Indices are obtained as follows:

- $\mu_j^* = \frac{1}{r}\sum_{i=1}^{r} |E_j^{(i)}|$ (mean of the absolute value of the elementary effects),
- $\sigma_j = \sqrt{\frac{1}{r}\sum_{i=1}^{r}\left(E_j^{(i)} - \frac{1}{r}\sum_{i=1}^{r} E_j^{(i)}\right)^2}$ (standard deviation of the elementary effects).

The interpretation of the indices is the following:

- μ_j^* is a measure of influence of the jth input on the output. The larger μ_j^* is, the more the jth input contributes to the dispersion of the output.
- σ_j is a measure of non-linear and/or interaction effects of the jth input. If σ_j is small, elementary effects have low variations on the support of the input. Thus the effect of a perturbation is the same all along the support, suggesting a linear relationship between the studied input and the output. On the other hand, the larger σ_j is, the less likely the linearity hypothesis is. Thus a variable with a large σ_j will be considered having non-linear effects, or being implied in an interaction with at least one other variable.

Then, a graph linking μ_j^* and σ_j allows to distinguish the three groups.

Morris method is applied on the flood example [Eqs. (5.2) and (5.3)] with $r = 5$ repetitions, which require $n = r(d+1) = 45$ model calls. Figure 5.2 plots results on the graph (μ_j^*, σ_j). This visualisation allows to make the following discussion:

- output S: inputs K_s, Z_v, Q, C_b et H_d are influent, while other inputs have no effects. In addition, the model output linearly depends on the inputs and there is no input interaction (because $\sigma_j \ll \mu_j^* \forall j$).

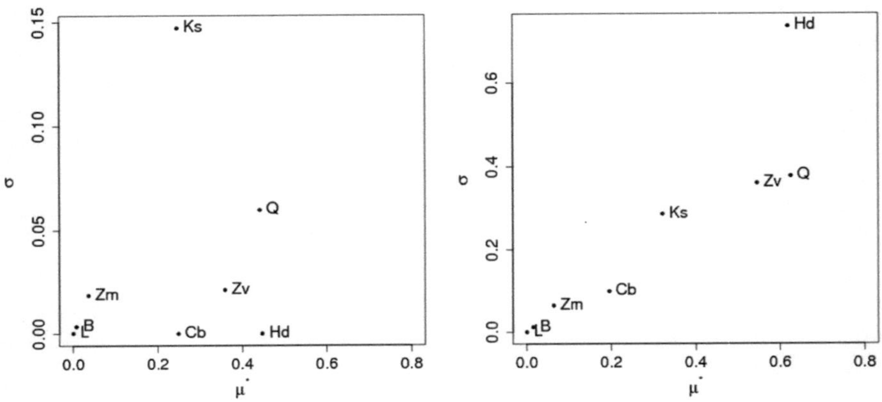

Fig. 5.2 Results of Morris method ($r = 5$ with 4 levels): outputs S (*left*) and C_p (*right*)

- output C_p: inputs H_d, Q, Z_v et K_s have strong influence with non-linear and/or interaction effects (because σ_j and μ_j^* have the same order of magnitude). C_b has an average influence while the other inputs have no influence.

Finally, after this screening phase, we have identified that three inputs (L, B and Z_m) have no influence on the two model outputs In the following, we fix these three inputs to their nominal values (which are the modes of their respective triangular distributions).

5.3 Importance Measures

5.3.1 *Methods Based on the Analysis of Linear Models*

If a sample of inputs and outputs $(\mathbf{X}^n, \mathbf{Y}^n) = \left(X_1^{(i)}, \ldots, X_d^{(i)}, Y_i\right)_{i=1..n}$ is available, it is possible to fit a linear model explaining the behaviour of Y given the values of $\mathbf{X}$, provided that the sample size n is sufficiently large (at least $n > d$). Some global sensitivity measures defined through the study of the fitted model are presented in the following. Main indices are:

- Pearson correlation coefficient:

$$\rho(X_j, Y) = \frac{\sum_{i=1}^{N}(X_j^{(i)} - \mathbb{E}(X_j))(Y_i - \mathbb{E}(Y))}{\sqrt{\sum_{i=1}^{N}\left(X_j^{(i)} - \mathbb{E}(X_j)\right)^2}\sqrt{\sum_{i=1}^{N}(Y_i - \mathbb{E}(Y))^2}}. \quad (5.5)$$

It can be seen as a linearity measure between variable X_j and output Y. It equals 1 or -1 if the tested input variable has a linear relationship with the output. If X_j and Y are independents, the index equals 0.

– Standard Regression Coefficient (SRC):

$$\mathrm{SRC}_j = \beta_j \sqrt{\frac{\mathrm{Var}(X_j)}{\mathrm{Var}(Y)}} \tag{5.6}$$

where β_j is the linear regression coefficient associated to X_j. SRC_j^2 represents a share of variance if the linearity hypothesis is confirmed.

– Partial Correlation Coefficient (PCC):

$$\mathrm{PCC}_j = \rho(X_j - \widehat{X_{-j}}, Y - \widehat{Y_{-j}}) \tag{5.7}$$

where $\widehat{X_{-j}}$ is the prediction of the linear model, expressing X_j with respect to the other inputs and $\widehat{Y_{-j}}$ is the prediction of the linear model where X_j is absent. PCC measures the sensitivity of Y to X_j when the effects of the other inputs have been canceled.

The estimation of these sensitivity indices is subject to an uncertainty estimation, due to the limited size of the sample. Analytical formulas can be applied in order to estimate this uncertainty (Christensen [15]).

These three indices are based on a linear relationship between the output and the inputs. Statistical techniques allow to confirm the linear hypothesis, as the classical coefficient of determination R^2 and the predictivity coefficient Q^2 (also called the Nash-Sutcliffe model efficiency):

$$Q^2 = 1 - \frac{\sum_{i=1}^{m} [Y_i^p - \hat{Y}(\mathbf{X}^{p(i)})]^2}{\sum_{i=1}^{m} [Y_i^p - \mathbb{E}(Y^p)]^2} \tag{5.8}$$

where $(\mathbf{X}^{p(i)}, Y_i^p)_{i=1..m}$ is a m-size test sample of inputs-output (not used for the model fitting) and $\hat{Y}(\cdot)$ is the predictor of the linear regression model. The value of Q^2 corresponds to the percentage of output variability explained by the linear regression model (a value equals to 1 means a perfect fit). If the input variables are independent, each SRC_j^2 expresses the part of output variance explained by the input X_j.

If the linear hypothesis is contradicted, one can use the same three importance measures (correlation coefficient, SRC and PCC) than previously using a rank transformation (Saltelli et al. [77]). The sample $(\mathbf{X}^n, \mathbf{Y}^n)$ is transformed into a sample $(\mathbf{R}_X^n, \mathbf{R}_Y^n)$ by replacing the values by their ranks in each column of the matrix. As importance measures, it gives the Spearman correlation coefficient ρ^S, the Standardized Rank Regression Coefficient (SRRC) and the Partial Rank Correlation Coefficient (PRCC). Of course, monotony hypothesis has to be validated as in the previous case, with the determination coefficient of the ranks (R^{2*}) and the predictivity coefficient of the ranks (Q^{2*}).

These linear and rank-based measures are part of the so-called sampling-based global sensitivity analysis method. This has been deeply studied by Helton and Davis [31] who have shown the interest to use a Latin Hypercube Sample (Mc Kay et al. [63]) in place of a Monte Carlo sample, in order to increase the accuracy of the sensitivity indices.

These methods are now applied on the flood example [Eqs. (5.2) and (5.3)] with the $d = 5$ inputs that have been identified as influent in the previous screening exercise. A Monte Carlo sample of size $n = 100$ gives 100 model evaluations. Results are the following:

- output S:

  $\mathrm{SRC}^2(Q) = 0.28$; $\mathrm{SRC}^2(K_s) = 0.12$; $\mathrm{SRC}^2(Z_v) = 0.15$; $\mathrm{SRC}^2(H_d) = 0.26$; $\mathrm{SRC}^2(C_b) = 0.03$ with $R^2 = 0.98$;
  $\mathrm{SRRC}^2(Q) = 0.27$; $\mathrm{SRRC}^2(K_s) = 0.12$; $\mathrm{SRRC}^2(Z_v) = 0.13$; $\mathrm{SRRC}^2(H_d) = 0.26$; $\mathrm{SRRC}^2(C_b) = 0.02$ with $R^{2*} = 0.95$;

- output C_p:

  $\mathrm{SRC}^2(Q) = 0.25$; $\mathrm{SRC}^2(K_s) = 0.16$; $\mathrm{SRC}^2(Z_v) = 0.18$; $\mathrm{SRC}^2(H_d) = 0.00$; $\mathrm{SRC}^2(C_b) = 0.07$ with $R^2 = 0.70$;
  $\mathrm{SRRC}^2(Q) = 0.26$; $\mathrm{SRRC}^2(K_s) = 0.19$; $\mathrm{SRRC}^2(Z_v) = 0.18$; $\mathrm{SRRC}^2(H_d) = 0.06$; $\mathrm{SRRC}^2(C_b) = 0.03$ with $R^{2*} = 0.73$.

For the output S, R^2 is close to one, which shows a good fit of linear model on the data. Analysis of regression residuals confirms this result. Variance-based sensitivity indices are given using SRC^2. For the output C_p, R^2 and R^{2*} are not close to one, showing that the relation is neither linear nor monotonic. SRC^2 and SRRC^2 indices can be used in a coarse approximation, knowing that it remains 30 % of non-explained variance. However, using another Monte Carlo sample, sensitivity indices values can be noticeably different. Increasing the precision of these sensitivity indices would require a large increase of the sample size.

5.3.2 *Functional Decomposition of Variance: Sobol' Indices*

When the model is non-linear and non-monotonic, the decomposition of the output variance is still defined and can be used for SA. Let us have $f(.)$ a square-integrable function, defined on the unit hypercube $[0, 1]^d$. It is possible to represent this function as a sum of elementary functions (Hoeffding [33]):

$$f(\mathbf{X}) = f_0 + \sum_{i=1}^{d} f_i(X_i) + \sum_{i<j}^{d} f_{ij}(X_i, X_j) + \cdots + f_{12\ldots d}(\mathbf{X}) . \tag{5.9}$$

This expansion is unique under conditions (Sobol [83]):

$$\int_0^1 f_{i_1\dots i_s}(x_{i_1},\dots,x_{i_s})dx_{i_k} = 0\ ,\ 1 \le k \le s,\ \{i_1,\dots,i_s\} \subseteq \{1,\dots,d\}\,.$$

This implies that f_0 is a constant.

In the SA framework, let us have the random vector $\mathbf{X} = (X_1,\dots,X_d)$ where the variables are mutually independent, and the output $Y = f(\mathbf{X})$ of a deterministic model $f(\cdot)$. Thus a functional decomposition of the variance is available, often referred to as functional ANOVA (Efron and Stein [22]):

$$\text{Var}(Y) = \sum_{i=1}^{d} D_i(Y) + \sum_{i<j}^{d} D_{ij}(Y) + \cdots + D_{12\dots d}(Y) \tag{5.10}$$

where $D_i(Y) = \text{Var}[\mathbb{E}(Y|X_i)]$, $D_{ij}(Y) = \text{Var}[\mathbb{E}(Y|X_i,X_j)] - D_i(Y) - D_j(Y)$ and so on for higher order interactions. The so-called "Sobol' indices" or "variance-based sensitivity indices" (Sobol [83]) are obtained as follows:

$$S_i = \frac{D_i(Y)}{\text{Var}(Y)},\quad S_{ij} = \frac{D_{ij}(Y)}{\text{Var}(Y)},\quad \cdots \tag{5.11}$$

These indices express the share of variance of Y that is due to a given input or input combination.

The number of indices growths in an exponential way with the number d of dimension: there are $2^d - 1$ indices. For computational time and interpretation reasons, the practitioner should not estimate indices of order higher than two. Homma and Saltelli [34] introduced the so-called "total indices" or "total effects" that write as follows:

$$S_{T_i} = S_i + \sum_{j\neq i} S_{ij} + \sum_{j\neq i,k\neq i,j<k} S_{ijk} + \ldots = \sum_{l\in\#i} S_l \tag{5.12}$$

where $\#i$ are all the subsets of $\{1,\dots,d\}$ including i. In practice, when d is large, only the main effects and the total effects are computed, thus giving a good information on the model sensitivities.

To estimate Sobol' indices, Monte Carlo sampling based methods have been developed: Sobol [83] for first order and interaction indices and Saltelli [73] for fist order and total indices. Unfortunately, to get precise estimates of sensitivity indices, these methods are costly in terms of number of model calls (rate of convergence in $\sqrt{n}$ where n is the sample size). In common practice, the value of 10^4 model calls can be required to estimate the Sobol' index of one input with an uncertainty of 10 %. Using quasi-Monte Carlo sequences instead of Monte Carlo samples can sometimes reduce this cost by a factor ten (Saltelli et al. [79]). The FAST method (Cukier et al. [16]), based on a multi-dimensional Fourier transform, is also used to reduce this cost. Saltelli et al. [76] have extended this technique to compute total Sobol' indices and Tarantola et al. [90] have coupled FAST with a Random Balance Design. Tissot and Prieur [91] have recently analyzed and improved these methods. However, FAST remains costly, unstable and biased when the number of inputs increases (larger than 10) (Tissot and Prieur [91]).

One advantage of using a Monte Carlo based method is that it provides error made on indices estimates via random repetition (Iooss et al. [37]), asymptotic formulas (Janon et al. [40]) or bootstrap methods (Archer et al. [1]). Thus, other Monte Carlo based estimation formulas have been introduced and greatly improved the estimation precision: Mauntz formulas (Sobol et al. [86], Saltelli et al. [74]) for estimating small indices, Jansen formula (Jansen [41], Saltelli et al. [74]) for estimating total Sobol' indices and Janon-Monod formula (Janon et al. [40]) for estimating large first-order indices.

To illustrate the estimation of the Sobol' indices on the flood exercise [Eqs. (5.2) and (5.3)] with $d = 5$ random inputs, we use Saltelli [73] formula with a Monte Carlo sampling. It has a cost $N = n(d + 2)$ in terms of model calls where n is the size of an initial Monte Carlo sample. Here, $n = 10^5$ and we repeat 100 times the estimation process to obtain confidence intervals (as boxplots) for each estimated indices. Figure 5.3 gives the result of these estimates, which have finally required $N = 7 \times 10^7$ model calls.

For the output S, the first order indices are almost equal to the total indices, and results seem very similar to those of SRC^2. The model is linear and the estimation of Sobol' indices is unnecessary in this case. For the output C_p, we obtain different information than those provided by SRC^2 and SRRC^2: the total effect of Q is about 50 % (twice than its SRC^2), the effect of H_d is about 20 %, while Q and K_s have non-negligible interaction effects. Second order Sobol' index between Q and K_s is worth 6 %.

5.3.3 Other Measures

From an independent and identically distributed sample (as a Monte Carlo one), other techniques can be used for SA. For example, statistical testing based techniques consist, for each input, to divide the sample into several sub-samples (dividing the considered input into equiprobable stratas). Statistical tests can then be applied to measure the homogeneity of populations between classes: common means (CMN) based on a Fisher test, common median (CMD) based on a χ^2-test, common variances (CV) based on a Fisher test, common locations (CL) based on the Kruskal-Wallis test, ...(Kleijnen and Helton [45], Helton et al. [32]). These methods do not require assumptions about the monotony of the output with respect to the inputs but lacks of some quantitative interpretation.

The indices of Sect. 5.3.2 are based on the second-order moment (i.e. the variance) of the output distribution. In some cases, variance poorly represents the variability of the distribution. Some authors have then introduced the so-called

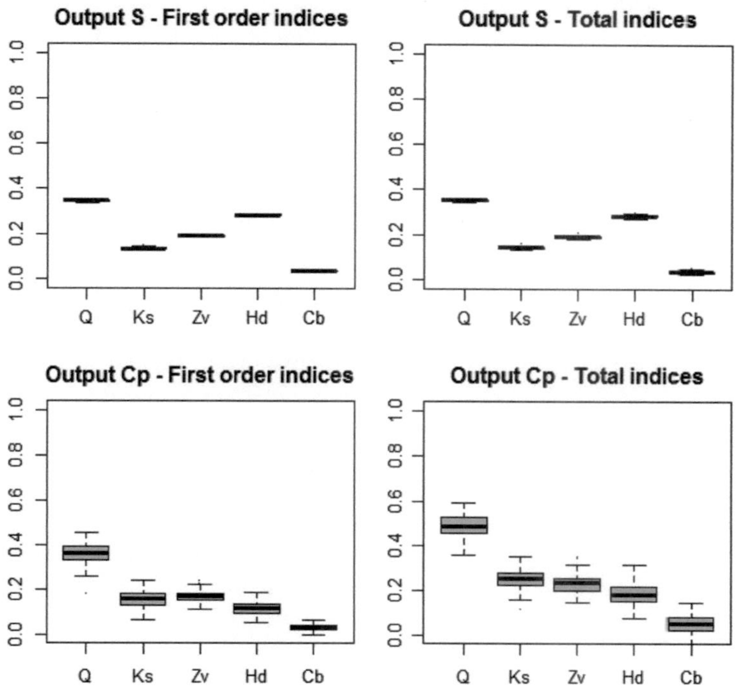

Fig. 5.3 Estimation of Sobol' indices on the flood example. Each boxplot corresponds to 100 independent estimates

moment independent importance measures, which do not require any computation of the output moments. Two kinds of indices have been defined:

- The entropy-based sensitivity indices (Krzykacz-Hausmann [47], Liu et al. [57], Auder and Iooss [3]),
- The distribution based sensitivity indices (Borgonovo [6], Borgonovo et al. [7]) which consider a distance or a divergence between the output distribution and the output distribution conditionally to one or several inputs.

It has been shown that these indices can provide complementary information than Sobol' indices. However, some difficulties arise in their estimation procedure.

5.4 Deep Exploration of Sensitivities

In this section, the discussed methods provide additional sensitivity information than just scalar indices. Moreover, for industrial computer codes with a high computational cost (from several tens of minutes to days), the estimation of Sobol' indices, even with sophisticated sampling methods, are often unreachable. This section also summarizes a class of methods for approximating the numerical model to estimate Sobol' indices at a low computational cost, while providing a deeper view of the input variables effects.

5.4.1 Graphical and Smoothing Techniques

Beyond Sobol' indices that only give a scalar value for the effect of an input X_i on the output Y, the influence of X_i on Y along its domain of variation is also of interest. In the literature, it is often referred to as main effects, but to avoid any confusion with the indices of the first order, it is preferable to talk about main effects visualization (or graph). The scatterplots (visualization of point cloud of any sample simulations $(\mathbf{X}^n, \mathbf{Y}^n)$ with the graphs of Y vs. $X_i, i = 1, \ldots, d$) meets this goal, but in a visual subjective manner. This is shown in Fig. 5.4, on the flood example and using the 100-size sample of Sect. 5.3.1.

Based on parametric or non-parametric regression methods (Hastie and Tibshirani [28]), the smoothing techniques aim to estimate the conditional moments of Y

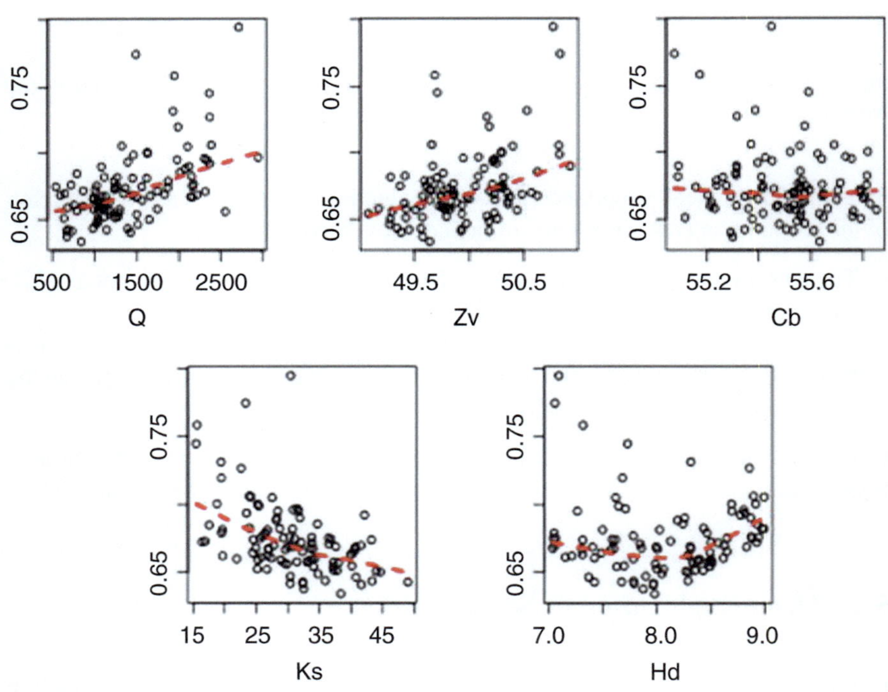

Fig. 5.4 Scatterplots on the flood example with the five inputs Q, Z_v, C_b, K_s, H_d and the output C_p. *Dotted curve* is a local polynomial based smoother

at first or higher order. SA is often restricted to the determination of the conditional expectation at first and second orders (Santner et al. [80]), in order to obtain:

- main effects graphs, between X_i and $\mathbb{E}(Y|X_i) - \mathbb{E}(Y)$ on the whole variation domain of X_i for $i = 1, \ldots, d$;
- interaction effects graphs, between (X_i, X_j) and $\mathbb{E}(Y|X_i X_j) - \mathbb{E}(Y|X_i) - \mathbb{E}(Y|X_j) - \mathbb{E}(Y)$ on all the variation domain of (X_i, X_j) for $i = 1, \ldots, d$ and $j = i + 1, \ldots, d$.

Storlie and Helton [87] conducted a fairly comprehensive review of non-parametric smoothing methods that can be used for SA: moving averages, kernel methods, local polynomials, smoothing splines, etc. In Fig. 5.4, the local polynomial smoother is plotted for each cloud of points, thereby clearly identifying the mean trend of the output versus each input.

Once these conditional expectations are modeled, it is easy to quantify their variance by sampling, and thus to estimate Sobol' indices [cf. Eq. (5.11)] of order one, two, or even higher orders. Da Veiga et al. [17] discuss the theoretical properties of local polynomial estimators of the conditional expectation and variance, and then deduce the theoretical properties of the Sobol' indices estimated by local polynomials. Storlie and Helton [87] also discuss the efficiency of additive models and regression trees to non-parametrically estimate $\mathbb{E}(Y|X_1, \ldots, X_d)$. This finally leads to build an approximate model of $f(\cdot)$, which is called a "metamodel". This will be detailed in the following section.

In SA, graphical techniques can also be useful. For example, all the scatterplots between each input variable and the model output can detect some trends in their functional relation (see Fig. 5.4). However scatterplots do not capture some interaction effects between the inputs. Cobweb plots (Kurowicka and Cooke [48]), also called parallel coordinate plots, can be used to visualize the simulations as a set of trajectories. In Fig. 5.5, the simulations leading to the 5 % largest values of the model output S have been highlighted. This allows to immediately understand that these simulations correspond to large values of the flowrate Q and small values of the Strickler coefficient K_s.

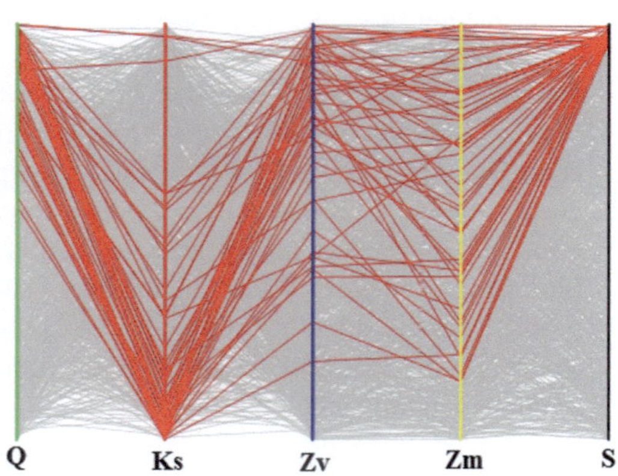

Fig. 5.5 Cobweb plot of 10, 000 simulations of the flood model

5.4.2 Metamodel-Based Methods

The metamodel concept is frequently used to simulate the behavior of an experimental system or a long running computational code based on a certain number of output values. Under the name of the response surface methodology, it was originally proposed as a statistical tool, to find the operating conditions of a process at which some responses were optimized (Box and Draper [8]). Subsequent generalizations led to these methods being used to develop approximating functions of deterministic computer codes (Downing et al. [21], Sacks et al. [71], Kleijnen and Sargent [46]). It consists in generating a surrogate model that fits the initial data (using for example a least squares procedure), which has good prediction capabilities and has negligible computational cost. It is thus efficient for uncertainty and SA requiring several thousands of model calculations (Iooss et al. [37]).

In practice, we focus on three main issues during the construction of a metamodel:

- the choice of the metamodel that can be derived from any linear regression model, non-linear parametric or non-parametric (Hastie et al. [29]). The most used metamodels include polynomials, splines, generalized linear models, generalized additive models, kriging, neural networks, SVM, boosting regression trees (Simpson et al. [82], Fang et al. [24]). Linear and quadratic functions are commonly considered as a first iteration. Knowledge on some input interaction types may be also introduced in polynomials (Jourdan and Zabalza-Mezghani [42], Kleijnen [44]). However, these kinds of models are not always efficient, especially in simulation of complex and non-linear phenomena. For such models, modern statistical learning algorithms can show much better ability to build accurate models with strong predictive capabilities (Marrel et al. [59]);
- the design of (numerical) experiments. The main qualities required for an experimental design are the robustness (ability to analyze different models), the effectiveness (optimization of a criterion), the goodness of points repartition (space filling property) and the low cost for its construction (Santner et al. [80], Fang et al. [24]). Several studies have shown the qualities of different types of experimental designs with respect to the predictivity metamodel (for example Simpson et al. [82]);
- the validation of the metamodel. In the field of classical experimental design, proper validation of a response surface is a crucial aspect and is considered with care. However, in the field of numerical experiments, this issue has not been deeply studied. The usual practice is to estimate global criteria (RMSE, absolute error, ...) on a test basis, via cross-validation or bootstrap (Kleijnen and Sargent [46], Fang et al. [24]). When the number of calculations is small and to overcome problems induced by the cross validation process, Iooss et al. [38] have recently studied how to minimize the size of a test sample, while obtaining a good estimate of the metamodel predictivity.

Some metamodel allows to directly obtain the sensitivity indices. For example, Sudret [89] has shown that Sobol' indices are a by-product result of the polynomial chaos decomposition. The formulation of the kriging metamodel provides also analytical formula for the Sobol' indices, associated with interval confidence coming from the kriging error (Oakley and O'Hagan [66], Marrel et al. [60], Le Gratiet et al. [51]). A simplest idea, widely used in practice, is to apply an intensive sampling technique (see Sect. 5.3.2) directly on the metamodel to estimate Sobol' indices (Santner et al. [80], Iooss et al. [37]). The variance proportion not explained by the metamodel [calculated by $1 - Q_2$, cf. Eq. (5.8)] gives us what is missing in the SA (Sobol [84]). Storlie et al. [88] propose a bootstrap method for estimating the impact of the metamodel error.

As in the previous section, we can be interested by visualizing main effects (Schonlau and Welch [81]). These can be directly given by the metamodel (this is the case with the polynomial chaos methods, kriging, additive models), or computed by simulating the conditional expectation $\mathbf{E}(Y|X_i)$.

To illustrate our purpose, we use the flood example [Eqs. (5.2) and (5.3)]. A kriging metamodel is built on a 100-size Monte Carlo sample with inputs Q, K_s, Z_v, H_d, C_b and on the output C_p. The metamodel consists in a deterministic term (simple linear model), and a corrective term modeled by a Gaussian stationary stochastic process, with a generalized exponential covariance (see Santner et al. [80] for more details). The technique for estimating the metamodel hyperparameters is described in Roustant et al. [69]. The predictivity coefficient estimated by leave-one-out is $Q^2 = 99\,\%$ compared with $Q^2 = 75\,\%$ obtained with a simple linear model. The kriging metamodel is then used to estimate Sobol' indices in the same manner as in Sect. 5.3.2: Saltelli's estimation formula, Monte Carlo sampling, $n = 10^5$, $r = 100$ repetitions. This requires $N = 7 \times 10^7$ metamodel predictions. In Table 5.2, we compare Sobol' indices (averaged over 100 repetitions) obtained with the metamodel to those obtained with the "real" flood model [Eqs. (5.2) and (5.3)]. Errors between these two estimates are relatively low: with only 100 simulations with the true model, we were able to obtain precise estimates (errors $< 15\,\%$) of first order and total Sobol' indices.

Table 5.2 Sobol' indices estimated by Monte Carlo sampling (cost of $N = 7 \times 10^7$ evaluations) using the flood model and a metamodel fitted on $N' = 100$ calls of the flood model

Indices (in %)	Q	K_s	Z_v	H_d	C_b
S_i model	35.5	15.9	18.3	12.5	3.8
S_i metamodel	38.9	16.8	18.8	13.9	3.7
S_{T_i} model	48.2	25.3	22.9	18.1	3.8
S_{T_i} metamodel	45.5	21.0	21.3	16.8	4.3

5.5 Synthesis and Conclusion

Although all SA techniques have not been listed, this review has illustrated the great variety of available methods, positioning in terms of assumptions and kind of results. Moreover, some recent improvements have not been explained, for example for the Morris method (Pujol [68]).

A synthesis is provided in Fig. 5.6 which has several levels of reading:

- distinction between screening methods (identification of non-influential variables among a large number) and more precise variance-based quantitative methods,
- positioning methods based on their cost in terms of model calls number (which linearly depends in the number of inputs for most of the methods),
- positioning methods based on their assumptions about the model complexity and regularity,
- distinction between the type of information provided by each method,
- identification of methods which require some a priori knowledge about the model behaviour.

Based on the characteristics of the different methods, some authors (de Rocquigny et al. [19], Pappenberger et al. [67]) have proposed decision trees to help the practitioner to choose the most appropriate method for its problem and its model. Figure 5.7 reproduces the flowchart of de Rocquigny et al. [19]. Although useful to fix some ideas, such diagrams are rather simple and should be used with caution.

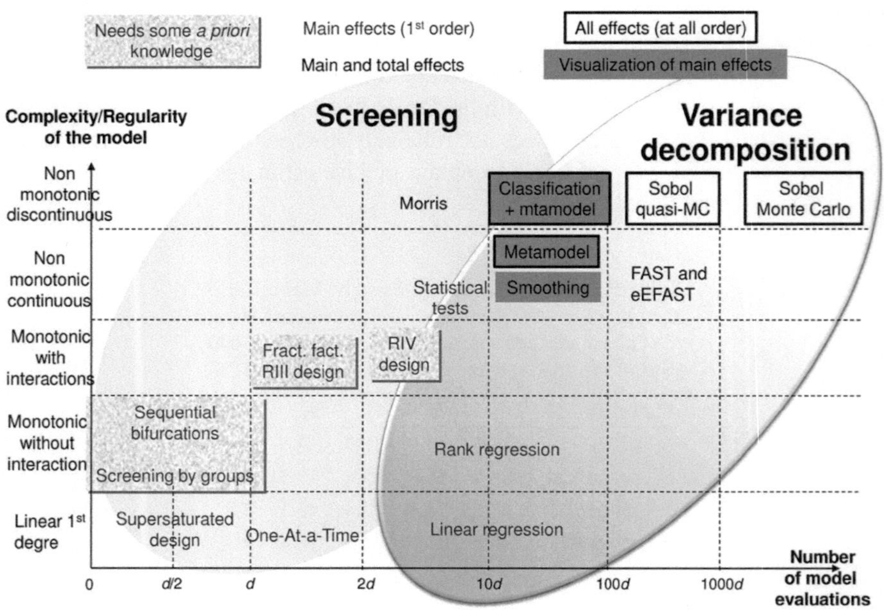

Fig. 5.6 SA methods graphical synthesis

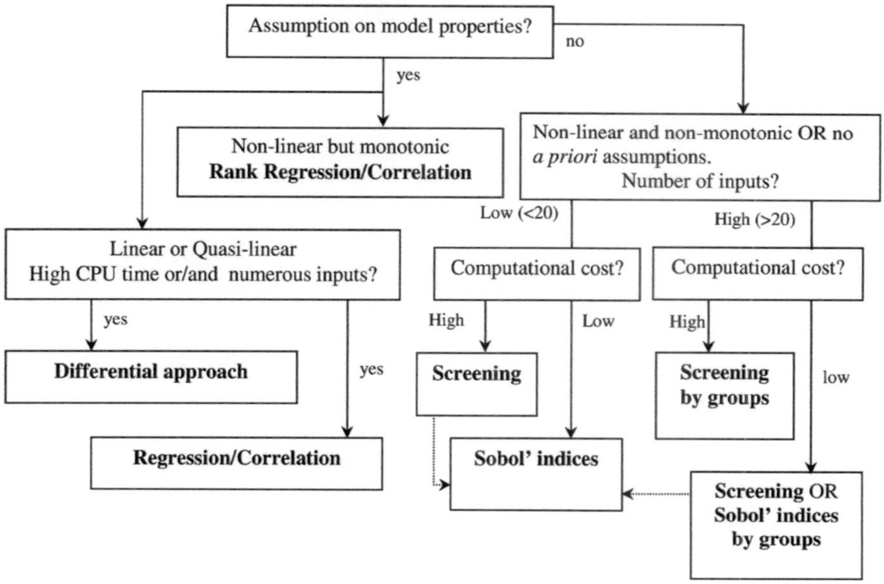

Fig. 5.7 Decision diagram for the choice of a SA method (from de Rocquigny et al. [19])

Several issues about SA remain open. For instance, recent theoretical results have been obtained on the asymptotical properties and efficiency of Sobol' indices estimators (Janon et al. [40]), but estimating total Sobol' indices at low cost is a problem of primary importance in applications (see Saltelli et al. [74] for a recent review on the subject). SA for dependent inputs has also been discussed by several authors (Saltelli and Tarantola [75], Jacques et al. [39], Xu and Gertner [93], Da Veiga et al. [17], Gauchi et al. [27], Li et al. [54], Chastaing et al. [14]), but this issue remains misunderstood.

This chapter has been focused on SA relative to the overall variability of model output. In practice, one can be interested by other quantities of interest, such as the output entropy (cf. Sect. 5.3.3), the probability that the output exceeds a threshold (Saltelli et al. [77], Frey and Patil [25], Lemaître et al. [53]) or a quantile estimation (Cannamela et al. [12]). This is an active area of research.

In many applications, the model output is not a single scalar but a vector or a function (temporal, spatial, spatio-temporal, ...). Campbell et al. [11], Lamboni et al. [50], Marrel et al. [61] and Gamboa et al. [26] have produced first SA results on such problems. The case of functional inputs also receives a growing interest (Iooss and Ribatet [36], Lilburne and Tarantola [55], Saint-Geours et al. [72]), but its treatment in a functional statistical framework remains to be done.

In some situations, the computer code is not a deterministic simulator but a stochastic one. This means that two model calls with the same set of input variables leads to different output values. Typical stochastic computer codes are queuing models, agent-based models, models involving partial differential equations applied to heterogeneous or Monte-Carlo based numerical models. For this type of codes, Marrel et al. [62] have proposed a first solution for dealing with Sobol' indices.

Finally, quantitative SA methods are limited to low-dimensional models, with no more than a few tens of input variables. On the other hand, deterministic methods, such as adjoint-based ones (Cacuci [10]), are well suited when the model includes a large number of input variables. A natural idea is to use the advantages of both methods. Recently introduced, Derivative-Based Sensitivity Measures (DGSM), consists in computing the integral of the square model derivatives for each input (Sobol and Kucherenko [85]). An inequality relation has been proved between total Sobol' indices and DGSM which allow to propose some interpretative results (Lamboni et al. [49], Roustant et al. [70]). It opens the way to perform global SA in high dimensional context.

Acknowledgements Part of this work has been backed by French National Research Agency (ANR) through COSINUS program (project COSTA BRAVA no. ANR-09-COSI-015). We thank Anne-Laure Popelin and Merlin Keller for providing the cobweb plot and the flood model figure.

References

1. Archer, G., Saltelli, A., Sobol, I.: Sensitivity measures, ANOVA-like techniques and the use of bootstrap. J. Stat. Comput. Simul. **58**, 99–120 (1997)
2. Auder, B., de Crécy, A., Iooss, B., Marquès, M.: Screening and metamodeling of computer experiments with functional outputs. Application to thermal-hydraulic computations. Reliab. Eng. Syst. Saf. **107**, 122–131 (2012)
3. Auder, B., Iooss, B.: Global sensitivity analysis based on entropy. In: Martorell, S., Guedes Soares, C., Barnett, J. (eds.), Safety, Reliability and Risk Analysis - Proceedings of the ESREL 2008 Conference, pp. 2107–2115. CRC Press, Valencia (2008)
4. Badea, A., Bolado, R.: Review of sensitivity analysis methods and experience. PAMINA 6th FPEC Project, European Commission (2008). http://www.ip-pamina.eu/downloads/pamina.m2.1.d.4.pdf
5. Bettonvil, B., Kleijnen, J.P.C.: Searching for important factors in simulation models with many factors: Sequential bifurcation. Eur. J. Oper. Res. **96**, 180–194 (1996)
6. Borgonovo, E.: A new uncertainty importance measure. Reliab. Eng. Syst. Saf. **92**, 771–784 (2007)
7. Borgonovo, E., Castaings, W., Tarantola, S.: Moment independent importance measures: new results and analytical test cases. Risk Anal. **31**, 404–428 (2011)
8. Box, G.E., Draper, N.R.: Empirical Model Building and Response Surfaces. Wiley Series in Probability and Mathematical Statistics. Wiley, New York (1987)
9. Cacuci, D.G.: Sensitivity theory for nonlinear systems. I. Nonlinear functional analysis approach. J. Math. Phys. **22**, 2794 (1981)
10. Cacuci, D.G.: Sensitivity and Uncertainty Analysis - Theory. Chapman & Hall/CRC, Boca Raton (2003)
11. Campbell, K., McKay, M.D., Williams, B.J.: Sensitivity analysis when model ouputs are functions. Reliab. Eng. Syst. Saf. **91**, 1468–1472 (2006)
12. Cannamela, C., Garnier, J., Iooss, B.: Controlled stratification for quantile estimation. Ann. Appl. Stat. **2**, 1554–1580 (2008)

13. Castaings, W., Dartus, D., Le Dimet, F.-X., Saulnier, G.-M.: Sensitivity analysis and parameter estimation for distributed hydrological modeling : potential of variational methods. Hydrol. Earth Syst. Sci. Discuss. **13**, 503–517 (2009)
14. Chastaing, G., Gamboa, F., Prieur, C.: Generalized Hoeffding-sobol decomposition for dependent variables - Application to sensitivity analysis. Electron. J. Stat. **6**, 2420–2448 (2012)
15. Christensen, R.: Linear Models for Multivariate, Time Series and Spatial Data. Springer, New York (1990)
16. Cukier, H., Levine, R.I., Shuler, K.: Nonlinear sensitivity analysis of multiparameter model systems. J. Comput. Phys. **26**, 1–42 (1978)
17. Da Veiga, S., Wahl, F., Gamboa, F.: Local polynomial estimation for sensitivity analysis on models with correlated inputs. Technometrics **51**(4), 452–463 (2009)
18. de Rocquigny, E.: La maîtrise des incertitudes dans un contexte industriel - 1ère partie : une approche méthodologique globale basée sur des exemples. Journal de la Société Française de Statistique **147**(3), 33–71 (2006)
19. de Rocquigny, E., Devictor, N., Tarantola, S. (eds.): Uncertainty in Industrial Practice. Wiley, Chichester (2008)
20. Dean, A., Lewis, S., (eds.): Screening - Methods for Experimentation in Industry, Drug Discovery and Genetics. Springer, New York (2006)
21. Downing, D.J., Gardner, R.H., Hoffman, F.O.: An examination of response surface methodologies for uncertainty analysis in assessment models. Technometrics **27**(2), 151–163 (1985)
22. Efron, B., Stein, C.: The jacknife estimate of variance. Ann. Stat. **9**, 586–596 (1981)
23. Faivre, R., Iooss, B., Mahévas, S., Makowski, D., Monod, H., (eds.): Analyse de sensibilité et exploration de modèles. Éditions Quaé, Versailles (2013)
24. Fang, K.-T., Li, R., Sudjianto, A.: Design and Modeling for Computer Experiments. Chapman & Hall/CRC, Boston (2006)
25. Frey, H.C., Patil, S.R.: Identification and review of sensitivity analysis methods. Risk Anal. **22**, 553–578 (2002)
26. Gamboa, F., Janon, A., Klein, T., Lagnoux, A.: Sensitivity indices for multivariate outputs. C. R. Acad. Sci. **351**, 307–310 (2013)
27. Gauchi, J.P., Lehuta, S., Mahévas, S.: Optimal sensitivity analysis under constraints. In: Procedia Social and Behavioral Sciences, vol. 2, pp. 7658–7659, Milan (2010)
28. Hastie, T., Tibshirani, R.: Generalized Additive Models. Chapman & Hall, London (1990)
29. Hastie, T., Tibshirani, R., Friedman, J.: The Elements of Statistical Learning. Springer, New York (2002)
30. Helton, J.C.: Uncertainty and sensitivity analysis techniques for use in performance assesment for radioactive waste disposal. Reliab. Eng. Syst. Saf. **42**, 327–367 (1993)
31. Helton, J.C., Davis, F.J.: Latin hypercube sampling and the propagation of uncertainty in analyses of complex systems. Reliab. Eng. Syst. Saf. **81**, 23–69 (2003)
32. Helton, J.C., Johnson, J.D., Salaberry, C.J., Storlie, C.B.: Survey of sampling-based methods for uncertainty and sensitivity analysis. Reliab. Eng. Syst. Saf. **91**, 1175–1209 (2006)
33. Hoeffding, W.: A class of statistics with asymptotically normal distributions. Ann. Math. Stat. **19**, 293–325 (1948)
34. Homma, T., Saltelli, A.: Importance measures in global sensitivity analysis of non linear models. Reliab. Eng. Syst. Saf. **52**, 1–17 (1996)
35. Iooss, B.: Revue sur l'analyse de sensibilité globale de modèles numériques. Journal de la Société Française de Statistique **152**, 1–23 (2011)
36. Iooss, B., Ribatet, M.: Global sensitivity analysis of computer models with functional inputs. Reliab. Eng. Syst. Saf. **94**, 1194–1204 (2009)
37. Iooss, B., Van Dorpe, F., Devictor, N.: Response surfaces and sensitivity analyses for an environmental model of dose calculations. Reliab. Eng. Syst. Saf. **91**, 1241–1251 (2006)
38. Iooss, B., Boussouf, L., Feuillard, V., Marrel, A.: Numerical studies of the metamodel fitting and validation processes. Int. J. Adv. Syst. Meas. **3**, 11–21 (2010)
39. Jacques, J., Lavergne, C., Devictor, N.: Sensitivity analysis in presence of model uncertainty and correlated inputs. Reliab. Eng. Syst. Saf. **91**, 1126–1134 (2006)

40. Janon, A., Klein, T., Lagnoux, A., Nodet, M., Prieur, C.: Asymptotic normality and efficiency of two sobol index estimators. ESAIM Probab. Stat. **18**, 342–364 (2013)
41. Jansen, M.J.W.: Analysis of variance designs for model output. Comput. Phys. Commun. **117**, 25–43 (1999)
42. Jourdan, A., Zabalza-Mezghani, I.: Response surface designs for scenario mangement and uncertainty quantification in reservoir production. Math. Geol. **36**(8), 965–985 (2004)
43. Kleijnen, J.P.C.: Sensitivity analysis and related analyses: a review of some statistical techniques. J. Stat. Comput. Simul. **57**, 111–142 (1997)
44. Kleijnen, J.P.C.: An overview of the design and analysis of simulation experiments for sensitivity analysis. Eur. J.Oper. Res. **164**, 287–300 (2005)
45. Kleijnen, J.P.C., Helton, J.C.: Statistical analyses of scatterplots to identify important factors in large-scale simulations, 1: review and comparison of techniques. Reliab. Eng. Syst. Saf. **65**, 147–185 (1999)
46. Kleijnen, J.P.C., Sargent, R.G.: A methodology for fitting and validating metamodels in simulation. Eur. J.Oper. Res. **120**, 14–29 (2000)
47. Krzykacz-Hausmann, B.: Epistemic sensitivity analysis based on the concept of entropy. In: Proceedings of SAMO 2001, pp. 31–35. CIEMAT, Madrid (2001)
48. Kurowicka, D., Cooke, R.: Uncertainty Analysis with High Dimensional Dependence Modelling. Wiley, Chichester (2006)
49. Lamboni, M., Iooss, B., Popelin, A.-L., Gamboa, F.: Derivative-based global sensitivity measures: general links with sobol' indices and numerical tests. Math. Comput. Simul. **87**, 45–54 (2013)
50. Lamboni, M., Monod, H., Makowski, D.: Multivariate sensitivity analysis to measure global contribution of input factors in dynamic models. Reliab. Eng. Syst. Saf. **96**, 450–459 (2011)
51. Le Gratiet, L., Cannamela, C., Iooss, B.: A Bayesian approach for global sensitivity analysis of (multifidelity) computer codes. SIAM/ASA J. Uncertain. Quantif. **2**, 336–363 (2014)
52. Lefebvre, S., Roblin, A., Varet, S., Durand, G.: A methodological approach for statistical evaluation of aircraft infrared signature. Reliab. Eng. Syst. Saf. **95**, 484–493 (2010)
53. Lemaître, P., Sergienko, E., Arnaud, A., Bousquet, N., Gamboa, F., Iooss, B.: Density modification based reliability sensitivity analysis. J. Stat. Comput. Simul. **85**, 1200–1223 (2015)
54. Li, G., Rabitz, H., Yelvington, P.E., Oluwole, O.O., Bacon, F., Kolb, C.E., Schoendorf, J.: Global sensitivity analysis for systems with independent and/or correlated inputs. J. Phys. Chem. **114**, 6022–6032 (2010)
55. Lilburne, L., Tarantola, S.: Sensitivity analysis of spatial models. Int. J. Geogr. Inf. Sci. **23**, 151–168 (2009)
56. Lin, D.K.J.: A new class of supersaturated design. Technometrics **35**, 28–31 (1993)
57. Liu, H., Chen, W., Sudjianto, A.: Relative entropy based method for probabilistic sensitivity analysis in engineering design. ASME J. Mech. Des. **128**, 326–336 (2006)
58. Makowski, D., Naud, C., Jeuffroy, M.H., Barbottin, A., Monod, H.: Global sensitivity analysis for calculating the contribution of genetic parameters to the variance of crop model prediction. Reliab. Eng. Syst. Saf. **91**, 1142–1147 (2006)
59. Marrel, A., Iooss, B., Van Dorpe, F., Volkova, E.: An efficient methodology for modeling complex computer codes with Gaussian processes. Comput. Stat. Data Anal. **52**, 4731–4744 (2008)
60. Marrel, A., Iooss, B., Laurent, B., Roustant, O.: Calculations of the Sobol indices for the Gaussian process metamodel. Reliab. Eng. Syst. Saf. **94**, 742–751 (2009)
61. Marrel, A., Iooss, B., Jullien, M., Laurent, B., Volkova, E.: Global sensitivity analysis for models with spatially dependent outputs. Environmetrics **22**, 383–397 (2011)
62. Marrel, A., Iooss, B., Da Veiga, S., Ribatet, M.: Global sensitivity analysis of stochastic computer models with joint metamodels. Stat. Comput. **22**, 833–847 (2012)
63. McKay, M.D., Beckman, R.J., Conover, W.J.: A comparison of three methods for selecting values of input variables in the analysis of output from a computer code. Technometrics **21**, 239–245 (1979)

64. Montgomery, D.C.: Design and Analysis of Experiments, 6th edn. Wiley, Hoboken (2004)
65. Morris, M.D.: Factorial sampling plans for preliminary computational experiments. Technometrics **33**, 161–174 (1991)
66. Oakley, J.E., O'Hagan, A.: Probabilistic sensitivity analysis of complex models: a Bayesian approach. J. R. Stat. Soc. Ser. B **66**, 751–769 (2004)
67. Pappenberger, F., Ratto, M., Vandenberghe, V.: Review of sensitivity analysis methods. In: Vanrolleghem, P.A., (ed.) Modelling Aspects of Water Framework Directive Implementation, pp. 191–265. IWA Publishing, London (2010)
68. Pujol, G. (2009). Simplex-based screening designs for estimating metamodels. Reliab. Eng. Syst. Saf. **94**, 1156–1160 (2009)
69. Roustant, O., Ginsbourger, D., Deville, Y.: DiceKriging, DiceOptim: Two R packages for the analysis of computer experiments by kriging-based metamodeling and optimization. J. Stat. Softw., **21** 1–55 (2012)
70. Roustant, O., Fruth, J., Iooss, B., Kuhnt, S.: Crossed-derivative-based sensitivity measures for interaction screening. **105**, 105–118 (2014)
71. Sacks, J., Welch, W.J., Mitchell, T.J., Wynn, H.P.: Design and analysis of computer experiments. Stat. Sci. **4**, 409–435 (1989)
72. Saint-Geours, N., Lavergne, C., Bailly, J.-S., Grelot, F.: Analyse de sensibilité de sobol d'un modèle spatialisé pour l'evaluation économique du risque d'inondation. Journal de la Société Française de Statistique **152**, 24–46 (2011)
73. Saltelli, A.: Making best use of model evaluations to compute sensitivity indices. Comput. Phys. Commun. **145**, 280–297 (2002)
74. Saltelli, A., Annoni, P.: How to avoid a perfunctory sensitivity analysis. Environ. Model. Softw. **25**, 1508–1517 (2010)
75. Saltelli, A., Tarantola, S.: On the relative importance of input factors in mathematical models: Safety assessment for nuclear waste disposal. J. Am. Stat. Assoc. **97**, 702–709 (2002)
76. Saltelli, A., Tarantola, S., Chan, K.: A quantitative, model-independent method for global sensitivity analysis of model output. Technometrics **41**, 39–56 (1999)
77. Saltelli, A., Chan, K., Scott, E.M. (eds.): Sensitivity Analysis. Wiley Series in Probability and Statistics. Wiley, New York (2000)
78. Saltelli, A., Tarantola, S., Campolongo, F., Ratto, M.: Sensitivity Analysis in Practice: A Guide to Assessing Scientific Models. Wiley, New York (2004)
79. Saltelli, A., Ratto, M., Andres, T., Campolongo, F., Cariboni, J., Gatelli, D., Salsana, M., Tarantola, S.: Global Sensitivity Analysis - The Primer. Wiley, New York (2008)
80. Santner, T., Williams, B., Notz, W.: The Design and Analysis of Computer Experiments. Springer, New York (2003)
81. Schonlau, M., Welch, W.J.: Screening the input variables to a computer model. In: Dean, A., Lewis, S., (eds.) Screening - Methods for Experimentation in Industry, Drug Discovery and Genetics. Springer, New York (2006)
82. Simpson, T.W., Peplinski, J.D., Kock, P.N., Allen, J.K.: Metamodel for computer-based engineering designs: Survey and recommandations. Eng. Comput. **17**, 129–150 (2001)
83. Sobol, I.M.: Sensitivity estimates for non linear mathematical models. Math. Model. Comput. Exp. **1**, 407–414 (1993)
84. Sobol, I.M.: Theorems and examples on high dimensional model representation. Reliab. Eng. Syst. Saf. **79**, 187–193 (2003)
85. Sobol, I.M., Kucherenko, S.: Derivative based global sensitivity measures and their links with global sensitivity indices. Math. Comput. Simul. **79**, 3009–3017 (2009)
86. Sobol, I.M., Tarantola, S., Gatelli, D., Kucherenko, S.S., Mauntz, W.: Estimating the approximation errors when fixing unessential factors in global sensitivity analysis. Reliab. Eng. Syst. Saf. **92**, 957–960 (2007)
87. Storlie, C.B., Helton, J.C.: Multiple predictor smoothing methods for sensitivity analysis: Description of techniques. Reliab. Eng. Syst. Saf. **93**, 28–54 (2008)
88. Storlie, C.B., Swiler, L.P., Helton, J.C., Salaberry, C.J.: Implementation and evaluation of nonparametric regression procedures for sensitivity analysis of computationally demanding models. Reliab. Eng. Syst. Saf. **94**, 1735–1763 (2009)

89. Sudret, B.: Uncertainty propagation and sensitivity analysis in mechanical models - Contributions to structural reliability and stochastics spectral methods. Mémoire d'Habilitation à Diriger des Recherches de l'Université Blaise Pascal - Clermont II (2008)
90. Tarantola, S., Gatelli, D., Mara, T.: Random balance designs for the estimation of first order global sensitivity indices. Reliab. Eng. Syst. Saf. **91**, 717–727 (2006)
91. Tissot, J.-Y., Prieur, C.: A bias correction method for the estimation of sensitivity indices based on random balance designs. Reliab. Eng. Syst. Saf. **107**, 205–213 (2012)
92. Volkova, E., Iooss, B., Van Dorpe, F.: Global sensitivity analysis for a numerical model of radionuclide migration from the RRC "Kurchatov Institute" radwaste disposal site. Stoch. Env. Res. Risk A. **22**, 17–31 (2008)
93. Xu, C., Gertner, G.: Extending a global sensitivity analysis technique to models with correlated parameters. Comput. Stat. Data Anal. **51**, 5579–5590 (2007)

Chapter 6
Connections Among Optimization Models with Uncertainties, ABC and RBV

Saverio Giuliani and Carlo Meloni

6.1 Introduction

Two of the main problems from applications of decision support methods in real problems are:

1. data gathering, collection and organization is one of the most expensive phases for a decisional process, in terms of time and resources
2. a pure deterministic world is not a real world.

The answer to the first problem is to build a mathematical model which is based as much as possible on data usually collected from organizations: we will focus our attention on data coming from the Activity Based Costing (ABC) system, that is an accounting technique used by many companies, both from private and public sector. In such a way we avoid to formulate a mathematical model which requires a lot of parameters and variables whose estimation cost is not well defined.

The answer to the second problem consists in using optimization models under uncertainty. In particular, we can refer to a stochastic programming approach,

S. Giuliani
Dipartimento di Economia, Università degli Studi di Foggia, Largo Giovanni Paolo II, 1 - 71100 Foggia, Italy
e-mail: s.giuliani@unifg.it

C. Meloni (✉)
Dipartimento di Ingegneria Elettrica e dell'Informazione, Politecnico di Bari, Via E. Orabona, 4 - 70125 Bari, Italy

Istituto per le Applicazioni del Calcolo "Mauro Picone" - CNR, Via Giovanni Amendola 122/I - 70126 Bari, Italy
e-mail: meloni@poliba.it

G. Dellino, C. Meloni (eds.), *Uncertainty Management in Simulation-Optimization of Complex Systems*, Operations Research/Computer Science Interfaces Series 59,
DOI 10.1007/978-1-4899-7547-8_6

where we define a probability distribution for unknown parameters of the problem and we find an optimal solution among the scenarios generated according to such distribution.

A problem that, for example, we can face is the strategic planning of resources, e.g., personnel, raw materials, etc., for an organization when demand is uncertain. For the classification of resources we can refer to the Resource Based View (RBV) of the firm theory, that can be applied for the interpretation of the results as well.

After a review of mathematical modeling with uncertainties and, in particular, stochastic programming, of ABC and of RBV, we will conclude analyzing the connections among them.

6.2 Mathematical Modeling with Uncertainties

6.2.1 Data-Driven Models

Theories formulating a mathematical model are audacious in scope, in large part because scholars proposing them are not inhibited by the ordeal of implementing and validating data-driven models.

By contrast, modeling practitioners are much more cautious in selecting the scope of a strategic planning model. Practitioners and managers commissioning modeling studies can benefit by challenging themselves to devise quantitative descriptions that actualize abstract concepts about strategy and incorporating them in data-driven models. Conversely, strategy theorists can profit from 'reality checks' provided by models and by refinements and extensions to their theories that will undoubtedly result. Between a mathematical model and reality there is statistics which allow us to check if a model is failing or not.

Data-driven models should be based as much as possible on real data that can be found in a firm. We will develop the case of data coming from the ABC system, that is a management accounting system for decision support having a wide diffusion, for which companies spend a certain amount of their financial resources and time, in terms of personnel directly working in accounting offices and managers involved in the estimation process: the use of such source of data, not only in an analytic way but also as a planning instrument, should be a must in order of having a return on such investment.

Moreover, it's not unusual that many models do not care about the effort and cost in gathering information needed for a mathematical model: the result is that some models are so full of coefficients whose detail is so hard to gather that, after an ad hoc implementation, its application is inevitably condemned to death. Therefore, it's very important to base a model as much as possible on the flow of data and information that firms produce: this is the case of the ABC system that is not an ad hoc flow of information but a continuous one. In this way, a mathematical model which stands on such solid basis, will have a high probability to be applied, and so tested and improved, in a continuous way.

6.2.2 Aggregation Levels

When a modeler starts implementing a mathematical model, the first problem he probably encounters is the choice of the proper level of aggregation. We can distinguish between:

1. Data aggregation (which reflects into variable aggregation in the model)
2. Model aggregation.

Concerning the first type, nowadays despite of an easy access to transactional data assembled by enterprise resource planning (ERP) and other transactional data systems, in many instances (see [43]) more than 80 % of such data is not relevant to decision making. Therefore we need to face 'tons' of data where data aggregation, descriptive models and other procedures are needed to transform the remaining 20 %, or less, into intelligence contained in the decision database. The choice of the proper level of aggregation, when possible, has to be made taking also into account the purposes of analysis for the model which takes as an input such data: in this way products can become groups of products, suppliers groups of suppliers, resources groups of resources, and so on. The general problem is: 'How and how much does the aggregation level affect solutions?' Such a problem seems to be almost ignored in the literature. Studies concerning robustness measure variations for perturbations of data; a very different task is to consider the level of aggregation of data. One paper which analyze the effect of data aggregation in a simulation framework is [29], while for ABC problems we can refer to [12].

The model aggregation problem arises because in real complex managerial problems, especially in production and inventory planning, we may have a huge number of items. If we want to limit the 'explosion' of the model we need of a compromise between complexity and approximation: in fact, relatively small scale approximations of much larger problems can be requested. The question is now: 'When is an aggregate model a reasonably good representation of the corresponding larger problem?' For planning problems, the so called 'aggregate planning' has been introduced where, for instance, some answers in some circumstances can be found in [15, 16, 20, 53]. A unified optimization methodology for planning problems which combines mathematical decomposition methods with heuristics has been shown in [43]: a decomposition method breaks a large-scale monolithic mixed-integer programming model down into several smaller submodels (a linear programming master submodel and several lagrangean submodels) and then the method iteratively reassembles subplans from these submodels in seeking an optimal global plan, that is an optimal solution to the original monolithic model.

6.2.3 Sources of Uncertainty

When a deterministic model does not satisfy the needs of a mathematical modeler, he has necessarily to face the uncertainty which characterize reality: Albert Einstein stated that "as far as a mathematical model refers to the reality is not certain, as far as reality refers to a mathematical model it is uncertain".

If we are interested in facing the problem of uncertainty by a stochastic model we have to deep its sources. In general, we can identify four main situations where uncertainty arises:

1. predict a specific event in the future
2. estimate a distribution and its parameters
3. identify the structure of a model
4. something we did not consider.

In order to build up a stochastic model we can identify four main steps of approximations, that is a way, according to the above categories, to face such kinds of uncertainty:

(a) Data
(b) Mathematical (stochastic) modeling
(c) Uncertainty distribution
(d) Solution methods.

In Fig. 6.1 we report a detail of the last four categories, where as internal or external we mean with respect to a given decisor, e.g., a company. Moreover, if we don't embody in a mathematical model qualitative aspects, which are usually missing or hidden in a quantitative approach, we have an additional source of uncertainty: the vice-versa can be true as well. Anyway, a mathematical model is in itself a source of uncertainty because it will never be able to reproduce reality in a perfect way. In general, the sum of all types of uncertainty, comprehensive of some possible interrelations among them, will determine the global uncertainty.

A not trivial task is to determine how much every type of these kinds of uncertainty affects the global uncertainty or, in other words, what is the percentage of contribution for every category to the final uncertainty. What we can say is that the attention is usually devoted to the last three categories while the uncertainty coming from data is almost hidden: maybe this happens as it is more difficult to treat such issue in a general way, being strictly dependent on the context of application. It is obvious that the uncertainty coming from data cannot be considered always null or almost null: sometimes it can be even greater than the other components.

6.2.4 Scenario Planning

In the previous sections we have seen different sources of uncertainty: now let's restrict our scope to the prediction of future events. The natural problem which

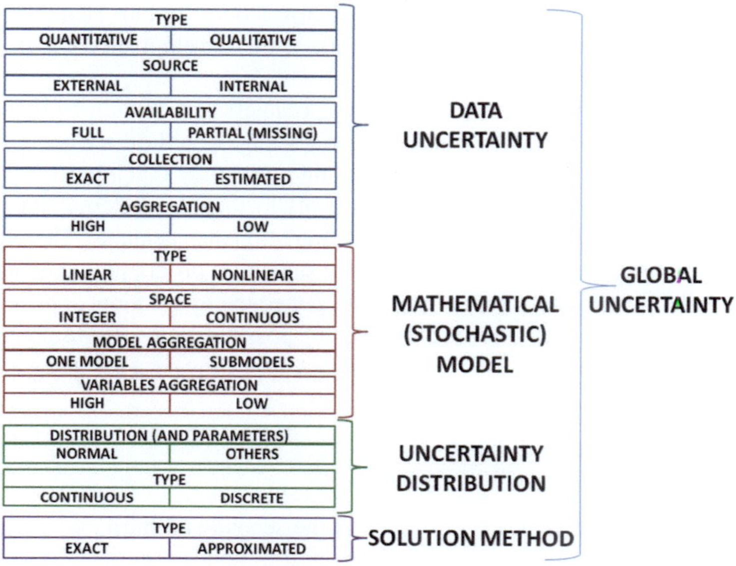

Fig. 6.1 Global uncertainty

arises in this case is: 'How to make predictions?'. The first answer to such question can be made choosing a probability distribution which represents in a good way the possible future behavior of the phenomenon object of study: usually we are aided by historical data or causal models or judgmental models which try to introduce subjective elements and hence qualitative aspects. In general we can identify (see [44]) the following *planning methods* to identify possible future scenarios:

1. *contingency planning*, which presents only one uncertainty, the base case, and an exception or contingency
2. *sensitivity analysis*, where we examine the effect of a change in one variable, keeping all other variables constant
3. *computer simulations*, based on a large number of possible outcomes a computer might generate.

A second, less quantitative and objective, answer to our initial question is possible, giving a wider space to decisor's intuition, experience, know how and ability to catch weak signals or, in one word, to subjective aspects based on human judgment. The 'ratio' of such approach is given from the fact that mathematical models are not able to adequately embody the just mentioned qualitative aspects and, in particular, they can fail or be less adequate than human judgment, when we operate in a highly complex environment where manifold (and difficult to capture and measure) elements interact among them: this is the field where *scenario planning* operates. On the opposite side, when relations among elements can be formalized with a sufficient degree of accuracy, the development of quantitative methods will be appropriate.

Scenario planning attempts to capture the richness and range of possibilities, stimulating decision makers to consider changes they would otherwise ignore. At the same time it organizes those possibilities into narratives that are easier to grasp and use than great volumes of data: it attempts to identify patterns and clusters among the millions of outcomes a computer simulation may generate. Therefore, we can say that scenario planning simplifies, in a stochastic programming context, the exponentially increasing number of scenarios generated by solution, approximation or sampling methods into a limited number of possible states. If we consider, in predicting future, three *classes of knowledge*:

1. things we know we know
2. things we know we don't know
3. things we don't know we don't know.

then scenario planning is devoted to analyze the second and third class, which are the main cause of possible bias and no failproof technique exist.

The *process for developing scenarios* in such approach can be subdivided into the following ten categories (see [44]):

1. Define the scope
2. Identify the major stakeholders
3. Identify basic trends
4. Identify key uncertainties
5. Construct initial scenario themes
6. Check for consistency and plausibility
7. Develop learning scenarios
8. Identify research needs
9. Develop quantitative methods
10. Evolve towards decision scenarios.

Such procedure should be repeated until we have not reached a good set of scenarios, in terms of relevance and consistency. Moreover, scenarios should describe generically different futures rather than variations on one theme, highlighting competing perspectives while focusing on interlinkages and the internal logic within each future.

Anyway, practical experiences show that scenarios proposed prior to modeling analysis can be far from exhaustive (see [43]) and the articulation of new scenarios can be due to unexpected results and relationships identified by optimization models exploring the space of strategic options. Therefore, we can conclude that interaction among scenario planning and optimization models, in particular stochastic programming, allows to achieve the best results.

6.2.5 Decision Making Under Uncertainty

Manifold real problems involve different aspects that can be known only with a certain degree of uncertainty; this means we need to embrace the paradigms of decision making under uncertainty. For instance, decision analysis, dynamic programming and stochastic control address similar problems to stochastic programming, and each one is effective in certain domains. Decision analysis is usually restricted to problems in which discrete choices are evaluated in view of sequential observations of discrete random variables: it allows the decision maker to use very general preference functions in comparing alternative courses of action, thus, both single and multiple objectives are incorporated in the decision analytic framework. Unfortunately, the need to enumerate all choices (decisions) as well as outcomes (of random variables) limits this approach to decision making problems in which only a few strategic alternatives are considered. These limitations are similar to methods based on dynamic programming, which also require finite action (decision) and state spaces: path dependence remains wedded to Markovian decision problems. Stochastic programming provides a general framework to model path dependence of the stochastic process within an optimization model and it permits uncountable many states and actions, together with constraints, time-lags, etc. Unlike dynamic programming, stochastic programming separates the model formulation activity from the solution algorithm: in this way it is not necessary for such models to all obey the same mathematical assumptions and this leads to a rich class of models for which a variety of algorithms can be developed. On the downside of the ledger, stochastic programming formulations can lead to very large scale problems, and methods based on approximation and decomposition become necessary. Anyway in order to allow calculations we heavily rely on convexity and this requires uncertain events to be exogenous: therefore a limitation is that actions taken cannot affect probability distributions (i.e., learning about demand by experimenting).

In order to 'jump' from a mathematical programming model to a *stochastic optimization* model, we can identify three different approaches:

1. Probabilistic
2. Fuzzy Sets
3. Interval Arithmetic.

In the first case we must define a probability distribution that model the uncertainty: stochastic programming deals to the such approach. In the second case, parameters are treated as fuzzy numbers and constraints are treated as fuzzy sets: some constraint violation is allowed and the degree of satisfaction of a constraint is introduced. In the interval arithmetic approach (not included among the stochastic optimization in [5, 39]) we put bounds on rounding errors in mathematical computation and thus developing numerical methods that yield very reliable results; where classical arithmetic defines operations on individual numbers, interval arithmetic defines a set of operations on intervals.

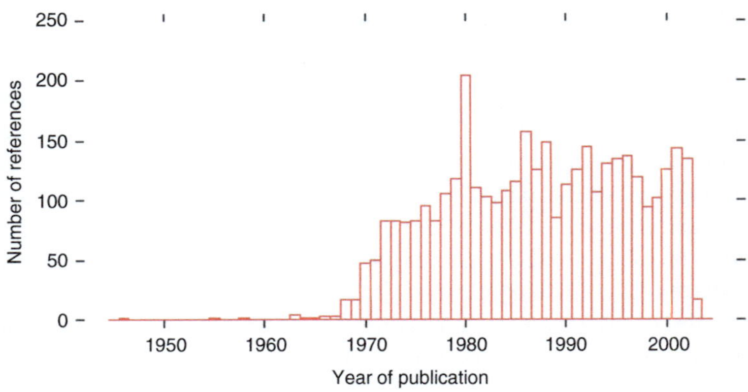

Fig. 6.2 Stochastic programming publication years

6.2.6 *Stochastic Programming Overview*

In order to have an idea of works concerning such field of research see Fig. 6.2 (source 'The Collection of Computer Science Bibliographies', available at http://www.stoprog.org) where the evolution of the articles along years is shown: it is clear the birth of stochastic programming, which dates back to the 1950s and early 1960s of the last century. A certain number of pioneers at that time contributed to the field, either by identifying stochastic linear programming problems in particular applications, or by formulating various model types and solution approaches for dealing adequately with linear programs containing random variables in their right-hand side, their technology matrix, and/or their gradient of the objective function; in particular three of the most pioneering works are given by [4, 6, 11]. In depth examination concerning the state of the art and relative applications can be found in [39], as well as in [5]; a comprehensive and periodically updated bibliography is available in [49]. At present, the most popular applications of stochastic programming seem to be in financial context (see [18, 50]). The list of further favorable application areas contains, for instance, planning and allocation of resources (including water), energy production and transmission, production planning and optimization of technological processes, logistics problems (including aircraft allocation and yield management) and telecommunications.

From a general point of view in stochastic programming we can introduce distinctions with respect to:

- Variables and relative probability

  1. Continuous
  2. Integer
  3. Singular (i.e., continuous but with an almost everywhere null derivative; it has only a theoretical interest)

- Functions
  1. Linear
  2. Nonlinear
- Constraints
  1. Deterministic
  2. Probabilistic (chance-constrained)
- Objective function
  1. Expected value (E-model)
  2. Probability with respect to a fixed threshold (P-model)
  3. Variance of some result (V-model)
  4. Quantile of a cumulative function
- Sequence of decisions
  1. Two-stage
  2. Multistage (Stochastic Dynamic Programming).

For everyone of the above classes we have different theoretical problems and solution methods developed in the literature: in the following sections we will treat only some of them, that are the most common approaches.

6.2.7 Stochastic Programming Problem Formulation

A stochastic programming problem can be defined in the following way:

$$F(x) = \min_{x \in D \subset \mathbb{R}^n} E(f(x, \xi)) \tag{6.1}$$

where D is a certain feasible set, $\xi \in \Omega$ is the elementary event in the probability space $(\Omega, \mathcal{F}, P_x)$ with P_x the measure defined by the probability (mass or density for discrete or continuous variables respectively) function $p(x, \cdot) : \mathbb{R}^n \times \Omega \longrightarrow \mathbb{R}_+$, and $f(x, \cdot) : \mathbb{R}^n \times \Omega \longrightarrow \mathbb{R}$, depending on the decision variable x in general and satisfying conditions of integrability and differentiability. For continuous variables (the discrete case will be analogous) we have:

$$F(x) = E(f(x, \xi)) = \int_{\mathbb{R}^n} f(x, y) \cdot p(x, y) dy \tag{6.2}$$

and the support of measure P_x is given by:

$$S(x) = \{y \mid p(x, y) > 0\}, \ x \in \mathbb{R}^n \tag{6.3}$$

The gradient of the objective function is expressed as:

$$\nabla_x F(x) = E(g(x, \xi)) \tag{6.4}$$

and is very useful for approximation and sampling solution techniques, being $g(x, \xi)$ obtained as a solution of a proper dual problem. We must notice that in (6.1) we consider the expectation E excluding the other approaches concerning the P-model, V-model and quantiles: this is why the E-model is the most popular and other approaches are usually treated in a separate way.

The most widespread model is the two-stage stochastic linear programming where we start in the first stage from a set of decisions (represented by the vector x) to be taken with a certain degree of uncertainty. Later, we have the information concerning the realization of a random vector ξ. Then, in the second stage, some corrective actions y are taken.

The two-stage stochastic linear programming problem with complete recourse can be formulated in the following way:

$$F(x) = \min_{x \in D_1 \subset \mathbb{R}^n_+} \left[c^T \cdot x + E(Q(x, \xi)) \right] \tag{6.5}$$

subject to the feasible set:

$$D_1 = \left\{ x \mid A \cdot x = b,\ x \in \mathbb{R}^n_+ \right\} \tag{6.6}$$

where:

$$Q(x, \xi) = \min_y \left\{ q^T \cdot y \mid W \cdot y + T \cdot x = h, y \in \mathbb{R}^m_+ \right\} \tag{6.7}$$

vectors b, q, h and full rank matrices A, W, T are of appropriate dimensionality. The feasible set D_1 is assumed to be nonempty and bounded. Vectors q, h and matrix T are random in general and consequently depending on an elementary event $\xi \in \Omega$ defined in the same way than in (6.1). Moreover we assume that the solution of the second stage problem (6.7) and the values of the function Q almost surely (a.s.) exist and are bounded. Notice that complete recourse is derived from the fact that W is fixed: it is possible to consider W random as well, but with a loss in many properties of the problem.

6.3 Activity Based Costing (ABC)

6.3.1 General Concepts

Companies, especially in a global market, have to face ever-increasing competition, which require, to be successful, a quick response to changing needs of demand, with high quality and low cost products or services. To make proper decisions, managers must have accurate and up to date costing information. Traditional costing systems based on volume-based allocation of overhead have lost relevance in a manufacturing environment that has seen a sharp increase in overhead and a subsequent decline in direct labor. In such situations the traditional costing systems tend to distort product costs and lead to poor strategic decision making. In order to deal with such deficiencies the costing method named Activity Based Costing (ABC) has been introduced: see the pioneering works by Robin Cooper, Robert Kaplan, and H. Thomas Johnson ([9, 10, 26, 27]).

Service companies are ideal candidates for ABC, even more than manufacturing ones, as Kaplan, Cooper and Young in [1] suggest: their justification for this statement is that most of the costs are indirect. For convenience, we will talk of products, but everything will be valid for services as well.

We can define ABC as a methodology of assigning the organization's resource costs through activities to the products and services provided to its customers, with the purposes of analyzing services, products and customer cost and profitability. It belongs to the broader area of management accounting for identifying, measuring, reporting and analyzing information about the economic events.

Main differences from traditional financial accounting are the following:

1. not historical but forward-looking
2. focused on the needs of management rather than for external reports
3. pragmatically computed instead of complying with accounting standards.

6.3.2 Methodology

The traditional model of Activity Based Costing is widely described in the literature: we can identify two main stages (see [9, 10]) for implementing an ABC model. In the first stage, costs are assigned to cost pools within an activity center, based on a cost driver. There is no equivalent step in a traditional costing approach. In the second stage, costs are allocated from the cost pools to a product based on the product's consumption of the activities. This stage is similar to a traditional costing approach except that the traditional approach uses solely volume related characteristics of the product without consideration for non-volume related characteristics. Some examples of cost drivers not related to volume include setup hours, number of setups, ordering hours, and number of orders. Allocating non-volume related costs using volume-based methods distorts the product costs.

In ABC model, overhead expense categories such as administration, rent, transportation, and insurance are identified. This cost data can be usually obtained from accounting. Such expense categories, referred to the traditional way in which a company divides overhead from general ledger, allow to identify resources: how to turn from expenses categories to resources can be a work of reclassification of expenses in order to have a meaningful classification for our scopes of analysis. In Fig. 6.3 we call this step 'stage zero' because it is not usually considered or

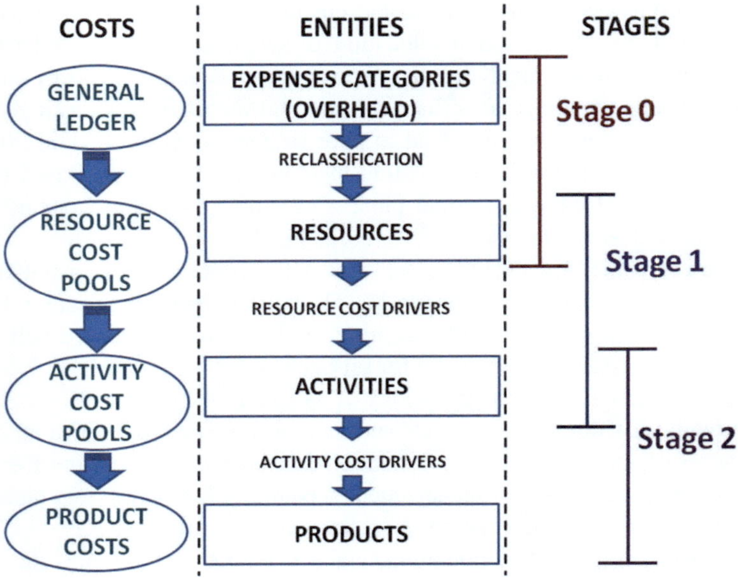

Fig. 6.3 ABC methodology

it remains hidden in the literature: but we think it should be underlined being extremely important for the subsequent analyses for which ABC exist. In this step it can be useful inheriting some concepts and ideas from the Resource Based View of the firm theory.

The next step is to determine the main activities that simplify the tracing of cost information. This can be accomplished by grouping actions into activities and activities (or cost pools) into activity centers using the ABC approach; a flowchart of the process or Integrated Definition IDEF0 modeling methods (see for instance [7]) are commonly used tools for identifying these main activities. Thus, in order to establish the needed activities, homogeneous processes must be grouped together: i.e., product driven activities and customer driven activities must be separated in different groups. Some examples of activities for a manufacturing company are: receiving a customer inquiry, customer quotes, production supervision and shipping products. Resources will be assigned to the previously defined activities via the (first stage) resource cost drivers.

In the following second stage, activity cost drivers are determined to allocate overhead to individual products. Figure 6.3 illustrates the hierarchical relationship among resources, activities, and products. This information will assist the company in validating that the total overhead calculated at the beginning of the process matches the total obtained when summing the overhead that is assigned to each individual product using ABC.

6.3.3 Information Gathering Procedures

Because the information needed for ABC is costly and firms are typically financially constrained, companies need to be very selective in the type of data and analysis that they use to determine overhead costs. Moreover, small businesses require specialized cost management approaches, in fact a 'small business is not a little big business' (see [37, 51]).

Gathering information is essential in order to achieve accuracy of final product costs. An important part of the required data is given by the proportions used in each stage of an ABC costing system. Each activity consumes a portion of an expense category. Similarly, each product consumes a portion of an activity.

In order of achieving a more general formulation, let's consider both direct and indirect (overhead) costs: a cost is defined as direct with respect to a cost object (in our case an activity or a product) if it is directly accountable to the cost object, otherwise it will be considered as indirect. If a cost is direct its cost driver is self evident (see [43]) and it will be the amount of resources, which will be directly accounted to the cost object: e.g., raw materials can be directly accounted to an activity or a product. In the latter case we do not need of ABC, passing through activities, to determine the portion of the cost accounted to the product. Anyway, if we are interested also in activities, we can consider direct and indirect costs together. Moreover, an overhead cost can be sometimes associated to a driver which can be directly accounted to the activities: e.g., number of hours devoted to the personnel to a given activity might be directly assigned to such activity by the information systems of the firm. While in ABC the activity is merely a step or an instrument, the cost of the activity can be an information of the same importance of the cost of products.

Now we can distinguish three types of information gathering procedures:

1. *Data collection.* They usually derive from the information systems of the firm and can be directly accounted to an activity or product. This is the case of direct costs or overhead costs with a cost driver directly accounted to the cost object.
2. *Unit coefficients estimation.* It is a costly procedure because timely and periodical interviews may be required. The results usually have to be analyzed using statistical methods. This is the case for instance of the cost driver 'time employed' for the resource 'personnel' where, after a subdivision in profiles, it is asked the (average) number of hours employed for every single activity. In the latter case we are referring to the so called time driven ABC [28] if estimates are made by managers rather than relying on time consuming and costly employee surveys.
3. *Percentages estimation.* When a data collection is not available and unit coefficients estimation is not financially justified we can proceed to a less accurate but less expensive estimation of the percentages of absorption of resources from activities and of activities from products. Educated guess can be made in order to obtain proportions: they can be done collaboratively by management, financial organizers, and operational employees associated with the costing center cf

interest. The level of accuracy obtained is based on a combination of the teams' diversity and their knowledge of the cost center of interest. A more scientific way to obtain the proportions for tracing costs is using a systematic technique such as Analytic Hierarchical Process (AHP) (see [38] for general methodology and [41] for an application to ABC): it is a suitable tool for pulling subjective individual opinion into more representative information. For example, let's assume that the allocation of a given gasoline resource is needed between three cost pools namely sales, delivery and maintenance: by questioning the departments that consume this resource and by asking them to evaluate what percentage of mileage they accumulate in a certain period of time, AHP can generate the percentage of this resource and allocate it to the appropriate cost pool.

The performance of different methods for handling uncertainty in ABC has been analyzed in [34]. In particular, they consider interval mathematics, Monte Carlo simulation with triangularly and normal distributed input parameters, and fuzzy sets theory. Based on a comparative cost/benefit analysis, Monte Carlo simulation and fuzzy sets theory are found to be superior to interval mathematics.

6.3.4 The ABC Matrices

Let us suppose of being in the first stage of the ABC process (see Fig. 6.3) and denote with $k = 1, \ldots, K$ the resources and with $j = 1, \ldots, J$ the activities.We can define a resources-activities matrix A_{kj} (see Fig. 6.4) that is a typical output/report from the ABC system (see also Expense-Activity-Dependence matrix in [37]), not necessarily limited to the overhead costs but eventually extended to all the resources of the firm. The k-th resource is a 'process' resource if all, or at least most of, the coefficients in the resources-activities matrix are positive; by contrast, the k-th resource is a 'facility' resource if only a limited number of coefficients in the matrix are non-zero (i.e., positive). In short, the distinction between facility and process resources and costs may be ambiguous and ultimately depends on human judgment.

Consider now the second stage of the ABC process (see Fig. 6.3) and denote with $j = 1, \ldots, J$ and $z = 1, \ldots, Z$ the activities and products (or services) respectively. In a similar way to the first stage, we can define the resources-activities matrix A_{jz} (see Fig. 6.4 where $A'_{j,z}$ is the transposed matrix) that is a typical output/report from the activity based costing system (see also Activity-Product-Dependence matrix in [37]). The j-th activity is a 'general' activity if all, or at least most of, the coefficients in the activities-products matrix are positive; by contrast, the j-th activity is a 'focused' activity if only a limited number of the coefficients in the matrix are non-zero (i.e., positive).

Note that both ABC matrices obtained assume that we have a unique resource or activity cost driver. Anyway, in real applications, to obtain a more precise imputation sometimes it is necessary to consider more than one driver. Multiple cost driver

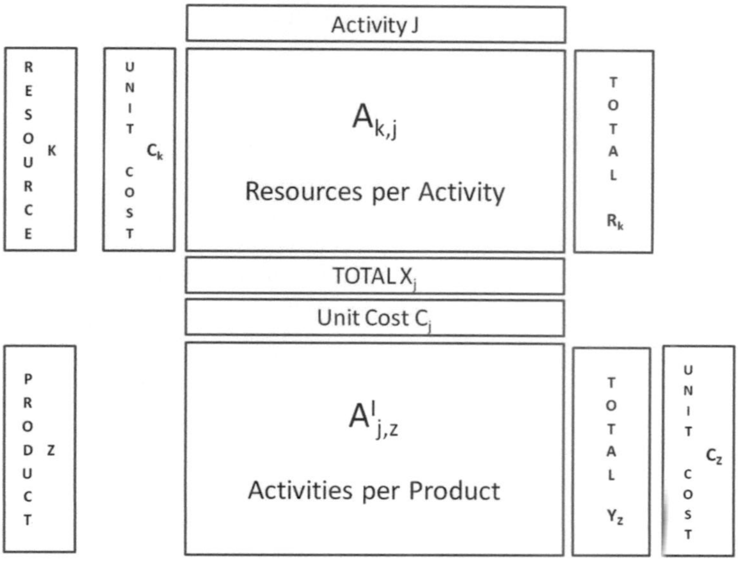

Fig. 6.4 ABC matrices

optimization has been analyzed in [2] while in [23] higher level cost drivers are introduced, that are a sort of heterogeneity drivers to improve the quality of ABC; the case of operational units with multiple cost drivers is considered in [47].

6.3.5 *Connections with Optimization Models*

ABC was not originally proposed in order to use it as a planning instrument (see [40]) but it can be used in such a way provided an acceptable precision level for estimated parameters; moreover the definition of resources from expenses (step zero in Fig. 6.3) should be made in a suitable way for subsequent analyses and measures chosen to be easily readable for decisors.

In the literature, connections among mathematical programming and ABC are analyzed in [42] and ABC implications for operations management in [21]. Some models which make use of ABC are present in the literature: in [46] a model for flexible manufacturing systems in a simulation framework, models for procurement in [13, 14] and for sourcing strategies in [13], a model for best product mix in [22] and for logistic process and tactical production planning in [8]. Note that all the models are developed in a deterministic context.

Equations which utilize matrices resources-activities allow to know the level of resources needed to make a given planned level of activities or to identify a set of possible level of activities given a planned level of resources. If we introduce an optimization model including such equations, which measure the absorption of resources, we must jointly consider budget constraints in order to take into account available financial resources. If we refer to a future period when some changes in the production process are planned, from the resource point of view, we can change in a proper way technical coefficients as well.

On the other hand equations which utilize matrices activities-products are the basis to know the level of activities needed to make a given planned level of products, or to identify a set of possible level of products given a planned level of activities. Such equations cover a fundamental role as they describe how activities are connected with products, that is the production model, from the products point of view: the equations as they are, without any change, are the basis for an optimization model which takes into account how activities are transformed into products.

6.4 The Resource Based View of the Firm (RBV)

6.4.1 Introduction

The Resource Based View of the firm (RBV) is an articulated theory whose origin dates to the seminal paper by Wernerfelt [52] although earlier publications anticipated some of the later work. The importance of resources to a company's strategic and tactical planning has been emphasized: our particular interest in RBV is due to its explicit treatment of the role of resources in strategy formation. RBV implicitly provides important insights about the construction and use of optimization models for management. It examines why companies with unique resources attain competitive advantage over other firms in the same market. We want to show in our research work that many concepts from the RBV can be captured and revealed by optimization models.

6.4.2 Main Concepts

According to RBV, a firm's sustainable competitive advantage depends mainly on its resources and how they are used. In particular, the theory assumes that superior firms possess *heterogeneous resources* that differentiate it from other firms and allow it to earn rents: i.e., the average and even marginal costs of their products are below, probably significantly below the market prices. The rents may be converted to sustainable profits if forces exist which limit competition for critical resources, once the market has recognized their value.

Two factors limiting competition are *imperfect imitability* and *imperfect substitutability* of heterogeneous resources. Such factors exist when there are barriers due to patents, contracts, learning effects, or market preferences that make imitation and substitution by other firms difficult or impossible.

Moreover, critical resources of the superior firm will be *perfectly immobile*, which means they are idiosyncratic and have no use in other firms, or *imperfectly mobile*, which means they can be traded but have higher value within the firm. Finally, the theory states that a firm can establish heterogeneous new resources only if there are limits to competition prior to efforts on the part of the firm to create them. Otherwise, the rents that the superior firm can realize will be dissipated by excessive costs of initial competition.

In reviewing connections between RBV and research on strategy, in [33] four types of rents belonging to the superior firm have been introduced. Ownership of scarce resources such as valuable land, production facilities near markets, or patents lead to *Ricardian rents*. As the result of collusion or government protection, the firm may achieve *monopoly rents*. Firms that undertake risky and entrepreneurial ventures in an environment of significant uncertainty or complexity may realize *Schumpeterian*, or *entrepreneurial rents*. Firms with idiosyncratic resources that are scarce, but less scarce and less sustainable than Ricardian resources, may receive *quasi-rents*.

In [17] the issue of sustainability has been addressed, being linked to characteristics of the stock asset (heterogeneous resource) accumulation process. They identify six phenomena affecting the efficacy of such processes.

Inefficiencies associated with attempting to create and exploit heterogeneous resources too quickly are called *time compression diseconomies*. The phenomena of 'success breeding success' in competitive endeavors leads to *asset mass efficiencies* and *learning effects*; they are forms of economies of scale and represent barriers to entry for late entrants in a market. When creation of a valuable asset does not necessarily lead to competitive advantage because complementary assets are absent, the firm has failed to recognize the *interconnectedness of stock assets*. A loss of competitive advantage through deterioration of heterogeneous resources is called *asset erosion*. Finally, *causal ambiguity* refers to the uncertainties and discontinuities associated with a successful effort in creating a heterogeneous resource. If the causes of success are difficult to identify, the firm may find obstacles in sustaining the ensuing advantage. Conversely, it may be difficult for competitors to replicate the resource.

The concept of a firm's *core competencies* is an important idea linked to RBV (see [36]). Core competencies refer to those heterogeneous resources that provide the superior firm with sustainable competitive advantage. Often, senior managers in a firm do not clearly understand the precise nature of its core competencies, how they should be protected, and how new ones should be created.

6.4.3 Taxonomy of Resources

Several categories are suggested in [3, 33], while in [42] are summarized in the following way:

1. physical resources (e.g., plants, distribution centers, inventories)
2. human resources (e.g., machine operators, production managers, scientists)
3. financial resources (e.g., cash flow, debt capacity, equity availability)
4. information technology resources (e.g., inventory management system, communication network, supply chain modeling system)
5. marketing resources (e.g., market share, brand recognition, goodwill)
6. organizational resources (e.g., training systems, corporate culture, supplier relationships)
7. legal resources (e.g., patents, copyrights, contracts).

Except for legal resources, these categories underlie much of the RBV literature: the latter has been suggested because the existence of patents or contracts protecting the firm's valuable resources can have a large impact on its competitive position, especially in an era of rapid technological change.

Another distinction concerns its measurability:

1. tangible resources (e.g., plants, machine operators, cash flow)
2. intangible resources (e.g., scientists or corporate culture).

A challenge for the modeling practitioner is to devise descriptive approaches for measuring the impact of intangible resources on the firm's strategy.

6.4.4 Connections with Strategic Planning and ABC

When attempting to understand sustainability due to heterogeneous resources, management will be interested in the impact of strategic decisions on the duration of a competitive advantage as well as its existence. In all likelihood, the duration will be dependent on the scenario being analyzed. If an optimization model is being used to evaluate such scenarios, the analyst must devise schemes for extracting meaningful insights from the results of multiple scenario runs. The dependence of sustainability on scenarios also suggest the use of stochastic programming models to identify strategies for hedging against uncertainties, such as market developments that might erode the firm's advantage.

Moreover one of the objectives of an optimization model for strategic planning is to assist management in identifying, measuring and tracking core competencies. Quantitative methods for identifying and measuring core competencies, based in part on ABC and stochastic programming models, can be pursued. The critical step, as described in [42, 43], is the use of ABC in developing forecasts of how costs will vary as functions of the cost drivers. In developing such functions, we distinguish between:

1. accounting resources
2. sustaining resources.

Concerning the first category, the cost driver is merely an accounting device and not a resource that will constrain the strategy while, in the second category, the cost driver is a resource that may be scarce and therefore may constrain an optimal strategy. We refer to the former functions as *cost/accounting functions*, and to the latter as *cost/resource functions*. For example, in a manufacturing company energy with total machine hours as the cost driver and packing supervision with packing setup hours as the cost driver might be accounting resources. This is because energy and packing supervision are commodities that may be acquired in any quantity at a homogeneous cost. By contrast, casting depreciation with machine hours as the cost driver and machining supervision with machining setup hours as the cost driver might be sustaining resources. This is because casting machine hours and machining supervision are potentially scarce resources that the company may be forced to allocate to production.

6.4.5 Connections with Optimization Models

Qualitative theories of strategy formation and analysis, such as the RBV, are important sources of ideas for elements to be incorporated in the formulation of an optimization model for strategic planning. They also provide a useful vocabulary for interpreting solutions about competitive strategies suggested by models. In other words, we can say that contribution from RBV to mathematical modeling is both from input and output of the model.

Connections among RBV and optimization models are both explicit and implicit. Optimization models accept explicit descriptions of many of the types of resources listed in the taxonomy and determine optimal levels for them in a strategic or tactical plan. Such descriptions include cost relationships describing investment, disposal, and fixed and variable costs as a function of the quantity of the resource made available, discarded, and/or consumed. The models also incorporate consumption rates for these resources as they are utilized by transformation and handling activities in manufacturing and distribution facilities.

Clearly, physical resources can be directly represented in a optimization model. Human resources as they relate to tangible activities, such as supervising a packaging line, maintaining machines, or dispatching, can also be directly represented. By their nature, financial resources readily admit objective, quantitative descriptions and can be explicitly incorporated in an optimization model. In fact, optimization models have long been proposed for corporate financial planning.

Understanding and evaluating the role of information technology (IT) resources in corporate strategy formation has proven difficult and ambiguous: some analyses, however, suggest that IT resources are necessary but not sufficient elements of a firm's competitive advantage (see [35]). IT resources are different than other types of resources because they serve only to manage other resources and have no intrinsic value per se. Investments in IT for improving manufacturing or distribution processes may be planning phenomena that are little different from investments in plants or production machines and should be therefore explicitly modeled.

Marketing resources are both tangible and intangible. Strategic planning model should involve demand management as well. Models for acquiring and allocating marketing resources should also reflect existing or potential conditions of Ricardian, monopoly, or entrepreneurial rents.

Organizational and legal resources are intangible and therefore difficult to represent in an optimization model. Modeling practitioners may find it possible and worthwhile to indirectly portray them in the structure of a model. For example, it may be important to represent suppliers in such a way that the model reflects their size and the relationship with the company. A large impersonal supplier may be represented by a simple cost-versus-volume curve. By contrast, a small but important supplier who is capable of making several key parts may be represented in a way that allows the model to determine the specific parts and volumes that the supplier will provide.

In general, each resource that the firm must acquire or divest, falls into one of the three following classes:

1. *heterogeneous resource*: critical to the firm's competitive advantage
2. *homogeneous resource*: its availability can be increased or decreased at a cost that is at or near the market cost
3. *stranded resource*: its value to the company is negative or well below market value.

Because modelers probably do not know the category in which each resource lies, they must treat them as equals and try to deduce their category from the optimal solution of the model.

Model optimization provides insights indicating that certain tangible resources may be heterogeneous and should be expanded, whereas other resources may be stranded and should be reduced. Homogeneous resources can be readily adjusted up or down to enhance profitability, while stranded resources are candidates for divestment as long as divestment costs are not too high. Consider a net revenue maximizing model for a manufacturing firm: a high shadow price on a resource at its maximal capacity in an optimal solution indicates that maximal net revenues could be significantly increased if more of that resource was available. Such a resource may be heterogeneous. Remember that the shadow price measures the marginal value of another unit of capacity: in a stochastic model we have to consider its value among all scenarios and so its expectation taking into account variability (e.g., standard deviation) as well.

Anyway we must be careful in drawing conclusions from shadow prices, and its expectation in stochastic models, because they measure only marginal values, which might decrease rapidly as more resources are made available. In a deterministic context we can re-optimize the model parametrically for capacities above current capacity, in other words we need to evaluate the sustainability of the resource as heterogeneous before proceeding with an investment. The extended model should recognize the danger of time compression diseconomies in trying to too quickly

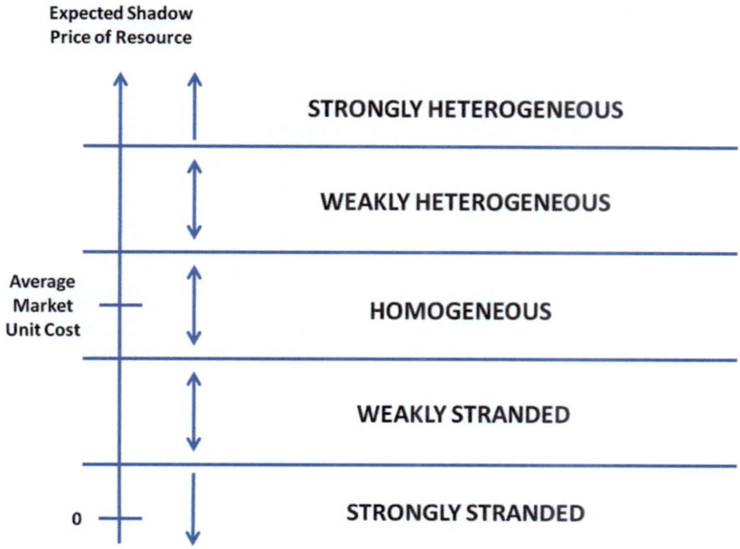

Fig. 6.5 Resources classification for stochastic models

exploit apparent heterogeneous resources. For example, is there sufficient time for human learning about using the additional machinery capacity to take place? The extended model should also be optimized under a variety of demand scenarios to see if increased net revenue will be sustained under a reasonable selection of scenarios: in a stochastic approach we can be able to consider all scenarios generated from the probability distribution for demand.

Extending to the stochastic case the categories proposed in [42], we can introduce an homogeneity scale according to the expected shadow price and an average market unit cost as presented in Fig. 6.5 where also the analysis of variability, for instance using a box plot chart, can suggest which classification of resource is more suitable. In every case the thresholds which differentiate such categories are not objective but fixed by decisors.

If the resource is unique to the firm and no meaningful market average unit cost exists, then we have only two ranges: heterogeneous if the shadow price is positive and stranded if the price is non-positive. Moreover, a cost/accounting function corresponds only to a homogeneous resource for which perfect markets allow expansion or contraction, virtually without limit, at approximately the market average unit cost of the resource.

Taking a look to the literature, in order to model competitiveness through quantitative analysis, in [32] it is considered the problem of how combining the degree and scope of determinant factors of competitive advantages and competitive strategic goals to maximize a firm's competitiveness. Moreover a model to explain the formation of strategic alliances and provide optimal resource allocation has been proposed in [24], while for best alliance partners and allocating optimal alliance resources we can refer to [25].

6.5 Connections Among Stochastic Programming, ABC and RBV

If we consider separately stochastic programming, ABC and RBV, they show a quite high number of papers devoted to them: in Fig. 6.6 a comparison among the number of published papers which have one of the three different topic has been reported, along the period from 1990 to 2008 (source: elaboration from ISI Web of Knowledge). It is easy to see that the number of papers devoted to stochastic programming is much higher than those devoted to RBV, which are in turn higher than those devoted to ABC: such ranking reflects their age as a significant number of papers devoted to stochastic programming can be found even before 1970 (see Fig. 6.2), while the birth of RBV and ABC can be fixed respectively to 1984 and 1987. Moreover, while the number of papers concerning ABC is quite stable with an increase in 2008, the trend is always increasing for stochastic programming and RBV.

But what happens if we consider papers facing the connections among them? Before answering to such a question let's consider the most common deterministic case, i.e., mathematical programming (MP): from Fig. 6.7 it is easy to see that their amount dramatically decreases, in a way that we can count them only using

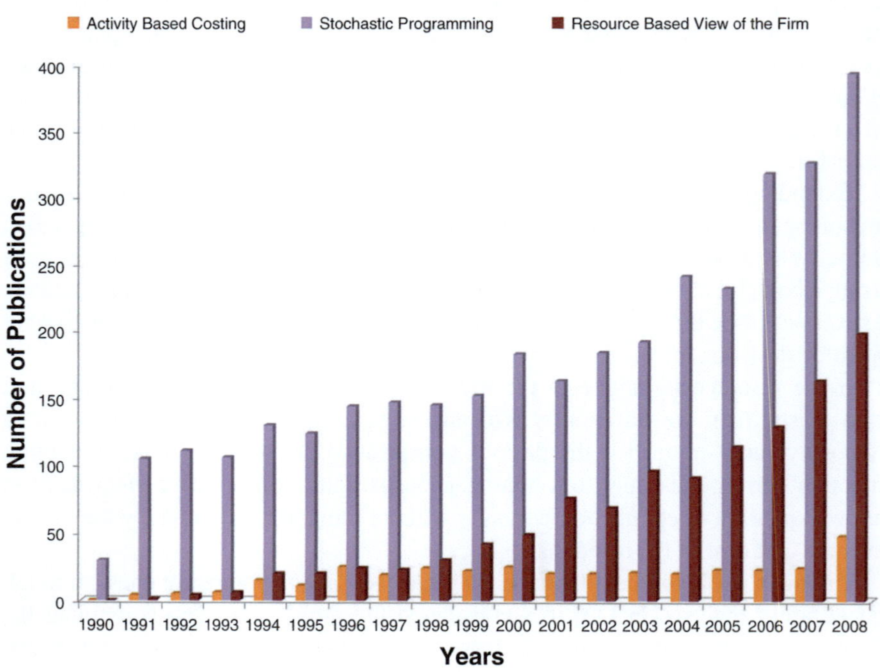

Fig. 6.6 Papers on stochastic programming, ABC and RBV

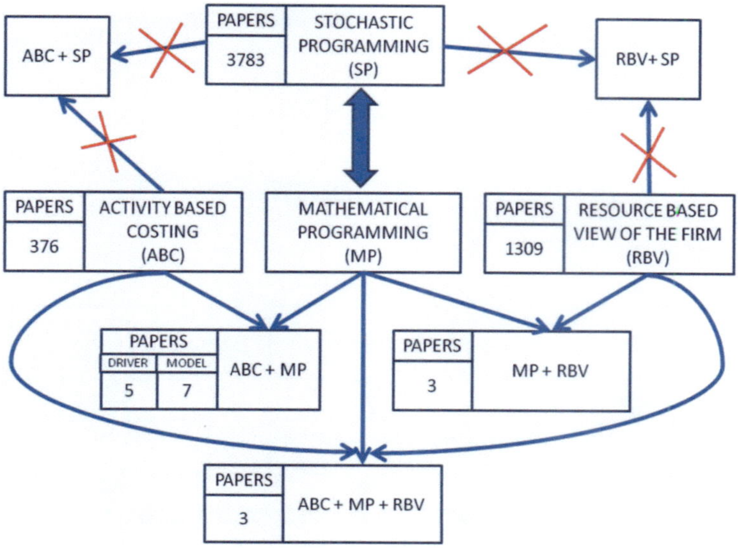

Fig. 6.7 Papers on connections among SP, ABC and RBV

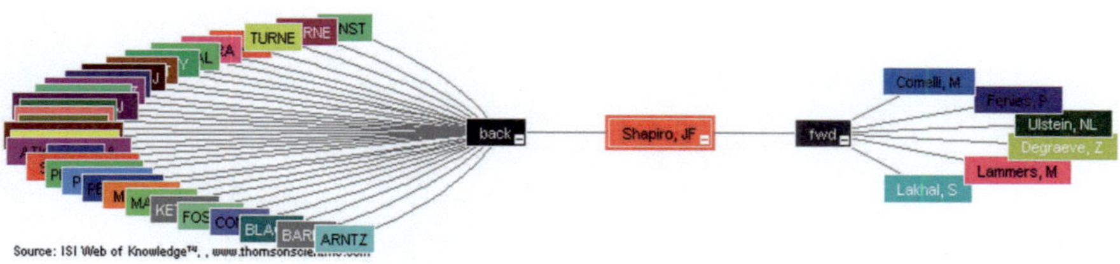

Fig. 6.8 Citation map: Shapiro J.F.

the fingers of one hand. Papers considering ABC and MP have been treated in Sect. 6.3.5, while the ones analyzing RBV and MP are discussed in Sect. 6.4.5.

Concerning the three papers which analyze simultaneously ABC, MP and RBV, the first pioneering work is by Shapiro [42]. In Fig. 6.8 we report (source: ISI Web of Knowledge) the citation map which shows, on the left, the references from the article (back) and, on the right, the articles which reference the paper object of analysis (forward).

The six articles which reference [42] are all devoted to a deterministic approach: in turn they are quoted from 0 to 4 times with the exception of the main subsequent work [31], quoted 21 times and which continues such approach, extended to networking decisions but always in a deterministic context. The citation map for [31] is reported in Fig. 6.9.

Concerning the subsequent 21 papers there is not anyone who is embracing a stochastic formulation. Coming back to the six articles which quote [42], the remaining ones are [8, 14], just described in Sect. 6.3.5 as they don't consider the

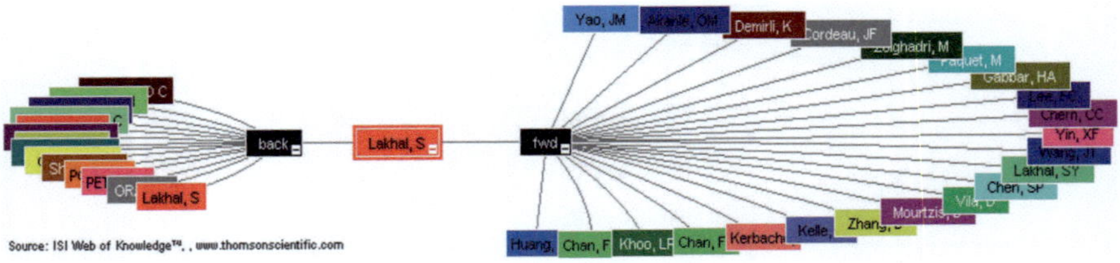

Fig. 6.9 Citation map: Lakhal S.

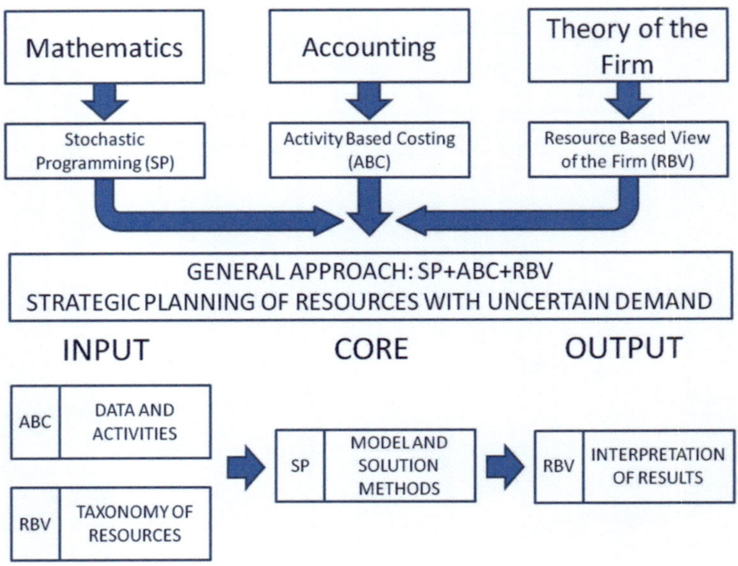

Fig. 6.10 General approach

connections with RBV, while papers [19, 48] are devoted respectively to applications in hospitals and manufacturing companies, and paper [30] extends the approach to a sourcing framework: all of them are developed in a deterministic context. The same can be stated for [45], the third article treating mathematical (linear) programming, ABC and RBV, whose approach shows many points in common with [42], that anyway is not mentioned.

But what about the connections among stochastic programming, ABC and RBV? As we can see from the top of Fig. 6.7 and from the just made analysis of the literature, there is no paper which extend the approach introduced in [42] to the stochastic context: the last paper suggests such extension and the same suggestion can be found in [14]. Therefore, future perspectives may concern an extension to a stochastic context, for instance, defining first and second stage variables and adding constraints on the uncertain demand.

In Fig. 6.10 a general approach is showed, where an attempt to go over the traditional walls which divide stochastic programming, ABC and RBV is made building up a stochastic programming model which inherits as input a taxonomy of resources from RBV and gathers data from the ABC system of the company: the output obtained in this way can be interpreted according to the RBV concepts.

The usefulness of the stochastic programming approach can be showed obtaining a positive value of the stochastic solution, i.e., the gain from using a stochastic approach with respect to a deterministic one (see [5]).

6.6 Conclusions

We have seen that it is possible to formulate stochastic programming models which make use of data coming from the ABC system and a taxonomy of resources from the RBV theory: for instance, the models can be applied to face situations where the strategic planning of resources is required when the demand of services is uncertain. The interpretation of the results can be made according to the RBV, which provides a framework for the analysis of resources according to their strategic value, that is extremely important in order to identify the competitiveness of an organization.

One of the main peculiarities of such kind of models is that they are based on data coming from the ABC system, that is an accounting technique quite widespread among both manufacturing and service companies: therefore data availability, accuracy and updating should be ensured to guarantee a possible implementation of the models, without an extensive effort in estimating difficult and expensive ad-hoc parameters and variables.

In the end, the connections among stochastic programming, ABC and RBV, show a multiplicative positive effect in order to use the potential of mathematical modeling: further research can amplify such potential. In general, future directions can exploit different type of models, e.g., having as deterministic variables suppliers, markets, etc. or having nonlinear functions and continuous distributions. Moreover, the introduction of multiple stochastic variables, beyond demand, can be useful for describing parameters such as prices, revenues or technical coefficients, in particular those estimated from the Activity Based Costing system.

References

1. Atkinson, A.A., Kaplan, R.S., Young, S.M.: Management Accounting, 4th edn. Prentice-Hall, Englewood Cliffs, NJ (2004)
2. Babad, Y.M., Balachandran, B.V.: Cost driver optimization in activity-based costing. Account. Rev. **68**(3), 563–575 (1993)
3. Barney, J.: Firm resources and sustained competitive advantage. J. Manag. **17**, 99–120 (1991)
4. Beale, E.: On minimizing a convex function subject to linear inequalities. J. R. Stat. Soc. B **17**, 173–184 (1955)

5. Birge, J.R., Louveaux, F.V.: Introduction to Stochastic Programming. Springer, New York (1997)
6. Charnes, A., Cooper, W.W.: Chance-constrained programming. Manag. Sci. **5**, 73–79 (1959)
7. Colquhoun, G.J., Baines, R.W., Crossley, R.: A state of the art review of IDEF0. Int. J. Comput. Integr. Manuf. **6**(4), 252–264 (1993)
8. Comelli, M., Féniès, P., Tchernev, N.: A combined financial and physical flows evaluation for logistic process and tactical production planning: application in a company supply chain. Int. J. Prod. Econ. **112**, 77–95 (2008)
9. Cooper, R.: The two-stage procedure in cost accounting - Part 1. J. Cost Manage. **1**(2), 43–51 (1987)
10. Cooper, R.: The two-stage procedure in cost accounting - Part 2. J. Cost Manage. **1**(3), 39–45 (1987)
11. Dantzig, G.B.: Linear programming under uncertainty. Manage. Sci. **1**, 197–206 (1955)
12. Datar, S., Gupta, M.: Aggregation, specification and measurement errors in product costing. Account. Rev. **69**, 567–591 (1994)
13. Degraeve, Z., Roodhooft, F.: A mathematical programming approach for procurement using activity based costing. J. Bus. Financ. Account. **27**(1–2), 69–98 (2000)
14. Degraeve, Z., Roodhooft, F., Van Doveren, B.: The use of total cost of ownership for strategic procurement: a company-wide management information system. J. Oper. Res. Soc. **56**, 51–59 (2005)
15. Dellino, G., Kleijnen, J.P.C., Meloni, C.: Robust optimization in simulation: Taguchi and response surface methodology. Int. J. Prod. Econ. **125**(1), 52–59 (2010)
16. Dellino, G., Kleijnen, J.P.C., Meloni, C.: Robust optimization in simulation: Taguchi and Krige combined. INFORMS J. Comput. **24**, 471–484 (2012)
17. Dierickx, I., Cool, K.: Asset stock accumulation and sustainability of competitive advantage. Manage. Sci. **35**, 1504–1511 (1989)
18. Dupačová, J.: Applications of stochastic programming: Achievements and questions. Eur. J. Oper. Res. **140**, 281–290 (2002)
19. Fenies, P., Gourgand, M., Rodier, S.: Interoperable and multi-flow software environment: application to health care supply chain. Bus. Process Manage. Workshops **4103**, 311–322 (2006)
20. Graves, S.C.: Using Lagrangean techniques to solve hierarchical production planning problems. Manage. Sci. **28**(3), 260–275 (1982)
21. Gupta, M., Galloway, K.: Activity-based costing/management and its implications for operations management. Technovation **23**, 131–138 (2003)
22. Gurses, A.P.: An activity-based costing and theory of constraints model for product - mix decisions. Ph.D. Thesis (1999)
23. Homburg, C.: Improving activity-based costing heuristics by higher-level cost drivers. Eur. J. Oper. Res. **157**, 332–343 (2004)
24. Huang, J.J., Tzeng, G.H., Ong, C.S.: Motivation and resource-allocation for strategic alliances through the de novo perspective. Math. Comput. Model. **41**, 711–721 (2005)
25. Huang, J.J., Tzeng, G.H., Ong, C.S.: Choosing best alliance partners and allocating optimal alliance resources using the fuzzy multi-objective dummy programming model. J. Oper. Res. Soc. **57**(10), 1216–1223 (2006)
26. Johnson, H.T.: The decline of cost management: a reinterpretation of 20th-century cost accounting history. J. Cost Manage. **1**(1), 5–12 (1987)
27. Johnson, H.T., Kaplan, R.S.: Relevance Lost: The Rise and Fall of Management Accounting. Harvard Business School Press, Boston (1987)
28. Kaplan, R.S., Anderson, S.R.: Time-driven activity-based costing. Harv. Bus. Rev. **82**, 131–138 (2004)
29. Kersebaum, K.C., Wenkel, K.O.: Modelling water and nitrogen dynamics at three different spatial scales – influence of different data aggregation levels on simulation results. Nutr. Cycl. Agroecosyst. **50**, 313–319 (1998)

30. Lammers, M.: Make, buy or share - combining resource based view, transaction cost economics and production economies to a sourcing framework. Wirtschaftsinformatik **46**(3), 204–212 (2004)
31. Lakhal, S., Martel, A., Kettani, O., Oral, M.: On the optimization of supply chain networking decisions. Eur. J. Oper. Res. **129**, 259–270 (2001)
32. Li, Y., Deng, S.: A methodology for competitive advantage analysis and strategy formulation: an example in a transitional economy. Eur. J. Oper. Res. **118**, 259–270 (1999)
33. Mahoney, J.T., Pandian, J.R.: The resource-based view within the conversation of strategic management. Strateg. Manag. J. **13**, 363–380 (1992)
34. Needy, K.L., Nachtmann, H.: Methods for handling uncertainty in activity based costing systems. Eng. Econ. **48**(3), 259–282 (2003)
35. Powell, T.C., Dent-Metcallef, A.: Information technology as competitive advantage: The role of human, business and technology resources. Strateg. Manag. J. **18**, 375–405 (1997)
36. Prahalad, C.K., Hamel, G.: The core competence of the corporation. Harv. Bus. Rev. **68**, 79–91 (1990)
37. Roztocki, N., Porter, J.D., Thomas, R.M., Needy, K.L.: A procedure for smooth implementation of activity based costing in small companies. Eng. Manage. J. **16**(4), 19–27 (2004)
38. Saaty, T.L.: Decision Making for Leaders. Lifetime Learning Publications, London (1982)
39. Sahinidis, N.V.: Optimization under uncertainty: state-of-the-art and opportunities. Comput. Chem. Eng. **28**, 971–983 (2004)
40. Schneeweiss, C.: On the applicability of activity based costing as a planning instrument. Int. J. Prod. Econ. **54**, 277–284 (1998)
41. Schniederjans, M.J., Garvin, T.: Using the analytic hierarchy process and multi-objective programming for the selection of cost drivers in activity-based costing. Eur. J. Oper. Res. **100**, 72–80 (1997)
42. Shapiro, J.F.: On the connections among activity-based costing, mathematical programming models for analyzing strategic decisions, and the resource-based view of the firm. Eur. J. Oper. Res. **118**, 295–314 (1999)
43. Shapiro, J.F.: Modeling the Supply Chain, 2nd edn. Duxbury, Pacific Grove (2007)
44. Schoemaker, P.J.H.: Scenario planning: a tool for strategic thinking. Sloan Manage. Rev. **36**(2), 25–40 (1995)
45. Singer, M., Donoso, P.: Strategic decision-making at a steel manufacturer assisted by linear programming. J. Bus. Res. **59**, 387–390 (2006)
46. Takakuwa, S.: The use of simulation in activity-based costing for flexible manufacturing systems. Proceedings of the 1997 Winter Simulation Conference (1997)
47. Troutt, M.D., Gribbin, D.W., Shanker, M., Zhang, A.: Cost efficiency benchmarking for operational units with multiple cost drivers. Decis. Sci. **31**(4), 813–832 (2000)
48. Ulstein, N.L., Christiansen, M., Gronhaug, R., Magnussen, N., Solomon, M.M.: Elkem uses optimization in redesigning its supply chain. Interfaces **36**(4), 314–325 (2006)
49. Van der Vlerk, M.H.: Stochastic programming bibliography. World Wide Web. http://www.mally.eco.rug.nl/spbib.html (1996/2007)
50. Wallace, S.W., Ziemba, W.T. (eds.): Applications of Stochastic Programming. Series in Optimization. MPS SIAM. SIAM, Philadelphia (2005)
51. Welsh, J.A., White, J.F.: A small business is not a little big business. Harv. Bus. Rev. **59**, 18–32 (1981)
52. Wernerfelt, B.: A resource based view of the firm. Strateg. Manage. J. **5**, 171–180 (1984)
53. Zipkin, P.: Exact and approximate cost functions for product aggregates. Manage. Sci. **28**(9), 1002–1012 (1982)

Chapter 7
Addressing Uncertainty in Complex Systems. The Case of Bio-Based Products Derived from Urban Bio-Waste Valorisation

Piergiuseppe Morone and Valentina Elena Tartiu

7.1 Introduction

With global climate change challenges and its various effects on ecosystems and on resource depletion, over the past decade the waste problem has been receiving increased attention. In particular, there is a general consensus that a holistic approach to waste management has positive consequences for GHG (Green House Gasses) emissions, as the prevention and recovery of waste (i.e. as secondary materials or energy) helps preventing emissions in all other sectors of the economy—agriculture, mining, transport, and manufacturing ([40]: 4).

In addition, the increasing costs of fossil-based raw materials and the need for more efficient and environmentally friendly production patterns (in line with the goals of sustainable development) have led to a search for alternatives, namely finding possible ways to obtain chemicals, fuels and solvents from other sources, such as biomass and bio-waste streams.

A growing body of literature tackles the role of biomasses in achieving sustainability goals. As a matter of fact, there is a plethora of international documents addressing the issue from different perspectives (e.g. [4, 18, 30]). In this study, we concentrate on bio-waste streams and its role in the shift towards a bio-based

P. Morone (✉)
DiGEF—Department of Law, Philosophy and Economics, Sapienza—University of Rome, Piazzale Aldo Moro 5, 00185 Rome, Italy
e-mail: piergiuseppe.morone@uniroma1.it

V.E. Tartiu
STAR∗AgroEnergy Group, University of Foggia, Via Gramsci 89/91, 71122 Foggia, Italy
e-mail: valentinatartiu@gmail.com

G. Dellino, C. Meloni (eds.), *Uncertainty Management in Simulation-Optimization of Complex Systems*, Operations Research/Computer Science Interfaces Series 59,
DOI 10.1007/978-1-4899-7547-8_7

economy—i.e. an economy which makes the most out of biomasses in terms of energy and production of other by-products. As we believe, this very area of enquiry is still under-investigated[1] and its applications are under-appreciated due to multiple uncertainties characterizing this sector—few examples of key sources of uncertainties are: heterogeneity of drivers of change; technology challenges in scaling-up; capital generation; weak market transparency; need to establish new and highly complex value chains; lack of information on bio-based production (BBP) among consumers and downstream producers; integration of new BBP into existing value chains; high price competition with traditional products; sustainability factors.

In order to outline a clear framework-of-action for the various stakeholders involved in bio-based production (investors, policy makers, owners of waste treatment plants, representatives of different industries, etc.), a better understanding of the above-mentioned sources of uncertainties and of their effects on the emerging BBP market, as well as of the hazards (and opportunities) they create, is needed.

Along these lines of reasoning, our research aims at addressing this very issue, mapping all sources of uncertainty associated with the urban bio-waste derived BBP system. This exercise is divided into three steps: first, we provide a theoretical discussion, reviewing the concept of uncertainty as it evolved over the years moving from traditional distinction between risk and uncertainty associated with neoclassical models to the most recent literature of uncertainty and complex-system models (Sect. 7.2); subsequently, we introduce the multi-dimensional framework within which our case study is developed (Sect. 7.3). Finally, we present the case study on BBP and assess the many sources of uncertainty associated with it (Sect. 7.4). Conclusions and further developments are presented in the last section (Sect. 7.5).

7.2 On Uncertainty and Risk in Complex Systems

Before exploring the impact of uncertainty on sustainability transitions, we shall first provide a general definition of this concept as it emerged in the economic literature. Moving from traditional definitions of risk and uncertainty, we will eventually consider how these concepts evolved to match the growing complexity of modern societies.

[1]The existing literature includes mainly institutional reports (e.g. [1, 9, 10, 16]; etc.) and to a lesser extent scientific papers (e.g. [20, 25, 29]). It addresses the bio-based products issues in a rather general way, focusing on drivers, market potential, green public procurement, recommendations, and indirectly also the bio-based products derived from bio-waste streams.

7.2.1 Defining Risk and Uncertainty: The Prolegomena to the Enquiry

Risk is associated, in the original definition of [24], with stochastic processes. A risky situation is one characterized by more than one outcome and the probability of each outcome is known to the decision makers. In this sense, problems of risk concern the stochastic variation in the outcome associated with a decision. As stated by Knight, however, "for logical accuracy and in order to understand the different kinds of situations and modes of dealing with them in practice, a further distinction must be drawn" (p. 12). Knight distinguishes between: (1) *a priori probability* and (2) *statistical probability*. The former is defined as an absolutely homogeneous classification of instances completely identical except for really indeterminate factors. This judgment of probability is on the same logical plane as the propositions of mathematics. In this sense, *a priori* probabilities can be attributed objectively by logical reasoning, without the need to perform any experiments or trials [6]. Statistical probability is defined as the empirical evaluation of the frequency of association between predicates, not analyzable into varying combinations of equally probable alternatives ([24]: 224).

Hence, *knightian risk* refers to a situation where the probability of the alternatives[2] is either known *ex-ante*, or can be reliably estimated. Anyway, in both cases it is possible to assign numerical probabilities to events on the basis of knowledge of the relevant 'chances' associated with alternative occurrences ([34]). However, Knight himself observes that the "mathematical or a priori type of probability is practically never met within business, while the second is extremely common" ([24]: 215–16).

Uncertainty refers to a situation in which a decision might have more than one outcome and the probability of possible outcomes is unknown or cannot be meaningfully estimated. The unpredictability of an outcome may be due to lack of reliable information, inadequate past experience, and high variability of the underlying process or incomplete knowledge of that process. Knights refers to this third situations as (3) *estimates*—"The distinction here is that there is no valid basis of any kind for classifying instances. This form of probability is involved in the greatest logical difficulties of all, and no very satisfactory account of it can be given" (1921: 224–5).

In 1954 Savage countered the knightian view, suggesting a subjective theory of probability that treats probability as a property of the way one thinks about the world. Savage approach takes account of the 'orthodox' subjective conception of probability widely regarded as stemming from the works of Bruno de Finetti (1937) and Frank Ramsey (1926). The underlying idea of this model is that "the probability of a proposition or event is the strength of the decision-maker's degree of belief in

---

[2]As suggested by Runde, *alternatives* in Knight's writing should be understood as outcomes in a real or imaginary experiment.

that proposition or event, and it is assumed that the decision-maker always behaves 'as if' he assigned numerical probabilities to the events impinging on her actions, and calculates the value of any risky option as the sum of the probability-weighted utility of its possible consequences" ([14]: 2). In other words, this theory claims that it is possible to assign precise numerical probabilities to virtually any proposition or event, so that Savage's uncertainty can be stretched to include Knightian risk.

This approach has been broadly advocated by many economists, especially those considered neoclassical. As put by Freedman, "In his seminal work, Frank Knight drew a sharp distinction between risk, as referring to events subject to a known or knowable probability distribution and uncertainty, as referring to events for which it was not possible to specify numerical probabilities. I have not referred to this distinction because I do not believe it is valid. I follow L. J. Savage in his view of personal probability, which denies any valid distinction along these lines. We may treat people as if they assigned numerical probabilities to every conceivable event" ([15]: 282).

7.2.2 Beyond Risk and Uncertainty: Ambiguity and Ignorance

Following [38, 39], the distinction between risk and uncertainty relates to 'knowledge about probabilities', this being unproblematic in the first case and problematic in the second case. However, there is another type of knowledge which is not always available to the decision maker, which is 'knowledge about the possibilities'. Whenever knowledge about possibilities is problematic, risk and uncertainty, as defined above, do not apply anymore. Under this condition we should refer to *ambiguity* and *ignorance*. Specifically, ambiguity refers to a situation in which it is not the probability but the characterization of all possible outcomes that is problematic. This condition can stem from two different situations: (1) the decision maker does not possess all the information/knowledge required to identify ex-ante all possible outcomes, or alternatively (2) events are certain (or have occurred already) but there is disagreements over the selection, partitioning, bounding, measurement, prioritization, or interpretation of outcomes ([38]: 99).

A more extreme condition is the one characterized by lack of knowledge both on the probabilities and on the outcomes. The problem is not merely that we do not have enough information to reliably attach probabilities to a given number of outcomes, but that there are events, that we cannot yet imagine, which may occur in the future. Stirling [38] refers to this condition as ignorance. This differs from uncertainty, which focuses on agreed known parameters. It also differs from ambiguity in that the parameters are not just contestable, under-characterized, or indeterminate in their relative importance, but are unbounded or at least partly unknown ([38]: 100).

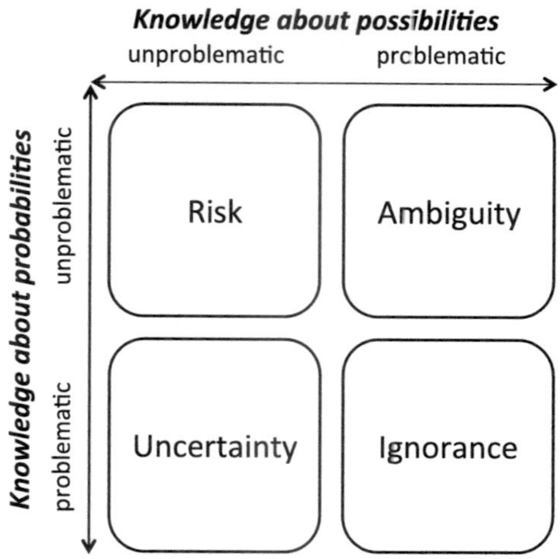

Fig. 7.1 Substantive uncertainty matrix. Source: Adapted from [39]

7.2.3 Addressing Uncertainty in Complex Innovation Systems

In order to categorise these four forms of uncertainty (i.e. risk, uncertainty, ambiguity and ignorance), [39] proposed an uncertainty matrix, which we report in Fig. 7.1. As discussed above, these four categories of uncertainty have to do with some kind of informational gap, which derives from lack of knowledge. Dosi and Egidi [8] refer to these as *substantive* forms of uncertainty. As put by the authors, "a quite diffused theoretical presumption in the economic analysis of information is that agents make the best possible use of the available information, which is generally taken to mean both that they utilize maximisation procedures and that these procedures are somewhat 'naturally' associated with their normal cognitive competences. That is, there is no competence gap in their information processing" ([8]: 149).

However, the complexity of the decision task characterizing most aspects of modern societies may easily determine a competence gap, in addition to the information gap associated with substantive uncertainty. Following [8], we shall refer to such circumstances whereby the decision-makers are constrained in their computational and cognitive capabilities as characterized by *procedural uncertainty*. Complex innovation systems are a case in point. In fact, introducing an innovation involves uncertainty at various levels. First, since an innovation is something not attempted before, its results are characterized by fundamental uncertainty at the time of decision. Moreover, since complex systems are characterized by a tight interrelation between parts and the collective behavior of the system, this produces further (procedural) uncertainty due to the "the density of structural linkages and interactions between the parts of an interdependent system" ([17]: 668–669).

Putting it differently, the mere possibility of the introduction of an innovation by someone constitutes a major source of fundamental uncertainty in the system. Moreover, given the underlying complexity of the system, cognitive gaps are most likely to occur, this producing further procedural uncertainty.

Within complex innovation systems, the notion of procedural uncertainty is compatible with, and complementary to, the notion of fundamental uncertainty: a reality that is subject to non-predetermined structural change may also be complex; and people who are capable of innovating may also have limited abilities [6]. Hence, we can agree that complex innovation systems are often characterized by *fundamental substantive uncertainty* as well as *procedural uncertainty*. In what follows we shall try to give an account of such forms of uncertainty characterizing complex innovation system in the specific case of sustainable transition. As we will show, the emerging complex system associated with sustainability transition is characterized by many sources of uncertainty related to the non-predetermined structure of the system as well as to the complex interdependence of the system itself.

7.3 Sustainability Transition: Setting the Framework of Analysis

7.3.1 Introducing the Problem

Currently, two economies co-exist side-by-side: fossil-economy being the dominant one and bio-economy which is "a complex socio-technical system undergoing rapid change" ([36]: 1). Moving from the former to the latter involves a sustainability transition.

In this respect, sustainability is increasingly becoming a core focus of innovation economics, lying at the intersection of several subfields such as geography, network theory, and political ecology. Yet, strategies for achieving this goal remain under investigated, mainly due to the complexity related to the manifold nature of concepts involved. However, "in the past decade, the literature on sustainability transitions has made a considerable contribution in understanding the complex and multi-dimensional shifts considered necessary to prepare and adapt societies for sustainable development" ([3]: 6). Van Den Bergh et al. [41] identified four theoretical frameworks that enable decision makers to gain an insight into how sustainability transitions emerge and evolve, namely: (1) the innovation systems approach, (2) the multi-level perspective approach, (3) the evolutionary economics approach combined with multi-agent modelling of transitions and (4) the transition management approach.

In order to outline a clear framework-of-action for the various stakeholders involved in bio-based production (investors, policy makers, owners of waste treatment plants, representatives of different industries, etc.), we decided to adopt the multi-level perspective (MLP) approach. The core novelty of this approach rests on the idea that the system can be seen as a nested framework formed by three linked levels: socio-technical regime (ST-regime), socio-technical landscape and innovation niches [32].

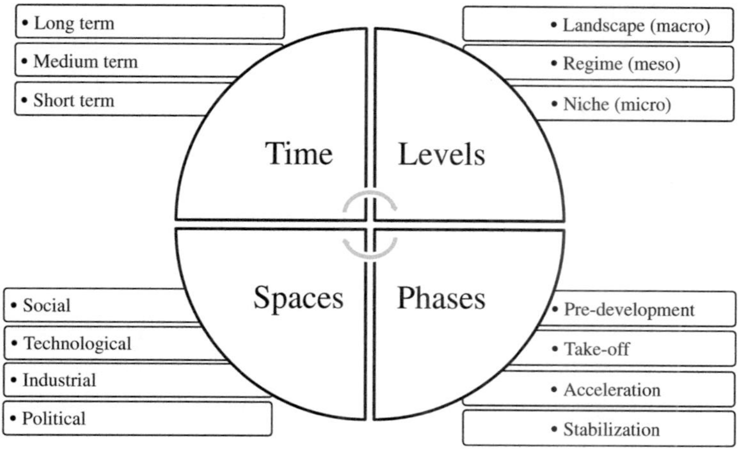

Fig. 7.2 Sustainability transition: a four-dimensional framework

Along with the multi-level perspective, we shall include in our analysis other three dimensions which, as we believe, complement the MLP creating a holistic approach to the sustainability transition problem. More specifically, we are using a four-dimensional transition framework[3] (see Fig. 7.2) that integrates:

1. Four *phases* of transition;
2. Three *levels* of transition;
3. Four *spaces* of transition;
4. Three *time-spans* of transition.

This will allow us to grasp the complexity associated with the transition patterns from traditional to bio-based production (that use "sub-products" derived from bio-waste valorisation as raw materials), and in turn assess all sources of uncertainty characterising such a complex innovation system.

7.3.2 A Four-Dimensional Transition Framework

The four-dimensional framework is built on the following considerations: (1) sustainability transition implies a long-term continuous change process with parallel developments, that take place in different phases (i.e. pre-development, take-off,

[3]We adapted this framework from [23]. We do not take into account here the governance functions that in the original framework are combined with the different transitions phases, levels and dimensions. In addition, here we include in the same framework the time, that is essential if we consider, for instance, that different technologies are likely to exist in parallel but in different phases of transition. Also [23] take into account time but not in the same framework, basically they substitute the phases of transition with time, keeping the three dimensional framework.

acceleration, stabilization); (2) sustainability transition implies developments at different levels, namely: landscape (macro), regime (meso), niche (micro) and (3) on each of these levels sustainability transition addresses technological, industrial, political and social changes ([23], p. 8). We shall now attempt to disentangle the four-dimensional framework presenting all its components.

7.3.2.1 Phases of Transition

From a conceptual point of view, the transition process can be disentangled into four different phases[4]: (1) ***pre-development (incubation)***—in which "the initial state does not visibly change but the shortcomings get recognized and the aspiration to solve these generally arises" ([37]: 6). In this phase the key actors involved in the transition process are still largely disconnected; (2) ***take-off***—some changes appear as a result of ad-hoc network formation that facilitates interaction and exchange of expectations. In this phase, the processes of learning are concentrated on technical aspects and user dimensions ([3]: 12); (3) ***acceleration***—the structural changes are occurring in a visible way as a result of "accumulation and implementation of political, economic, institutional and socio-cultural changes" ([37]: 6). In this phase "collective action becomes prevalent and group-based rules are established", while also the focus of the learning processes shifts from technical aspects to governmental policy, and environmental impact ([3]: 12). As a consequence, returns from scale economies increase, supporting in this way the diffusion of new solutions and leading to structural changes [23]; (4) ***stabilization***—in this phase "the niche has evolved into a regime that consists of established networks, shared expectations and collectively endorsed institutions" ([3]: 12), and original shortcomings are solved.

7.3.2.2 Levels of Transition

The socio-technical transition takes place through the interactions of three different levels [22], namely: (1) the ***regime level***; (2) the ***landscape level***; (3) the ***niche level***. Within this framework, the regime is defined as a relatively stable configuration of institutions, techniques and artefacts (such as hardware and infrastructures), as well as rules, practices and networks that determine the 'normal' development and use of technologies. Any regime represents the meso-level unit of analysis, which is nested in a wider context that influences its performance. Such context consists of a set of deep structural trends and variables which go beyond the direct influence of regime actors. In the MLP these elements form the landscape level, which is the second level of the analysis. At the bottom of this multi-levelled structure lie innovation niches, which represents the niche level. Niches are protected spaces for

---

[4]For a discussion on these phases see among others: [23, 26, 33, 37, 42].

the development and use of promising technologies by means of experimentation ([21]: 186). We can see niches as 'incubation rooms' for novelties because they are protected or insulated from 'normal' market selection in the regime [35].

7.3.2.3 Spaces of Transition

Further to phases and levels, we shall now look into the four dimensions of the socio-technical transition (on this point see: [23]: 15–16): (1) ***social space***—since the success of new technologies depends also on the experience and response of the end-users, social change occurring as a consequence of the transition process might stimulate the demand for the emerging technology. However, social changes introduced by the adoption of a new technology might also generate counter-productive social behaviours, that could eventually jeopardise the whole implementation process by increasing the system inertia; (2) ***technological space***—in order to improve understanding not only of the current state of the transition process, but also of the major technological bottlenecks and opportunities, it is essential to identify the linkages between physical technologies and their different phases of maturity (from emerging to dominant design technologies); (3) ***industrial space***—on the one hand, "the identification of networks of technology developers, providers and appliers (users) and related financing services (investors) improves the understanding of the key drivers and barriers for change in the system", while on the other,"the analysis of lobbying and standardisation efforts provides important information on the industry dynamics"; (4) ***political space***—this is the broad institutional and legal framework which can act both as a barrier or as a driver for a socio-technical transition. On the one hand, policy makers may act simply as optimization-oriented actors and, in this way, may reinforce lock-in conditions to existing systems. On the other hand, policy-makers might attempt to shape institutional context through their strategic actions of creating and claiming value [31] and can help create new social networks and agreements which can open up possibilities for novel innovations.

7.3.2.4 Time-Spans of Transition

Another key element of the four-dimensional framework is **time**. This is indeed an essential feature of each system, and in our case is even more so if we consider, for example, that different technologies are likely to co-exist in parallel but at different phases of transition. As our goal is to map all the uncertainties associated with the socio-technical transition, we took into account three different time-spans: the short term, the medium term and the long term, being aware that there are multiple sources of uncertainty that can emerge and evolve in different time spans.

7.4 Assessing Uncertainty in Sustainability Transitions: The Case of Bio-Based Production

Mapping the uncertainties according to their source is essential since: (1) they have a major influence on the decisions and also on the behaviour of the stakeholders; (2) the different sources require adopting a different way of action in order to cope with the associated uncertainties; (3) it represents a useful starting point for the development of policies and strategies.

Although a lot of research has dealt with the concept of uncertainty, currently, there is no consensus about the definition and operationalization of uncertainty, because each discipline (e.g. economics, sociology, computer science, mathematics, engineering, risk management, organizational management, innovation management, etc.) studies particular aspects of the uncertainty concept and has developed its own way of addressing it.

Because socio-technical transition implies both the adoption and the development of innovation, we decided to use the taxonomy of uncertainty developed by [19] who carried out a systematic review of innovation literature. Thus, according to [19], we can distinguish among the following types of uncertainty: technological uncertainty, market uncertainty, regulatory/institutional uncertainty, political uncertainty, acceptance/legitimacy uncertainty, managerial uncertainty, timing uncertainty and consequence uncertainty. Furthermore, we consider here also another important type of uncertainty for the case study under investigation, namely resource uncertainty.

In order to give a complete and comprehensive view of the case study, it would be useful to apply this taxonomy of uncertainty within the four-dimensional framework of socio-technical transition, by showing which type of uncertainty applies to each of the four dimensions described above. However, before doing this, we first present the taxonomy of uncertainty, emerged from the innovation literature.

7.4.1 *A Taxonomy of Uncertainty*

Technological uncertainty: According to [27], this type of uncertainty can be represented by: (1) *uncertainty about the technology itself*, which is greatly influenced by the stakeholders' perception of the technology itself and which may hinder a proper assessment of the innovation and thus postpone or even encourage abandoning the innovation decision; (2) *uncertainty about the relation between the technology and the infrastructure* within which the new technology will be integrated. Firms will hesitate to invest in a technology that requires a new infrastructure or in a new infrastructure when the technology that complements it is still lacking; (3) *uncertainty about the availability of alternative technological solutions*— typically, "technological change creates uncertainty with respect to the speed of new technologies' development and improvement relative to current state-of-the-art technologies, as well as uncertainty about the possibility that future technologies can cause older technologies to become obsolete" ([27]: 12).

Market uncertainty: This is one of the most influential types of uncertainty that acts within socio-technical transition, if we consider that an innovation that has no market quickly disappear. It can be subdivided into the following elements: (1) *consumer uncertainty*—which refers both to the consumer preferences and characteristics as well as to the demand pattern (especially the demand size and the time span which takes to make it become stable); (2) *supplier uncertainty*—encompasses mainly the uncertainty about partners, for instance in a joint venture. This type of uncertainty increases significantly in the case of innovations that require the establishment of a new supply chain, and therefore new relations; (3) *competitive uncertainty*—if related to lack of awareness to the prospective actions of competitors, we refer to *innocent* competitive uncertainty, while when some stakeholders deliberately create uncertainty for their competitors in order to gain an advantage, we refer to *strategic* competitive uncertainty [27].

Regulatory/institutional uncertainty: This source of uncertainty may act as an obstacle if it provides unclear and/or contradictory signals, that mislead both the developers of the new technology and the investors, leading to the postponement or even the abandonment of the innovation. By the same token, a pro-active and supportive regulatory/institutional framework can facilitate or speed-up the development of the new technology.

Political uncertainty: Whenever policies implemented at different levels (e.g. supra-national, national and local) are incoherent, this leads to confusion and inertia, generating a barrier for the innovation process. However, coherent and well crafted policies might be an important driver for the development of new technologies.

Acceptance/legitimacy uncertainty: This source of uncertainty appears when "necessary skills and knowledge invalidate existing skills and knowledge possessed by users" or when "innovation threatens individuals basic values and/or organizational norms" ([19]: 28).

Managerial uncertainty: Often this type of uncertainty arises as a consequence of: (1) lack of knowledge concerning the effectiveness of activities meant to support innovative behaviour in risky context which may lead to a failure; (2) lack of managerial tools required to deal with risks inherent to an innovation process.

Timing uncertainty: This type of uncertainty arises from: (1) "lack of information in the early phases of innovation", creating difficulties for firms in finding the optimal timing for an investment decision; (2) ambiguous information in the late phases of innovation; (3) temporal complexity faced by innovators ([19]: 31).

Resource uncertainty: This type of uncertainty appears whenever firms encounter difficulties in making accurate forecasts on resources availability (raw materials, human and financial resources), required to scale up the innovation and take it from the laboratory to the market. Uncertainty regarding human resources has to do with the availability of knowledge and skills necessary to carry out the innovation ([27]: 13).

7.4.1.1 Uncertainty in the Four-Dimensional Framework: The Bio-Based Production Case

After emerging as a policy concept within the OECD at the beginning of this century, the *bio-based economy* is currently recognized as a potential driver for the achievement of the sustainable development goals.[5] However, several hurdles are still impeding the deployment of its full potential:

1. Although in the last 10 years the potential of a bio-based production of chemicals and materials has been extensively documented, the investment in industrial biotechnology and biorefineries across Europe is still low [5].
2. Moreover, despite the abundance of EU-funded projects aiming at the advancement of bio-based industries, producers haven't succeeded in reaching a critical mass sufficient to overcome fragmentation and to create integrated bio-based industry value chains in Europe ([11]: 4–5).
3. Finally, and probably most importantly, most of the efforts in this very area have been channelled towards the production of bio-based products, which make use of biomasses obtained from dedicated crops as opposed to valuable compounds[6] obtained from bio-waste valorisation processes.

Approximately 120 to 140 million tonnes of bio-waste are produced every year only in the EU and about 40 % of this entire amount is landfilled—up to 100 % in some Member States [12]. As a consequence, making the bio-waste handling more environmentally friendly has become a key objective for policy makers.

Across the world, the most used practices to treat urban bio-waste are anaerobic digestion and composting, allowing the re-use (complete or partial) of the waste at the end of the treatment process. However, these techniques lead to low value products, having only marginal economic value. Hence, the valorisation of bio-waste could have many advantages, but mostly it solves a critical waste management issue[7] and represents a sustainable renewable resource, making it doubly green.

As a matter of fact, more advanced technologies (through the identification and isolation of valuable components present in the bio-waste streams) have the potential to recover higher value products for use in chemical, agriculture, pharmaceutical or other industries [7, 25, 29]. In spite of this encouraging evidence, the uptake of new bio-based products derived from bio-waste valorisation processes

[5]Policy makers' interest in BBP took form in a series of policy initiatives (e.g. Innovating for Sustainable Growth: A Bioeconomy for Europe, 2012; National Bioeconomy Blueprint-USA, 2012; European Innovation Partnership for Agricultural Productivity and Sustainability, 2012; The Bioeconomy to 2030: Designing a Policy Agenda, Main Findings—[30]; etc.).

[6]Such as: soluble bio-organic substances (SBO), phenolics, fatty acids, triglycerides, proteins, carbohydrates, etc.

[7]By decreasing the amount of waste landfilled, reducing uncontrolled GHG emissions as well water contamination through leaching of inorganic matter, etc.

is hindered by multiple uncertainties, that come up at different levels (i.e. macro, meso, micro), during different phases (i.e. pre-development, take-off, acceleration, stabilization), emerging and evolving in different points in time and spaces.

When speaking about bio-based products derived from bio-waste valorisation processes we mostly have in mind *bio-based chemicals* that can be further used for obtaining different products such as: bio-plastics packaging, detergents, emulsifiers, foaming agents, photo-sensitizers, nanostructured materials, textiles auxiliaries, fertilizers. Bearing this in mind, we will now explore the links between the different types of uncertainty and the components of the four-dimensional framework in the case of bio-based chemicals (derived from bio-waste valorisation processes).

Currently, bio-based chemicals have to face a "fierce" battle against well-established petrochemicals, which can rely on already existing refineries, economies of scale, reliable supply chains, and longstanding customer relationships ([2]: 6).

Uncertainty is highly pertinent in the case of bio-based chemicals at least for two sets of reasons. On the one hand, there is *the problem of funding instability*; for instance, in order to reach the *stabilization phase*, new bio-based chemicals need "5 to 10 years longer than most investors can tolerate without revenues or profits. Venture capitalists and risk-oriented equity investors may be willing to wait several years, but they have not been willing to put up the billions of dollars needed for commercial scale-up. Banks and bond investors have traditionally financed big projects that offer modest but predictable annual returns over many years, but they do not want to take on technology risk or untested markets" ([2]: 7).

The risk-aversion toward new bio-based chemicals is not manifested only by banks, venture capitalists or bond investors, but also by existing petrochemical companies. Archer Daniels Midland (ADM), an agrichemical giant, is a case in point, abandoning a high-profile joint venture with a young biomass company (Metabolix) to manufacture and market bio-plastics. Although they have booked a $300 million charge against earnings on the joint venture, they decided to give up saying that Metabolix's fermentation technology had 'performed well' but cited 'uncertainty around projected capital and production costs, combined with the rate of market adoption' ([2]: 9).

The need of large investments required to make the shift from laboratory to industrial scale is coupled with *uncertainty on technology performance*. In other words, "uncertainty will not only arise about the technology itself, which still needs to be shaped, but also about the socio-institutional setting in which the emerging technology will be embedded [...]. Technology developers will perceive uncertainty about user requirements and market demand, whereas potential users will perceive uncertainty about what the new technology might have to offer" ([28]: 1224). In addition, we have the *uncertainty related to the potential market size* and the need to set new, complex value chains which require a long term-perspective.

On the other hand, there is a wide range of stakeholders who have different levels of expertise and knowledge that can lead to the accumulation of perceived uncertainties and loss of motivation, and invariably to different ways of understanding the decision making process. "Negative interactions between different sources of perceived uncertainty and factors in the internal and external project environment (such as changes in the constitution of actors involved, institutional change or external technological developments) appeared to play a crucial role in this" ([28]: 1223).

New bio-based chemicals must also take account of stringent regulations, seeing that the chemical industry is increasingly under scrutiny of national and international bodies due to concerns of toxicity effects of chemicals. The European Union is an example in this regard, adopting a rigorous regulation (EC-no. 2006/1907) on the Registration Evaluation Authorisation and Restriction of Chemicals (REACH).[8] As observed, "despite provisions that enable producers/importers to share the cost of obtaining all the necessary hazard and risk data required to register the same substance, the testing and administrative costs of achieving a registration are nonetheless considerable. Small(er) scale producers in the EU, particularly of any novel substances/mixtures resulting from food waste reprocessing, may ultimately find the compliance costs of REACH legislation a major barrier to the commercial viability of the process" ([25]: 9). Moreover, the regulation procedure for bio-based chemicals is a complex one and sometimes "more onerous than rules governing petrochemicals", for instance "a single bio-based chemical can be subject to regulations at more than one agency, making compliance with the law complicated, uncertain, and expensive—especially for startups" ([2]: 10).

Bearing all this in mind, we provide in Fig. 7.3 a visual representation of the uncertainty sources affecting BBP within the four-dimensional framework sketched above. Through this figure we can recombine in one single framework the whole system—considering the complex and interlinked system as a whole.

We built Fig. 7.3 being aware that: (1) in order to cope with uncertainties that characterize the BBP system it is essential to distinguish between the different sources of uncertainty (i.e. market, technological, and so on) because each source of uncertainty should be tackled differently; (2) there is a practical concern of minimising uncertainties from decision makers' horizon (as a matter of fact, investors, waste treatment entrepreneurs and innovating firms managers, all perceive uncertainties as a fundamental obstacle). As a consequence, in order to narrow the gap between theory and practice, we tried to capture in Fig. 7.3 all the sources of uncertainty that are most likely to emerge during the socio-technical transition from fossil-fuels chemicals and products to bio-based chemicals and products. Thus, based on the literature review and empirical evidences, we illustrated for each source of uncertainty the level(s), the phase(s), space(s) and the time span(s) in which it can appear and evolve.

As we can see, the first two phases of socio-technical transition (pre-development and take-off) entail most of the types of uncertainty (described in Sect. 7.4.1): (1) *technological uncertainty*: "in the pre-development phase, technology-

[8]"This requires all those who manufacture in the EU in quantities of one tonne or more per annum per manufacturer (or who meet the threshold criteria in an importer capacity) to obtain a registration for the chemical concerned, without which the substance cannot be placed on the market within the EU" ([25]: 9).

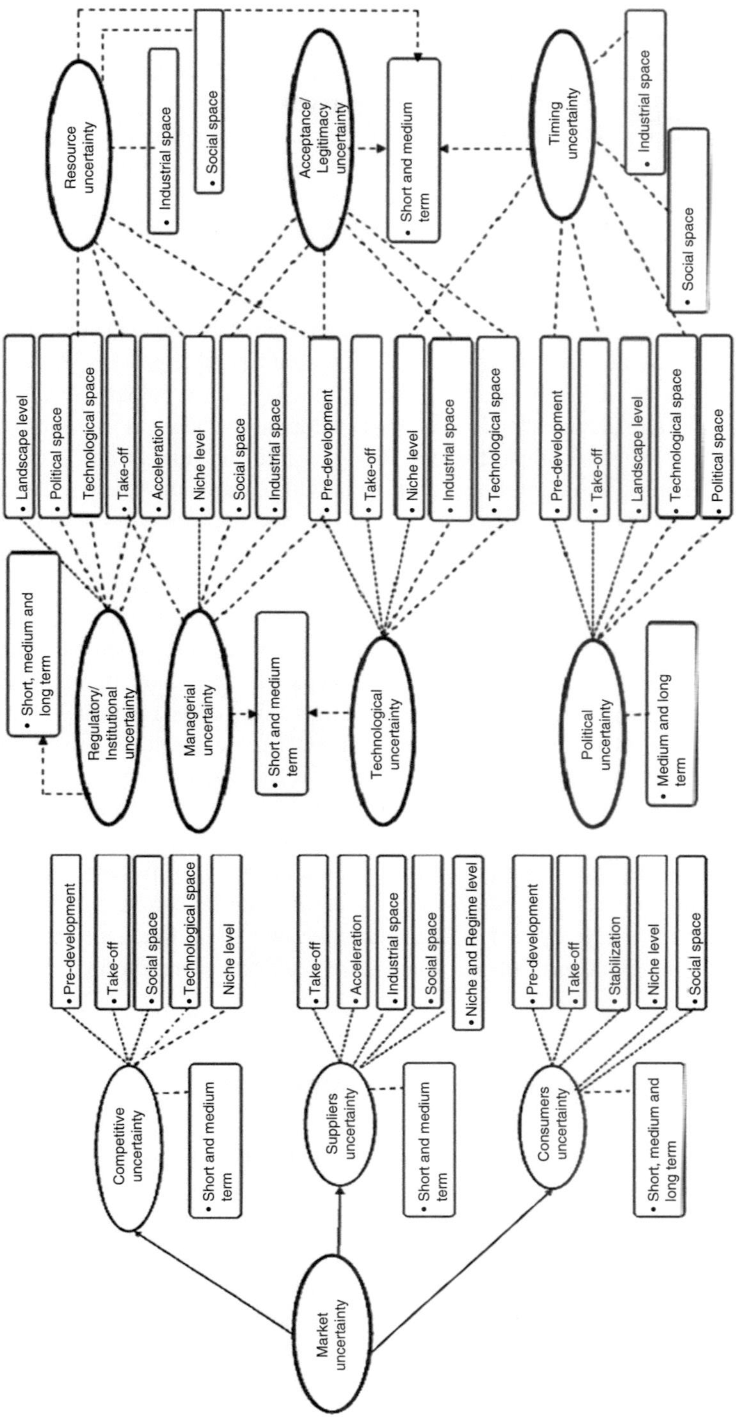

Fig. 7.3 The impact of uncertainty in the four-dimensional framework

developers are searching in various directions and the uncertainty about what is possible and which direction to choose is very high. In the take-off phase, it is still unclear which technology will dominate on what technical parameters" ([27]: 17). In addition, technological uncertainty can hinder the proper evaluation of the innovation and consequently affect the innovation decision (facilitating the appearance of *managerial uncertainty*); (2) *political uncertainty* can play a significant role both in the pre-development and take-off phases if we take into account that policy can guide or facilitate the speed and direction of sustainability transition towards bio-based chemicals by different means such as fiscal instruments or niche management measures. In addition, "at the landscape level, one of the key challenges for transition policy is to find leverage to enhance the attractiveness of alternative system options, so increase potential for change" ([13]: 12); (3) *market uncertainty*, through all its components—but most notably *competitive uncertainty*—is already present in the pre-development phase, as it is uncertain which firm will bring a competitive technologies into the market and how these competing technologies will perform. In the take-off phase competitive uncertainty is most dominant as new technologies have to compete with both established and competing new technologies ([27]: 18); *supplier uncertainty*—has a more significant role in the take-off phase when for instance, innovating firms have to find reliable suppliers that are able to deliver high-quality components in large quantities, that assure commercialization; *consumer uncertainty* is perceived by the innovating firms in the first two phases in a strong way, since "potential consumers are unable to clearly articulate their expectations and needs regarding the new technology" ([27]: 18) and also the new products that are meant to substitute the traditional ones; (4) *acceptance/legitimacy uncertainty* appears in these two phases when necessary skills and knowledge outdo existing skills and knowledge possessed by the users ([19]: 28); (5) *timing uncertainty* is perceived by the innovating firms, especially when they are confronted with the lack of managerial tools required to deal with the inherent risk; (6) *resource uncertainty* about human resources is most dominant in the pre-development phase, while the one about financial uncertainty is most evident in the take-off phase, when there is a fierce competition [27].

7.5 Conclusions and Further Developments

Managing risk and uncertainty is a challenge which has drawn the attention of economists, policy analysts, entrepreneurs and policy makers. In this paper we attempt to provide some guidelines for identifying and handling uncertainty in a complex system within a sustainability transition framework.

Specifically, we aimed at providing insight into how different types of uncertainty characterising the bio-based production system (we identified eight types of uncertainty, all of which have different implications for the various stakeholders) affect the development of bio-based chemicals derived from bio-waste valorisation processes and, more generally, how it affects the shift towards a bio-based economy.

In this sense, in order to outline a clear framework-of-action for the stakeholders involved in bio-based chemicals production (investors, policy makers, owners of waste treatment plants, representatives of different industries, etc.), we decided to adopt a *four-dimensional framework*, building it on the following considerations: (1) socio-technical transition implies a long-term continuous change process with parallel developments that take place in different phases (i.e. pre-development, take-off, acceleration, stabilization); (2) socio-technical transition implies developments at different levels, namely: landscape (macro), regime (meso), niche (micro) and (3) on each of these levels it might entail technological, industrial, political and social changes ([23]: 8) occurring at (4) different times (short, medium and long term).

Within this framework, the main contribution of our investigation was to apply the *uncertainty taxonomy* to this four-dimensional framework, emphasizing which type of uncertainty could emerge within each dimension. We believe this can be very helpful in the process of designing management strategies, both at entrepreneurial and policy-making level.

Our assessment provided a holistic approach to uncertainty within the complex system investigated. This, in turn, allowed us to depict the intricate web of links connecting uncertainty to the various elements composing the four-dimensional framework of the analysis. This exercise turned out to be important, as it sets out guidelines for a more informed management of risk and uncertainty, leaving for future research the task of identifying ways to reduce them.

In fact, as we believe, additional research and empirical work is needed in order to establish how different types of uncertainty evolve within different levels (i.e. macro, meso, micro) and spaces (i.e. social, technological, industrial, political), during the four phases of the socio-technical transition and time spans. It is also a challenge for future research to assess how each source of uncertainty affects the involved stakeholders (i.e. investors, waste treatment plant owners, etc.), the types of bio-based chemicals adopted on the market and the timing of adoption.

References

1. ADEME: Guide de l'achat public eco-responsable. http://www.campusresponsables.com/sites/default/files/ressources/guide_achats_eco-responsables.pdf (2004). Accessed 7 Feb 2013
2. Andrews, E., MacLean, C., Kurtzman, J.: Unleashing the power of the bioeconomy. financial innovations lab® report, Milken Institute, Feb 2013. http://www.milkeninstitute.org/pdf/BioEconFIL.pdf (2013). Accessed 26 Aug 2013
3. Avdeitchikova, S., Coenen, L.: Commercializing clean technology innovations – the emergence of new business in an agency-structure perspective, paper no. 2013/06, Centre for Innovation, Research and Competence in the Learning Economy (CIRCLE) Lund University. http://www.circle.lu.se/?wpfb_dl=7 (2013). Accessed 10 July 2013
4. BTG: Sustainability criteria & certification systems for biomass production. Final report prepared for DG- TREN European comission. http://www.rpd-mohesr.com/uploads/custompages/sustainability_criteria_and_certification_systems.pdf (2008). Accessed 6 Feb 2013

5. Carus, M., Carrez, D., Kaeb, H., Ravenstijn, J., Venus, J.: Policy paper on bio-based Economy in the EU: level playing field for bio-based chemistry and materials. http://www.bio-based.eu/policy/en/ (2011). Accessed 23 Feb 2013
6. Dequech, D.: Uncertainty: a typology and refinements of existing concepts. J. Econ. Iss. **XLV**(3), 621–640 (2011)
7. D'Hondt, E., Voorspoels, S.: Maximising value making the most of biowaste. http://www.waste-management-world.com/articles/print/volume-13/issue-1/features/maximising-value-making-the-most-of-biowaste.html (2012). Accessed 6 Feb 2013
8. Dosi, G., Egidi, M.: Substantive and procedural uncertainty. J. Evol. Econ. **1**(1), 145–198 (1991)
9. EPEC: Detailed assessment of the market potential and demand for an EU ETV scheme. Business case annexes. http://www.ec.europa.eu/environment/etv/pdf/ETV%20Final%20Report%20Business%20Case%20Annexes.pdf (2011). Accessed 6 Feb 3013
10. European Commission: Accelerating the development of the market for bio-based products in Europe. Report of the taskforce on bio-based products. http://www.ec.europa.eu/enterprise/policies/ innovation/ files/ lead-market-initiative/ bio_based_products_taksforce_report_en.pdf (2007). Accessed 5 Feb 2013
11. European Commission: Proposal for a council regulation on the bio-based industries joint undertaking, Brussels, 10.7.2013, COM (2013) 496 final. http://www.eur-lex.europa.eu/LexUriServ/LexUriServ.do?uri=COM:2013:0496:FIN:en:PDF (2013). Accessed 26 Aug 2013
12. EU: Supporting Environmentally sound decisions for bio-waste management a practical guide to life cycle thinking (LCT) and life cycle assessment (LCA), JRC scientific and technical reports. http://www.lct.jrc.ec.europa.eu/pdf-directory/D4A-Guidance-on-LCT-LCA-applied-to-BIO-WASTE-Management-Final-ONLINE.pdf (2011). Accessed 6 Feb 2013
13. Faber, A., Alkemade, F.: Success or failure of sustainability transition policies. A framework for the evaluation and assessment of policies in complex systems. DIME final conference, Maastricht. http://www.final.dime-eu.org/files/Faber_Alkemade_C5.pdf (2011). Accessed 26 Aug 2013
14. Feduzi, A., Runde, J., Zappia, C.: De Finetti on the insurance of risks and uncertainties. Br. J. 603 Philos. Sci. **63**, 329–356 (2012)
15. Friedman, M.: Price Theory: A Provisional Text. Aldine, Chicago (1976)
16. Friends of Europe: The rise of the bio-based economy. Report of the greening Europe forum (GEF) roundtable. http://www.friendsofeurope.org/Portals/13/Documents/Reports/2012/FoE_2012_The_rise_of_the_bio-based_economy_Report_WEB.pdf (2012). Accessed 5 Feb 2013
17. Hodgson, G.F.: The ubiquity of habits and rules. Camb. J. Econ. **21**(6), 663–684 (1997)
18. IEA Bioenergy: Economic sustainability of biomass feedstock supply. Technical report. http://142.150.176.36/task43/library/otherreports/IEA_Bioenergy_Task43_TR2013-01.pdf (2013). Accessed 15 Feb 2013
19. Jalonen, H.: The uncertainty of innovation: a systematic review of the literature. J. Manag. Res. **4**(1), E12 (2012)
20. van Haveren, J., Scott, E.L., Sanders, J.: Review: bulk chemicals from biomass. Biofuels Bioprod. Biorefin. **2**, 41–57 (2008)
21. Kemp, R., Schot, J., Hoogma, R.: Regime shifts to sustainability through processes of niche formation. The approach of strategic niche management. Tech. Anal. Strat. Manag. **10**(2), 175–195 (1998)
22. Kemp, R.: The Dutch energy transition approach. IEEP **7**(2–3), 291–316 (2010)
23. Könnölä, T., Van der Have, R., Carrillo-Hermosilla, J.: System transition. Concepts and framework for analysing nordic energy system research and governance, VTT working papers 99. http://www.vtt.fi/inf/pdf/workingpapers/2008/W99.pdf (2008). Accessed 10 July 2013
24. Knight, F.: Risk, Uncertainty and Profit. University of Chicago Press, Chicago (1921)
25. Lin, C.S.K., et al.: Food waste as a valuable resource for the production of chemicals, materials and fuels. Current situation and global perspective. Energy Environ. Sci. (2012). doi:10.1039/C2EE23440H

26. Loorbach, D., Rotmans, J.: Managing transitions for sustainable development. In: Olsthoorn, X., Wieczorek, A. J. (eds.) Understanding industrial transformations: views from different disciplines, pp. 187–205. Springer, Dordrecht (2006)
27. Meijer, I.S.M., Hekkert, M.P., Faber, J., Smits, R.E.H.M.: Perceived uncertainties regarding socio-technological transformations: towards a typology. Working paper for the Druid Winter 2005 Ph.D. conference. http://www2.druid.dk/conferences/viewpaper.php?id=2534&cf=17 (2005). Accessed 27 June 2013
28. Meijer, I.S.M., Koppenjan, J.F.M., Pruyt, E., Negro, S.O., Hekkert, M.P.: The influence of perceived uncertainty on entrepreneurial action in the transition to a low-emission energy infrastructure: the case of biomass combustion in the Netherlands. Technol. Forecast. Soc. Chang. **77**, 1222–1236 (2010)
29. Montoneri, E., Mainero, D., Boffa, V., Perrone, D.G., Montoneri, C.: Biochemenergy: a project to turn an urban wastes treatment plant into biorefinery for the production of energy, chemicals and consumer's products with friendly environmental impact. Int. J. Glob. Environ. Iss. **11**(2), 170–195 (2011)
30. OECD: The Bioeconomy to 2030: designing a policy agenda. Main findings and policy conclusions. http://www.oecd.org/futures/long-termtechnologicalsocietalchallenges/42837897.pdf (2009). Accessed 6 Feb 2013
31. Powell, W.W., DiMaggio, P.J.: The New Institutionalism in Organizational Analysis. University of Chicago Press, Chicago (1991)
32. Rip, A., Kemp, R.: Technological change. In: Rayner, S., Malone, L. (eds.) Human Choice and Climate Change. Resources and Technology, vol. 2, pp. 327–399. Battelle Press, Washington (1998)
33. Rotmans, J., Kemp, R., et al.: More evolution than revolution: transition management in public policy. Foresight: J. Futur. Stud. Strateg. Think. Policy **3**(1), 15–32 (2001)
34. Runde, J.: Clarifying Frank Knight's discussion of the meaning of risk and uncertainty. Camb. J. Econ. **22**(5), 539–546 (1998)
35. Schot, J.W.: The usefulness of evolutionary models for explaining innovation. The case of the Netherlands in the nineteenth century. Hist. Technol. **14**, 173–200 (1998)
36. Sorasalmi, T., Nieminen-Sundell, R., Ylén, J.P.: A dynamic analysis of socio-technical transition towards bio-economy, VTT Technical Research Centre of Finland. http://www.systemdynamics.org/web.portal?P1285+0 (2013). Accessed 30 June 2013
37. Sporri, A.: Integrating and structuring expert knowledge for sustainability transitions in socio-technical systems. Applied to swiss waste management. http://www.e-collection.library.ethz.ch/eserv/eth:1357/eth-1357-02.pdf (2009). Accessed 27 June 2013
38. Stirling, A.: Science, precaution, and the politics of technological risk. Converging implications in evolutionary and social scientific perspectives. Ann. N. Y. Acad. Sci. **1128**, 95–110 (2008)
39. Stirling, A.: Keep it complex. Nature **468**(7327), 1029–1031 (2010)
40. UNEP: Waste and climate change: global trends and strategy framework. http://www.unep.org/ietc/Portals/136/Publications/Waste%20Management/Waste&ClimateChange.pdf (2010). Accessed 25 Jan 2013
41. Van Den Bergh, J.C.J.M., Truffer, B., Kallis, G.: Environmental innovation and societal transitions: Introduction and overview. Environ. Innov. Soc. Trans. **1**, 1–23 (2011)
42. Wiek, A., Lang, D.J., Siegrist, M.: Qualitative system analysis as a means for sustainable governance of emerging technologies: the case of nanotechnology. J. Clean. Prod. **16**(8–9), 988–999 (2008)

Part III
Methods and Applications

Chapter 8
Global Optimization of Simulation Based Complex Systems

Giampaolo Liuzzi, Stefano Lucidi, and Veronica Piccialli

8.1 Introduction

Many real world problem can be cast as global optimization problems where the objective function value is produced by possibly expensive simulation codes. Mathematically, the problem can be stated as

$$\min_{x \in \mathcal{F} \subseteq \Re^n} f(x), \tag{8.1}$$

where $f : \Re^n \rightarrow \Re$.

In this work we focus on simulation-based global optimization problems with the following common features:

- they can be formulated as single objective optimization problems;
- they require the execution of simulation programs to compute the performance measures which define the problem;

G. Liuzzi
Istituto di Analisi dei Sistemi ed Informatica "A. Ruberti", CNR, via dei Taurini 19, 00185 Roma, Italy
e-mail: giampaolo.liuzzi@iasi.cnr.it

S. Lucidi
Dipartimento di Ingegneria Informatica, Automatica e Gestionale "A. Ruberti", "Sapienza" Università di Roma, via Ariosto 25, 00185 Roma, Italy
e-mail: lucidi@dis.uniroma1.it

V. Piccialli (✉)
Dipartimento di Ingegneria Civile e Ingegneria Informatica, Università degli Studi di Roma "Tor Vergata", viale del Politecnico 1, 00133 Roma, Italy
e-mail: veronica.piccialli@gmail.com

G. Dellino, C. Meloni (eds.), *Uncertainty Management in Simulation-Optimization of Complex Systems*, Operations Research/Computer Science Interfaces Series 59,
DOI 10.1007/978-1-4899-7547-8_8

- some of the functions defining the problem are of the black box type, hence derivative information is unavailable or unreliable;
- there are many uninteresting local minima besides the global ones.

Some further characteristics can be envisaged which can influence the difficulty of the problem and hence can be used to choose the solution algorithm. These are:

- the simulation codes are computationally expensive;
- the global minimum (or an approximation to it) must be computed with an high accuracy;
- the global minimum point has a very narrow region of attraction;
- there are many local minima with a value of the objective function very close to each other.

As significant examples we report four real-world applications arising in different fields. The first one concerns the structural comparison and alignment of protein surface patches which is a basic problem for protein-ligand binding site recognition. This problem is not particularly expensive, has potentially many local minima but the global one has a reasonably large region of attraction.

The second one consists in the design of a small low-cost, low-field multipolar magnet for Magnetic Resonance Imaging with a high field uniformity. In this case the computation of the objective function is the result of an expensive magnetic field simulation. Since high field uniformity is sought, the global minimum must be computed with a high precision.

The third one is connected with a ship design problem, namely the reduction of the amplitude of the heave motion of a ship advancing in head seas. Also in this case the objective function computation can be very expensive and many local minima with objective function value close to each other exist.

Finally, the fourth application arises in the detection of gravitational waves emitted by coalescing binary systems of compact objects. This problem is particularly difficult from a global optimization point of view because the global minimum has a very narrow region of attraction.

To handle the difficulties of the above applications, different solution approaches can be defined taking into proper account as much as possible both the nature of the problem and (if available) any a priori knowledge on it. In particular we present algorithms that have been successfully applied to these applications and that belong to different classes of global optimization algorithms. Below we briefly recall three main classes of global optimization methods.

8.1.1 Population Based Algorithms

Among the various approaches for solving real-world global optimization problems, stochastic methods [45, 48] proved to be extremely robust and sufficiently reliable in many practical problems, see e.g. [4, 7, 8, 11, 14, 19, 22, 26, 36, 37, 41, 42, 49, 52]. These algorithms use a population of M individuals (points). The initial population is randomly generated on the feasible set. At each iteration, the population is evolved by generating new individuals exploiting the information on the objective function given by the current population. As the algorithm proceeds, the cloud of points tends to cluster more and more around the global minimum points of the problem. Typically, these algorithms can locate a good approximation of the global minimum in a few generations. However, they potentially require many function evaluations especially when high accuracy in the final solution is needed. An Adaptive Controlled Random Search (ACRS) algorithm belonging to this class has been used for solving the protein structural alignment problem [4].

8.1.2 Multistart-Type Algorithms

Another class is defined by those methods which repeatedly use efficient local minimization algorithms in order to produce good approximations of minimum points [2, 28]. However, when a local algorithm starts far from a global minimum, it can be trapped into a local one. To overcome this problem, we consider two possible approaches resulting in two different subclasses of methods:

(1) *Globalization via simulated annealing*. The starting points of the local searches are chosen at random according to a probability density function which is updated during the iterates of the algorithm so as to be concentrated around a global minimum point of the problem. Indeed, a simulated annealing acceptability criterion is used: the basic idea is to let a local minimization start from points chosen at random according to a suitable probability density function. A distributed algorithm belonging to this class has been applied to the MRI problem in [26].

(2) *Globalization via filled functions*. Once determined a first stationary point x_1^* of problem (8.1), a perturbation of the objective function, called filled function [15], is built such that its stationary points satisfy the relation $f(x) < f(x_1^*)$. In this way, by minimizing the filled function it is possible to find a stationary point of the filled function with a value of the original objective function lower than $f(x_1^*)$. Starting a local minimization from this stationary point, a new local minimum of problem (8.1) is produced with lower objective function value and the process is iterated until the global minimum has been located. Such an algorithm has been applied to the solution of the ship hull design problem in [8].

8.1.3 Partition-Based Algorithms

If the objective function of problem (8.1) is not too expensive to evaluate, it is possible to use algorithms whose convergence is guaranteed in a deterministic fashion: as an example we consider partition based global optimization algorithms [27]. The idea is to perform a sampling of the feasible domain on a set of points that becomes dense in the limit, thus guaranteeing strong theoretical convergence properties. Due to their deterministic nature, partition based algorithms may require a considerable number of function evaluations to find sufficiently good approximation of a global minimum thus resulting inefficient for most simulation-based global optimization problems. This sort-of intrinsic inefficiency can be overcome by modifying the standard partition based algorithms in some suitable way. A first possibility is to select, at every iteration, a set of "promising" points and start an efficient local optimization algorithm from them. A second choice could be to adapt as much as possible the partition strategy to the problem by exploiting, for example, any previous information on the objective function behaviour. A partition-based algorithm based on this latter strategy has been used to solve the gravitational waves detection problem in [46].

8.2 Simulation Based Applications

In this section we report four significant simulation-based applications from different fields. In particular we consider a problem arising in protein structural alignment, two optimal design problems, one in Magnetic Resonance Imaging and the other concerning ship hull optimization, and finally a challenging problem in astrophysics.

8.2.1 Protein Structural Alignment

Given two protein structures $\mathcal{P}$ and $\mathcal{Q}$, let us denote by P and Q the two finite sets of points corresponding to the atoms of the active sites of the two structures $\mathcal{P}$ and $\mathcal{Q}$, respectively. We let $n = |P| \quad \text{and} \quad m = |Q|$ and assume, without loss of generality, that $n \le m$. The set P is conventionally representative of a query shape while Q defines a reference model shape.

An isometric transformation in three-dimensional space can be defined by a unit quaternion $a_r = (a_0, a_1, a_2, a_3)^\top \in \Re^4$ ($\|a_r\| = 1$) and by a translation vector $a_t \in \Re^3$. Let $a^\top = (a_r^\top \; a_t^\top)$ be the transformation defining vector and denote by T_a the corresponding transformation, so that

$$y = T_a(x) = R(a_r)x + a_t$$

for every $x \in \Re^3$, where $R(a_r)$ is the rotation matrix defined by the unit quaternion a_r.

Let $\Theta \subset \Re^7$ be the set of all vectors $a \in \Re^7$ defining an isometric transformation in $\Re^3$. Given a transformation vector $a \in \Theta$, let $T_a(P) = P_a$ denote the set of points obtained by applying the transformation T_a to every point of P, that is

$$T_a(P) = P_a = \{y : y = R(a_r)p + a_t, \; \forall \; p \in P\}.$$

Let $\psi : P \to Q$ denote a point to point mapping that associates to every point of P a point of Q. Since, as assumed above, P and Q are finite sets, the class Ψ of all mappings ψ has finite cardinality given by $|\Psi| = m^n$.

Let $\psi \in \Psi$ be a given mapping and a be a vector defining an isometric transformation, then the mean square error function between P and Q is the following

$$f(\psi, a) = \frac{1}{n} \sum_{p \in P} \|\psi(p) - R(a_r)p - a_t\|^2.$$

Let us denote by $\psi(a) = \arg\min_{\psi \in \Psi} f(\psi, a)$ the closest point mapping [5] and $g(a) = f(\psi(a), a)$. Then, the surface alignment problem can be posed as

$$\min_{a \in \Theta} g(a). \tag{8.2}$$

Every global solution a^* of (8.2) is, by definition, a solution such that $f(\psi(a^*), a^*) \leq f(\psi(a), a)$, for all $a \in \Theta$. Problem (8.2) is a global optimization problem with a black-box objective function, a feasible set Θ described by box constraints and some "easy" constraints (i.e. $\|a_r\| = 1$). Furthermore, numerical experiments show that the problem has many local minima and a global minimum exists with reasonably large basin of attraction.

8.2.2 *Magnetic Resonance Imaging*

Magnetic Resonance Imaging (MRI) or Magnetic Resonance Tomography (MRT) [9, 18, 23] is a powerful diagnosis instrument especially because of its non-invasive nature, its high resolution and its ability to scan even soft tissues. Patients undergoing an MRI exam lie flat on a scanning table and are placed in a magnetic field created by a huge magnet.

Over the past few years, MRI equipments have been devised with the purpose of lowering the cost of MRI analysis. This requires new technology developments, particularly in the magnet design. The main purpose is to build economical MRI systems focused to dedicated applications, e.g. low-field MRI systems for orthopedic applications.

Naturally, low field apparatus are inherently less sensitive than high field ones. However, this drawback can be overcome by a high uniformity of the magnetic field which results in high resolution images.

In [26] a model (M) of the multipolar magnet which has the shape of a cylinder with an elliptical base has been considered. The elliptical shape of the magnet basis has been chosen to maximize the possibility of use in different situations (such as for the peripheral skeleton and paediatrics).

The magnet (M) is composed of 12 elliptical iron rings with 18 small permanent magnets screwed on each of them. In particular, the following optimization variables have been considered:

1. the positions $(x_1, \dots, x_6)$ of the rings along the cylinder axis (see Fig. 8.1b);
2. the angular positions (see Fig. 8.1a) of each row of small permanent magnets $(x_7, \dots, x_{10})$, being a row constituted by magnets occupying the same position but on different rings (as shown by Fig. 8.1c);
3. the offsets $(x_{11}, \dots, x_{14})$ of the four outermost rings with respect to the two innermost ones (see Fig. 8.1b).

In spite of its simple structure and due to the high nonlinearities introduced by the iron yoke, the field generated by model (M) can not be analytically computed. For this reason, the multipolar magnet model, corresponding to a feasible choice of the above mentioned variables, is computer rendered within a field simulation program which predicts the behavior of the magnetic field by means of a sophisticated finite element analysis (the RADIA [10, 12] finite element simulator of the *European Synchrotron Radiation Facility*).

Let XYZ be a system of Cartesian coordinates with origin at the center of the structure, X axis parallel to the cylinder axis and, Z and Y axes directed, respectively, along the shortest and longest semi-axes of the cylinder base. As already said, we want the magnetic field $\mathbf{B}$ generated by the multipolar magnet to be as uniform as possible within the target region and directed along the Z axis.

In order to measure the uniformity of the magnetic field within the target region, we just sample the three components of $\mathbf{B}$ on a grid of N_p points uniformly distributed inside the cylindrical region of interest. Let $B_X^{(i)}(x)$, $B_Y^{(i)}(x)$ and $B_Z^{(i)}(x)$ be the three components of the magnetic field measured at the ith point of the grid, the objective function will be

$$U(x) = \frac{\sum_{i=1}^{N_p} \left((B_Z^{(i)}(x) - \bar{B}_Z(x))^2 + (B_X^{(i)}(x))^2 + (B_Y^{(i)}(x))^2 \right)}{\bar{B}_Z(x)^2},$$

where $x = (x_1 \dots x_{14})^\top$ and

$$\bar{B}_Z(x) = \frac{\sum_{i=1}^{N_p} B_Z^{(i)}(x)}{N_p}.$$

Furthermore, there are also a number of constraints (i.e. 49 constraints) to be considered which enforce physical realizability of the magnetic apparatus and in particular: (1) box constraints on the variables, (2) linear constraints to ensure rings to be separated one from another and to enforce ordering of the magnets angular positions, and (3) nonlinear non-convex constraints to prevent magnets to overlap onto each other. Hence, the resulting problem is

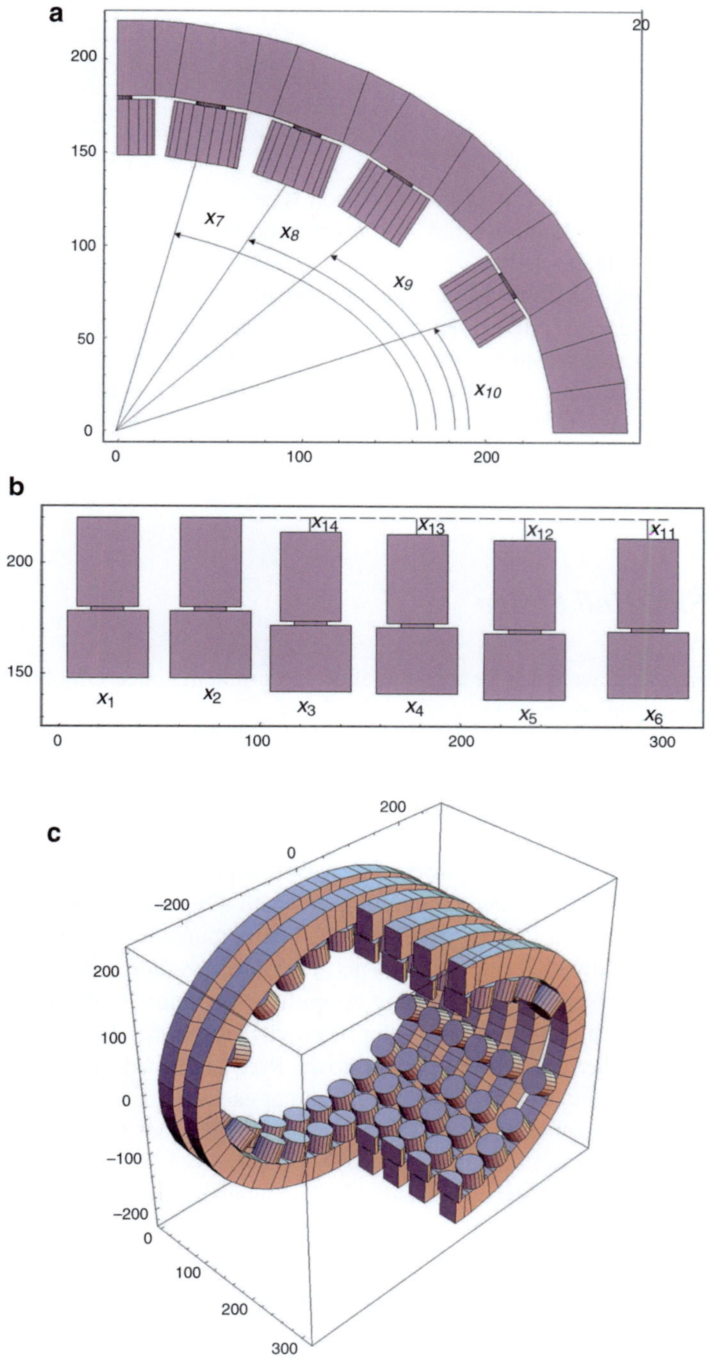

Fig. 8.1 Optimization variables. (**a**) Angles. (**b**) Displacements and offsets. (**c**) Multipolar magnet structure

$$\begin{aligned} &\min\ U(x) \\ &s.t.\ \ell \le x \le u, \\ &\qquad g(x) < 0, \end{aligned}$$

which has the properties listed below:

(1) the objective function is of the black-box type in the sense that apart from its continuity in the feasible set, no information on its structure is available and its computation is expensive;
(2) the objective function is not defined outside of the feasible set and the constraints are continuous but non convex; on the other hand it is "relatively" easy to generate feasible points and to remain in the feasible set;
(3) it is possible to find a feasible point $\tilde{x}$ such that the set $\{x \in R^n : g(x) < 0, \ell \le x \le u, U(x) \le U(\tilde{x})\}$ is compact;
(4) the objective function does not satisfy any convexity assumptions and hence the problem has local minimizers.

8.2.3 Ship Hull Design

In this subsection, we consider an optimal design problem concerning the design of the hull of a containership [8].

A frequent request from shipyards and navies is to limit the vertical motion and acceleration while the ship is advancing in irregular seas. The prediction of this behavior is typically obtained by studying the problem in the frequency domain, under two major assumptions: it is assumed that (1) the irregular sea waves can be represented as a sum of a simple sine waves with specified amplitudes (from selected spectral densities) and random phases (with uniform distributions) and (2) the response of the ship to irregular waves can be obtained as the sum of the ship responses to the individual sine components. The objective function selected for this application is the peak of the Response Amplitude Operator (RAO) for the heave motion (the vertical motion of the center of gravity) when the ship is advancing at constant speed in head seas. For a given ship the RAO is defined as the square of the amplitude of the regular wave transfer function at each frequency of the incoming sea, i.e. the transfer function of the ship for all the six motions under any incoming wave of assigned relative direction.

In particular, the ship considered is the S175 containership[1] while it is advancing at the speed of 16 knots in head seas. The minimum of the response is searched for

[1] It has been adopted by the ITTC (Int. Towing Tank Conf., an international organization of the naval hydrodynamic community) Seakeeping Committee as a benchmark test.

non-dimensional frequencies higher than 0.4 and for a ship speed of $Fr = 0.198$ (the Froude number Fr is defined as the ratio of inertial to gravitational force).

The seakeeping performances of the S175 containership are numerically evaluated with a simulation code based on the *strip* theory (see [35]). With this approach the hull is represented as a series of two-dimensional slices and the model for the fluid is based on potential flow assumptions. The output is the transfer function of the ship for all the six motion under any incoming wave of assigned relative direction.

Hull shape parameterization is performed according to [39] and a Béziér patch is superimposed to the original hull shape. Six control points of the patch are used as design variables to modify the hull shape. The patch acts in the y (transversal) direction only. As a consequence, the keel line is left unchanged during the optimization process.

In order to come up with a problem having the characteristics of a real design case, some geometrical constraints must hold. Three different constraints are adopted, in particular a range of variation for the displacement, Δ, and for the beam, B are defined:

$$2398t \leq \Delta(x) \leq 2460t \tag{8.3}$$

$$25m \leq B(x) \leq 26m \tag{8.4}$$

Finally, in order to avoid unreliable hull form, a maximum range of variation for the design variables x_i is imposed:

$$-20.0 \leq x_i \leq 20.0 \quad i = 1, \ldots, 6 \tag{8.5}$$

Note, however, that in this optimal design problem, it is known that the global minimum point x^* is strictly feasible, that is $g(x^*) < 0$ and $l < x^* < u$.

The resulting global optimization problem has a computationally expensive black-box objective function. It presents many local minima with a value close to each other and a global minimum with a narrow region of attraction. Further, we note that, on the one hand the feasible set is non-convex, and, on the other hand, the objective function is defined also on infeasible points.

8.2.4 Gravitational Waves Detection

The detection of Gravitational Waves (GWs) is a very ambitious goal in modern astrophysics, because it will provide a validation of the General Relativity Theory of Einstein and a new type of information on the Universe [47]. Networks of detectors have been deployed, but GWs have not yet been observed because of many difficulties in the detection process. Such difficulties are related to the weakness of the GWs, the rarity of the events that generate them, and the instrumental noise of the detectors. For these reasons, sophisticated data analysis techniques are required. Furthermore, because of the huge quantity of data acquired by the detectors twenty-four hours a day, a real-time on-line data analysis is needed.

We focus on the detection of GWs emitted by coalescing binary systems, which are very promising sources. The technique generally used for this problem is the matched filter, which exploits the waveform of the gravitational signal and assumes that the instrumental noise be a stationary Gaussian stochastic process. The computational kernel of the matched filter is the solution of a hard box-constrained global optimization problem, in which the objective function is a stochastic process because of the presence of noise. In practice, the output data of a detector contain a sample of noise, thus the optimization problem corresponding to that sample must be solved.

The problem of detecting GWs consists in deciding if the output of a detector contains a gravitational signal or it is made of noise only. This output is generally modeled as

$$x(t) := r(t) + h(t; \boldsymbol{\theta}),$$

where t is the time, $r(t)$ is the noise, $h(t; \boldsymbol{\theta})$ is the gravitational signal, and $\boldsymbol{\theta}$ is a vector of parameters. We assume that $r(t)$ be strictly white noise, i.e. a wide-sense stationary Gaussian stochastic process with mean 0 and variance 1. We are interested in gravitational signals emitted by coalescing binary systems of compact objects (neutron stars and/or black holes), which are one of the most promising sources for ground-based laser interferometric detectors. In this case, a relative large number of events per year is expected (tens per year within a few hundred Mpc) [32], and a model of the emitted waves is available, i.e. the so-called *chirp* signal in which both the frequency and the amplitude increase with time until the two objects of the system are close enough to merge [33]. The corresponding vector of parameters is $\boldsymbol{\theta} := (A, \varphi_0, t_0, m_1, m_2)$, where A is the amplitude, φ_0 the initial phase, and t_0 the arrival time of the signal, while m_1 and m_2 are the masses of the binary system; all of them are unknown. In practice, the output of the detector is sampled with a certain time step, thus a segment of data is available, which is an N-dimensional vector $\boldsymbol{x} := (x[0], \ldots, x[N-1])$; the corresponding sampled gravitational signal, if present, is an M-dimensional vector $\boldsymbol{h} := (h[0], \ldots, h[M-1])$, with $M < N$ (the dependence on $\boldsymbol{\theta}$ has been neglected for simplicity).

The most widely used detection technique is the matched filter, which is an optimal linear filter for detecting signals of known shape in stationary Gaussian noise [3]. It basically consists of three steps:

1. correlating the output of the detector with a family of templates, consisting of chirp signals $\boldsymbol{h}(\boldsymbol{\theta})$, with $\boldsymbol{\theta}$ varying in a suitable set;
2. finding the maximum of the correlation with respect to all the parameters;

3. comparing this maximum with a suitable threshold to decide if the output of the detector contains a gravitational signal (a detection is announced if the maximum exceeds the threshold).

This procedure is based on the observation that the highest Signal-to-Noise Ratio (SNR) of the filter output is achieved when the values of the parameters identifying the template are the same as in the signal, and that this SNR is equal to the maximum of the mean value of the correlation [34]. The choice of the threshold is related to the probability of false alarm, i.e. of stating a detection in the absence of a signal, and to the probability of detection, i.e. of stating a detection when the output contains a gravitational signal [34].

We note that the amplitude and the initial phase corresponding to the maximum in step 2 can be expressed in terms of the optimal values of the remaining parameters; therefore the maximization of the correlation must be actually performed with respect to the masses (m_1, m_2) and the index $n_0 \in I = \{0, \ldots, N - M\}$ of the sample corresponding to the arrival time of the signal. Furthermore, given (m_1, m_2), the maximum with respect to n_0 can be easily computed [3]. Thus, step 2 can be formulated as the following box-constrained global optimization problem:

$$\underset{(m_1,m_2)\in\Omega}{\text{maximize}}\, F(m_1, m_2), \tag{8.6}$$

with

$$\Omega := \{(m_1, m_2) \in \Re^2 \;:\; l \le m_1, m_2 \le u\}$$

and

$$F(m_1, m_2) := \sqrt{\max_{n_0 \in I} \left(C_0^2(n_0, m_1, m_2) + C_{\pi/2}^2(n_0, m_1, m_2) \right)},$$

where $C_0(n_0, m_1, m_2)$ and $C_{\pi/2}(n_0, m_1, m_2)$ are the correlations between $\boldsymbol{x}$ and the so-called normalized quadrature components of the template, $\hat{\boldsymbol{h}}_0(m_1, m_2)$ and $\hat{\boldsymbol{h}}_{\pi/2}(m_1, m_2)$ [34], i.e.

$$C_0(n_0) := \sum_{k=n_0}^{n_0+M-1} x[k]\hat{h}_0[k - n_0] \qquad C_{\pi/2}(n_0) := \sum_{k=n_0}^{n_0+M-1} x[k]\hat{h}_{\pi/2}[k - n_0],$$

where the dependence on m_1 and m_2 has been neglected for simplicity of notations.

The solution of problem (8.6) presents the following characteristics: the objective function F is highly nonlinear, it has many local maxima and its derivatives are not available (see Fig. 8.2). Furthermore, the evaluation of F is quite expensive, since it requires the solution of two ordinary differential equations (ODEs) to generate the quadrature components of each template [6], and the execution of three FFTs of length N to compute the correlations of $\boldsymbol{x}$ with them [34]. Furthermore, computing

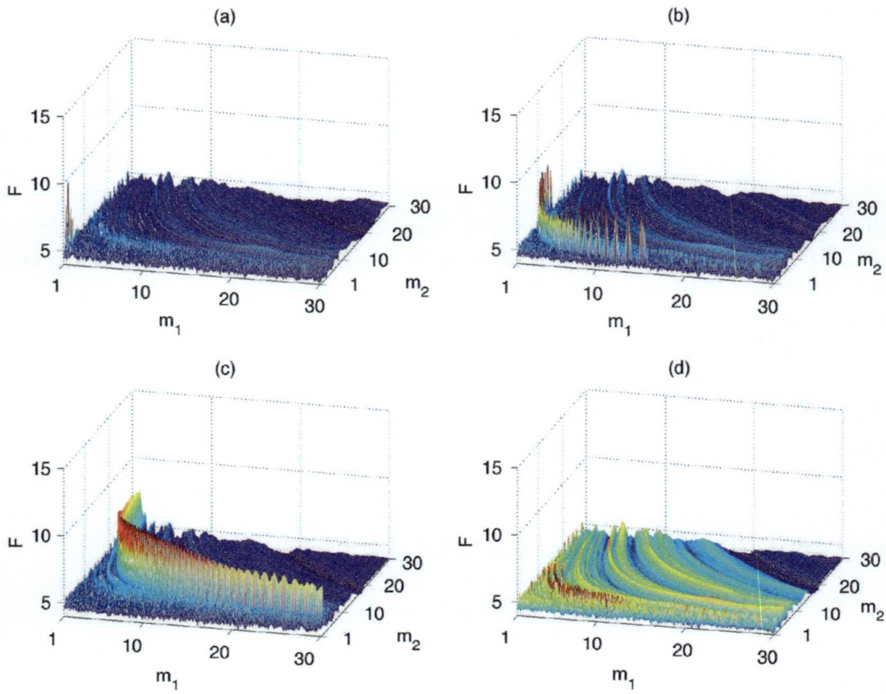

Fig. 8.2 3D plot of the objective function F, corresponding to noise plus gravitational signal from different pairs of masses $(\bar{m}_1, \bar{m}_2)$, or to noise only: (**a**) $\bar{m}_1 = \bar{m}_2 = 1.4\ M_\odot$, (**b**) $\bar{m}_1 = 1.4\ M_\odot$, $\bar{m}_2 = 10\ M_\odot$, (**c**) $\bar{m}_1 = 5\ M_\odot$, $\bar{m}_2 = 10\ M_\odot$, (**d**) noise only. $M_\odot$ is the solar mass; the SNR is equal to 10

the maximum of F with accuracy is crucial in the detection process, because a large error may correspond to a value of F which is under the threshold, thus preventing the detection of the signal [38].

8.2.5 Problems Formulation and Constraints Handling

The four applications that have been presented in the preceding subsections can be formulated as the following constrained global optimization problem

$$\begin{aligned} &\min\ f(x) \\ &\text{s.t. } g(x) \le 0 \\ &\quad\ l \le x \le u. \end{aligned}$$

The feasible set, and in particular the constraints $g(x) \leq 0$, can be further characterized depending on the particular application. More precisely, it is possible to identify the following classes:

(a) there are no general constraints, so that the feasible set is described only by the bound constraints on the variables, like e.g. in the gravitational waves detection problem (see Sect. 8.2.4);
(b) there general constraints are "easy" in the sense that the projection operator on the feasible set can be easily computed, like e.g. in the protein structural alignment problem (see Sect. 8.2.1);
(c) the general constraints are "soft" constraints in the sense that they can be relaxed so that the objective function can be computed also on infeasible points, like e.g. in the ship hull design problem (see Sect. 8.2.3);
(d) the general constraints are "hard" constraints, meaning that they must always be satisfied (otherwise the objective function is not defined), like e.g. in the magnetic resonance imaging problem (see Sect. 8.2.2). We recall that in the MRI problem the general constraints, though hard, are easy to satisfy.

While the bound constraints are treated explicitly, the handling of the general constraints (if any) must take into proper account the above classification. In particular, in case (b) the solution algorithm directly exploits the projection operator so that only feasible points are produced. In case (c) a "classical" nonsmooth penalty function can be employed. Finally in case (d) it is possible to resort to an extreme barrier approach, namely $f(x) = +\infty$ whenever x is infeasible.

In the following sections we present four classes of global optimization algorithms which are well-suited for the solution of the problems discussed in this section.

8.3 Population Based Algorithms

Population-based algorithms for global optimization are a subclass of stochastic methods and can be viewed as improvements of the fundamental Random Search (RS) method proposed in [44]. They are (mostly) based on two distinct major steps,i.e. a sampling step and a refinement (or optimization) step.

In the *sampling step* the algorithm tries to extract information on the "global" behaviour of the objective function by sampling the objective function on an initial set of randomly generated feasible points that constitute the initial population. Then, by repeatedly executing the *refinement step*, the algorithm tries to iteratively improving the initial population by means of approximated local minimizations. In this way the set of sample points should cluster more and more round the subregions which are more likely to contain a global minimizer of the objective function.

In this section we shall describe in some details a special class of population-based algorithms which are known as Controlled Random Search (CRS) algorithms. The basic CRS algorithm, which we report below for the sake of completeness, has been proposed in [40].

Algorithm 8.3.1: CRS

Data: A positive integer $m \geq n + 1$.
Sampling Step: Set $k := 0$; determine the initial set $S^k = \{x_1^k, \ldots, x_m^k\}$ of points chosen at random over $\mathcal{F}$.
Repeat (the following **Refinement Step**)
Determine the points x_{max}^k, x_{min}^k and the values f_{max}^k and f_{min}^k such that

$$\bar{f}_{max}^k = f(x_{max}^k) = \max_{x \in S^k} f(x),$$

$$f_{min}^k = f(x_{min}^k) = \min_{x \in S^k} f(x).$$

Choose at random $n + 1$, $x_{i_0}^k, \ldots, x_{i_n-1}^k, x_{i_n}^k$, over S^k.
Compute the centroid c^k of the n points, $x_{i_1}^k, \ldots, x_{i_n-1}^k, x_{i_n}^k$, that is

$$c^k = \frac{1}{n} \sum_{j=1}^{n} x_{i_j}^k.$$

Compute the trial point $\tilde{x}^k = \mathcal{P}_{\mathcal{F}}(c^k - (x_{i_0}^k - c^k))$ and $f(\tilde{x}^k)$.
If $(f(\tilde{x}^k) < f_{max}^k)$ **then** $S^{k+1} := S^k \cup \{\tilde{x}^k\} \setminus \{x_{max}^k\}$.
else $S^{k+1} := S^k$.
Set $k := k + 1$.
Until (Stopping criterion is satisfied)

In the above scheme, $\mathcal{P}_{\mathcal{F}}(x)$ denotes projection of x onto the feasible set.

Starting from the above CRS method proposed in [40], several new CRS algorithms have been proposed (see, e.g., [1, 7, 11, 25, 41, 43, 49]). The modifications introduced in these algorithms, which concern the refinement step, have the common aim of exploiting, as much as possible, the information on the minimization problem obtained during the iterates of the algorithm.

In the following we describe an improvement of the CRS algorithm which, though preserving a good global search, has improved local search abilities which is called Adaptive CRS Algorithm.

Algorithm 8.3.2: Adaptive CRS Algorithm (ACRS)

Data: A positive integer $m \geq n+1$.
Set $k := 0$; determine a set $S^k = \{x_1^k, \ldots, x_m^k\}$ of points chosen at random over $\mathcal{F}$.
Repeat

Determine $f_{max}^k = \max_{x \in S^k} f(x)$ and $f_{min}^k = \min_{x \in S^k} f(x)$.
Choose $x_{i_1}^k, \ldots, x_{i_n}^k, x_{i_{n+1}}^k$ by the *weighted random procedure* and let

$$f(x_{i_{n+1}}^k) \geq f(x_{i_j}^k), \quad j = 1, \ldots, n.$$

Determine the *weighted centroid* c^k

$$c^k = \sum_{j=1}^{n+1} w_j^k x_{i_j}^k,$$

where $w_j^k \geq 0$ for $j = 1, \ldots, n$ and $\sum_{j=1}^n w_j^k = 1$.

Compute the trial point $\tilde{x}^k$ by a *weighted reflection* of $x_{i_{n+1}}^k$ through c^k

$$\tilde{x}^k = \mathcal{P}_{\mathcal{F}}(c^k - \alpha^k (x_{i_{n+1}}^k - c^k)),$$

where $\alpha^k > 0$.
If $(f(\tilde{x}^k) < f_{max}^k)$ **then**

$$S^{k+1} := S^k \cup \{\tilde{x}^k\} \setminus \{x_{max}^k\}.$$

Else

$$S^{k+1} := S^k.$$

End if
Set k:= k+1.
Until (Stopping criterion is satisfied)

Algorithm 8.3.3: Weighted Random Procedure

Data: A set $S^k = \{x_1^k, \ldots, x_m^k\}$ such that $f(x_i^k) \leq f(x_{i+1}^k)$, $i = 1, \ldots, m-1$.
For $j := 1, \ldots, n+1$ **do**

Repeat
Generate a random number r_j uniformly distributed in $[0, 1]$ and compute

$$i_j = \lceil m(2^{r_j} - 1) \rceil .$$

Until $i_j \neq i_l \quad l = 1, \ldots, j-1.$

End for
Select the set $\{x_{i_1}^k, \ldots, x_{i_n}^k, x_{i_{n+1}}^k\}$ such that the point $x_{i_j}^k$, $j = 1, \ldots, n+1$, is the i_j-th element of the set S^k.

The algorithm produces a sequence $\{S^k\}$ of sets of m points. Initially ($k = 0$), the set S^k is chosen at random on the feasible set $\mathcal{F}$. At each iteration, the algorithm tries to "improve" the set S^k by replacing the point of the set S^k corresponding to the biggest function value with a new point where the objective function value is improved. The search of such a point is performed by exploiting the information contained in the set S^k, in particular:

(a) $n+1$ points are chosen over the set S^k by using a weighted random procedure which privileges the points corresponding to smaller objective function values;
(b) given these samples, the point, $x_{i_{n+1}}^k$, with the biggest function value is selected and the weighted centroid c^k is computed;
(c) the function values computed at the selected $n+1$ points should give a good representation of the local behavior of the objective function around point c^k and the vector $c^k - x_{i_{n+1}}^k$ should identify a good descent direction of the objective function at point c^k;
(d) the new trial point $\tilde{x}^k$ is obtained by performing a suitable movement from c^k along direction $c^k - \tilde{x}_{i_{n+1}}^k$, where the function should decrease, at least locally.

In order to complete the description of the algorithm, we have to specify how to compute the weights w_j^k, $j = 1, \ldots, n+1$, and the steplength α^k. These quantities are adaptively updated in such a way to find a good balance between the global search and the local one.

In the early stages of optimization, when a global search is to be preferred, this quantities should be such that the weighted centroid and the new trial point are computed without privileging any particular point $x_{i_1}^k, \ldots, x_{i_{n+1}}^k$. Namely, when $f_{max}^k - f_{min}^k$ is large we should have $w_j^k \simeq 1$, $j = 1, \ldots, n+1$, and $\alpha^k \simeq 1$.

As the number of iterations increases, more information on the problem becomes available, and an efficient local search should be preferred. Therefore, the centroid should be defined by weighting more and more the points with smaller function values and the trial point should be produced closer and closer to such points.

A suitable choice for w_j^k, $j = 1, \dots, n+1$, and α^k is the following.

$$w_j^k = \frac{\eta_j^k}{\sum_{j=1}^{n+1} \eta_j^k}, \qquad \eta_j^k = \frac{1}{f(x_{i_j}^k) - f(x_{min}^k) + \phi^k}$$

and

$$\alpha^k = 1 - \frac{f(x_{i_{n+1}}^k) - \sum_{j=1}^{n+1} w_j^k f(x_{i_j}^k)}{f(x_{max}^k) - f(x_{min}^k) + \phi^k},$$

where

$$\phi^k = \gamma \frac{\left(f(x_{max}^k) - f(x_{min}^k)\right)^2}{f(x_{max}^0) - f(x_{min}^0)}.$$

As concerns the value of the constants used in the statement of algorithm ACRS, in [25] they are $m = 25n$, $p = 2$, $\gamma = n$, and tol $= 10^{-6}$.

Population based algorithms thus, in particular, the ACRS algorithm, are particularly efficient for the solution of global optimization problems with easy constraints and a global minimum with a reasonably large region of attraction.

Indeed, in [4], Algorithm ACRS has been successfully applied to the solution of the protein structural alignment problem described in Sect. 8.2.1. We report in Fig. 8.3 an example of a computed alignment between the two proteins 1atp and 1hck.

8.4 Simulated Annealing-Type Algorithms

Multistart algorithms are based on the repeated use of local minimization algorithms as local search engine of a global minimization. In fact, it is well-known that good approximations of minimum points can be obtained by using efficient local minimization algorithms.

When a local algorithm starts far from a global minimum point, it can be trapped into a local minimum. In order to overcome this last difficulty, one possibility is the approach proposed in [26] where:

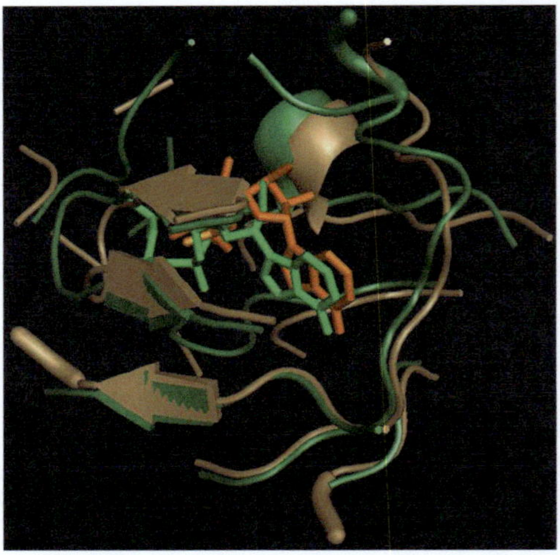

Fig. 8.3 Example of the superimposition obtained for the binding sites of ligand ATP of proteins 1atp and 1hck

- the starting points of the local searches are chosen at random according to a probability density function which is updated during the iterates of the algorithm so as to be concentrated around a global minimum point of the problem;
- the local searches are performed by an algorithm which has the property that it is attracted by any global minimum point.

The derivative-free local minimization is performed by means of the algorithm proposed in [31]. This algorithm is based on the use of linesearches along the coordinate axes which try to enforce sufficient decrease of the objective function. In order to better describe the distributed simulated annealing algorithm we introduce the procedure $DF(x, \alpha)$ which starting from point x performs a linesearch along all of the coordinate axes using as initial stepsizes $\alpha \in \Re^n$, $\alpha > 0$. Further, we also recall procedure $DFA(x, \alpha_{tol})$ which, starting from x, repeatedly applies procedure DF until a stationarity measure less than α_{tol} is reached. DFA is attracted by any global minimum point of the objective function provided that the starting point is sufficiently close to a global minimum point [26]. In order to ensure that this happens, in the following algorithm (DDFSA) the simulated annealing acceptability criterion proposed in [30] is used. In particular, the basic idea is to let a local minimization start from points chosen at random according to a probability density function proportional to $e^{\frac{-(f(x)-f_{\min})^+}{T}}$, where T is a parameter called "annealing temperature", which is progressively decreased during the minimization process, and $f_{\min}$ is the current estimate of the global minimum value.

In order to obtain good coverage of the feasible set and an high precision of the solution using as few function evaluations as possible in [26] a *working set* W of m triples $(x, f(x), \alpha)$ has been introduced. In particular, α is the current step of the derivative free algorithm at x. The working set W can be updated either by performing a single step of the derivative free algorithm (using Procedure DF) or by replacing the worst point, namely the one with highest objective function value, with a point produced by a partial minimization carried out by means of Procedure DFA starting from a point accepted by the simulated annealing criterion.

Algorithm DDFSA

1. Data: $\alpha^\circ > 0$.
2. Compute an initial temperature T°, set $k := 0$.
3. Generate the initial working set $W^k = \{(x_i, f(x_i), \alpha_i)^k,\ i = 1, 2, \dots m\}$.
4. Set

$$(x_{\min}, f_{\min}, \alpha_{\min})^k := (\bar{x}, \bar{f}, \bar{\alpha}) \in W^k : \bar{f} = \min_{(x, f(x), \alpha) \in W^k} f(x),$$

$$(x_{\max}, f_{\max}, \alpha_{\max})^k := (\bar{x}, \bar{f}, \bar{\alpha}) \in W^k : \bar{f} = \max_{(x, f(x), \alpha) \in W^k} f(x),$$

$$\alpha^k_{\text{stop}} = \max_{(x, f(x), \alpha) \in W^k} \alpha.$$

5. Randomly choose a feasible point $x^k \in \Re^n$ and a scalar $z^k \in (0, 1)$.
6. If $z^k > e^{\frac{-(f(x^k) - f_{\min})^+}{T^k}}$ compute T^{k+1} and go to step 9.
7. Compute $(\tilde{x}^k, \tilde{\alpha}^k) = \text{DFA}(x^k, \alpha^k_{\text{stop}})$.
8. If $f(\tilde{x}^k) < f^k_{\max}$ then set

$$W^{k+1} := (W^k \setminus \{(x_{\max}, f_{\max}, \alpha_{\max})^k\}) \cup \{(\tilde{x}^k, f(\tilde{x}^k), \tilde{\alpha}^k)\},$$

   $k := k + 1$ and go to step 4.
9. For every triple $(x_i, f(x_i), \alpha_i)^k \in W^k$, set $(\tilde{x}_i^k, \tilde{\alpha}_i^k) = DF(x_i^k, \alpha_i^k)$. Set

$$W^{k+1} := \bigcup_{i=1}^{m} \{\tilde{x}_i^k, f(\tilde{x}_i^k), \tilde{\alpha}_i^k)\},$$

   $k := k + 1$ and go to step 4.

As concerns the updating of the temperature parameter T^k at Step 6, we refer to the updating rule reported in [30].

Recalling [26] it is possible to prove that, for every global minimum point $x^\star$ of $f(x)$ on $\mathcal{F}$, a point x^k sufficiently close to $x^\star$ is accepted in a finite number of steps with probability one. Hence, the local minimization starting from such a point is attracted by the global minimum.

Algorithm DDFSA is suitable for the solution of the Magnetic Resonance Imaging problem because: (a) the use of efficient derivative-free local searches guarantees high precision in the computation of the global minimum point, and

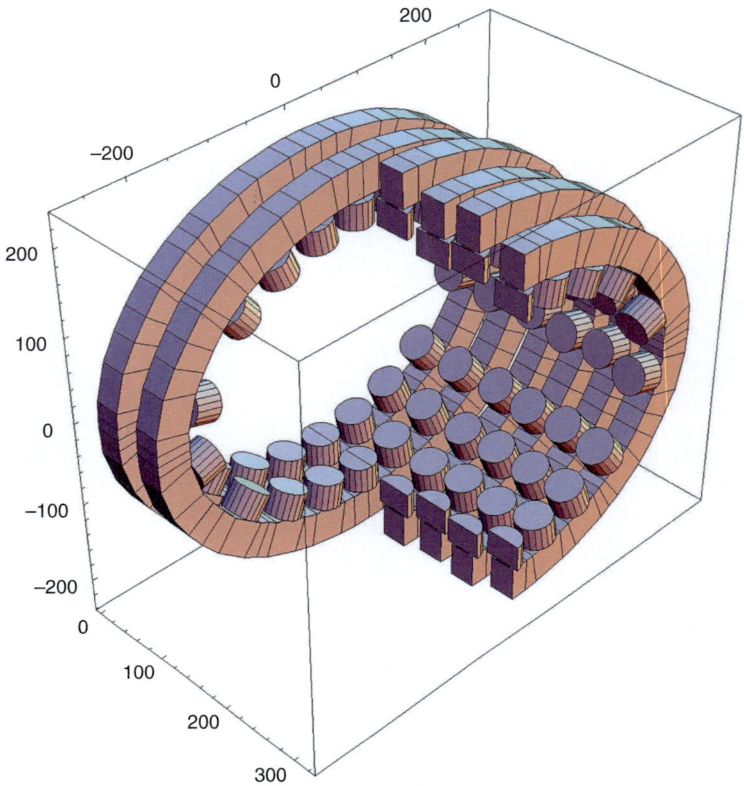

Fig. 8.4 Optimal design

(b) its distributed nature allows to considerably reduce the number of function evaluations required to solve the problem.

Indeed, the method has been applied to the Magnetic Resonance optimal design problem described in Sect. 8.2.2 by handling the general constraints through an extreme barrier approach, producing a point with a function value of $1.095 \cdot 10^{-7}$ which corresponds to a uniformity of 17 ppm for the z component, 10 ppm for the x component and 9 ppm for the y component of the magnetic field within the uniformity region.

The z component of the magnetic field has an average value of $\bar{B}_z = 743.5$ Gauss. In Fig. 8.4 we report the optimal structure as determined by the optimization procedure.

The global optimization algorithm allowed us to obtain a satisfactory field uniformity. We recall that existing low-field small MR magnets present 50 ppm of field uniformity. To have an idea of the achieved improvement in the field uniformity level, we plot the field behavior on the YZ-plane. Figure 8.5b corresponds to the optimal structure detected by DDFSA, whereas Fig. 8.5a, corresponds to a comparative configuration with a field uniformity of approximately 28 ppm for the z component.

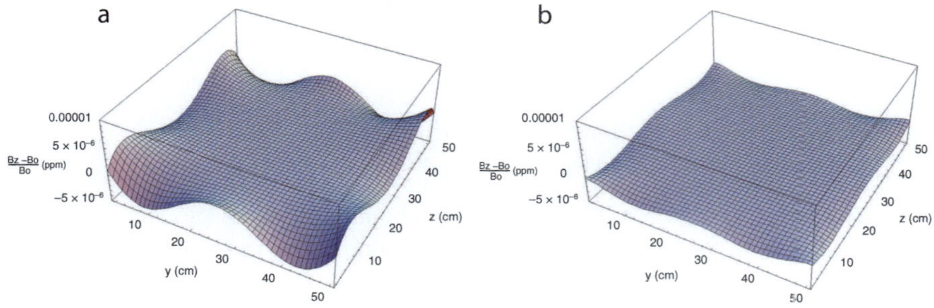

Fig. 8.5 Comparison between suboptimal and optimal field uniformities. (**a**) Configuration with 28 ppm z component uniformity. (**b**) Optimal configuration with 17 ppm z component uniformity

8.5 Filled Function Based Algorithms

The main difficulty of multi-start approaches is to escape from a "strong" local minimum. One possibility is to build a perturbation of the original objective function, called filled function, such that its stationary points satisfy $f(x) < f(x_k^*)$ where x_k^* is the current best local minimum. In this way, by minimizing the filled function it is possible to find a stationary point of the filled function with a value of the original objective function lower than $f(x_k^*)$. More formally, a scheme of a general algorithm based on a filled function can be stated as follows:

Algorithm 8.5.1: FILLED

Data: $x_0 \in \Re^n$. Set $k \leftarrow 0$.
Step 1. Compute x_k^* by applying a local minimization algorithm to the solution of problem (8.1) starting from x_k.
Step 2. Define a filled function $U_k(x)$.
Step 3. Choose a point $\bar{x}$ and find

$$y \in \arg\min_{x \in \Re^n} U_k(x)$$

by using a local minimization algorithm starting from $\bar{x}$.
Step 4. If $f(y) < f(x_k^*)$ then set $x_{k+1} \leftarrow y$, $k \leftarrow k + 1$ and goto Step 1.
Otherwise goto Step 3.

The concept of filled function has been introduced in [15] and since this paper many extensions/improvements have been proposed. Depending on the paper different definitions have been introduced of filled functions, corresponding to different expressions. The general structure of a filled function is composed by two terms $\eta_k(x)$ and $\phi_k(x)$, that can be combined in two different ways, giving rise to different filled functions:

- multiplicative filled functions: $U_k(x) = \phi_k(x)\eta_k(x)$;
- additive filled functions: $U_k(x) = \phi_k(x) + \eta_k(x)$.

The term $\phi_k(x)$ has the role to remove the stationary points of problem (8.1) that are not interesting, i.e. the ones corresponding to objective function values greater or equal to $f(x_k^*)$.

The term $\eta_k(x)$ has the role to ensure that the point x_k^* can be used as a starting point for the minimization of the filled function. This can be done in two ways: either making x_k^* a strict local maximum of the filled function ("filling" its basin of attraction) or making sure that the gradient of the filled function is different from zero in x_k^*. In the first case, it is ensured that a local minimization started from x_k^* will produce a point sufficiently different from x_k^*. In the second case, the term $\eta_k(x)$ ensures "good" structural properties to the filled function, like coercivity.

Depending on the choice of the structure of the function, on the role of the term $\eta_k(x)$ and on the number of parameters of the filled functions, different algorithms can be obtained [15–17, 24, 29, 50, 51].

A new filled function for unconstrained optimization for solving the ship hull optimal design problem has been introduced in [8] with the following expression:

$$Q(x, x_k^*, \tau, \varrho) = \exp\left(-\frac{\|x - x_k^*\|^2}{\gamma^2}\right) + 1 - \exp\left(-\tau\left[f(x) - f(x_k^*) + \varrho\right]\right), \quad (8.7)$$

where $\gamma > 0$ is a constant, and $\varrho > 0$ and $\tau \geq 1$ are real parameters.

This filled function is an additive one, where the first term makes point x_k^* a local maximum of the filled function $Q(x, x_k^*, \tau, \varrho)$, while the second term filters the stationary points of $f(x)$ which have objective value greater or equal to $f(x_k^*)$ and ensures that, for right values of the parameters, $Q(x, x_k^*, \tau, \varrho)$ has a local minimum point in a point with lower objective value than $f(x_k^*)$. In order to take into account the constraints (8.3)–(8.5), an ℓ_∞–Penalty function is used. The resulting problem is

$$\begin{aligned} \min\ & p_\epsilon(x) = f(x) + \frac{1}{\epsilon}\max\{0, g_1(x), \ldots, g_m(x)\} \\ & l \leq x \leq u, \end{aligned} \quad (8.8)$$

where $\epsilon > 0$ is a *penalty parameter* which should be chosen sufficiently small in order for Problem (8.8) to be equivalent to Problem (8.1).

A critical aspect of algorithm `FILLED` resides in Step 3. Namely, depending on the starting point $\bar{x}$ it could happen that point y produced by Step 3 does not satisfy condition $f(y) < f(x_k^*)$. This because the sequence of points produced by the local minimization algorithm leaves the level set $\mathcal{L}_f(x_0)$. Therefore, it could be necessary

Table 8.1 Results for the RAO's heave motion peak optimization obtained by `FILLDIR`

maxnf = $100n$			maxnf = $1000n$		
f_{min}	improv. (%)	nf	f_{min}	improv. (%)	nf
0.8796	33.36	320	0.8572	35.06	982

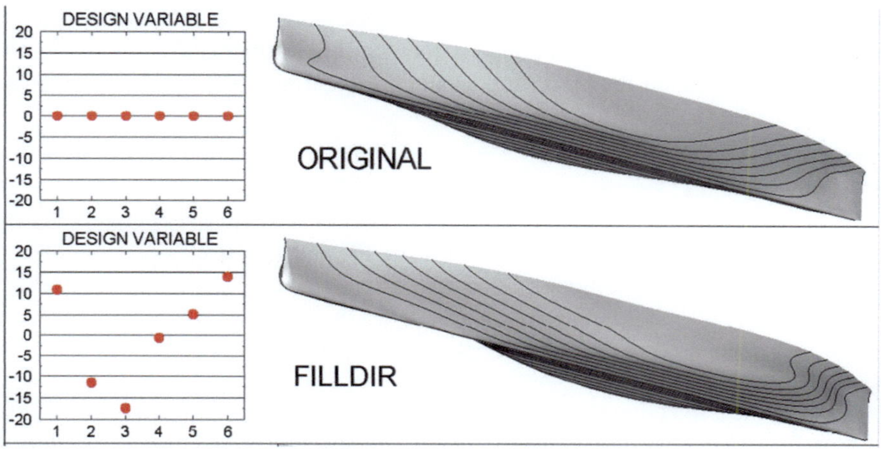

Fig. 8.6 S175 original and optimal hull shapes and design variables (maxnf = $100n$)

to reiterate Step 3 by choosing a different starting point $\bar{x}$. In general, the needed starting points are extracted from a pseudo-random sequence. In [8], a different selection rule is proposed that is based on a deterministic generation of points. In particular, the generation strategy is based on the `DIRECT` algorithm (described in Sect. 8.6). The idea is selecting the starting points required by the filled algorithm from the sequence of centroids generated by `DIRECT` when applied to a constant objective function. In this way the points are guaranteed to be sufficiently uniformly distributed over the feasible set. The resulting algorithm is called `FILLDIR`.

In Table 8.1 we report the objective function values computed by `FILLDIR` when $100n$ or $1000n$ maximum function evaluations are allowed. We also report the percentage improvement (improv.) of the computed shape with respect to the initial one.

Figure 8.6 shows the original and the optimized hull forms of the S175 containership and the corresponding design variables values in the case of maxnf = $100n$. As a consequence of the small differences in the numerical results among `DIRECT` and `DDFPSO` (i.e. design variable values and objective function optima) their corresponding optimized hull shapes are similar.

8.6 Partition Based Algorithms

If the objective function of problem (8.1) is not too expensive to evaluate, it is possible to use algorithms whose convergence is guaranteed in a deterministic fashion: as an example we consider partition based global optimization algorithms. The idea is to perform a sampling of the feasible domain on a set of points that becomes dense in the limit, thus guaranteeing strong theoretical convergence properties.

Algorithm 8.6.1: Partition Based Algorithm (PBA)

Step 0: Set $\mathcal{D}^0 = \mathcal{F}$, $l^0 = l$, $u^0 = u$, $I_0 = \{0\}$ and $k = 0$.
Step 1: Given the partition $\{\mathcal{D}^i : i \in I_k\}$ of $\mathcal{F}$ with

$$\mathcal{D}^i = \{x \in R^n : l^i \leq x \leq u^i\}, \quad \text{for all} \quad i \in I_k,$$

Use a selection strategy to choose a particular subset $I_k^* \subseteq I_k$.
Step 2: Use a partition strategy to divide each subinterval $\mathcal{D}^h$, $h \in I_k^*$, thus generating I_{k+1}.
Step 3: Update the current partition $\{\mathcal{D}^i : i \in I_{k+1}\}$.
Step 4: Set $k = k + 1$ and go to Step 1.

At each iteration PBA produces a new partition of the set $\mathcal{F}$. The choice of the set I_k^* of the hyperintervals to be partitioned, can be driven by information on the objective function.

On the basis of the particular selection and partition strategies, various algorithms showing different theoretical and computational performances can be obtained. In this respect, one significant example is the well-known DIRECT (i.e. DIvide RECTangles) algorithm [21].

At the generic kth iteration, a partition of $\mathcal{F}$ into hyperrectangles is built, by subdividing a set of *potentially optimal* hyperrectangles of the previous partition. The identification of a potentially optimal hyperrectangle is based on some measure of the hyperrectangle itself and on the value of f at its center. The refinement of the partition continues until a prescribed number of function evaluations has been performed, or another stopping criterion is satisfied. The minimum of f over all the centers of the final partition, and the corresponding centers, provide an approximate solution to the problem.

The DIRECT algorithm is specified once the following issues are defined:

- the way to measure the hyperrectangles (size);
- the way to select the potentially optimal hyperrectangles (selection strategy);
- the way to divide the hyperrectangles (partitioning strategy).

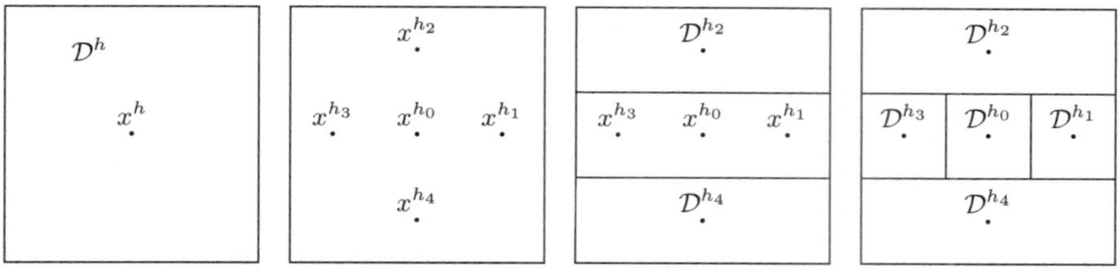

Fig. 8.7 Hyperrectangle partitioning example

In the original version of the algorithm, the size of a hyperrectangle is set as the distance d from its center to a vertex, i.e. half the diameter of the hyperrectangle [21].

Concerning the partition strategy, `DIRECT` divides a potentially optimal interval by trisection along the directions of the longest edges, as shown in Fig. 8.7. A rule based on the objective function value is proposed in [21] to choose among multiple longest sides; this rule ensures that smaller function values are in larger hyperrectangles, which, according to the selection strategy described below, are more likely to be divided at the next iterations. A simpler rule is described in [20].

In the selection strategy, a hyperrectangle $\mathcal{D}^h$ (having centroid x^h and size measure d^h) is defined potentially optimal if there exists $\alpha > 0$ such that

$$f(x^h) - \alpha d^h \leq f(x^i) - \alpha d^i \quad \forall\, \mathcal{D}^i, i \in I_k, \tag{8.9}$$

$$f(x^h) - \alpha d^h \leq f_{min} - \varepsilon |f_{min}|, \tag{8.10}$$

where f_{min} is the smallest value of f found so far, and ε is a parameter whose value is set at the beginning of the algorithm. A graphical interpretation of the selection criteria (8.9)–(8.10) can be given, as shown in Fig. 8.8. Each hyperrectangle is represented as a black dot with coordinates (d, f); criteria (8.9)–(8.10) select hyperrectangles on the lower-right convex hull of the points in the graph. In other words, the hyperrectangles are grouped according to their sizes, and the best ones (i.e. with smallest function values) in some of these groups are selected. This partitioning strategy allows a balance between local and global search, since it selects both small and large hyperrectangles, by weighting their function values with respect to the center-vertex distance. The parameter ε is a safeguard against excessive local search [13]; the larger it is, the higher the probability to exclude hyperrectangles with very good function values, but rather small sizes. Conversely, a small value of ε biases the algorithm to select small hyperrectangles as potentially optimal, thus forcing local search. In that sense, ε can be interpreted as a tuning parameter, to further control the balance between local and global search [13].

At each iteration `DIRECT` samples a set of points of $\mathcal{F}$, i.e. the centers of the hyperrectangles of the domain partition; its convergence is based on the fact that, as the number of iterations goes to infinity, the set of sampled points becomes everywhere dense in $\mathcal{F}$ [21].

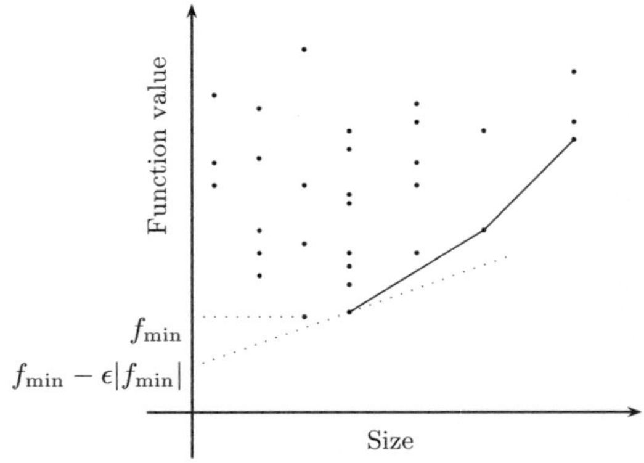

Fig. 8.8 Potentially optimal hyperrectangles

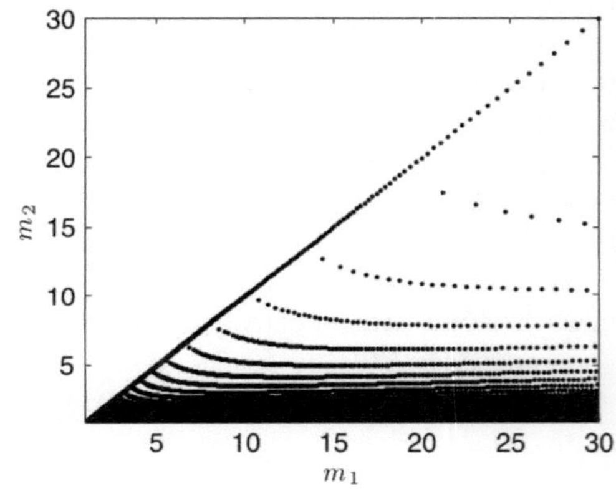

Fig. 8.9 A grid in the space of the masses

Partition based algorithms may be inefficient for most simulation-based global optimization problems since they typically require a high number of function evaluations to explore the feasible set. This sort-of intrinsic inefficiency can be overcome in different ways. For instance, a possibility is to adapt as much as possible the partition strategy to the problem by exploiting, for example, any previous information on the objective function behaviour as done for the gravitational waves detection problem (described in Sect. 8.2.4) in [46]. In particular, such an information can be obtained by performing a suitable discretization of the feasible domain that is known as "grid search" which is the reference algorithm in the astrophysics community for this problem [3].

The above discretization gives raise to a grid G of "promising" points (see Fig. 8.9) which contains significant information about the behaviour of the objective function but whose complete exploration requires an excessive number of function evaluations. The idea proposed in [46] is to exploit the grid information to drive the partitioning strategy of `DIRECT`.

We start from the observation that, if at some iteration of `DIRECT`, two hyperrectangles H_i and H_j have the same diameter, they are grouped together and discriminated against each other just on the basis of their representative function values. Nevertheless, given the highly nonuniform distribution of the points of G in Ω (see Fig. 8.9), it may happen that

$$|G \cap H_i| >> |G \cap H_j|,$$

where $|A|$ denotes the cardinality of a set A. In this case, if the representative function values $f(c_i)$ and $f(c_j)$ are close, it seems reasonable giving higher priority to H_i for further investigation, and hence subdivision, in the next iterations. This simple observation suggests that, in selecting the potentially optimal hyperrectangles, the algorithm should consider also the number of grid points that fall into them. Since the selection criteria are based on the representative function values and the sizes of the hyperrectangles, the most straightforward way to embody grid-driven information in the selection process is to modify the definition of hyperrectangle size. Specifically, in the selection criteria (8.9)–(8.10) the center-vertex distance d is substituted in [46] with

$$d^* := \begin{cases} |G \cap H| & \text{if } |G \cap H| > 1, \\ d & \text{otherwise.} \end{cases} \tag{8.11}$$

It is worth noting that, for every hyperrectangle, $d^* \geq d$ and, in particular, for those hyperrectangles having $d^* = d$, it results $d^* < 1$ (since $n = 2$).

With this choice, the hyperrectangles are grouped according to the number of grid points they contain, if this number is greater than one, otherwise according to the diameter length. This modified version of DIRECT is called DIRECT-G.

In Fig. 8.10 we report the set of points generated, after 3,000 function evaluations, by the two algorithms (DIRECT and DIRECT-G) applied to an instance of problem (8.6) with optimal solution $(\bar{m}_1, \bar{m}_2) = (1.4, 1.4)$. We see that DIRECT tends to uniformly cover the feasible domain, by oversampling regions

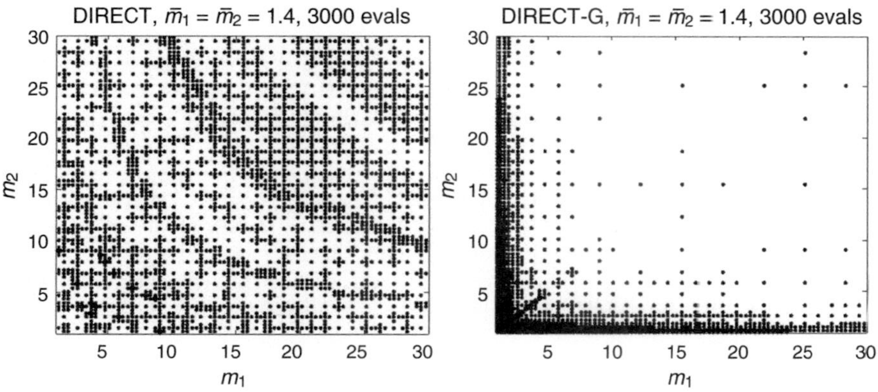

Fig. 8.10 Points of the feasible domain generated by DIRECT (*left*) and DIRECT-G (*right*) after 3,000 objective function evaluations, for a problem with solution $(\bar{m}_1, \bar{m}_1) = (1.4, 1.4)$

where G has very few points (see Fig. 8.9), and therefore $F(x)$ has very little variability. Conversely, DIRECT-G forces the partitioning strategy to follow the spatial distribution of the points of G, thus speeding up the progress toward the optimal point.

Numerical experiments on different test problems showed that DIRECT-G largely outperforms DIRECT and the grid search, the latter being the reference algorithm for the astrophysics community; in particular, DIRECT-G resulted very efficient on the hardest test problems.

8.7 Conclusions

In this chapter, we revised four real world applications arising from different fields that result in challenging simulation-based global optimization problems. Consequently we described four ad-hoc solution algorithms, belonging to significant classes of methods in the literature. In doing so, we identified some peculiar properties of each problem and matched them to the characteristics of the solution methods. In conclusions, the four case-studies indicate that the more the algorithm is tailored to the specific application, the more satisfactory are the results both in terms of computational effort and of solution quality.

References

1. Ali, M.M., Törn, A., Viitanen, S.: A numerical comparison of some modified controlled random search algorithms. J. Glob. Optim. **11**, 377–385 (1997)
2. Archetti, F., Schoen, F.: A survey on the global optimization problem: General theory and computational approaches. Ann. Oper. Res. **1**(2), 87–110 (1984)
3. Babak, S., Balasubramanian, R., Churches, D., Cokelaer, T., Sathyaprakash, B.S.: A template bank to search for gravitational waves from inspiralling compact binaries I: physical models. Classical Quantum Gravity **23**, 5477–5504 (2006)
4. Bertolazzi, P., Guerra, C., Liuzzi, G.: A global optimization algorithm for protein surface alignment. BMC Bioinf. **11**, 488 (2010). doi:10.1186/1471-2105-11-488
5. Besl, P.J., McKay, N.D.: A method for registration of 3-d shapes. IEEE Trans. Pattern Anal. Mach. Intell. **14**, 239–255 (1992)
6. Blanchet, L., Rlyer, B., Wiseman, A.G.: Gravitational waveforms from inspiralling compact binaries to second-post-Newtonian order. Classical Quantum Gravity **13**, 575–584 (1996)
7. Brachetti, P., De Felice Ciccoli, M., Di Pillo, G., Lucidi, S.: A new version of the Price's algorithm for global optimization. J. Glob. Optim. **10**, 165–184 (1997)
8. Campana, E.F., Liuzzi, G., Lucidi, S., Peri, D., Piccialli, V., Pinto, A.: New global optimization methods for ship design problems. Optim. Eng. **10**, 533–555 (2009)
9. Cho, Z., Jones, J.P., Singh, M.: Foundations of Medical Imaging. Wiley, New York (1993)
10. Chubar, O., Elleaume, P., Chavanne, J.: A 3d magnetostatics computer code for insertion devices. J. Synchrotron Radiat. **5**, 481–484 (1998)
11. Cirio, L., Lucidi, S., Parasiliti, F., Villani, M.: A global optimization approach for the synchronous motors design by finite element analysis. J. Appl. Electromagn. Mech. **16**, 13–27 (2002)

12. Elleaume, P., Chubar, O., Chavanne, J.: Computing 3d magnetic field from insertion devices. In: Proceedings of the PAC97 Conference, pp. 3509–3511 (1997)
13. Gablonsky, J.M., Kelley, C.T.: A locally-biased form of the DIRECT algorithm. J. Glob. Optim. **21**(1), 27–37 (2001)
14. Garcia, I., Ortigosa, P.M., Casado, L.G., Herman, G.T., Matej, S.: Multidimensional optimization in image reconstruction from projections. In: Bomze, I.M., Csendes, T., Horst, R., Pardalos, P. (eds.) Developments in Global Optimization, pp. 289–300. Kluwer, Dordrecht (1997)
15. Ge, R.P.: A filled function method for finding a global minimizer of a function of several variables. Math. Program. **46**(1–3), 191–204 (1990)
16. Ge, R.P., Qin, Y.: The globally convexized filled functions for global optimization. Appl. Math. Comput. **35**(2), 131–158 (1990)
17. Ge, R.P., Qin, Y.F.: A class of filled functions for finding global minimizers of a function of several variables. J. Optim. Theory Appl. **54**(2), 241–252 (1987)
18. Haacke, E.M., Brown, R.W., Thompson, M.R., Vankatesan, R.: Magnetic Resonance Imaging: Physical Principles and Sequence Design. Wiley, New York (1999)
19. Hendrix, E., Ortigosa, P., Garcia, I.: On success rates for controlled random search. J. Glob. Optim. **21**, 239–263 (2001)
20. Jones, D.R.: DIRECT global optimization. In: Floudas, C.A., Pardalos, P.M. (eds.) Encyclopedia of Optimization, pp. 725–735. Springer, New York (2009)
21. Jones, D.R., Perttunen, C.D., Stuckman, B.E.: Lipschitzian optimization without the Lipschitz constant. J. Optim. Theory Appl. **79**(1), 157–181 (1993)
22. Klepper, O., Rousse, D.I.: A procedure to reduce parameter uncertainty for complex models by comparison with real system output illustrated on a potato growth model. Agric. Syst. **36**, 375–395 (1991)
23. Liang, Z., Lauterbur, P.C.: Principles of Magnetic Resonance Imaging: A Signal Processing Approach. IEEE Press, New York (2000)
24. Liu, X.: Finding global minima with a computable filled function. J. Glob. Optim. **19**(2), 151–161 (2001)
25. Liuzzi, G., Lucidi, S., Parasiliti, F., Villani, M.: Multi-objective optimization techniques for the design of induction motors. IEEE Trans. Magn. **39**, 1261–1264 (2003)
26. Liuzzi, G., Lucidi, S., Piccialli, V., Sotgiu, A.: A magnetic resonance device designed via global optimization techniques. Math. Program. **101**(2), 339–364 (2004)
27. Liuzzi, G., Lucidi, S., Piccialli, V.: A partition-based global optimization algorithm. J. Glob. Optim. **48**, 113–128 (2010)
28. Locatelli, M., Schoen, F.: Global Optimization: Theory, Algorithms, and Applications. MOS-SIAM Series on Optimization. SIAM, Philadelphia (2013)
29. Lucidi, S., Piccialli, V.: New classes of globally convexized filled functions for global optimization. J. Glob. Optim. **24**(2), 219–236 (2002)
30. Lucidi, S., Piccioni, M.: Random tunneling by means of acceptance-rejection sampling for global optimization. J. Optim. Theory Appl. **62**, 255–279 (1989)
31. Lucidi, S., Sciandrone, M.: A derivative-free algorithm for bound constrained optimization. Comput. Optim. Appl. **21**(2), 119–142 (2002)
32. Milano, L., Barone, F., Milano, M.: Time domain amplitude and frequency detection of gravitational waves from coalescing binaries. Phys. Rev. D **55**(8), 4537–4554 (1997)
33. Mohanty, S.D.: Hierarchical search strategy for the detection of gravitational waves from coalescing binaries: extension to post-newtonian waveforms. Phys. Rev. D **57**(2), 630–658 (1998)
34. Mohanty, S.D., Dhurandhar, S.V.: Hierarchical search strategy for the detection of gravitational waves from coalescing binaries. Phys. Rev. D **54**(12), 7108–7128 (1996)
35. Newman, J.N.: Marine Hydrodynamics. Wei Cheng Cultural Enteroprise Company, Taipei (1977)

36. Nsakanda, A.L., Diaby, M., Price, W.L.: Hybrid genetic approach for solving large-scale capacitated cell formation problems with multiple routings. Eur. J. Oper. Res. **171**(3), 1051–1070 (2006)
37. Nsakanda, A.L., Price, W.L., Diaby, M., Gravel, M.: Ensuring population diversity in genetic algorithms: A technical note with application to the cell formation problem. Eur. J. Oper. Res. **178**(2), 634–638 (2007)
38. Owen, B.J.: Search templates for gravitational waves from inspiraling binaries: choice of template spacing. Phys. Rev. D **53**(12), 6749–6761 (1996)
39. Peri, D., Rossetti, M., Campana, E.F.: Design optimization of ship hulls via cfd techniques. J. Ship Res. **45**(2), 140–149 (2001)
40. Price, W.L.: A controlled random search procedure for global optimization. In: Dixon, L., Szego, G. (eds.) Towards Global Optimization, vol. 2. North-Holland, Amsterdam (1978)
41. Price, W.L.: Global optimization algorithms for a CAD workstation. J. Optim. Theory Appl. **55**, 133–146 (1983)
42. Price, W.L., Woodhams, F.: Optimising accelerator for CAD workstations. IEEE Proc. Comput. Digit. Tech. **135**(4), 214–221 (1988)
43. Price, W.L.: Global optimization by controlled random search. J. Optim. Theory Appl. **40**, 333–348 (1983)
44. Rastrigin, L.A.: The convergence of the random search method in the extremal control of a many parameter system. Autom. Remote Control **24**(10), 1337–1342 (1963)
45. Schoen, F.: Stochastic techniques for global optimization: a survey of recent advances. J. Glob. Optim. **1**(3), 207–228 (1991)
46. Serafino, D., Liuzzi, G., Piccialli, V., Riccio, F., Toraldo, G.: A modified dividing rectangles algorithm for a problem in astrophysics. J. Optim. Theory Appl. **151**(1), 175–190 (2011)
47. Thorne, K.S.: Gravitational radiation. In: Hawking, S.W., Israel, W. (eds.) 300 Years of Gravitation, pp. 330–458. Cambridge University Press, Cambridge (1987)
48. Törn, A., Ali, M., Viitanen, S.: Stochastic global optimization: Problem classes and solution techniques. J. Glob. Optim. **14**, 437–447 (1999)
49. Villani, M., Daidone, A., Parasiliti, F., Lucidi, S.: A new method for the design optimization of three-phase induction motors. IEEE Trans. Magn. **34**, 2932–2935 (1998)
50. Xu, Z., Huang, H.X., Pardalos, P.M., Xu, C.X.: Filled functions for unconstrained global optimization. J. Glob. Optim. **20**(1), 49–65 (2001)
51. Zhang, L.-S., Ng, C.-K., Li, D., Tian, W.-W.: A new filled function method for global optimization. J. Glob. Optim. **28**(1), 17–43 (2004)
52. Zinflou, A., Gagné, C., Gravel, M., Price, W.L.: Pareto memetic algorithm for multiple objective optimization with an industrial application. J. Heuristics **14**(4), 313–333 (2008)

Chapter 9
Personnel Scheduling in Queues with Time-varying Arrival Rates: Applications of Simulation-Optimization

Mieke Defraeye and Inneke Van Nieuwenhuyse

9.1 Introduction

In many service systems, customer arrival rates fluctuate over time (e.g., over the course of a day or a week): for instance in emergency departments (EDs) [46, 79] and call centers [27, 53], but also in airline terminals [54, 71], in restaurants [14, 39], and in retail stores [51, 55]. Consider for instance Fig. 9.1, which shows the hourly arrival rate of patients at the ED of a regional Belgian hospital: as evident from the plot, this ED is confronted with peak demand in the morning hours and early afternoon; demand then stays relatively high until 8 p.m., after which it declines rather steeply during the evening hours and stays low during the night. The peaks in the demand may cause waiting times to increase severely if personnel capacity is not adjusted accordingly. In service systems with time-varying demand, appropriate capacity planning thus is the natural means to control customer waiting times.

Thompson [82] specifies two managerial challenges for personnel planning in service systems: shift schedules need to be constructed so that they deliver the desired quality of service in an inexpensive way, or alternatively, to maximize the performance using the available capacity [82]. The capacity planning problem can thus be decomposed into two components [41]: *performance measurement* aims to quantify the customer quality of service (waiting time, queue length, abandonment percentage) that follows from a given personnel schedule, while the actual *capacity optimization* refers to the search procedure that identifies good schedules among a (potentially large) set of alternatives.

M. Defraeye • I. Van Nieuwenhuyse (✉)
Department of Decision Sciences and Information Management, Research Center for Operations Management, KU Leuven, Naamsestraat 69, 3000 Leuven, Belgium
e-mail: mieke.defraeye@kuleuven.be; inneke.vannieuwenhuyse@kuleuven.be

G. Dellino, C. Meloni (eds.), *Uncertainty Management in Simulation-Optimization of Complex Systems*, Operations Research/Computer Science Interfaces Series 59,
DOI 10.1007/978-1-4899-7547-8_9

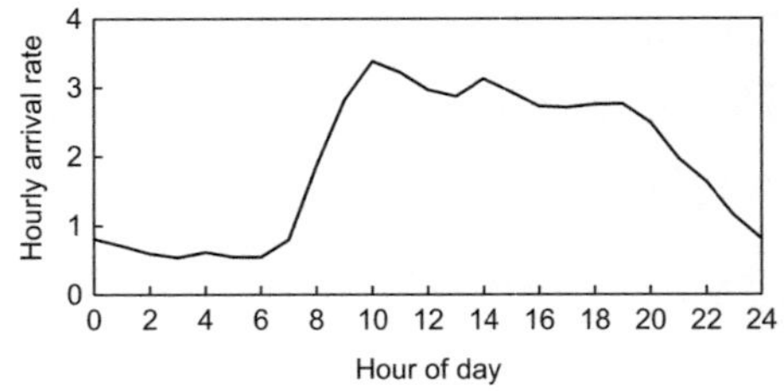

Fig. 9.1 Time-varying arrival rate at a Belgian ED

This chapter explores the opportunities of discrete-event simulation in optimizing capacity for $M(t)/G/s(t) + G$ service systems with an exhaustive service policy (i.e., servers work overtime if service is ongoing at the time that the server is scheduled to go off duty). Following the Kendall notation [52], the $M(t)/G/s(t) + G$ queue represents a system with time-varying Poisson arrivals (the $M(t)$), a general service time distribution (the first G), time-varying capacity levels (the $s(t)$), and abandonments that follow a general distribution (the last G). The system assumptions (which are further detailed in Sect. 9.2) make this setting highly realistic and thus relevant for many real-life settings. Furthermore, as detailed in Sect. 9.3, discrete-event simulation is the only methodology that allows an accurate estimation of system performance in this setting, and therefore is particularly appealing to insert into an optimization framework. In Sect. 9.4, we then discuss two approaches (a fast two-step heuristic and a more involved branch-and-bound method) that search for minimum cost schedules in view of meeting a predefined customer service level over the time horizon. A detailed comparison of these methods follows in Sect. 9.5: both methods are compared in terms of the final solution's shift cost and the number of simulations that is required to run the algorithm to completion. The heuristic generally yields solutions close to the estimated optimum (that results from the branch-and-bound method); moreover, these can often be improved with little computational effort by the branch-and-bound method. In addition, we check the sensitivity of the methods to the number of replications that is used in the simulation model. Section 9.6 summarizes the opportunities for further research.

9.2 Problem Setting and Notation

Consider a single-stage multiserver service system, as depicted in Fig. 9.2. The current time is represented as t and ranges between 0 and time horizon T (i.e., the opening hours of the service system). The *arrivals* of customers to the system follow a Poisson distribution with time-varying rate $\lambda(t)$; this arrival rate is assumed to follow a recurrent (and, hence, predictable) pattern. The shape of the arrival curve is commonly observed to be trimodal, bimodal or unimodal [8, 33, 81]: i.e., arrival patterns display three peaks per day (e.g., restaurants), two peaks per day (such as at traffic toll booths), or one peak per day. The Poisson assumption for the arrival process is supported by empirical observations [9, 35]. Alternatively, we might have

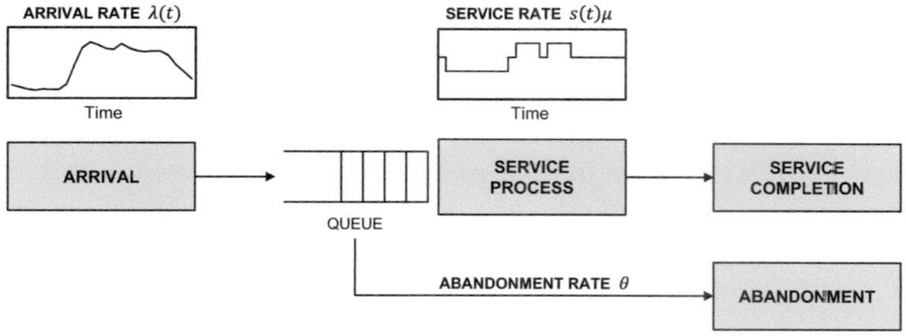

Fig. 9.2 Schematic representation of a single-stage queueing system with time-varying demand

opted to model the arrival rate as a piecewise constant function. This is often done in the literature when real-life data are available on an aggregated basis (e.g., per hour or half hour, as in [3, 35, 46]).

The patience of customers is limited; they may opt to leave the queue. This behavior is commonly referred to as *abandonment* [17], and is mainly caused by long waiting times (e.g., Johnson et al. [50] report that almost 77 % of untreated patients in an emergency department state that they abandoned because of long waiting times). In call centers and EDs, abandonments are prevalent. Though abandonments should be avoided, they tend to have a stabilizing effect by reducing the load on the system [36, 88]. We assume that each customer that leaves the system is “lost". The service and abandonment processes follow a *general distribution*, with the per server service rate μ and the abandonment rate θ, respectively. Prior research commonly assumes exponential service and abandonment distributions (see [28, 43, 91], among others). This assumption may facilitate the evaluation of customer waiting times by analytical (e.g., queueing) models. Non-exponential distributions, however, appear to be more common in practice: e.g., [9, 12] observe Lognormal and Erlang distributions, respectively (both articles study a call center context).

Changes in the available capacity are allowed only at fixed points in time. The intervals during which capacity remains constant are referred to as *staffing intervals*, with length Δ_s. There are I_s staffing intervals in the observed time horizon; set $\mathbf{I}_s = \{1, \ldots, I_s\}$ contains the staffing interval indices. We assume that the service policy is exhaustive: when the service provider is scheduled to leave (because the shift ends), he/she completes the ongoing service (if any) before leaving and thus works overtime if required. This type of policy is relevant in many real-life customer service systems. Yet, prior literature often implicitly assumes a preemptive service policy, where customers in service rejoin the queue when the service provider is scheduled to leave. As shown by [40], disregarding the exhaustive policy can severely bias the estimated waiting time (in particular if the number of servers changes frequently and when service times are long).

The customers in the system are treated following a first-in, first-out policy. We define $W(t)$, the waiting time that a customer would experience upon arrival at time t, and assume the maximum acceptable waiting time is τ. The probability of excessive waiting, $\Pr(W(t) > \tau)$, then provides a measure for the customer quality of service (QoS), at any given time t (note that the probability of excessive waiting is the complement of the customer service level, see e.g., [27, 36]). We require this probability to consistently lie below a user-defined target α:

$$\Pr(W(t) > \tau) \leq \alpha \qquad \forall t \in [0, T]. \tag{9.1}$$

In this way, we ensure a minimum QoS level to all customers, regardless of the time of arrival. Prior literature often focused on the time-varying delay probability [25, 35] which may be too crude as a metric in many service systems, as it does not take the length of the waiting time into consideration (often, small waiting times are acceptable). The probability of excessive waiting is often more relevant.

In this chapter, two approaches are compared that clearly show how simulation and optimization can be combined successfully for shift scheduling with time-varying demand for service. We solve a shift scheduling problem with a stochastic performance constraint (given by Expression 9.1). We assume that K eligible shift types exist (these are assumed to be known in advance). Each shift type specifies the start time of a work shift, its duration and the timing of breaks within that shift. Shift vector $\mathbf{w} = \{w(1), \ldots, w(K)\}$ defines how many workers are assigned to each of the K shift types. c_w represents the resulting shift cost (expressed in man-hours). We then tackle the shift scheduling problem, under a (stochastic) service level constraint:

$$\begin{aligned} \min c_w = & \sum_{i_s=1}^{I_s} \sum_{j=1}^{K} a(j, i_s) w(j) & \\ \text{s.t. } & \Pr(W(t) > \tau) \leq \alpha & \forall t \in [0, T] \\ & w(j) \geq 0 \text{ and integer}, & \forall j = 1, \ldots, K, \end{aligned} \tag{9.2}$$

with $a(j, i_s)$ the elements of the shift specification matrix $\mathbf{A}$. Variable $a(j, i_s)$ equals 1 if interval i_s is an active period in shift j; otherwise, $a(j, i_s)$ equals 0.

Note that the system under study assumes that customers and servers are homogeneous (there is only a single customer class, and all servers have the same skills; [27]). This is in fact still a simplification of reality: in real-life, service systems are often characterized by heterogeneity in customers and/or servers (in an ED, for instance, not all customers have the same priority or service requirements; at the same time, not all service providers have the same skills). Moreover, the system only considers a single service step: in reality, many service systems consist of a network of service steps.

9.3 Implications for Performance Measurement and Capacity Planning

Performance measurement specifies how to evaluate the time-dependent customer quality of service pertaining to any given staffing or scheduling solution. Many methodologies have been put forward to evaluate performance in systems with time-varying demand; Table 9.1 contains a summary. For each methodology, the table indicates whether we found articles that account for abandonments (AB), general distributions for the service and/or abandonment process (G), and an exhaustive service policy (EXH), which are the main assumptions of the system under study. Furthermore, it indicates if the methodology could be applied to systems with heterogeneous customers or servers (HE), and a network of process steps (N).

Stationary approximations (SA) are by far the most popular approach. These divide the time horizon in smaller intervals and approximate the nonstationary system by a series of stationary queueing models. Numerous SAs exist, such as the pointwise stationary approximation (PSA, [29, 30, 34, 85]), the stationary independent period-by-period approach (SIPP, [32]), and the modified offered load approximation (MOL, [19, 25, 47, 48, 58, 72, 73]); see also the review papers by [20, 36, 89] for further references. In theory, stationary approximations can be applied to any nonstationary model, provided that the stationary counterpart can be evaluated. However, when departing from the typical assumptions (e.g., exponential service and abandonment times), the stationary models are often difficult to solve, necessitating the use of approximations (e.g., [86] and [44] approximate the performance metrics of the $M/G/s + G$ queue). Moreover, decomposing the problem in several stationary models implies that the latter are implicitly assumed to be independent. This assumption tends to be less valid as service times increase [32]. Finally, SAs are unable to take into account the impact of the exhaustive service policy on performance.

Numerical integration of ODEs is particularly ill-suited for our type of system, because it cannot take into account abandonments or exhaustiveness of the service policy. The method typically assumes exponential service time distributions.

Table 9.1 Performance evaluation in queues with time-varying arrival rates

Methodology	Key references	AB	G	EXH	HE	N
Stationary approximations	[20, 36, 89]	x	x		x	x
Numerical integration of ODEs	[31, 42, 54]					
Randomization approaches	[16, 40]	x	x	x		
Closure approximations	[15, 74, 78, 80]		x		x*	x*
Discrete-time modeling	[13, 83, 84, 90]	x	x			
Fluid and diffusion approximations	[2, 49, 60, 64, 66, 68–70, 77, 87]	x	x		x	x
Discrete-event simulation	[5, 6, 11, 26, 56]	x	x	x	x	x

x*: only for infinite server queues

Moreover, [42] and [45] have shown that, even for the $M(t)/M/s(t)$ queue, the randomization approach is preferred over numerical integration of the ODEs because it yields similar accuracy and requires significantly less computational effort. The randomization approach by Creemers et al. [16] extends the method of Ingolfsson [40] to nonstationary queues with general arrival, service and abandonment times and an exhaustive service policy, by approximating the $G(t)/G(t)/s(t) + G(t)$ queue using phase-type distributions. They report that long computation times may be required to achieve accurate performance estimates, especially if the service and abandonment process are not Poisson distributed. Closure approximations [15, 74, 78, 80] approximate the (infinite) set of differential equations by a limited number of equations (e.g., two in [78] or five in [15]), hence they are said to "close" the set of differential equations. We did not find articles that address networks with a finite number of servers (though [74] applies the approach to multiclass networks of $Ph(t)/Ph(t)/\infty$ queues). Closure approximations, however, are cumbersome to implement and dominated by other methods in terms of both accuracy and computation speed [42]. Discrete-time modeling approaches (DTM) allow for general service times (see [84] and [90] for further references), but require long computation times [45]. To the best of our knowledge, all existing DTM papers study systems with capacity levels that are constant over time.

Fluid models tend to be more applicable in systems with many servers and high traffic intensity; they may fail to capture system dynamics accurately [2, 4, 49] if the system is underloaded. Fluid models have been rigorously studied in prior literature (fluid approximations for exponential service and/or abandonment time can be found in [49, 64, 67–70, 77]; models for general service/abandonment times can be found in [59–63, 67, 87] provide models applicable to networks).

Discrete-event simulation is a widely adopted methodology; it enables to model complexities that go beyond the capabilities of analytical and numerical methods. This particularly holds for the $M(t)/G/s(t)+G$ queue that is studied in this chapter, for which no closed-form results are available. We refer to [56] for a comprehensive textbook on discrete-event simulation; reviews concerning simulation-optimization approaches can be found in [5, 6, 11, 26]. Simulation-optimization approaches that target systems with nonstationary arrivals are presented in [3, 7, 21, 25, 46, 79, 92]. Some authors present optimization approaches that rely on general simulation models (e.g.,[7, 21, 25]), whereas others insert a context-specific simulation model into the optimization framework (e.g., [3, 46, 79] focus on emergency departments; [92] targets bed capacity planning in long-term care).

The performance evaluation methods in Table 9.1 provide a means to evaluate the quality of service of a given a personnel schedule; *capacity planning*, on the other hand, defines how good staffing solutions can be identified in a potentially large solution space. If a stochastic performance constraint is specified (e.g., a target service level), capacity optimization typically uses an iterative approach. Any of the performance evaluation methods described in Sect. 9.3 can be applied in an iterative capacity optimization algorithm (see for instance [43], who use a randomization approach for $M(t)/M/s(t)$ queues). Yet, discrete-event simulation is clearly the preferred method when analyzing realistic systems, because it provides great flexibility in terms of model assumptions. While the randomization approach by [16] captures all complexities in the system studied, its accuracy is found to be variable (depending on the squared coefficient of variation of the service and abandonment distribution, see [16]). Moreover, the long computation times render the method less practical in iterative optimization algorithms.

9.4 Methodology

We start with a description of the simulation model (in Sect. 9.4.1), that is used to evaluate the feasibility of the chance-constraint in Problem 9.2. Section 9.4.2 describes a fast heuristic that decomposes the problem in two stages by first selecting the staffing requirements that meet the performance constraint (first step), and then fitting a shift schedule to these staff requirements (second step). Then in Sect. 9.4.3, we describe a branch-and-bound approach that further improves on the heuristic solution to obtain an estimated optimal solution.

9.4.1 Performance Evaluation

The probability of excessive waiting, $\Pr(W(t) > \tau)$, is measured from the simulation model by means of *virtual waiting times*. The virtual waiting time corresponds to the time between t and the earliest time at which a (scheduled) server becomes available, because all customers that arrived before t have been served [37, 57, 65]:

$$W(t) = \min\{w : \left(N^t(t + w) \leq s(t + w) - 1\right) \wedge (w \geq 0)\}, \tag{9.3}$$

with $s(t + w)$ the capacity at time $t + w$ and $N^t(t + w)$ the number of customers arrived before time t that are still in system at time $t + w$. Note that the virtual waiting time is measured at a particular time instant (as opposed to *observed* waits, which are measured over an interval). The virtual waiting time distribution can be measured in a straightforward way through simulation. We insert a virtual (dummy) customer into the system at each time $t \in \mathbf{t}_p$ in replication r, such that the virtual waiting time $W_r(t)$ equals the time at which this dummy customer would enter service. Let R represent the total number of replications in the simulation run. Define $\delta_r(t)$ as a binary variable that signals whether the virtual waiting time exceeds the target τ for a given time t and replication r:

$$\delta_r(t) = \begin{cases} 1 \text{ if } W_r(t) > \tau, \\ 0 \text{ otherwise}. \end{cases}$$

The probability of excessive waiting at time t then can be estimated as:

$$\Pr(W(t) > \tau) = \frac{1}{R}\sum_{r=1}^{R} \delta_r(t)\,. \tag{9.4}$$

9.4.2 Heuristic Approach: Two-Step Sequential Method

A vast majority of the shift scheduling literature presumes the minimum staffing requirements are known in advance. A feasible—yet not necessarily optimal—solution can thus be found by searching for the minimum required capacity (i.e., ignoring the shift constraints) and inserting these minimum staffing requirements in a traditional shift scheduling algorithm. Though this decomposition scheme results in a heuristic solution, the stochastic performance constraint is (conveniently) accounted for during the staffing step, such that shift scheduling becomes a deterministic problem. As staffing and scheduling problems are solved in a sequential manner, we refer to this approach as the two-step heuristic.

The minimum staffing requirement problem minimizes the total staffing cost (c_s, expressed in man-hours), in view of meeting the performance constraint in Expression (9.1) at any time t over the time horizon:

$$\begin{aligned} &\min\ c_s \\ &\text{s.t.}\ \Pr(W(t) > \tau) \leq \alpha && \forall t \in [0, T] \\ &\qquad s(i_s) \geq 0 \text{ and integer}, && \forall i_s \in \mathbf{I}_s\,. \end{aligned} \tag{9.5}$$

The staffing vector $\mathbf{s}$ specifies the required available capacity $s(i_s)$ during each staffing interval i_s; the staffing cost c_s represents the total number of man-hours corresponding to $\mathbf{s}$.

We applied the ISA(τ) heuristic [21] to solve Problem (9.5). This simulation-optimization heuristic determines the minimum capacity that is needed to meet the performance target. In doing so, shift constraints are not taken into consideration. In ISA(τ) the staffing vector is altered iteratively, based on the estimated customer performance (see Fig. 9.3). The probability of excessive waiting that corresponds to a given staffing solution is estimated using a discrete-event simulation model. The deviation between the realized probability of excessive waiting, $\Pr(W(t) > \tau)$, and the target α, is then used to alter the staffing function. In each staffing interval, we multiply the staffing vector by an amplification factor: larger deviations from the target give rise to more drastic changes in the capacity level. ISA(τ) is inspired by the Iterative Staffing Algorithm (ISA) of Feldman et al. [25], a promising simulation-based technique for determining staffing requirements (in view of stabilizing *delay* probability).

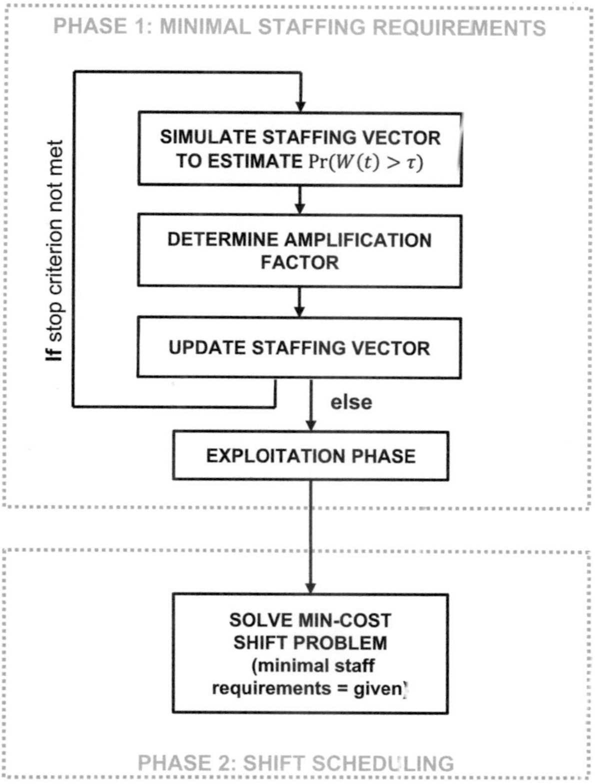

Fig. 9.3 Schematic representation of the two-step heuristic

In a second phase, personnel schedules are constructed that meet the shift constraints (see Fig. 9.3). The shift scheduling algorithm takes the minimum staffing requirements as given inputs. We apply the traditional min-cost shift problem, as suggested by Dantzig [18] (more sophisticated models can be found in [10, 76]; see [23, 24] for an extensive review and bibliography):

$$\begin{aligned} &\min\ c_w \\ &\text{s.t.} \sum_{j=1}^{K} a(j, i_s) w(j) \geq s(i_s)\ \forall i_s \in \mathbf{I}_s \\ &w(j) \geq 0 \text{ and integer} \qquad \forall j = 1, \ldots. K \end{aligned} \tag{9.6}$$

The two-step method is a heuristic: the strict separation of the staffing problem and the shift scheduling problem may give rise to suboptimal solutions (different staffing solutions may result in shift solutions that, while they are all feasible, vary widely in cost). To evaluate how severely this shortcoming affects the solution quality, we compare the heuristic to an estimated optimal shift schedule, which is found by the branch-and-bound approach that is discussed in the next section.

9.4.3 Branch-and-Bound Method

The branch-and-bound algorithm suggested in [22] improves on the heuristic solution described above, through the application of a simulation-based branch-and-bound algorithm. The algorithm consists of an enumerative search procedure that targets $M(t)/G/s(t) + G$ systems with limited opening hours and an exhaustive service policy. A search tree is constructed, in which each node represents a staffing vector. An illustration of the tree structure is presented in Fig. 9.4, for 3 staffing intervals. Each node in the tree represents a staffing vector **s**, with corresponding

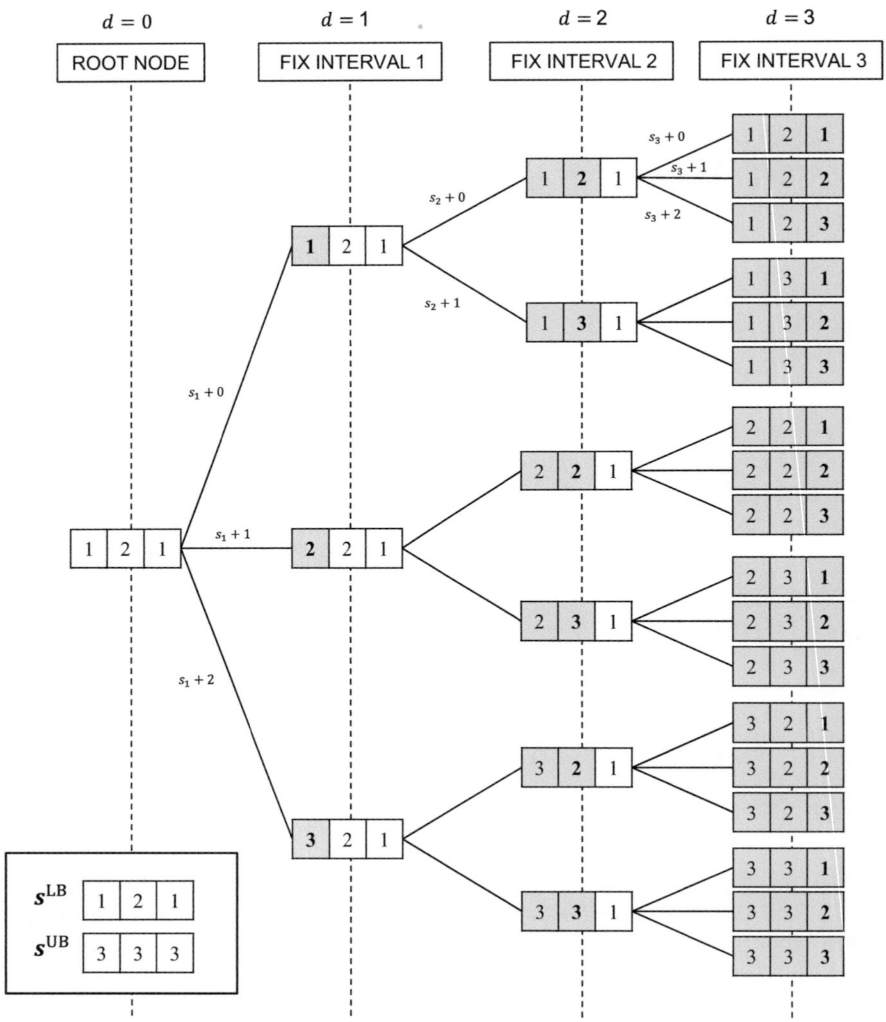

Fig. 9.4 Illustration of the tree structure in the branch-and-bound approach

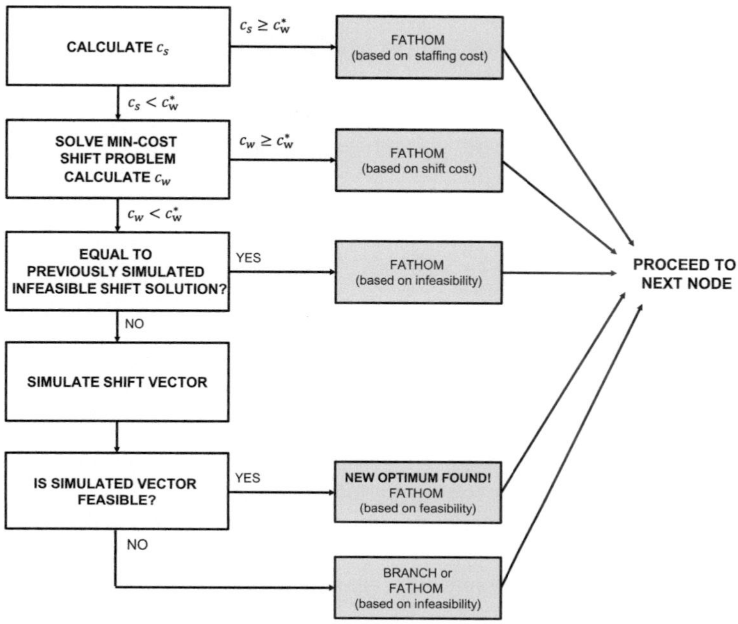

Fig. 9.5 Schematic representation of node exploration in the branch-and-bound approach

staffing cost c_s. The root node of the tree is initialized to a lower bound, $\mathbf{s}^{LB}$ (staffing vectors with capacity smaller than $\mathbf{s}^{LB}$ in at least one interval are infeasible, they need not be considered in the search tree). Starting from the root node, $\mathbf{s}$ is increased throughout the search tree. Each level in the tree is denoted by its depth $d = 0, \ldots, I_s$ ($d = 0$ represents the depth of the root node). Child nodes are generated from a parent node by adding capacity to a given staffing interval; the staffing levels in the other intervals are identical to those of the parent node. Throughout the algorithm, the best (feasible) shift vector found so far is stored ($\mathbf{w}^*$, with shift cost c_w^*).

As shown in Fig. 9.5, each node is explored in a step-wise manner in view of limiting the number of simulations, and to identify the regions of the solution space that cannot contain the optimum. For each node (or, staffing vector) the corresponding shift vector is retrieved from Problem (9.6); it is solved only for nodes with $c_s < c_w^*$. A simulation run is performed only if the solution can improve the optimum in terms of cost (i.e., if $c_w < c_w^*$), unless we know form previous simulation runs that the solution will be infeasible because it contains insufficient capacity in given time periods. In that case, checking the performance constraint through simulation is redundant (for more details, see [22]). The use of discrete-event simulation implies that we *estimate* the feasibility of the chance constraint. Although reducing the accuracy of the simulation model (through a lower number of replications per simulation run) only affected the optimal cost to a limited extent, the performance constraint may no longer be met (see Sect. 9.5).

The branch-and-bound algorithm requires an initial feasible solution; though we use the algorithm here to improve on the heuristic solution obtained from the two-step approach, other initial feasible solutions can also be inserted. As shown in [22], the algorithm succeeds in finding the estimated optimum with limited computational effort in small-scale systems (with an average offered load, $\bar{\lambda}/\mu$, ranging between 5 and 15).

9.5 Numerical Results

We assess to what extent solutions of the heuristic approach (i.e., the two-step method; Sect. 9.4.2) differ from the estimated optimum (obtained by means of the branch-and-bound algorithm; Sect. 9.4.3). Additionally, we examine how the number of replications affects the shift cost and the number of simulation runs needed in the simulation-optimization algorithms.

The test set consists of 972 instances and is constructed by varying the parameters in Table 9.6. We assume that the service system is open 12 h per day ($T = 12$) and that all arrival rates follow a sinusoidal pattern with 2 peaks per day, fluctuating around the average rate $\bar{\lambda}$:

$$\lambda(t) = \bar{\lambda}\left(1 + 0.5\sin\left(\frac{2\pi t}{12}\right)\right). \tag{9.7}$$

Different settings for the average arrival rate, the distribution of service and abandonment rates, the performance target α, the maximum allowed waiting time, and the staffing interval length are included in the test set (see Table 9.6). Our numerical experiment assumes that the arrival process follows a nonstationary Poisson distribution; as performance is evaluated by means of simulation, any general arrival process could be used. Experiments are performed for a small number of replications per simulation run (i.e., 100, as suggested in [7]) and a larger number (2,500, as suggested in [21]), to assess the impact of this parameter on the estimated optimal solution and on computation speed. We use the same shift set as [22]: a shift is 4, 6, or 8 h long and may include a 1-h break. This yields a set of five shifts for $\Delta_s = 240$ min, a set of 12 shifts for $\Delta_s = 120$ min, and a set of 45 shifts for $\Delta_s = 60$ min (the shifts set is provided in the appendix). The exhaustive service policy may cause overtime to occur in our experiments each time a shift ends (Table 9.2).

Two-Step Heuristic vs. Branch-and-Bound Approach Table 9.3 presents the main results of the branch-and-bound algorithm, for different settings of the staffing interval length, and for $R = 2,500$. Figure 9.6 represents the performance of the branch-and-bound approach graphically, for $R = 2,500$: each cell displays the percentage of problem instances in the test set that requires a given amount of simulations while exploring the branch-and-bound tree (i.e., the rows) and the cost reduction compared to the initial feasible solution that was realized in doing

Table 9.2 Experimental setting

Parameter	Parameter values
Service rate (customers/hour)	$\{1, 2, 4\}$
Offered load	$\{5, 10, 15\}$
Abandonment rate (customers/hour)	$\{0, \mu\}$
Max wait τ (min)	$\{0, 10, 20\}$
Squared coefficient service and abandonment times	$\{0.5, 1, 2\}$
Staffing interval Δ_s (min)	$\{240, 120, 60\}$
Performance interval Δ_p (min)	5
Number replications per simulation run R	$\{100, 2, 500\}$
Target α	$\{0.2\}$

Table 9.3 Results branch and bound algorithm, aggregated over all settings for the staffing interval length Δ_s (Total), and for separate values of Δ_s (240, 120, 60), for $R = 2,500$

	Total (all values of Δ_s aggregated)	$\Delta_s = 240$	$\Delta_s = 120$	$\Delta_s = 60$
Solved to optimality	87.9 %	100.0 %	100.0 %	63.6 %
Solved to optimality and initial solution within 5 % of optimum	49.8 %	46.9 %	60.5 %	42.0 %
Solved to optimality and initial solution optimal	5.1 %	6.8 %	5.6 %	3.1 %
Poor performance region (> 1,000 simulations and ≤ 10 % improvement)	18.1 %	0.0 %	0.0 %	54.3 %

% COST IMPROVEMENT (W.R.T. INITIAL SOLUTION)

NB SIMULATIONS (IN B&B TREE)	0	]0,0.05]	]0.05,0.1]	]0.1,0.15]	]0.15,0.2]	>0.2	
25000	0.00%	5.56%	5.76%	0.82%	0.00%	0.00%	**12.14%**
]10000,24999]	0.00%	0.82%	1.23%	0.00%	0.00%	0.00%	**2.06%**
]1000,10000]	0.41%	2.26%	2.06%	0.21%	0.00%	0.00%	**4.94%**
]100,1000]	0.00%	3.29%	2.88%	0.00%	0.00%	0.00%	**6.17%**
]10,100]	0.62%	8.23%	4.32%	0.00%	0.00%	0.00%	**13.17%**
]1,10]	0.21%	12.55%	5.35%	1.44%	0.00%	0.00%	**19.55%**
]0,1]	1.03%	17.49%	11.73%	8.02%	0.82%	0.00%	**39.09%**
0	2.88%	0.00%	0.00%	0.00%	0.00%	0.00%	**2.88%**
	5.14%	**50.21%**	**33.33%**	**10.49%**	**0.82%**	**0.00%**	*100.00%*

Fig. 9.6 Simulation runs performed in branch-and-bound algorithm vs. percent improvement of the initial solution ($R = 2,500$)

so (i.e., the columns). Higher percentages are indicated by a darker shade. Recall that the heuristic approach serves as the initial solution in the branch-and-bound approach. As such, Fig. 9.6 and Table 9.3 shed light on the difference between the two-step heuristic and branch-and-bound approach in terms of the optimal shift cost and computational effort.

The branch-and-bound algorithm is terminated if an estimated optimal solution has not been found after 25,000 simulations (in that case, we have no guarantee that the best solution found so far is indeed the estimated optimum.). The top row in Fig. 9.6 contains the instances that could not be solved to optimality; this was the case for 12.14 % of the instances. The staffing interval length plays a key role here: Table 9.3 reveals that instances with $\Delta_s = 60$ could not always be optimally solved within 25,000 simulation runs (although cost reductions of 10 to 15 % could be realized). The heuristic approach was optimal in only 5.1 % of the instances (which means that the initial solution could not be improved). Yet, the heuristic solution lies within 5 % of the optimal solution in approximately 50 % of the instances. This leads us to conclude that in many cases, the heuristic provides a solution that is sufficiently close to the optimal solution.

Searching for an estimated optimum is worthwhile only if this can be found with limited additional computation time, or alternatively, if substantial improvements can be realized compared to the heuristic solution. Figure 9.6 shows that further improving the heuristic solution—or validating its optimality—often requires very few additional simulations. We define a region that represents "poor performance" in the branch-and-bound algorithm (marked in Fig. 9.6 by a bold-lined box): it contains instances that require more than 1,000 simulations in the branch-and-bound tree *and* for which the algorithm does not succeed in achieving at least a 10 % cost reduction. On the whole, 18 % of instances in the test set fall in this region (all with $\Delta_s = 60$).

Similar results hold for $R = 100$, as is shown in Fig. 9.7 and Table 9.4. Although limiting the number of replications reduces the computation time per simulation run, the estimated optimum found by the algorithm may then turn out to be infeasible because the estimate of the chance constraint is less accurate (we explore this more in detail, in the next section).

Impact of Number of Replications In simulation-based optimization, the (in)accuracy in the simulated performance may affect the solution that is returned by the algorithm. The branch-and-bound approach may be particularly sensitive to estimation error with regard to the feasibility of the chance constraint: large

NB SIMULATIONS (IN B&B TREE) \ % COST IMPROVEMENT (W.R.T. INITIAL SOLUTION)	0	]0,0.05]	]0.05,0.1]	]0.1,0.15]	]0.15,0.2]	>0.2	
25000	0.00%	5.35%	5.14%	0.21%	0.00%	0.00%	**10.70%**
]10000,24999]	0.00%	0.41%	0.82%	0.00%	0.00%	0.00%	**1.23%**
]1000,10000]	0.00%	2.06%	2.26%	0.41%	0.00%	0.00%	**4.73%**
]100,1000]	0.21%	3.70%	1.85%	0.21%	0.00%	0.00%	**5.97%**
]10,100]	0.21%	8.02%	5.56%	0.41%	0.00%	0.00%	**14.20%**
]1,10]	1.03%	13.99%	7.61%	1.03%	0.00%	0.00%	**23.66%**
]0,1]	1.65%	16.26%	12.96%	4.94%	0.21%	0.00%	**36.01%**
0	3.50%	0.00%	0.00%	0.00%	0.00%	0.00%	**3.50%**
	6.58%	**49.79%**	**36.21%**	**7.20%**	**0.21%**	**0.00%**	*100.00%*

Fig. 9.7 Simulation runs performed in branch-and-bound algorithm vs. percent improvement of the initial solution ($R = 100$)

Table 9.4 Results branch-and-bound algorithm, aggregated over all settings for the staffing interval length Δ_s (Total), and for separate values of Δ_s (240, 120, 60), for $R = 100$

	Total (all values of Δ_s aggregated)	$\Delta_s = 240$	$\Delta_s = 120$	$\Delta_s = 60$
Solved to optimality	89.3 %	100.0 %	100.0 %	67.9 %
Solved to optimality and initial solution within 5 % of optimum	51.0 %	50.6 %	61.7 %	40.7 %
Solved to optimality and initial solution optimal	6.6 %	11.7 %	6.8 %	1.2 %
Poor performance region (> 1,000 simulations and ≤ 10 % improvement)	16.0 %	0.0 %	0.0 %	48.1 %

Table 9.5 Sensitivity of optimal solution to the number of replications

	Two-step heuristic		Branch-and-bound approach	
	Δc_w^*	Δ SIM	Δc_w^*	Δ SIM
Min	0.0 %	0	0.0 %	0
$p_{0.05}$	0.0 %	0	0.0 %	0
Med	1.8 %	2	1.4 %	1
$p_{0.95}$	6.9 %	6	6.4 %	6,215
Max	15.4 %	12	13.3 %	24,958
Avg	2.3 %	2	2.0 %	807

parts of the solution space are pruned based on the performance estimates, so inaccurate estimates potentially have a large impact and cause the algorithm to miss the optimum. We compare between $R = 100$ and $R = 2,500$, to assess the extent to which the number of replications (and thus, the accuracy) affects the optimization process.

We consider the difference in the number of simulations that is required to run the heuristic or branch-and-bound algorithm to completion, when using 100 versus 2,500 replications in the simulation model:

$$\Delta\text{SIM} \equiv |\text{SIM}(R = 100) - \text{SIM}(R = 2,500)|. \tag{9.8}$$

We define the cost difference (in percent) for the two-step heuristic or branch-and-bound approach:

$$\Delta c_w^* \equiv \frac{\left|c_w^*(R = 100) - c_w^*(R = 2,500)\right|}{c_w^*(R = 100)}. \tag{9.9}$$

Table 9.5 shows that the number of simulations is not affected in the heuristic approach, but may differ severely in the branch-and-bound approach. This implies that the computational effort (in terms of number of simulations) displays high variability, depending on the number of replications that is used. The difference in cost, by contrast, is far less outspoken: increasing the number of replications has only a limited impact on the cost of the final solution. In the heuristic (optimal) approach, using a smaller amount of replications yields a c_w^* that differs by 2.3 % (2 %) on average. If such deviations are considered acceptable, $R = 100$ is preferred because it requires significantly less computation time per simulation run. However, we found that in 33.7 % of the instances, the final solutions obtained with $R = 100$ appear to be infeasible if they are evaluated with $R = 2,500$. Though the performance constraint was typically violated in only a limited number of performance intervals, this shows that R should be large in settings where the performance constraint is strict.

For the branch-and-bound approach, we measured the confidence interval (CI) around $\Pr(W(t) > \tau)$, at each point in time. The confidence intervals are determined through the Wilson score interval for a binomial proportion ([1, 75]; for alternative methods see [38]). The time-averages of the CI halfwidth ranged between 0.032 and 0.062 on average, for $R = 100$. The half-widths are smaller if more replications are used: they range between 0.005 and 0.012 on average, if $R = 2,500$.

9.6 Conclusion

In this chapter, we discussed the challenges for capacity planning in systems where the customers arrive according to a time-varying arrival pattern. Discrete-event simulation turns out to be the most appealing methodology to measure the time-varying quality of service in such settings, in particular when other realistic system characteristics are taken into consideration (such as customer abandonments, general distributions for the service and abandonment process, and an exhaustive end-of-shift policy). We proposed a two-step heuristic and a branch-and bound approach to solve the shift scheduling problem with time varying demand. The outcomes of the numerical experiment confirm that the heuristic commonly results in good schedules (if desired, these can be improved further using the branch-and-bound algorithm).

A downside of the branch-and-bound algorithm is that it can only be applied to systems with limited opening hours (due to the choice of the fathoming rules); the heuristic also applies to continuously operating systems. Surprisingly, the number of replications in the simulation model generally did not have a great impact on the optimal cost, in our computational experiment. However, accurately estimating the chance constraint is important to guarantee the feasibility of the final solution: to keep the estimation error in the chance constraint acceptable, the amount of replications needs to be sufficiently large.

Acknowledgements This research was supported by the Research Foundation-Flanders (FWO) (grant no G.0547.09).

Table 9.6 Shift specifications (all breaks are assumed to be 1 h). K represents the size of the shift set for problem instances with staffing interval length Δ_s

Staffing interval length (number of shifts)	Shift specification {start time, end time, start time break}
$\Delta_s = 240$ ($K = 5$)	$\{0,4,-\}, \{4,8,-\}, \{8,12,-\}, \{0,8,-\}, \{4,12,-\}$
$\Delta_s = 120$ ($K = 12$)	$\{0,4,-\}, \{2,6,-\}, \{4,8,-\}, \{6,10,-\}, \{8,12,-\}, \{0,6,-\}, \{2,8,-\}, \{4,10,-\}, \{6,12,-\}, \{0,8,-\}, \{2,10,-\}, \{4,12,-\}$
$\Delta_s = 60$ ($K = 45$)	$\{0,4,-\}, \{1,5,-\}, \{2,6,-\}, \{3,7,-\}, \{4,8,-\}, \{5,9,-\}, \{6,10,-\}, \{7,11,-\}, \{8,12,-\}, \{0,6,2\}, \{1,7,3\}, \{2,8,4\}, \{3,9,5\}, \{4,10,6\}, \{5,11,7\}, \{6,12,8\}, \{0,6,3\}, \{1,7,4\}, \{2,8,5\}, \{3,9,6\}, \{4,10,7\}, \{5,11,8\}, \{6,12,9\}, \{0,6,4\}, \{1,7,5\}, \{2,8,6\}, \{3,9,7\}, \{4,10,8\}, \{5,11,9\}, \{6,12,10\}, \{0,8,3\}, \{1,9,4\}, \{2,10,5\}, \{3,11,6\}, \{4,12,7\}, \{0,8,4\}, \{1,9,5\}, \{2,10,6\}, \{3,11,7\}, \{4,12,8\}, \{0,8,5\}, \{1,9,6\}, \{2,10,7\}, \{3,11,8\}, \{4,12,9\}$

Appendix: Shift Specifications

See Table 9.6.

References

1. Agresti, A., Coull, B.A.: Approximate is better than "exact" for interval estimation of binomial proportions. Am. Stat. **52**(2), 119–126 (1998)
2. Aguir, S., Karaesmen, F., Akskin, O.Z., Chauvet, F.: The impact of retrials on call center performance. OR Spectr. **26**(3), 353–376 (2004)
3. Ahmed, M.A., Alkhamis, T.M.: Simulation optimization for an emergency department healthcare unit in Kuwait. Eur. J. Oper. Res. **198**(3), 936–942 (2009)
4. Altman, E., Jiménez, T., Koole, G.: On the comparison of queueing systems with their fluid limits. Probab. Eng. Inf. Sci. **15**, 165–178 (2001)
5. April, J., Glover, F., Kelly, J.P., Laguna, M.: Practical introduction to simulation optimization. In: Proceedings of the Winter Simulation Conference, pp. 71–78 (2003)
6. April, J., Better, M., Glover, F., Kelly, J.: New advances and applications for marrying simulation and optimization. In: Proceedings of the 36th Winter Simulation Conference (2004)
7. Atlason, J., Epelman, M.A., Henderson, S.G.: Optimizing call center staffing using simulation and analytic center cutting-plane methods. Manag. Sci. **54**(2), 295–309 (2008)
8. Aykin, T.: A composite branch and cut algorithm for optimal shift scheduling with multiple breaks and break windows. J. Oper. Res. Soc. **49**(6), 603–615 (1998)
9. Brown, L., Gans, N., Mandelbaum, A., Sakov, A., Shen, H., Zeltyn, S., Zhao, L.: Statistical analysis of a telephone call center: a queueing perspective. J. Am. Stat. Assoc. **100**(469), 36–50 (2005)
10. Brunner, J.O., Bard, J.F., Kolisch, R.: Midterm scheduling of physicians with flexible shifts using branch and price. IIE Trans. **43**(2), 84–109 (2010)
11. Carson, Y., Maria, A.: Simulation optimization: methods and applications. In: Proceedings of the 29th Winter Simulation Conference, pp. 118–126 (1997)

12. Castillo, I., Joro, T., Li, Y.Y.: Workforce scheduling with multiple objectives. Eur. J. Oper. Res. **196**(1), 162–170 (2009)
13. Chassioti, E., Worthington, D., Glazebrook, K.: Effects of state-dependent balking on multi-server non-stationary queueing systems. J. Oper. Res. Soc. Forthcoming (2013)
14. Choi, K., Hwang, J., Park, M.: Scheduling restaurant workers to minimize labor cost and meet service standards. Cornell Hosp. Q. **50**(2), 155–167 (2009)
15. Clark, G.M.: Use of Polya distributions in approximate solutions to nonstationary $M/M/s$ queues. Commun. ACM **24**(4), 206–217 (1981)
16. Creemers, S., Defraeye, M., Van Nieuwenhuyse, I.: G-RAND: a phase-type approximation for the nonstationary $G(t)/G(t)/s(t) + G(t)$ queue. *Performance Evaluation, accepted* (2013)
17. Dai, J.G., He, S.: Customer abandonment in many-server queues. Math. Oper. Res. **35**(2), 347–362 (2010)
18. Dantzig, G.: A comment on Edie's traffic delay at toll booths. Oper. Res. **2**, 339–341 (1954)
19. Davis, J.L., Massey, W.A., Whitt, W.: Sensitivity to the service-time distribution in the nonstationary erlang loss model. Manag. Sci. **41**(6), 1107–1116 (1995)
20. Defraeye, M., Van Nieuwenhuyse, I.: Setting staffing levels in an emergency department: opportunities and limitations of stationary queuing models. Rev. Bus. Econ. **56**(1), 73–100 (2011)
21. Defraeye, M., Van Nieuwenhuyse, I.: Controlling excessive waiting times in small service systems with time-varying demand: An extension of the ISA algorithm. Decis. Support Syst. **54**(4), 1558–1567 (2013)
22. Defraeye, M., Van Nieuwenhuyse, I.: A branch-and-bound algorithm for shift scheduling with nonstationary demand. Research report KBI_1322, KU Leuven, Leuven (2013)
23. Ernst, A.T., Jiang, H., Krishnamoorthy, M., Sier, D.: Staff scheduling and rostering: a review of applications, methods and models. Eur. J. Oper. Res. **153**(1), 3–27 (2004)
24. Ernst, A.T., Jiang, H., Krishnamoorthy, M., Owens, B., Sier, D.: An annotated bibliography of personnel scheduling and rostering. Ann. Oper. Res. **127**, 21–144 (2004)
25. Feldman, Z., Mandelbaum, A., Massey, W.A., Whitt, W.: Staffing of time-varying queues to achieve time-stable performance. Manag. Sci. **54**(2), 324–338 (2008)
26. Fu, M.C., Glover, F.W., April, J.: Simulation optimization: a review, new developments, and applications. In: Proceedings of the Winter Simulation Conference (2005)
27. Gans, N., Koole, G., Mandelbaum, A.: Telephone call centers: tutorial, review, and research prospect. Manuf. Serv. Oper. Manag. **5**(2), 79–141 (2003)
28. Gans, N., Sheng, H., Zhou, Y.-P., Korolev, N., McCord, A., Ristock, H.: Parametric stochastic programming models for call-center workforce scheduling. Working paper, University of Washington (2012). Available online at http://faculty.washington.edu/
29. Green, L.V., Kolesar, P.J.: The pointwise stationary approximation for queues with nonstationary arrivals. Manag. Sci. **37**(1), 84–97 (1991)
30. Green, L.V., Kolesar, P.J.: The lagged PSA for estimating peak congestion in multiserver Markovian queues with periodic arrival rates. Manag. Sci. **43**(1), 80–87 (1997)
31. Green, L.V., Soares, J.: Computing time-dependent waiting time probabilities in $M(t)/M/s(t)$ queueing systems. Manuf. Serv. Oper. Manag. **9**(1), 54–61 (2007)
32. Green, L.V., Kolesar, P.J., Soares, J.: Improving the SIPP approach for staffing service systems that have cyclic demands. Oper. Res. **49**(4), 549–564 (2001)
33. Green, L.V., Kolesar, P.J., Soares, J.: An improved heuristic for staffing telephone call centers with limited operating hours. Prod. Oper. Manag. **12**(1), 46–61 (2003)
34. Green, L.V., Kolesar, P.J., Svoronos, A.: Some effects of nonstationarity on multiserver Markovian queueing systems. Oper. Res. **39**(3), 502–511 (1991)

35. Green, L.V., Soares, J., Giglio, J.F., Green, R.A.: Using queueing theory to increase the effectiveness of emergency department provider staffing. Acad. Emerg. Med. **13**(1), 61–68 (2006)
36. Green, L.V., Kolesar, P.J., Whitt, W.: Coping with time-varying demand when setting staffing requirements for a service system. Prod. Oper. Manag. **16**(1), 13–39 (2007)
37. Gross, D., Shortle, J.F., Thompson, J.M., Harris, C.M.: Fundamentals of Queueing Theory, 4th edn. Wiley Series in Probability and Statistics. Wiley-Blackwell, Hoboken (2008)
38. Guan, Y.: A generalized score confidence interval for a binomial proportion. J. Stat. Plan. Inf. **142**, 785–793 (2012)
39. Hueter, J., Swart, W.: An integrated labor-management system for Taco Bell. Interfaces **28**(1), 75–91 (1998)
40. Ingolfsson, A.: Modeling the $M(t)/M/s(t)$ queue with an exhaustive discipline. Working paper, University of Alberta (2005). Available online on http://www.business.ualberta.ca/aingolfsson/publications.htm
41. Ingolfsson, A., Haque, A., Umnikov, A.: Accounting for time-varying queueing effects in workforce scheduling. Eur. J. Oper. Res. **139**(3), 585–597 (2002)
42. Ingolfsson, A., Akhmetshina, E., Budge, S., Li, Y.: A survey and experimental comparison of service level approximation methods for non-stationary M(t)/M/s(t) queueing systems with exhaustive discipline. INFORMS J. Comput. **19**(2), 201–214 (2007)
43. Ingolfsson, A., Campello, F., Wu, X., Cabral, E.: Combining integer programming and the randomization method to schedule employees. Eur. J. Oper. Res. **202**(1), 153–163 (2010)
44. Iravani, F., Balcioğlu, B.: Approximations for the $M/GI/N+GI$ type call center. Queueing Syst. **58**(2), 137–153 (2008)
45. Izady, N.: On queues with time-varying demand. PhD Thesis, Lancaster University (2010)
46. Izady, N., Worthington, D.J.: Setting staffing requirements for time-dependent queueing networks: The case of accident and emergency departments. Eur. J. Oper. Res. **219**, 531–540 (2012)
47. Jagerman, D.L.: Nonstationary blocking in telephone traffic. Bell Syst. Tech. **54**, 625–661 (1975)
48. Jennings, O.B., Mandelbaum, A., Massey, W.A., Whitt, W.: Server staffing to meet time-varying demand. Manag. Sci. **42**(10), 1383–1394 (1996)
49. Jiménez, T., Koole, G.: Scaling and comparison of fluid limits of queues applied to call centers with time varying parameters. OR Spectr. **26**(3) 413–422 (2004)
50. Johnson, M., Myers, S., Wineholt, J., Pollack, M., Kusmiesz, A.L.: Patients Who Leave the Emergency Department Without Being Seen. J. Emerg. Nurs. **35**(2), 105–108 (2009)
51. Kabak, Ö., Ülengin, F., Aktaş, E., Önsel, Ş, Topcu, Y.I.: Efficient shift scheduling in the retail sector through two-stage optimization. Eur. J. Oper. Res. **184**(1), 76–90 (2008)
52. Kendall, D.G.: Stochastic processes occurring in the theory of queues and their analysis by the method of the imbedded Markov chain. Ann. Math. Stat. **24**(3), 338–354 (1953)
53. Koole, G., Pot, A.: An overview of routing and staffing algorithms in multi-skill customer contact centers. Working paper, VU University, Amsterdam (2006). Available online at http://www.math.vu.nl/
54. Koopman, B.O.: Air-Terminal queues under time-dependent conditions. Oper. Res. **20**(6), 1089–1114 (1972)
55. Lam, S., Vandenbosch, M., Pearce, M.: Retail sales force scheduling based on store traffic forecasting. J. Retail. **74**(1), 61–88 (1998)
56. Law, A.M., Kelton, W.D.: Simulation Modeling and Analysis. McGraw-Hill Series in Industrial Engineering and Management Science. McGraw-Hill, Boston (2000)
57. Le Minh, D.: The discrete-time single-server queue with time-inhomogeneous compound Poisson input and general service time distribution. J. Appl. Probab. **15**, 590–601 (1978)
58. Liu, Y., Whitt, W.: Stabilizing customer abandonment in many-server queues with time-varying arrivals. Working paper, Columbia University, New York (2009). Available online at http://www.columbia.edu/~ww2040/recent.html

59. Liu, Y., Whitt, W.: A Fluid Approximation for the $GI(t)/GI/s(t) + GI$ Queue. Working paper, Columbia University, New York (2010). Available online at http://www.columbia.edu/~ww2040/allpapers.html
60. Liu, Y., Whitt, W.: A Network of Time-Varying Many-Server Fluid Queues with Customer Abandonment. Oper. Res. **59**(4), 835–846 (2011)
61. Liu, Y., Whitt, W.: Large-Time Asymptotics for the $G_t/M_t/s_t+GI_t$ Many-Server Fluid Queue with Abandonment. Queueing Syst. **67**(2), 145–182 (2011)
62. Liu, Y., Whitt, W.: The $G_t/GI/s_t + GI$ many-server fluid queue. Queueing Syst. **71**(4), 405–444 (2012)
63. Liu, Y., Whitt, W.: A many-server fluid limit for the $G_t/GI/s_t + GI$ queueing model experiencing periods of overloading. OR Lett. **40**, 307–312 (2012)
64. Mandelbaum, A., Massey, W.A.: Strong approximations for time-dependent queues. Math. Oper. Res. **20**(1), 33–64 (1995)
65. Mandelbaum, A., Momğilović, P.: Queues with many servers: the virtual waiting-time process in the QED regime. Math. Oper. Res. **33**(3), 561–586 (2008)
66. Mandelbaum, A., Massey, W.A., Reiman, M.I.: Strong approximations for Markovian service networks. Queueing Syst. **30**(1), 149–201 (1998)
67. Mandelbaum, A., Massey, W., Reiman, M.: Strong approximations for Markovian service networks. Queueing Syst. **30**(1), 149–201 (1998)
68. Mandelbaum, A., Massey, W.A., Reiman, M.I., Rider, B.: Time varying multiserver queues with abandonments and retrials. In: Proceedings of the 16th International Teletraffic Conference, vol. 3, pp. 355–364 (1999)
69. Mandelbaum, A., Massey, W.A., Reiman, M.I., Stolyar, A.: Waiting time asymptotics for time varying multiserver queues with abandonment and retrials. In: Proc. 37th Allerton Conf. Monticello, pp. 1095–1104 (1999)
70. Mandelbaum, A., Massey, W.A., Reiman, M.I., Stolyar, A., Rider, B.: Queue lengths and waiting times for multiserver queues with abandonment and retrials. Telecommun. Syst. **21**(2–4), 149–171 (2002)
71. Mason, A.J., Ryan, D.M., Panton, D.M.: Integrated simulation, heuristic and optimisation approaches to staff scheduling. Oper. Res. **46**(2), 161–175 (1998)
72. Massey, W.A., Whitt, W.: An analysis of the modified offered-load approximation for the nonstationary erlang loss model. Ann. Appl. Probab. **4**(4), 1145–1160 (1994)
73. Massey, W.A., Whitt, W.: Peak congestion in multi-server service systems with slowly varying arrival rates. Queueing Syst. **25**(1), 157–172 (1997)
74. Nelson, B.L., Taafe, M.R.: The $[Ph_t/Ph_t/\infty]^K$ queueing system: Part II—The multiclass network Part II – The multiclass network. INFORMS J. Comput. **16**(3), 275–283 (2004)
75. Newcombe, R.G.: Two-sided confidence intervals for the single proportion: comparison of seven methods. Stat. Med. **17**, 857–872 (1998)
76. Rekik, M., Cordeau, J.-F., Soumis, F.: Implicit shift scheduling with multiple breaks and work stretch duration restrictions. J. Schedul. **13**(1), 49–75 (2010)
77. Ridley, A.D., Fu, M.C., Massey, W.A.: Customer relations management: call center operations: Fluid approximations for a priority call center with time-varying arrivals. In: Proceedings of the 35th Conference on Winter Simulation, New Orleans, vol. 2, pp. 1817–1823 (2003)
78. Rothkopf, M.H., Oren, S.S.: A closure approximation for the nonstationary M/M/s queue. Manag. Sci. **25**(6), 522–534 (1979)
79. Sinreich, D., Jabali, O.: Staggered work shifts: a way to downsize and restructure an emergency department workforce yet maintain current operational performance. Health Care Manag. Sci. **10**, 293–308 (2007)
80. Taaffe, M., Ong, K.: Approximating nonstationary $Ph(t)/Ph(t)/l/c$ queueing systems. Ann. Oper. Res. **8**(1), 103–116 (1987)
81. Thompson, G.M.: Accounting for the multi-period impact of service when determining employee requirements for labor scheduling. J. Oper. Manag. **11**(3), 269–287 (1993)
82. Thompson, G.M.: Labor staffing and scheduling models for controlling service levels. Naval Res. Log. **44**(8), 719–740 (1997)

83. Wall, A.D., Worthington, D.J.: Using discrete distributions to approximate general service time distributions in queueing models. J. Oper. Res. Soc. **45**(12), 1398–1404 (1994)
84. Wall, A.D., Worthington, D.J.: Time-dependent analysis of virtual waiting time behaviour in discrete time queues. Eur. J. Oper. Res. **178**(2), 482–499 (2007)
85. Whitt, W.: The pointwise stationary approximation for $M(t)/M(t)/s$ queues is asymptotically correct as the rates increase. Manag. Sci. **37**(3), 307–314 (1991)
86. Whitt, W.: Engineering solution of a basic call-center model. Manag. Sci. **51**(2), 221–235 (2005)
87. Whitt, W.: Staffing a call center with uncertain arrival rate and absenteeism. Prod. Oper. Manag. **15**(1), 88–102 (2006)
88. Whitt, W.: Fluid models for multiserver queues with abandonments. Oper. Res. **54**(1), 37–54 (2006)
89. Whitt, W.: What you should know about queueing models to set staffing requirements in service systems. Naval Res. Log. **54**(5), 476–484 (2007)
90. Worthington, D., Wall, A.: Using the discrete time modelling approach to evaluate the time-dependent behaviour of queueing systems. J. Oper. Res. Soc. **50**(8), 777–788 (1999)
91. Zeltyn, S., Marmor, Y.N., Mandelbaum, A., Carmeli, B., Greenshpan, O., Mesika, Y., Wasserkrug, S., Vortman, P., Shtub, A., Lauterman, T., Schwartz, D., Moskovitch, K., Tzafrir, S., Basis, F.: Simulation-based models of emergency departments: Operational, tactical, and strategic staffing. ACM Trans. Model. Comput. Simul. **21**(4), 1–25 (2011)
92. Zhang, Y., Puterman, M.L., Nelson, M., Atkins, D.: A simulation optimization approach to long-term care capacity planning. Oper. Res. **60**(2), 249–261 (2012)

Chapter 10
Stochastic Dual Dynamic Programming Solution of a Short-Term Disaster Management Problem

Ebru Angün

10.1 Introduction

Every year, more than 500 disasters are estimated to strike our planet, causing the deaths of around 75,000 people, and impacting more than 200 million others [1]. To decrease the number of deaths and disaster-affected people, the design of an efficient and effective emergency logistics system is vital. The inefficiency in such a system in Haiti after the 2010 earthquake had the following results: Various on-field journalists [2, 3] reported that relief efforts were stalling in the logistics network and that, therefore, much aid remained undelivered. This caused more than 3 million affected people, 200,000 deaths, and more than one million wounded.

Disaster operations represent the set of all activities performed before, during, and after a disaster in order to diminish its impacts. Traditionally, the life cycle of disaster operations is divided into four stages, namely risk mitigation, preparedness, response, and recovery. The risk mitigation operations are performed before the disaster occurs, and they aim at reducing vulnerability to the disaster impacts such as injuries, and loss of life and property. The preparedness operations involve those activities performed before the disaster occurs in order to accomplish a more efficient response. The response operations are performed upon the occurrence of the disaster, and they address immediate threats presented by the disaster, including saving lives, meeting humanitarian needs (food, shelter, clothing, public health and safety), evacuating people from the disaster affected area, etc. Finally, recovery operations are performed after a disaster occurs, and they refer to short-term or

E. Angün (✉)
Department of Industrial Engineering, Galatasaray University, Çırağan Cad.
Ortaköy, 34349 Istanbul, Turkey
e-mail: eangun@gsu.edu.tr

G. Dellino, C. Meloni (eds.), *Uncertainty Management in Simulation-Optimization of Complex Systems*, Operations Research/Computer Science Interfaces Series 59,
DOI 10.1007/978-1-4899-7547-8_10

long-term activities to restore the normal functioning of the community. Two recent reviews on the Disaster Operations Management and on the optimization models used in emergency logistics are given by [4, 5], respectively.

In the rest of this section, we present early works that cover preparedness and/or response phases of the disaster life cycle, where only natural (and not man-made) disasters are considered.

The following papers focused only on post-disaster operations such as relief distribution and evacuation. The paper [6] considered the problem of distributing relief commodities after a disaster and formulated a multi-commodity, multi-modal network flow problem with time windows as a large-scale, mixed-integer programming problem on a time-space network, which accounted for the dynamic decision process. Furthermore, [6] solved a multi-period, deterministic optimization problem which minimized the sum of the different types of costs. Later, [7] extended that work to consider uncertainties in available supplies, demands, and arc capacities through definition of a set of scenarios. Moreover, [7] formulated the relief distribution problem as a two-stage stochastic programming problem which minimized the expected sum of the different types of costs; the decisions in [7] (i.e., the amounts of distributed commodities) were static. The paper [8] considered a no-notice mass evacuation problem, and proposed a multi-period, deterministic traffic flow optimization model which was formulated as a linear programming problem. This model minimized the total system travel time and simultaneously solved the optimal evacuation destination, traffic assignment, and evacuation departure schedule. Finally, the paper [9] considered an integrated problem of locating temporary medical centers, relief distribution, and evacuation and transfer of wounded people to emergency centers. Furthermore, [9] proposed a mixed-integer multi-commodity network flow model which minimized delay in providing prioritized relief commodities and health care services to the prioritized groups of people; the model was multi-period and deterministic. Unlike [6–8], [9] did not consider the cost criterion.

The paper [10] focused only on pre-disaster operations, and considered a stochastic inventory pre-positioning problem for relief commodities. Lodree and Taskin [10] formulated the problem as an optimal stopping time problem to obtain the optimal quantity and the timing of the inventory decisions. This paper assumed random wind speed with a known prior distribution with some unknown parameters, which were updated through Bayesian updates. The problem was solved through dynamic optimization, and the optimal solutions provided a trade-off between the forecast cost, which was decreasing in time, and the order/production cost, which was increasing in time.

The papers [11–14] considered both pre- and post-disaster phases. Balcik et al. [11] considered a last mile distribution system in which a local distribution center stored and distributed relief commodities to a number of demand locations using a fixed set of vehicles. The problem was formulated through a variant of multi-item inventory routing model to determine a delivery schedule for each vehicle and to make inventory allocation decisions by taking into account supply, vehicle capacity, and delivery time restrictions. Furthermore, [11] used a rolling horizon approach to capture the multi-periodicity of the problem. The papers [12, 13] considered an integrated problem of facility location for storage facilities, inventory pre-positioning for emergency commodities, and relief distribution. Rawls and Turnquist [12] formulated this problem through a two-stage stochastic programming model, and [13] extended the static two-stage model to a multi-period model and solved it dynamically. Both [12, 13] assumed that the random demands, arc capacities, etc. had a known, joint, discrete distribution. Different from all papers above, [14] considered explicitly young, elderly, disabled, and low-income residents, who did not have access to an automobile for evacuation. In the pre-disaster phase, [14] determined the locations of the permanent pick-up facilities—which were subject to disruptions with the same probability—for disaster evacuees. In the post-disaster phase, [14] determined the evacuee-to-facility assignment, and the allocation of the evacuation vehicles to functioning facilities and their schedules; the numbers of evacuees arriving at the pick-up facilities were assumed to be deterministic. Then, [14] formulated and solved this problem as a medium size linear integer programming problem.

10.1.1 Contributions and Structure of Paper

In our problem, we consider both pre- and post-disaster phases of a disaster life cycle, and formulate a multistage stochastic optimization model for the disaster preparedness and the relief distribution problem. The first-stage is an integrated facility location and inventory pre-positioning problem. We formulate the problems at later stages as variants of capacitated multi-commodity network flow problems with fractional flows; in fact, our model is an extension of the two-stage stochastic optimization model of [12]. Based on the literature survey in Sect. 10.1, our paper contributes in the following directions.

- Many papers in Sect. 10.1 formulate multi-period optimization models for the disaster management problems. Due to the consideration of the multi-periodicity, these models are dynamic. The model in this paper is also dynamic, but this is due to the consideration of the multistage; i.e., we update dynamically the first-stage inventory decisions at later stages as well as updating the realizations of the random quantities.
- The random quantities in Sect. 10.1 are dealt through the definition of a given set of scenarios. We, however, assume to have continuous distributions for the random demands and road capacities; i.e., we have originally infinitely many scenarios. Then, we discretize these distributions and obtain scenario trees with a huge (but finite) number of scenarios through different sampling techniques such as Crude Monte Carlo Sampling (CMCS) and Latin Hypercube Sampling (LHS). Furthermore, the computationally untractable expectations, which require multi-dimensional integrations, are estimated through their Sample Average Approximations (SAA).

- Under some assumptions, the multistage model is solved through the Stochastic Dual Dynamic Programming (SDDP) algorithm, which provides non-anticipative policies; i.e., the tth-stage policies are determined based on the realizations of the randomness observed up to that stage, and they do not consider the future realizations of the random quantities. In that sense, these policies are implementable. This issue has not been mentioned in the disaster management literature so far.
- To the best of our knowledge, this is one of the first few papers (together with [15]) that uses different sampling techniques (i.e., CMCS or LHS) in the multistage stochastic optimization framework.

In this paper, simulation is the add-on to generate scenarios for the mathematical programming problem from an infinite number of possible realizations. Therefore, our use of simulation is different from the simulation-based optimization, in which an optimization subroutine is an add-on to a stochastic discrete-event simulator, and provides candidate solutions to the simulator; see [16].

The remainder of this paper is organized as follows. Section 10.2 introduces the formulation of a general multistage stochastic linear optimization problem and describes the LHS. Section 10.3 explains in detail the SDDP algorithm for the problem introduced in Sect. 10.2, and provides two pseudocodes for the backward and forward passes of the algorithm. Section 10.4 introduces the disaster preparedness and the short-term relief distribution problem that considers only the first 72 h in the aftermath of an earthquake, and presents the computational results. Finally, Sect. 10.5 summarizes the results and provides some future research directions.

Throughout the paper, $\mathbb{E}[.]$, "$\prime$", $\equiv$, $:=$, and $|.|$ denote the expectation, the transpose of a vector or a matrix (with the exception in Sect. 10.4, where (i', j') denotes an arc in the transportation network), the equivalence, "is defined by", and the cardinality of a set, respectively.

10.2 Mathematical Formulation

We consider a T-stage stochastic program in which a sequence of decisions $\{\mathbf{x}_t\}_{t=1}^T$ is made with respect to a random process $\left\{\tilde{\boldsymbol{\xi}}_t\right\}_{t=1}^T$ as follows. At stage t, the decision $\mathbf{x}_t$ is made with only the knowledge of past decisions $\mathbf{x}_1, \mathbf{x}_2, \ldots, \mathbf{x}_{t-1}$, and the realizations of the random vectors $\tilde{\boldsymbol{\xi}}_1, \tilde{\boldsymbol{\xi}}_2, \ldots, \tilde{\boldsymbol{\xi}}_t$, where the history of the random process up to stage t is denoted by $\tilde{\boldsymbol{\xi}}_{[t]} = \left(\tilde{\boldsymbol{\xi}}_1, \tilde{\boldsymbol{\xi}}_2, \ldots, \tilde{\boldsymbol{\xi}}_t\right)$. That is, $\mathbf{x}_1$ is a function of $\tilde{\boldsymbol{\xi}}_1$ only, $\mathbf{x}_2$ is a function of $\mathbf{x}_1$ and $\tilde{\boldsymbol{\xi}}_2$, and hence it is a function of $\tilde{\boldsymbol{\xi}}_{[2]}$, and so on. In general, this is denoted by $\mathbf{x}_t\left(\tilde{\boldsymbol{\xi}}_{[t]}\right)$. Furthermore, the decision $\mathbf{x}_t$ at stage

t does not depend on the future realizations of the random vectors $\tilde{\boldsymbol{\xi}}_{t+1}$, $\tilde{\boldsymbol{\xi}}_{t+2}$, $\ldots$, $\tilde{\boldsymbol{\xi}}_T$; i.e., the decision process is non-anticipative. Such an $\mathbf{x}_t\left(\tilde{\boldsymbol{\xi}}_{[t]}\right)$ is called an (implementable) policy in [17].

We make the following two assumptions for $\tilde{\boldsymbol{\xi}}_t$.

(A1) The distribution P_t of $\tilde{\boldsymbol{\xi}}_t$ is known, and this P_t is supported on a set $\Xi_t \subset \mathbb{R}^{d_t}$.

(A2) The random process $\left\{\tilde{\boldsymbol{\xi}}_t\right\}_{t=1}^T$ is stagewise independent; i.e., $\tilde{\boldsymbol{\xi}}_{t+1}$ is independent of its history $\tilde{\boldsymbol{\xi}}_{[t]}$.

We formulate the T-stage problem through the following dynamic programming equations. At stage $t = 1$, the problem is

$$\begin{aligned} &\underset{\mathbf{x}_1 \geq \mathbf{0}}{\text{Min}}\ \mathbf{c}_1'\mathbf{x}_1 + \mathbb{E}\left[Q_2\left(\mathbf{x}_1, \tilde{\boldsymbol{\xi}}_2\right)\right] \\ &\text{s.t.}\quad \mathbf{A}_1\mathbf{x}_1 = \mathbf{b}_1 \end{aligned} \tag{10.1}$$

where for later stages $t = 2, \ldots, T-1$ and for a realization $\boldsymbol{\xi}_t^s$ of $\tilde{\boldsymbol{\xi}}_t$, the cost-to-go (or value) functions $Q_t\left(\mathbf{x}_{t-1}, \boldsymbol{\xi}_t^s\right)$ are given by

$$\begin{aligned} Q_t\left(\mathbf{x}_{t-1}, \boldsymbol{\xi}_t^s\right) = &\underset{\mathbf{x}_t \geq \mathbf{0}}{\text{Min}}\ \mathbf{c}_t'\mathbf{x}_t + \mathbb{E}\left[Q_{t+1}\left(\mathbf{x}_t, \tilde{\boldsymbol{\xi}}_{t+1}\right)\right] \\ &\text{s.t.}\quad \mathbf{B}_t^s\mathbf{x}_{t-1} + \mathbf{A}_t\mathbf{x}_t = \mathbf{b}_t^s\ . \end{aligned} \tag{10.2}$$

Note that under the Assumption (A2), $Q_t\left(\mathbf{x}_{t-1}, \boldsymbol{\xi}_t^s\right)$ does not depend on the history $\boldsymbol{\xi}_{[t]}^s$. The random vector $\tilde{\boldsymbol{\xi}}_t$ consists of the random components from $\tilde{\mathbf{B}}_t$ and $\tilde{\mathbf{b}}_t$, where a realization is denoted by $\mathbf{B}_t^s$ and $\mathbf{b}_t^s$, respectively. At stage $t = 1$, $\tilde{\boldsymbol{\xi}}_{[1]} \equiv \tilde{\boldsymbol{\xi}}_1 \equiv \mathbf{b}_1$ is deterministic. At stage $t = T$, $Q_T\left(\mathbf{x}_{T-1}, \boldsymbol{\xi}_T^s\right)$ is

$$\begin{aligned} Q_T\left(\mathbf{x}_{T-1}, \boldsymbol{\xi}_T^s\right) = &\underset{\mathbf{x}_T \geq \mathbf{0}}{\text{Min}}\ \mathbf{c}_T'\mathbf{x}_T \\ &\text{s.t.}\quad \mathbf{B}_T^s\mathbf{x}_{T-1} + \mathbf{A}_T\mathbf{x}_T = \mathbf{b}_T^s \end{aligned} \tag{10.3}$$

where we set $\mathbb{E}\left[Q_{T+1}\left(\mathbf{x}_T, \tilde{\boldsymbol{\xi}}_{T+1}\right)\right] = 0$.

In (10.1) through (10.3), $\mathbf{c}_t$ and $\mathbf{b}_t^s$ (hence, $\tilde{\mathbf{b}}_t$) are $(n_t \times 1)$- and $(m_t \times 1)$-dimensional vectors, and $\mathbf{A}_t$ and $\mathbf{B}_t^s$ (hence, $\tilde{\mathbf{B}}_t$) are $(m_t \times n_t)$- and $(m_t \times n_{t-1})$-dimensional matrices, respectively, where n_t is the dimension of $\mathbf{x}_t$ and m_t is the number of constraints at stage t.

Note that the Assumption (A2) includes the case where the vector $\tilde{\mathbf{b}}_t$ is modeled through a first-order autoregressive process $\tilde{\mathbf{b}}_t = \boldsymbol{\Phi}_t\mathbf{b}_{t-1} + \tilde{\boldsymbol{\eta}}_t$ with a given matrix $\boldsymbol{\Phi}_t$ of appropriate dimensions, where the $\tilde{\boldsymbol{\eta}}_t$'s are the stagewise independent residual vectors (see [18]).

There are two problems related with the formulations in (10.1) through (10.3).

(P1) These formulations provide a risk-neutral approach to the problem; i.e., the random cost-to-go functions $Q_t\left(\mathbf{x}_{t-1}, \tilde{\xi}_t\right)$ are only minimized on average.

(P2) The expectation in (10.1) [or in (10.2)] usually requires the computation of a multi-dimensional integration, which can make the "true" (expected value) problem untractable.

One way to deal with the problem (P1) is to add chance (or probabilistic) constraints to the problems in (10.1) and (10.2), because these constraints ensure that the random cost-to-go functions do not exceed given upper bounds with high probability for different realizations of the random process. However, it is well-known that the chance constraints usually define non-convex feasible sets which make the minimizations of (10.1) and (10.2) highly problematic. Hence, the issue of risk aversion is left for future research.

A possible way to handle the problem (P2) (i.e., make the "true" problem tractable) is to replace the expectation by its Sample Average Approximation (SAA); i.e., sample $\tilde{\boldsymbol{\xi}}_t$ from its known distribution P_t through some sampling techniques to obtain a sample $\mathcal{S}_t := \left\{\boldsymbol{\xi}_t^1, \ldots, \boldsymbol{\xi}_t^{N_t}\right\}$ for $t = 2, \ldots, T$, where N_t is the sample size at stage t, and then estimate the expectation by the following SAA

$$\hat{\mathcal{Q}}_t\left(\mathbf{x}_{t-1}\right) = \frac{1}{N_t}\sum_{s=1}^{N_t} Q_t\left(\mathbf{x}_{t-1}, \boldsymbol{\xi}_t^s\right) . \tag{10.4}$$

Note that at $t = 1$, $\mathcal{S}_1$ is a singleton; i.e., $\mathcal{S}_1 := \{\mathbf{b}_1\}$. The sampling techniques that will be used in this paper are *Crude Monte Carlo Sampling* (CMCS) and *Latin Hypercube Sampling* (LHS).

The LHS was proposed in [19], and its theoretical properties and numerical efficacy have been thoroughly studied in [20–22]. For a single component $\tilde{\xi}_{t,k}$ of $\tilde{\boldsymbol{\xi}}_t$, the technique can be described as follows. The interval [0, 1] is divided into N_t non-overlapping intervals (strata) of equal probability, and inside each interval a single value, which is uniform on that interval, is sampled. The inverse transform method is then used to convert the uniform value into the one that has the same distribution as $\tilde{\xi}_{t,k}$. The above procedure is repeated for all components of $\tilde{\boldsymbol{\xi}}_t$, and the resulting set of values are randomly permuted to give $\mathcal{S}_t$. Figure 10.1 shows an example of $N_t = 100$ sample points obtained through the LHS and the CMCS of an uniformly distributed vector on $[0, 1]^2$. In this figure, n_I, n_{II}, n_{III}, and n_{IV} show respectively the number of sample points that fall into their corresponding subregions, where the sample points on the horizontal boundary belong to the upper subregions and those on the vertical boundary belong to the subregions on the right; it is obvious from this figure that the LHS provides more uniformity over $[0, 1]^2$ than the CMCS does, where for the CMCS, one observes clusters of points in the third subregion (i.e., $n_{III} = 30$) and "holes" in the fourth subregion (i.e., $n_{IV} = 20$).

Both the LHS and the CMCS discretize the true distribution P_t $(t = 2, \ldots, T)$ and replace it by an empirical distribution $\hat{P}_t$, where now each realization $\boldsymbol{\xi}_t^s$ occurs

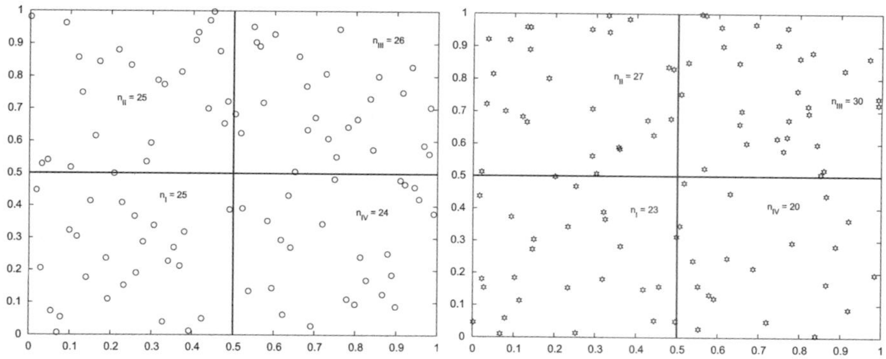

Fig. 10.1 An example of 100 sample points obtained through the LHS (*on the left*) and the CMCS (*on the right*) of a two-dimensional uniform vector on $[0, 1]^2$

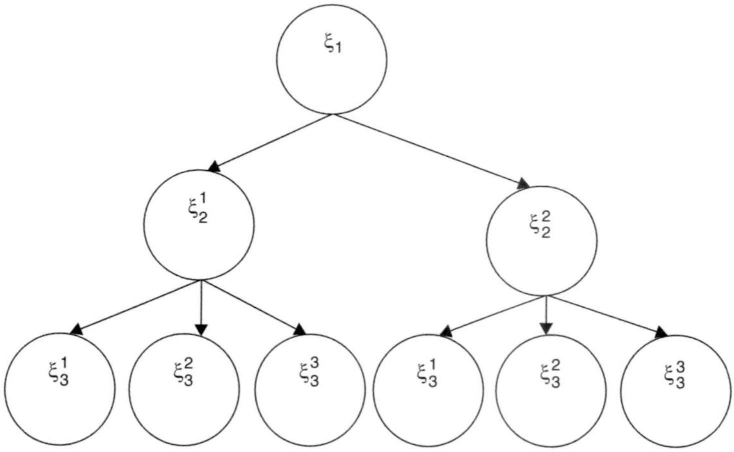

Fig. 10.2 A simple example of a scenario tree which preserves stagewise independence with $\mathcal{S}_2 := \{\xi_2^1, \xi_2^2\}$ and $\mathcal{S}_3 := \{\xi_3^1, \xi_3^2, \xi_3^3\}$

with probability $1/N_t$. Furthermore, the samples $\mathcal{S}_2, \ldots, \mathcal{S}_T$ form a scenario tree, which preserves the stagewise independence of $\tilde{\boldsymbol{\xi}}_t$; a simple example of such a tree is given in Fig. 10.2. The total number of scenarios in this tree is equal to $N_2 \times \ldots \times N_T$; i.e., the number of scenarios grows exponentially with the number of stages T. However, it will be seen in Sects. 10.3.1 and 10.3.2 that the number of times optimization is performed in a single iteration of the algorithm is much less than the total number of scenarios in the tree; this important property is due to the stagewise independence of $\tilde{\boldsymbol{\xi}}_t$.

We replace the possibly untractable expectations in (10.1) and (10.2) by their SAA's in (10.4), and obtain the following so-called SAA problems. At $t = 1$ the problem is

$$\begin{aligned} &\underset{\mathbf{x}_1 \geq \mathbf{0}}{\text{Min}}\ \mathbf{c}_1'\mathbf{x}_1 + \hat{\mathcal{Q}}_2\left(\mathbf{x}_1\right) \\ &\text{s.t.}\quad \mathbf{A}_1\mathbf{x}_1 = \mathbf{b}_1\ . \end{aligned} \tag{10.5}$$

At $t = 2, \ldots, T-1$ and for a specific realization $\boldsymbol{\xi}_t^s$, the problem is

$$\begin{aligned} &\underset{\mathbf{x}_t \geq \mathbf{0}}{\text{Min}}\ \mathbf{c}_t'\mathbf{x}_t + \hat{\mathcal{Q}}_{t+1}\left(\mathbf{x}_t\right) \\ &\text{s.t.}\quad \mathbf{B}_t^s\mathbf{x}_{t-1} + \mathbf{A}_t\mathbf{x}_t = \mathbf{b}_t^s\ . \end{aligned} \tag{10.6}$$

At $t = T$ and for a specific realization $\boldsymbol{\xi}_T^s$, the problem is

$$\begin{aligned} &\underset{\mathbf{x}_T \geq \mathbf{0}}{\text{Min}}\ \mathbf{c}_T'\mathbf{x}_T \\ &\text{s.t.}\quad \mathbf{B}_T^s\mathbf{x}_{T-1} + \mathbf{A}_T\mathbf{x}_T = \mathbf{b}_T^s\ . \end{aligned} \tag{10.7}$$

10.3 Stochastic Dual Dynamic Programming Algorithm

This section gives a brief description of the Stochastic Dual Dynamic Programming (SDDP) algorithm. More comprehensive discussions can be found in [23–25]. Recent applications of the SDDP can be found in [15, 26]. The SDDP is a sampling-based algorithm for solving multistage stochastic linear problems. The algorithm can be divided into two steps, namely backward and forward passes, that are repeated iteratively until a termination criterion is satisfied. In the backward pass which is introduced in Sect. 10.3.1, the algorithm starts at the last stage and passes information to the previous stage with respect to the expected total future costs until the first stage is reached. That information comes in the form of a Benders cut, which is an outer linear approximation of the expected cost-to-go function. At the end of the backward pass, the algorithm updates the lower bound on the objective value of the T-stage problem. In the forward pass which is introduced in Sect. 10.3.2, the algorithm samples a group of scenarios—from the second to the last stage—which is called a sample path; then, starting at the first stage and proceeding to the next one, it optimizes the T-stage problem over this path. The forward pass is repeated for a number of times to update the estimate of an upper bound on the objective value of the T-stage problem. Algorithm 2 presents an overview of the SDDP algorithm.

For the rest of the paper, we make the following standard assumption of the SDDP literature.

(A3) The problems in (10.5) through (10.7) have relatively complete recourse; i.e., given any feasible $\mathbf{x}_{t-1}\left(\boldsymbol{\xi}_{[t-1]}^s\right)$ to any $(t-1)$ th-stage problem defined by a realization $\boldsymbol{\xi}_{[t-1]}^s$ of the random data, there exists $\mathbf{x}_t$ that solves $\mathbf{B}_t^s\mathbf{x}_{t-1} + \mathbf{A}_t\mathbf{x}_t = \mathbf{b}_t^s$ for almost every (a.e.) realization $\boldsymbol{\xi}_t^s \in \Xi_t$.

Algorithm 2: An overview of the SDDP algorithm

Require: $\epsilon > 0$ (accuracy), $\{\mathcal{S}_t\}_{t=2,\ldots,T}$ (scenario tree)
Initialize: iteration $\leftarrow 0$, $\hat{\phi}_{\text{up}} = \infty$ (upper bound), $\phi_{\text{low}} = -\infty$ (lower bound), $\{\mathcal{K}_t \equiv \emptyset\}_{t=1,\ldots,T}$ (cut index sets)
while $\hat{\phi}_{\text{up}} - \phi_{\text{low}} > \epsilon$ **do**
  Perform the forward pass: Update the upper bound $\hat{\phi}_{\text{up}}$
  Perform the backward pass: Update the lower bound ϕ_{low}
  Update the iteration number: iteration $\leftarrow$ iteration + 1
end while

10.3.1 Backward Pass

In this section, it is assumed that a sequence $\{\overline{\mathbf{x}}_{t-1}\}_{t=2}^{T}$ of trial solutions was already obtained through the forward pass; in fact, the forward pass gives M such sequences, where M is the number of sample paths. The procedure below is described for a single sequence, but it can be straightforwardly applied to the M sequences separately.

At $t = T$, for a given $\overline{\mathbf{x}}_{T-1}$, the backward pass solves (10.7) for all $\boldsymbol{\xi}_T^s \in \mathcal{S}_T$:

$$\begin{aligned} &\operatorname*{Min}_{\mathbf{x}_T \geq \mathbf{0}} \ \mathbf{c}_T' \mathbf{x}_T \\ &\text{s.t.} \quad \mathbf{A}_T \mathbf{x}_T = \mathbf{b}_T^s - \mathbf{B}_T^s \overline{\mathbf{x}}_{T-1} \ . \end{aligned} \tag{10.8}$$

Let $Q_T(\overline{\mathbf{x}}_{T-1}, \boldsymbol{\xi}_T^s)$ be the optimal value of (10.8), and suppose that $Q_T(\mathbf{x}_{T-1}, \tilde{\boldsymbol{\xi}}_T)$ is finite for a.e. $\boldsymbol{\xi}_T^s \in \Xi_T$ (e.g., the feasible set in (10.8) is bounded). Then, both $Q_T(\mathbf{x}_{T-1}, \boldsymbol{\xi}_T^s)$ and its SAA $\hat{\mathcal{Q}}_T(\mathbf{x}_{T-1})$ are convex in $\mathbf{x}_{T-1}$ (in fact, they are piecewise linear). The Benders cut (or simply the cut) follows from the following gradient inequality that holds for all $\mathbf{x}_{T-1}$ because of the convexity of $Q_T(\mathbf{x}_{T-1}, \boldsymbol{\xi}_T^s)$

$$Q_T(\mathbf{x}_{T-1}, \boldsymbol{\xi}_T^s) \geq Q_T(\overline{\mathbf{x}}_{T-1}, \boldsymbol{\xi}_T^s) + (\mathbf{x}_{T-1} - \overline{\mathbf{x}}_{T-1})' \, \mathbf{g}_T^s \tag{10.9}$$

where $\mathbf{g}_T^s = -\mathbf{B}_T^{s\prime} \boldsymbol{\pi}_T^s$ is a subgradient of $Q_T(\mathbf{x}_{T-1}, \boldsymbol{\xi}_T^s)$ at a point $\overline{\mathbf{x}}_{T-1}$ and $\boldsymbol{\pi}_T^s$ is the vector of dual variables corresponding to the constraints in (10.8). The inequality (10.9) can also be written for $\hat{\mathcal{Q}}_T(\mathbf{x}_{T-1})$, where now $Q_T(\overline{\mathbf{x}}_{T-1}, \boldsymbol{\xi}_T^s)$ and $\mathbf{g}_T^s$ are replaced by $\hat{\mathcal{Q}}_T(\overline{\mathbf{x}}_{T-1})$ and $\hat{\mathbf{g}}_T$ computed through

$$\hat{\mathcal{Q}}_T(\overline{\mathbf{x}}_{T-1}) = \frac{1}{N_T} \sum_{s=1}^{N_T} Q_T(\overline{\mathbf{x}}_{T-1}, \boldsymbol{\xi}_T^s) \text{ and } \hat{\mathbf{g}}_T = \frac{1}{N_T} \sum_{s=1}^{N_T} \mathbf{g}_T^s \ .$$

This cut is shared by all $(T-1)$th stage problems; see [18] and also Fig. 10.2.

In (10.6) at stage $t = T-1$, $\hat{\mathcal{Q}}_T(\mathbf{x}_{T-1})$ is replaced by the maximum of a collection of cuts added to the problem during the course of the algorithm. Let $\mathcal{K}_{T-1}$ be the index set of these cuts. That is, a variable $\hat{\theta}_T \in \mathbb{R}$ is defined such that

$$\hat{\theta}_T := \max_{k_{T-1} \in \mathcal{K}_{T-1}} \left\{ \mathbf{x}'_{T-1} \hat{\mathbf{g}}_{T,k_{T-1}} + \hat{\beta}_{T,k_{T-1}} \right\}$$

where $\hat{\beta}_{T,k_{T-1}}$ is the intercept, and for a specific cut, it is computed through $\hat{\beta}_T = \hat{\mathcal{Q}}_T(\overline{\mathbf{x}}_{T-1}) - \overline{\mathbf{x}}'_{T-1}\hat{\mathbf{g}}_T$. Then, for a given trial solution $\overline{\mathbf{x}}_{T-2}$, the backward pass solves the following problem for all $\boldsymbol{\xi}^s_{T-1} \in \mathcal{S}_{T-1}$:

$$\begin{aligned} \underset{\mathbf{x}_{T-1} \geq \mathbf{0}, \hat{\theta}_T \in \mathbb{R}}{\text{Min}} \quad & \mathbf{c}'_{T-1}\mathbf{x}_{T-1} + \hat{\theta}_T \\ \text{s.t.} \quad & \mathbf{A}_{T-1}\mathbf{x}_{T-1} = \mathbf{b}^s_{T-1} - \mathbf{B}^s_{T-1}\overline{\mathbf{x}}_{T-2} \\ & -\mathbf{x}'_{T-1}\hat{\mathbf{g}}_{T,k_{T-1}} + \hat{\theta}_T \geq \hat{\beta}_{T,k_{T-1}} \quad k_{T-1} \in \mathcal{K}_{T-1} \, . \end{aligned} \tag{10.10}$$

Let $\underline{\mathcal{Q}}_{T-1}\left(\overline{\mathbf{x}}_{T-2}, \boldsymbol{\xi}^s_{T-1}\right)$ be the optimal value of (10.10) and $\hat{\underline{\mathcal{Q}}}_{T-1}(\overline{\mathbf{x}}_{T-2})$ its SAA. This $\hat{\underline{\mathcal{Q}}}_{T-1}(\overline{\mathbf{x}}_{T-2})$ is only a lower bound on the optimal value of (10.6) because $\hat{\theta}_T$ approximates $\hat{\mathcal{Q}}_T(\mathbf{x}_{T-1})$ from below. Then, the cut which is passed to all $(T-2)$th stage problems is found where now the dual vector $\boldsymbol{\pi}^s_{T-1}$ corresponds to the constraints $\mathbf{A}_{T-1}\mathbf{x}_{T-1} = \mathbf{b}^s_{T-1} - \mathbf{B}^s_{T-1}\overline{\mathbf{x}}_{T-2}$, and the same steps are repeated for stages $t = T-2, \ldots, 2$.

At stage $t = 1$, the backward pass solves the following problem:

$$\begin{aligned} \underset{\mathbf{x}_1 \geq \mathbf{0}, \hat{\theta}_2 \in \mathbb{R}}{\text{Min}} \quad & \mathbf{c}'_1\mathbf{x}_1 + \hat{\theta}_2 \\ \text{s.t.} \quad & \mathbf{A}_1\mathbf{x}_1 = \mathbf{b}_1 \\ & -\mathbf{x}'_1\hat{\mathbf{g}}_{2,k_1} + \hat{\theta}_2 \geq \hat{\beta}_{2,k_1} \; k_1 \in \mathcal{K}_1 \, . \end{aligned} \tag{10.11}$$

Note that the optimal value ϕ_{low} of (10.11) is a lower bound on the optimal value of the whole T-stage SAA problems [i.e., (10.5) through (10.7)], and this ϕ_{low} is utilized in the termination criterion of the SDDP algorithm; see Algorithm 2. Moreover, at each iteration, a new cut is added to (10.11) so that ϕ_{low} is non-decreasing. Solving (10.11) terminates the backward pass per iteration. Algorithm 3 presents a pseudocode for the backward pass.

10.3.2 Forward Pass

This section summarizes the forward pass which provides trial solutions to the backward pass and estimates an upper bound on the objective value of the whole T-stage SAA problems. Unlike the backward pass, the forward pass is not performed over the whole scenario tree, but it samples a sequence of scenarios from the second till the last stage; this sampling can be done either from the true distribution P_t for $t = 2, \ldots, T$ or from the fixed scenario tree $\mathcal{S}_2, \ldots, \mathcal{S}_T$, which is called an internal sampling. The convergence of the SDDP algorithm, however, requires the sampling

Algorithm 3: Backward pass of the SDDP algorithm for M trial solutions

Require: $\left\{\overline{\mathbf{x}}_1, \overline{\mathbf{x}}_2^m, \ldots, \overline{\mathbf{x}}_{T-1}^m\right\}_{m=1,\ldots,M}$ (trial solutions)
for $t = T \to 2$ **do**
  for $m = 1 \to M$ **do**
    for $s = 1 \to N_t$ **do**
      Solve stage t problem ($\hat{\theta}_{T+1} = 0$, $\mathcal{K}_T \equiv \emptyset$, $\underline{Q}_T\left(\overline{\mathbf{x}}_{T-1}^m, \boldsymbol{\xi}_T^s\right) = Q_T\left(\overline{\mathbf{x}}_{T-1}^m, \boldsymbol{\xi}_T^s\right)$, $\hat{\underline{\mathcal{Q}}}_T\left(\overline{\mathbf{x}}_{t-1}^m\right) = \hat{\mathcal{Q}}_T\left(\overline{\mathbf{x}}_{t-1}^m\right)$):
      $\left(\underline{Q}_t\left(\overline{\mathbf{x}}_{t-1}^m, \boldsymbol{\xi}_t^s\right), \boldsymbol{\pi}_t^{s,m}\right) \leftarrow \min_{\mathbf{x}_t \geq \mathbf{0}, \hat{\theta}_{t+1} \in \mathbb{R}} \left\{\mathbf{c}_t'\mathbf{x}_t + \hat{\theta}_{t+1} :\right.$
      $\left.\mathbf{A}_t\mathbf{x}_t = \mathbf{b}_t^s - \mathbf{B}_t^s\overline{\mathbf{x}}_{t-1}^m, -\mathbf{x}_t'\hat{\mathbf{g}}_{t+1,k_t}^m + \hat{\theta}_{t+1} \geq \hat{\beta}_{t+1,k_t}^m k_t \in \mathcal{K}_t\right\}$
      Compute $\mathbf{g}_t^{s,m}$: $\mathbf{g}_t^{s,m} = -\mathbf{B}_t^{s\prime}\boldsymbol{\pi}_t^{s,m}$
    end for
    Compute $\hat{\mathbf{g}}_t^m$, $\hat{\underline{\mathcal{Q}}}_t\left(\overline{\mathbf{x}}_{t-1}^m\right)$, and $\hat{\beta}_t^m$:
    $\hat{\mathbf{g}}_t^m = \frac{1}{N_t}\sum_{s=1}^{N_t}\mathbf{g}_t^{s,m}$, $\hat{\underline{\mathcal{Q}}}_t\left(\overline{\mathbf{x}}_{t-1}^m\right) = \frac{1}{N_t}\sum_{s=1}^{N_t}\underline{Q}_t\left(\overline{\mathbf{x}}_{t-1}^m, \boldsymbol{\xi}_t^s\right)$,
    $\hat{\beta}_t^m = \hat{\underline{\mathcal{Q}}}_t\left(\overline{\mathbf{x}}_{t-1}^m\right) - \overline{\mathbf{x}}_{t-1}^{m\prime}\hat{\mathbf{g}}_t^m$
    Add the new cut $-\mathbf{x}_{t-1}'\hat{\mathbf{g}}_t^m + \hat{\theta}_t \geq \hat{\beta}_t^m$ to all $(t-1)$th stage problems
  end for
end for
Update the lower bound: Solve stage 1 problem
$\phi_{\text{low}} \leftarrow \min_{\mathbf{x}_1 \geq \mathbf{0}, \hat{\theta}_2 \in \mathbb{R}} \left\{\mathbf{c}_1'\mathbf{x}_1 + \hat{\theta}_2 : \mathbf{A}_1\mathbf{x}_1 = \mathbf{b}_1, -\mathbf{x}_1'\hat{\mathbf{g}}_{2,k_1} + \hat{\theta}_2 \geq \hat{\beta}_{2,k_1} k_1 \in \mathcal{K}_1\right\}$

be done from the fixed scenario tree; see Proposition 3.1 in [25]. Hence, in the rest of the paper, we only consider the internal sampling.

To keep the notation simple, the forward pass below is described for a generic path, omitting the path index m. The forward pass starts by solving

$$\begin{aligned} \operatorname*{Min}_{\mathbf{x}_1 \geq \mathbf{0}, \hat{\theta}_2 \in \mathbb{R}} \quad & \mathbf{c}_1'\mathbf{x}_1 + \hat{\theta}_2 \\ \text{s.t.} \quad & \mathbf{A}_1\mathbf{x}_1 = \mathbf{b}_1 \\ & -\mathbf{x}_1'\hat{\mathbf{g}}_{2,k_1} + \hat{\theta}_2 \geq \hat{\beta}_{2,k_1} \; k_1 \in \mathcal{K}_1 \; . \end{aligned} \tag{10.12}$$

For later stages $t = 2, \ldots, T$, it solves

$$\begin{aligned} \operatorname*{Min}_{\mathbf{x}_t \geq \mathbf{0}, \hat{\theta}_{t+1} \in \mathbb{R}} \quad & \mathbf{c}_t'\mathbf{x}_t + \hat{\theta}_{t+1} \\ \text{s.t.} \quad & \mathbf{A}_t\mathbf{x}_t = \mathbf{b}_t^\iota - \mathbf{B}_t^\iota\overline{\mathbf{x}}_{t-1} \\ & -\mathbf{x}_t'\hat{\mathbf{g}}_{t+1,k_t} + \hat{\theta}_{t+1} \geq \hat{\beta}_{t+1,k_t} \; k_t \in \mathcal{K}_t \end{aligned} \tag{10.13}$$

where $\hat{\theta}_{T+1} = 0$. Notice that at iteration 0, the index sets $\mathcal{K}_t$ of cuts are all empty for $t = 1, \ldots, T-1$, and hence to have finite optimal values in (10.12) and (10.13), lower bounds on $\hat{\theta}_t$ are required.

Solving (10.12) through (10.13) terminates the forward pass per path. This results in a sequence of policies $\left\{\bar{\mathbf{x}}_1, \bar{\mathbf{x}}_2\left(\boldsymbol{\xi}^{\iota}_{[2,m]}\right), \bar{\mathbf{x}}_3\left(\boldsymbol{\xi}^{\iota}_{[3,m]}\right), \ldots, \bar{\mathbf{x}}_T\left(\boldsymbol{\xi}^{\iota}_{[T,m]}\right)\right\}$, which is used as trial solutions by the backward pass in Sect. 10.3.1. By construction, these policies are feasible for the SAA problems in (10.5) through (10.7). Let ϕ^m be the T-stage objective value of these policies; i.e.,

$$\phi^m = \mathbf{c}_1'\bar{\mathbf{x}}_1 + \sum_{t=2}^{T} \mathbf{c}_t'\bar{\mathbf{x}}_t\left(\boldsymbol{\xi}^{\iota}_{[t,m]}\right).$$

The forward pass is repeated for the M independent sample paths, each resulting in a new ϕ^m. Then, an unbiased estimator of an upper bound of the whole T-stage SAA problems and its variance are given by

$$\hat{\phi} = \frac{\sum_{m=1}^{M}\phi^m}{M} \text{ and } \hat{\sigma}^2_{\phi} = \frac{\sum_{m=1}^{M}\left(\phi^m - \hat{\phi}\right)^2}{M-1}.$$

By the Central Limit Theorem, this $\hat{\phi}$ has approximately a normal distribution for a large M (in practice, M should be bigger than 30). It was suggested in [25] to estimate an upper bound on the whole T-stage SAA problems through the following $100(1-\alpha)\%$-upper confidence bound

$$\hat{\phi}_{\text{up}} = \hat{\phi} + z_{\alpha}\hat{\sigma}_{\phi}/\sqrt{M}$$

where z_α is the $(1-\alpha)$-quantile of the standard normal distribution, and to terminate the SDDP algorithm if the difference between the upper bound $\hat{\phi}_{\text{up}}$ and the lower bound ϕ_{low} is less than a prescribed accuracy level $\epsilon > 0$; see Algorithm 2. Algorithm 4 presents a pseudocode for the forward pass.

10.4 Disaster Preparedness and Short-Term Relief Distribution Problem

In this section, we assume that we are given a transportation network with a node set $\mathcal{N}$ and an arc set $\mathcal{A}$. The node set $\mathcal{N}$ is partitioned into two sets I and J; the nodes in I are the possible locations for storage facilities and the nodes in J are the shelters. Furthermore, we assume that there exists a path connecting every pair of nodes $i', j' \in \mathcal{N}$ in the network. Our decisions at different stages $t = 1, \ldots, T$ can be summarized as follows. The decisions at stage 1 are pre-disaster decisions and they are made before observing any randomness; these decisions belong to the disaster preparedness phase. Our decisions at stage 1 determine the locations and the size categories of the storage facilities, and the amounts of emergency commodities of different types to be pre-positioned at the opened facilities. The decisions at later

---

Algorithm 4: Forward pass of the SDDP algorithm for M sample paths

---

Require: Finite lower bounds on $\hat{\theta}_t$ for $t = 2, \ldots, T$
for $m = 1 \rightarrow M$ **do**
  Solve stage 1 problem:
  $\overline{\mathbf{x}}_1 \leftarrow \arg\min_{\mathbf{x}_1 \geq \mathbf{0}, \hat{\theta}_2 \in \mathbb{R}} \left\{ \mathbf{c}_1' \mathbf{x}_1 + \hat{\theta}_2 : \mathbf{A}_1 \mathbf{x}_1 = \mathbf{b}_1, -\mathbf{x}_1' \hat{\mathbf{g}}_{2,k_1} + \hat{\theta}_2 \geq \hat{\beta}_{2,k_1} k_1 \in \mathcal{K}_1 \right\}$
  for $t = 2 \rightarrow T$ **do**
    Generate path m: $(\boldsymbol{\xi}^{\iota}_{2,m}, \boldsymbol{\xi}^{\iota}_{3,m}, \ldots, \boldsymbol{\xi}^{\iota}_{T,m})$
    Solve stage t problem ($\hat{\theta}_{T+1} = 0$):
    $\overline{\mathbf{x}}_t^m \leftarrow \arg\min_{\mathbf{x}_t \geq \mathbf{0}, \hat{\theta}_{t+1} \in \mathbb{R}} \left\{ \mathbf{c}_t' \mathbf{x}_t + \hat{\theta}_{t+1} : \right.$
    $\left. \mathbf{A}_t \mathbf{x}_t = \mathbf{b}^{\iota}_{t,m} - \mathbf{B}^{\iota}_{t,m} \overline{\mathbf{x}}^m_{t-1}, -\mathbf{x}_t' \hat{\mathbf{g}}_{t+1,k_t} + \hat{\theta}_{t+1} \geq \hat{\beta}_{t+1,k_t} k_t \in \mathcal{K}_t \right\}$
  end for
  Compute the T-stage objective value:
  $\phi^m \leftarrow \mathbf{c}_1' \overline{\mathbf{x}}_1 + \sum_{t=2}^{T} \mathbf{c}_t' \overline{\mathbf{x}}_t \left(\boldsymbol{\xi}^{\iota}_{[t,m]} \right)$
end for
Compute the sample average $\hat{\phi}$ and the sample variance $\hat{\sigma}^2_{\phi}$:
$\hat{\phi} = \frac{\sum_{m=1}^{M} \phi^m}{M}$ and $\hat{\sigma}^2_{\phi} = \frac{\sum_{m=1}^{M} (\phi^m - \hat{\phi})^2}{M-1}$
Update the upper bound:
$\hat{\phi}_{\text{up}} \leftarrow \hat{\phi} + z_\alpha \hat{\sigma}_{\phi} / \sqrt{M}$

---

stages $t = 2, \ldots, T$ are post-disaster decisions and the tth stage decisions are made after observing that stage's randomness $\tilde{\boldsymbol{\xi}}_t$; these decisions belong to the disaster response phase. Our decisions at stages $t = 2, \ldots, T$ determine the amounts of emergency commodities to be purchased to update the previous stage's inventories and the amounts of commodities to be distributed to the disaster victims.

There are two sources of randomness in our problem, namely the demands for emergency commodities at shelters and the arc capacities, which correspond to the total amount of all commodities that can be transported through those arcs. At any stage t, we denote the demand and capacity vectors by $\tilde{\boldsymbol{\nu}}_t$ and $\tilde{\boldsymbol{\kappa}}_t$, respectively, so $\tilde{\boldsymbol{\xi}}_t = \left(\tilde{\boldsymbol{\nu}}_t', \tilde{\boldsymbol{\kappa}}_t' \right)'$. We assume that a component $\tilde{\nu}^k_{tj}$ of $\tilde{\boldsymbol{\nu}}_t$, which is the random demand for commodity k at shelter j at stage t, is modeled as follows.

$$\tilde{\nu}^k_{tj} = \delta^k_t \left(\varsigma_{t-1,j} + \tilde{\varsigma}_{t,j} \right) \text{ for } t = 2, \ldots, T,\ j \in J \tag{10.14}$$

where δ^k_t is the amount of commodity k needed by a single individual during stage t, $\varsigma_{t-1,j}$ is the number of evacuees who were expected to arrive at shelter j at the end of stage $(t-1)$, and $\tilde{\varsigma}_{t,j}$ is the random additional number of evacuees who arrive at shelter j at stage t. We consider only the first and most critical 72 h in the aftermath of a disaster (an earthquake). Hence, if the total number of stages is three (i.e., $T = 3$), both stages 2 and 3 are assumed to last for 36 h, and the δ^k_t's are determined accordingly. Furthermore, in the literature the number of evacuees

Table 10.1 Notation for the problems in (10.16) through (10.18)

L	:	Set of size categories indexed by l
K	:	Set of commodity types indexed by k
F_{il}	:	Fixed cost of opening a facility of size category l in location i
q_t^k	:	Unit acquisition cost of commodity k at stage t
b^k	:	Unit space requirement for commodity k
M_l	:	Overall capacity of a facility of size l
$d_{ti'j'}^k$	:	Unit transportation cost of commodity k at stage t through an arc (i', j')
p_t^k	:	Unit shortage cost of commodity k at stage t
h_T^k	:	Unit holding cost of commodity k at stage T due to spoilage

accumulated in time is usually modeled through an S-shaped curve (see [27]). Hence, we assume a normal distribution—whose cumulative distribution function is an S-shaped curve—and a lognormal distribution—whose right tail is thicker than the one of a normal distribution—for $\tilde{\varsigma}_{t,j}$.

After an earthquake occurs, we assume that all arcs in $\mathcal{A}$ can still be used for transportation, and hence the network remains connected. However, the average speed of a vehicle is reduced due to the partial blockage of an arc (e.g., because of a collapsed building). Moreover, we assume that a component $\tilde{\kappa}_{ti'j'}$ of $\tilde{\boldsymbol{\kappa}}_t$, which is the random capacity for any arc (i', j') at stage t, is modeled through:

$$\tilde{\kappa}_{ti'j'} = \eta * \frac{\tau(t)}{\omega(i',j')/\tilde{\gamma}_{ti'j'}} \text{ for } t = 2, \ldots, T, (i', j') \in \mathcal{A} \tag{10.15}$$

where η is the capacity of a single vehicle, $\tau(t)$ is the length of stage t (i.e., if $T = 3$, then $\tau(t) = 36$), $\omega(i', j')$ is the actual distance between nodes i' and j', and $\tilde{\gamma}_{ti'j'}$ is the random speed of the vehicle. In (10.15) it is assumed that there is a single vehicle type, and that the random speed $\tilde{\gamma}_{ti'j'}$ remains constant over stage t. Because the speeds have been found empirically to be normally distributed in [28], $\tilde{\gamma}_{tij}$ is assumed to have a normal distribution.

We now present the mathematical formulations for all T stages for which the notation is given in Table 10.1. Our approach extends the problem in [12] in the following two senses: (1) The problem in [12] was formulated and solved as a two-stage (static) stochastic programming problem; ours, however, is formulated and solved as a multistage (dynamic) stochastic programming problem. Hence, our results will reflect the effects of the dynamic updates of the acquisition decisions at stages $t = 2, \ldots, T - 1$ as well as the effects of the dynamic updates of the random demands and road capacities. (2) It was assumed in [12] that $\tilde{\boldsymbol{\xi}}_t$ has a finite support. In our problem, however, we have an infinite number of realizations for $\tilde{\nu}_{tj}^k$ and $\tilde{\kappa}_{ti'j'}$. Through the CMCS or the LHS in Sect. 10.2, we generate a (finite) scenario tree (i.e., ν_{tj}^{ks} and $\kappa_{ti'j'}^s$ for $t = 2, \ldots, T$ and $s = 1, \ldots, N_t$), and then solve the problem over this tree. Obviously, our results will depend on the generated tree, and hence in Sect. 10.4.1, we will apply the SDDP algorithm over a number of generated trees and present the median, lower, and upper quartiles of the results.

Now, the stage 1 SAA problem in (10.5) is

$$\begin{aligned}
\text{Min} \quad & \sum_{i \in I} \sum_{l \in L} F_{il} y_{il} + \sum_{k \in K} \sum_{i \in I} q_1^k r_{1i}^k + \hat{\mathcal{Q}}_2(\mathbf{x}_1) \\
\text{s.t.} \quad & \sum_{k \in K} b^k r_{1i}^k \leq \sum_{l \in L} M_l y_{il} \forall i \in I \qquad (10.16a) \\
& \sum_{l \in L} y_{il} \leq 1 \forall i \in I \qquad (10.16b) \\
& y_{il} \in \{0,1\} \, \forall i \in I, l \in L, r_{1i}^k \geq 0 \forall i \in I, k \in K
\end{aligned}$$

where y_{il} are the variables for location i and size category l of the storage facilities, r_{1i}^k are the variables for the amounts of emergency commodity k to be pre-positioned at storage facility i, and $\mathbf{x}_1$ is the vector whose components are the y_{il}'s and the r_{1i}^k's. Furthermore, the constraints (10.16a) are for the capacities of the storage facilities, and the constraints (10.16b) restrict the number of storage facilities per node to at most one. Note that in Sect. 10.4.1, the binary restrictions on y_{il}'s are relaxed; i.e., $y_{il} \in [0,1]$. For later stages $t = 2, \ldots, T-1$ and for realizations $\boldsymbol{\varsigma}_t^s$ and $\boldsymbol{\kappa}_t^s$ from the scenario tree, whose components are the ς_{tj}^s's and the $\kappa_{ti'j'}^s$'s, respectively, the stage t SAA problem in (10.6) is

$$\begin{aligned}
\text{Min} \quad & \sum_{k \in K} \sum_{i \in I} q_t^k r_{ti}^k + \sum_{(i',j') \in \mathcal{A}} \sum_{k \in K} d_{ti'j'}^k m_{ti'j'}^k + \sum_{j \in J} \sum_{k \in K} p_t^k w_{tj}^k + \hat{\mathcal{Q}}_{t+1}(\mathbf{x}_t) \\
\text{s.t.} \quad & z_{ti}^k + \sum_{(i,j') \in \mathcal{A}} m_{tij'}^k - \sum_{(j',i) \in \mathcal{A}} m_{tj'i}^k = r_{t-1,i}^k + z_{t-1,i}^k \forall i \in I, k \in K \qquad (10.17a) \\
& \sum_{(i',j) \in \mathcal{A}} m_{ti'j}^k - \sum_{(j,i') \in \mathcal{A}} m_{tji'}^k + w_{tj}^k = \delta_t^k \left(\varsigma_{t-1,j} + \varsigma_{t,j}^s \right) \qquad (10.17b) \\
& \forall j \in J, k \in K \\
& \sum_{k \in K} b^k \left(m_{ti'j'}^k + m_{tj'i'}^k \right) \leq \kappa_{ti'j'}^s \forall (i',j') \in \mathcal{A} \qquad (10.17c) \\
& \sum_{k \in K} b^k \left(z_{ti}^k + r_{ti}^k \right) \leq \sum_{l \in L} M_l y_{il} \forall i \in I \qquad (10.17d) \\
& r_{ti}^k, m_{ti'j'}^k, w_{tj}^k, z_{ti}^k \geq 0 \forall i \in I, j \in J, k \in K, (i',j') \in \mathcal{A}
\end{aligned}$$

where r_{ti}^k are the variables for the amounts of commodity k to be purchased at storage facility i with $q_t^k > q_1^k$, $m_{ti'j'}^k$ are the variables for the amounts of commodity k to be transported through arc (i', j'), z_{ti}^k and w_{tj}^k are the auxiliary variables for the inventory amounts of commodity k at facility i and shortage amounts of commodity k at shelter j, respectively, and $\mathbf{x}_t$ is the vector whose components are the r_{ti}^k's and the z_{ti}^k's. Moreover, the constraints (10.17a) represent the flow conservation constraints, where we set $z_{1,i}^k = 0 \forall i \in I, k \in K$, (10.17b) are the demand satisfaction constraints, and (10.17c) and (10.17d) are the capacity constraints for the arcs and the storage facilities, respectively.

The stage T SAA problem in (10.7) has the same constraints as in (10.17a) through (10.17c), but there are no more acquisition decisions at that stage and the remaining inventories are penalized through a unit holding (spoilage) cost. Hence, the objective function at $t = T$ is changed to

$$\text{Min} \sum_{k\in K}\sum_{i\in I} h_T^k z_{Ti}^k + \sum_{(i',j')\in\mathcal{A}}\sum_{k\in K} d_{Ti'j'}^k m_{Ti'j'}^k + \sum_{j\in J}\sum_{k\in K} p_T^k w_{Tj}^k . \tag{10.18}$$

Note that the formulation in (10.17) satisfies the relatively complete recourse assumption (A3) in Sect. 10.3; in fact, (10.17) has complete recourse. This is achieved by making the demand satisfaction constraints (10.17b) feasible for a.e. realization of $\tilde{\varsigma}_{t,j}$ through adding the shortage variables w_{tj}^k's.

Below, we give the necessary details for the application of the backward pass in Sect. 10.3.1 of the SDDP algorithm; more specifically, we present the matrix $\mathbf{B}_t$ and the dual vector $\boldsymbol{\pi}_t$ at all stages $t = 2, \ldots, T$. At stage $t = 2$, from (10.17), $\mathbf{B}_2$ is the matrix that is partitioned as

$$\mathbf{B}_2 = \begin{bmatrix} \mathbf{D}_{2,1} & \mathbf{0} \\ \mathbf{0} & \mathbf{D}_{2,2} \end{bmatrix}$$

where $\mathbf{D}_{2,1}$ is the $(|I| * |K|)$-dimensional (square) diagonal matrix with -1 on the diagonal, $\mathbf{D}_{2,2}$ is the $|I| \times (|I| * |L|)$-dimensional matrix given by

$$\mathbf{D}_{2,2} = \begin{bmatrix} -M_1 & -M_2 & \ldots & -M_{|L|} & 0 & 0 & \ldots 0 & \ldots 0 & 0 & \ldots 0 \\ 0 & 0 & \ldots 0 & & -M_1 & -M_2 & \ldots & -M_{|L|} & \ldots 0 & 0 & \ldots 0 \\ . & . & \ldots . & & . & . & \ldots . & \ldots . & . & \ldots . \\ 0 & 0 & \ldots 0 & & . & . & \ldots . & \ldots -M_1 & -M_2 & \ldots -M_{|L|} \end{bmatrix}$$

and the $\mathbf{0}$'s are the zero matrices of appropriate dimensions. The dual vector $\boldsymbol{\pi}_2$ consists of the dual variables corresponding to the constraints in (10.17a) and (10.17d). For later stages $t = 3, \ldots, T$, from (10.17), $\mathbf{B}_t$ is the matrix that is partitioned as

$$\mathbf{B}_t = \begin{bmatrix} \mathbf{D}_{2,1} & \mathbf{D}_{2,1} \end{bmatrix}$$

and the dual vector $\boldsymbol{\pi}_t$ consists of the dual variables corresponding to the constraints in (10.17a).

10.4.1 Computational Results

We consider three consumable emergency commodity types, namely water, food, and medical kits, and 10 potential locations for storage facilities; the data for costs and volumes of commodities are given in Table 10.2, and the data for costs and

Table 10.2 Unit purchase price at stage 1, volume occupied, and transportation costs for commodities

Commodity	q_1^k ($ per unit)	b^k (ft^3 per unit)	Transport cost ($ per unit-mile)
Water (1,000 gals)	647.7	144.6	0.3
Food (1,000 MREs)	5420	83.33	0.04
Medical kits	140	1.16	5.80e−04

Table 10.3 Categories, fixed costs, and storage capacity for facilities

Size category	Descriptor	F_l ($)	M_l (ft^3)
1	Small	19,600	36,400
2	Medium	188,400	408,200
3	Large	300,000	780,000

Table 10.4 Estimated numbers of non-damaged (*ND*), slightly damaged (*SD*), medium damaged (*MD*), extensively damaged (*ED*), and completely damaged (*CD*) buildings in the two boroughs of Istanbul (source for Avcilar and Kucukcekmece: [30], source for Istanbul's total: [29])

	ND buildings	SD buildings	MD buildings	ED buildings	CD buildings
Avcilar	2,572	5,220	4,919	1,550	736
Kucukcekmece	8,104	11,916	11,828	3,800	1,757
Istanbul's total	155,288	183,522	154,193	46,379	23,291

capacities of storage facilities are given in Table 10.3 (the same data as in [12]). Moreover, we consider 30 shelters that are schools or hospitals in the two boroughs of Istanbul, namely Avcilar and Kucukcekmece; in the network representation, there are all together 40 nodes and 75 arcs linking these nodes. These boroughs were found to be very vulnerable to the earthquakes in [29] because of their soil conditions. The same work estimated the total numbers of buildings that are prone to be damaged at various levels in all boroughs of Istanbul for an earthquake of magnitude 7.3 on the Richter scale; see Table 10.4. Furthermore, [29] estimated the total number of casualties as 85,087 within all boroughs of Istanbul. According to the Turkish Statistical Institute [31], the population of Avcilar in 2012 was 395,274, and the population of Kucukcekmece was 721,911.

We consider $T = 3$ stages, and we assume that each stage lasts for $\tau(t) = 36\,\text{h}$. Furthermore, in (10.14), we set $\delta_t^k = 1.585$ gals per capita, $\delta_t^k = 4$ units per capita, and $\delta_t^k = 2.5$ units per capita for water, food, and medical kits, respectively. We further assume that in the aftermath of an earthquake, those people living in the medium-damaged buildings in both boroughs are distributed equally among the 30 shelters. The estimated total number of these people is given by $= (16747/52402) * (395274 + 721911) = 357037.846$, where from Table 10.4, 16,747 and 52,402 are respectively the total number of medium-damaged buildings and the total number of all buildings in both boroughs. Hence, at stage 2 in (10.14) $\varsigma_{1,j}$ is estimated through $\varsigma_{1,j} = 357037.846/30 = 11901.262 \forall j \in J$. For later stages, we assume that $\tilde{\varsigma}_{t,j}$ are identically distributed across shelters; hence, the means of the normal $\tilde{\varsigma}_{2,j}$ and $\tilde{\varsigma}_{3,j}$ are assumed to be given by $((17136/52402)*$

Table 10.5 Sampling strategies for the scenario tree of the SDDP

Case	Scenario tree	Distribution of $\tilde{\varsigma}_{t,j}$ in (10.14)
1	CMCS	Normal
2	LHS	Normal
3	CMCS	Lognormal
4	LHS	Lognormal

$(395274 + 721911))/30 = 12177.705$ and $((10676/52402) * (395274 + 721911))/30 = 7586.903$, respectively, where from Table 10.4, 17,136 and 10,676 are respectively the total number of slightly damaged buildings and the total number of non-damaged buildings in both boroughs. Moreover, the variances of $\tilde{\varsigma}_{2,j}$ and $\tilde{\varsigma}_{3,j}$ are assumed to be 10 % and 20 % of their corresponding means; i.e., the third stage data are assumed to be noisier than the second stage data. For the lognormal $\tilde{\varsigma}_{2,j}$ and $\tilde{\varsigma}_{3,j}$, we assume the same means (i.e., 12,177.705 and 7,586.903) and the same variances as the normal $\tilde{\varsigma}_{2,j}$ and $\tilde{\varsigma}_{3,j}$. Then, to generate the lognormal samples, the means and the variances of the corresponding normal random variables are computed; see, for example, [32].

In (10.15), we set $\eta = 28.252\text{ft}^3$. We also assume that $\tilde{\gamma}_{tij}$ are identically distributed across arcs, the means of the normal $\tilde{\gamma}_{2ij}$ and $\tilde{\gamma}_{3ij}$ are both assumed to be 24.855 miles per hour, and the variances are again assumed to be 10 % and 20 % of their means, respectively. In (10.17) and (10.18), the acquisition price q_2^k at stage 2, the penalty costs p_2^k and p_3^k at stages 2 and 3, and the holding cost z_3^k at stage 3 are set as $q_2^k = 3q_1^k$, $p_2^k = 10q_1^k$, $p_3^k = 10q_2^k$, and $z_3^k = 0.25q_2^k\ \forall k \in K$. Note that all numerical values are selected for illustration purpose only, and they may not match values that might be estimated by the ultimate users of the model.

We use CMCS or LHS to generate a scenario tree and consider the following cases summarized in Table 10.5. To measure the variability in the performances of the SDDP algorithm, we generate 10 scenario trees for each case in Table 10.5, and then apply the SDDP algorithm for each tree. The sample sizes for stages 2 and 3 are selected as $N_2 = N_3 = 300$, and hence, each scenario tree contains $300^2 = 90,000$ scenarios.

For the stopping criterion, the accuracy parameter ϵ is set to $\epsilon = 0.001$. However, because of the very slow convergence of the SDDP algorithm, we also fix the maximum number of iterations to 500, and we make the algorithm stop if at the 500th iteration, the original stopping criterion in Algorithm 2 is not satisfied; we observed that in all four cases and for all trees, the SDDP algorithm stopped because the maximum number of iterations was reached. Furthermore, to speed up the procedure, we make the SDDP algorithm run the forward pass once every 10 iterations. The number of sample paths generated for the forward pass is $M = 30$.

All computational experiments are conducted on a workstation with Windows 2008 Server, three Intel(R) Xeon(R) CPU E5-2670 CPUs of 2.60 GHz, and 4 GB RAM. The linear programming problems are solved by ILOG CPLEX Callable Library 12.2.

Figure 10.3 shows the third best (i.e., fastest) performance of the SDDP algorithm over the 10 scenario trees for all cases. To smooth out the fluctuations in the estimated upper bounds, we also consider the moving averages of the estimated upper bounds. It is obvious from Fig. 10.3 that most of the improvements (i.e., increases) in the lower bounds are made up to the first 1,000 CPU seconds, which correspond to the first 200 iterations. The numerical details for Fig. 10.3 are given in Table 10.6. In that table, the absolute gap is the criterion that is checked by the stopping criterion of the algorithm in Algorithm 2; i.e., the absolute gap is $\hat{\phi}_{\text{up}} - \phi_{\text{low}}$, where we consider the moving average of the estimated upper bounds for $\hat{\phi}_{\text{up}}$. For all cases at 500th iteration, the SDDP algorithm is far from satisfying the stopping criterion in Algorithm 2, which stops the SDDP when the absolute gap is less than or equal to $\epsilon = 0.001$. We define the percent relative gap in Table 10.6 as

$$\text{Percent Relative Gap} = \frac{\hat{\phi}_{\text{up}} - \phi_{\text{low}}}{\phi_{\text{low}}} * 100$$

where we again use the moving average of the estimated upper bounds for $\hat{\phi}_{\text{up}}$. In Table 10.6, it is clear that the decreases in the percent relative gap are more substantial, especially in the first 200 iterations. Hence, in the applications of the SDDP algorithm, it is better to use the percent relative gap than the absolute gap in the stopping criterion, and stop the SDDP when this percent gap is less than, for example, 5 %.

To compare Cases 1 and 2, we apply the paired t-tests, where the null and the alternative hypotheses for the three tests are given by

H_0: Mean of (percent relative gap for Case 2 – percent relative gap for Case 1) = 0
H_1: Mean of (percent relative gap for Case 2 – percent relative gap for Case 1) > 0,

H_0: Mean of ("optimal" 3-stage cost for Case 2 – "optimal" 3-stage cost for Case 1) = 0
H_1: Mean of ("optimal" 3-stage cost for Case 2 – "optimal" 3-stage cost for Case 1) > 0,

and

H_0: Mean of (CPU time for Case 1 – CPU time for Case 2) = 0
H_1: Mean of (CPU time for Case 1 – CPU time for Case 2) > 0,

where the "optimal" 3-stage cost is the moving average of the estimated upper bounds at the 500th iteration (i.e., because both the absolute and percent relative gaps are minimum for the 500th iteration, the ultimate users should consider either the estimated upper bound or the moving average of the upper bounds at the 500th iteration as the "optimal" 3-stage cost). The p-values are found to be 0.3113, 0.3368, and 0.3337, respectively; see also Table 10.7 and Fig. 10.4. Hence, for all "reasonable" values of the significance level (i.e., $\alpha = 1\,\%$, $\alpha = 5\,\%$, and $\alpha = 10\,\%$), the three null hypotheses cannot be rejected; in fact, to reduce the

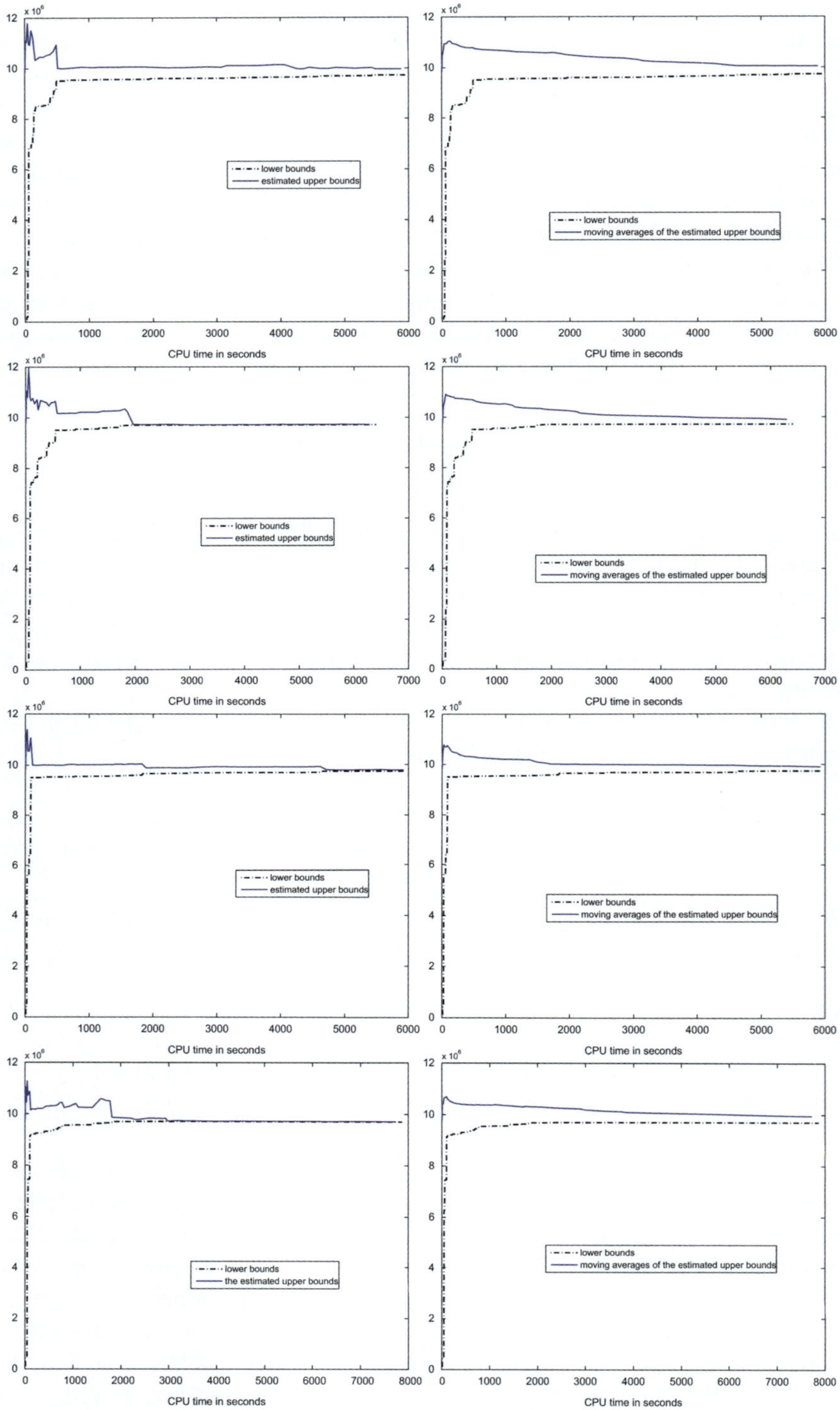

Fig. 10.3 Changes in bounds for the third fastest performance of the SDDP for Cases 1, 2, 3, and 4, respectively

Table 10.6 Improvements in the absolute and percent relative gaps over iterations corresponding to Fig. 10.3

Case	Iteration	Lower bound	Moving average of upper bounds	Absolute gap	Percent relative gap (%)
1	50	6,849,561.008	10,942,760.920	4,093,199.912	59.759
	100	8,519,613.644	10,957,160.021	2,437,546.377	28.611
	200	9,549,194.168	10,708,404.027	1,159,209.859	12.139
	350	9,636,998.992	10,218,123.122	581,124.130	6.030
	500	9,724,593.911	10,035,679.425	311,085.514	3.199
2	50	7,324,940.251	10,881,379.401	3,556,439.150	48.552
	100	8,445,593.177	10,744,304.566	2,298,711.389	27.218
	200	9,518,002.455	10,588,523.394	1,070,520.939	11.247
	350	9,705,782.196	10,292,149.092	586,366.896	6.041
	500	9,705,988.903	9,895,185.518	189,196.615	1.949
3	50	6,393,689.078	10,681,129.175	4,287,440.097	67.057
	100	9,520,065.086	10,444,020.568	923,955.482	9.705
	200	9,545,683.221	10,223,817.687	678,134.466	7.104
	350	9,675,491.422	9,998,380.536	322,889.114	3.337
	500	9,735,599.691	9,900,368.370	164,768.679	1.692
4	50	7,459,438.678	10,655,083.954	3,195,645.276	42.841
	100	9,241,570.677	10,481,877.804	1,240,307.127	13.421
	200	9,454,208.016	10,378,381.131	924,173.115	9.775
	350	9,698,366.587	10,306,273.237	607,906.650	6.268
	500	9,706,567.404	9,954,845.953	248,278.549	2.558

high noises in Table 10.7, the time-consuming SDDP algorithm has to be run over more scenario trees. However, the ultimate users of this procedure are going to run the SDDP algorithm over a single scenario tree. Then, it is advisable to generate the scenario tree through the LHS, because this sampling technique results in less variability on the percent relative gaps, the "optimal" 3-stage costs, and the CPU times over different scenario trees; see Fig. 10.4.

We also compare Cases 3 and 4 through the paired t-tests, where now the null and the alternative hypotheses are given by

H_0: Mean of (percent relative gap for Case 3 − percent relative gap for Case 4) = 0
H_1: Mean of (percent relative gap for Case 3 − percent relative gap for Case 4) > 0,

H_0: Mean of ("optimal" 3-stage cost for Case 3 − "optimal" 3-stage cost for Case 4) = 0
H_1: Mean of ("optimal" 3-stage cost for Case 3 − "optimal" 3-stage cost for Case 4) > 0,

and

H_0: Mean of (CPU time for Case 4 − CPU time for Case 3) = 0
H_1: Mean of (CPU time for Case 4 − CPU time for Case 3) > 0.

Table 10.7 Variabilities of the percent relative gaps, "optimal" 3-stage costs, and CPU times over 10 scenario trees for Cases 1 and 2 (see Fig. 10.4)

	Percent relative gap	"Optimal" 3-stage cost	CPU times (in seconds)
Case 1			
Minimum value	0.2972	9.7684e+006	5.1571e+003
Lower quartile	0.5542	9.7802e+006	5.7502e+003
Median	0.7761	9.7854e+006	6.1390e+003
Upper quartile	3.7351	1.0076e+007	7.4038e+003
Maximum value	5.3436	1.0197e+007	9.6930e+003
Sample average	2.0511	9.9141e+006	6.7156e+003
Sample standard deviation	2.1709	1.9337e+005	1.7479e+003
Case 2			
Minimum value	1.9493	9.8952e+006	5.9596e+003
Lower quartile	2.1717	9.9150e+006	6.1643e+003
Median	2.2947	9.9286e+006	6.4033e+003
Upper quartile	3.1180	1.0008e+007	6.6744e+003
Maximum value	3.1548	1.0012e+007	6.7112e+003
Sample average	2.5501	9.9527e+006	6.3937e+003
Sample standard deviation	1.0923	5.2959e+004	311.1915

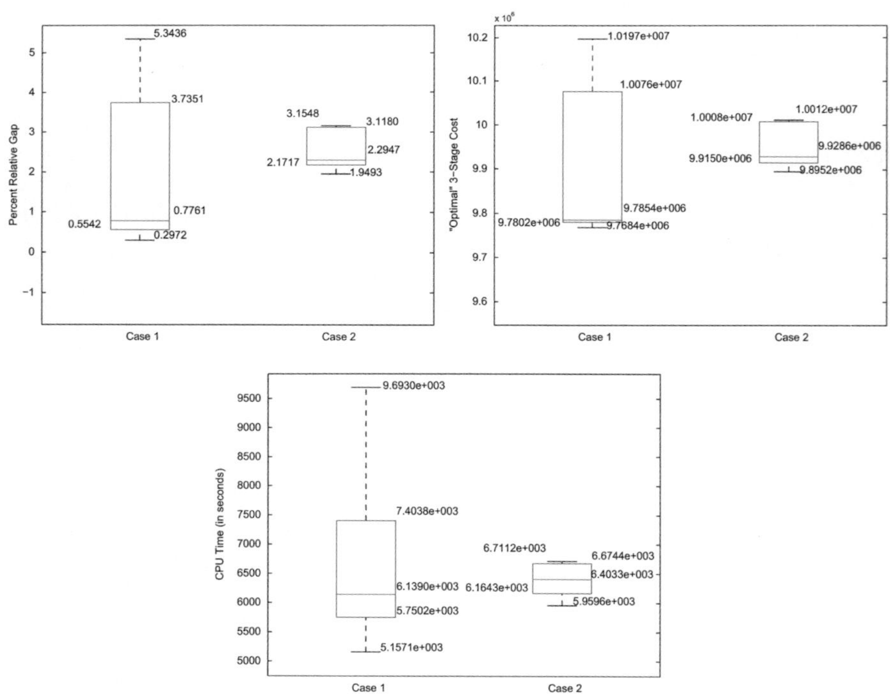

Fig. 10.4 *Box plots* to show the variabilities in the relative percent gaps, the "optimal" 3-stage costs, and the CPU times for Cases 1 and 2

Table 10.8 Variabilities of the percent relative gaps, "optimal" 3-stage costs, and CPU times over 10 scenario trees for Cases 3 and 4 (see Fig. 10.5)

	Percent relative gap	"Optimal" 3-stage cost	CPU times (in seconds)
Case 3			
Minimum value	0.2778	9.7671e+006	4.8335e+003
Lower quartile	0.5560	9.7775e+006	4.8574e+003
Median	5.0889	1.0081e+007	6.4847e+003
Upper quartile	6.5955	1.0214e+007	7.4521e+003
Maximum value	8.5499	1.0264e+007	8.9429e+003
Sample average	4.1019	1.0018e+007	6.4163e+003
Sample standard deviation	3.5602	2.3225e+005	1.7022e+003
Case 4			
Minimum value	0.1627	9.7221e+006	5.0865e+003
Lower quartile	1.6937	9.8694e+006	5.9245e+003
Median	2.5578	9.9548e+006	6.2149e+003
Upper quartile	5.4115	1.0195e+007	8.0328e+003
Maximum value	7.7221	1.0313e+007	8.5246e+003
Sample average	3.4576	1.0013e+007	6.7797e+003
Sample standard deviation	2.8646	2.2759e+005	1.3918e+003

Now the p-values are again very high, namely, 0.3236, 0.4768, and 0.2717, respectively; see also Table 10.8 and Fig. 10.5. Again, the three null hypotheses cannot be rejected for $\alpha = 1\,\%$, or $\alpha = 5\,\%$, or $\alpha = 10\,\%$. Furthermore, the variabilities of the percent relative gaps, the "optimal" 3-stage costs, and the CPU times are very similar for both cases; see Fig. 10.5. Hence, either the CMCS or the LHS should be used to generate the scenario tree without any obvious preference for one sampling technique over the other.

10.5 Conclusions and Future Research

In this paper, we consider a disaster preparedness and short-term response planning problem. We formulate this problem through a multistage stochastic optimization model, where the first-stage problem is formulated to determine the locations of the storage facilities and their sizes, and the amounts of the emergency commodities to be pre-positioned at the opened facilities. The later stages problems are formulated as variants of the capacitated multi-commodity network flow problems with fractional flows, and they determine the amounts of the emergency commodities to be distributed to the disaster victims and to be purchased to update the inventories at the storage facilities. Furthermore, we assume that the demands at the shelters and the road capacities are stage-dependent and random, where we consider the

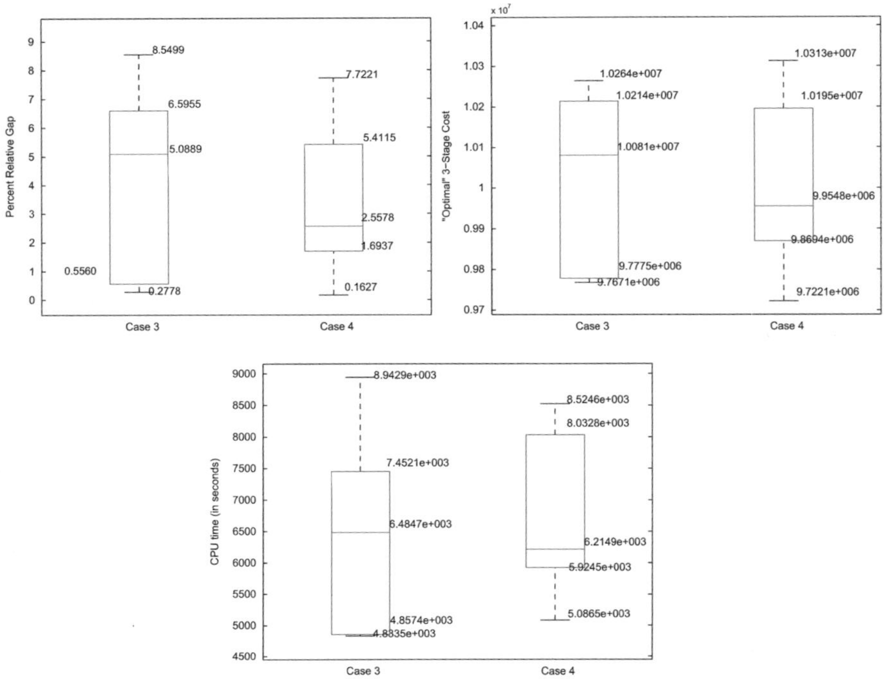

Fig. 10.5 *Box plots* to show the variabilities in the relative percent gaps, the "optimal" 3-stage costs, and the CPU times for Cases 3 and 4

normal and lognormal distributions for the random quantities. To overcome the problem of having infinitely many scenarios, we discretize the normal and the lognormal distributions, and hence build a scenario tree through the Crude Monte Carlo Sampling (CMCS) or the Latin Hypercube Sampling (LHS). Moreover, to overcome the problem of the computation of a multi-dimensional integration, we replace the computationally untractable expectations through their Sample Average Approximation (SAA) estimators. The resulting SAA problems are solved through the Stochastic Dual Dynamic Programming (SDDP) algorithm over a scenario tree, which consists of 90,000 scenarios. Because the solution depends on the generated scenario tree, we repeat the procedure over a number of different trees generated through the CMCS or the LHS. In all computational experiments, we observe that after the first few hundred iterations, there is almost no improvement in the absolute gap, which forms the stopping criterion of the algorithm. Therefore, instead of the absolute gap, the percent relative gap can perform better as the stopping criterion in the applications of the SDDP algorithm. Moreover, we compare the results of the CMCS and the LHS through the paired t-tests, and we find that when the demands and the road capacities are both normally distributed, the LHS's results are more robust with respect to the variabilities in scenario trees.

Several points present themselves as directions for further work. First of all, the multistage stochastic model in this paper is risk-neutral. A better model for disaster management studies should include risk measures such as chance constraints, conditional value-at-risk type constraints, etc. For example, such a constraint can ensure that the probability of not satisfying certain percentage of the total demand does not exceed a given upper bound with high probability for different realizations of the random demands. Moreover, humanitarian criteria such as maximizing the total saved lives or minimizing the total delivery times of the emergency commodities should be considered in the multistage stochastic models. Furthermore, more research has to be done to improve the slow convergence of the SDDP algorithm after the first few hundred iterations.

Acknowledgements The author thanks Atilla Ansal and Mustafa Erdik (Boğaziçi University Kandilli Observatory and Earthquake Research Center) for giving their data of the estimated number of buildings that will be damaged at various levels after an earthquake in Istanbul. This research has been financially supported by Galatasaray University Research Fund.

References

1. Wassenhove, L.N.V.: Humanitarian aid logistics: supply chain management in high gear. J. Oper. Res. Soc. **57**(5), 475–489 (2006)
2. Hedgpeth, D.: U.S. task force commander for Haitian relief says logistics remain stumbling block. Washington Post, 18 Jan 2010. http://www.washingtonpost.com/wp-dyn/content/article/2010/01/18/AR2010011804059.html. Accessed 13 Dec 2013
3. BBC News: Logistical nightmare hampers Haiti aid effort, 22 Jan 2010. http://www.news.bbc.co.uk/go/pr/fr/-/2/hi/americas/8460787.stm. Accessed 13 Dec 2013
4. Galindo, G., Batta, R.: Review of recent developments in OR/MS research in disaster operations management. Eur. J. Oper. Res. **230**, 201–211 (2013)
5. Caunhye, A.M., Nie, X., Pokharel, S.: Optimization models in emergency logistics. Socio Econ. Plan. Sci. **46**(1), 4–13 (2012)
6. Haghani, A., Oh, S.-C.: Formulation and solution of a multi-commodity, multi-modal network flow model for disaster relief operations. Transp. Res. Part A **30**(3), 231–250 (1996)
7. Barbarosoğlu, G., Arda, Y.: A two-stage stochastic programming framework for transportation planning in disaster response. J. Oper. Res. Soc. **55**, 43–53 (2004)
8. Chiu, Y-C., Zheng, H., Villalobos, J., Gautam, B.: Modeling no-notice mass evacuation using a dynamic traffic flow optimization model. IIE Trans. **39**, 83–94 (2007)
9. Yi, W., Özdamar, L.: A dynamic logistics coordination model for evacuation and support in disaster response activities. Eur. J. Oper. Res. **179**, 1177–1193 (2007)
10. Lodree, E.J., Taskin, S.: Supply chain planning for hurricane response with wind speed information updates. Comput. Oper. Res. **36**, 2–15 (2009)
11. Balcik, B., Beamon, B.M., Smilowitz, K.: Last mile distribution in humanitarian relief. J. Intell. Transp. Syst. **12**(2), 51–63 (2008)
12. Rawls, C.G., Turnquist, M.A.: Pre-positioning of emergency supplies for disaster response. Transp. Res. Part B **44**, 521–534 (2010)
13. Rawls, C.G., Turnquist, M.A.: Pre-positioning and dynamic delivery planning for short-term response following a natural disaster. Socio Econ. Plan. Sci. **46**(1), 46–54 (2012)
14. An, S., Cui, N., Li, X., Ouyang, Y.: Location planning for transit-based evacuation under the risk of disruptions. Transp. Res. Part B 54, 1–16 (2013)

15. Homem-de-Mello, T., de Matos, V.L., Finardi, E.C.: Sampling strategies and stopping criteria for stochastic dual dynamic programming: a case study in the long-term hydrotermal scheduling. Energy Syst. **2**, 1–31 (2011)
16. Fu, M.: Optimization for simulation: theory vs. practice. INFORMS J. Comput. **14**(3), 192–215 (2002)
17. Shapiro, A., Dentcheva, D., Ruszczyński, A.: Lectures on Stochastic Programming: Modeling and Theory. SIAM, Philadelphia (2009)
18. Infanger, G., Morton, D.P.: Cut sharing for multistage stochastic linear programs with interstage dependency. Math. Program. **75**, 241–256 (2006)
19. McKay, M.D., Beckman, R.J., Conover, W.J.: A comparison of three methods for selecting values of input variables in the analysis of output from a computer code. Technometrics **21**, 239–245 (1979)
20. Loh, W.: On Latin hypercube sampling. Ann. Stat. **24**(5), 2058–2080 (1996)
21. Owen, A.B.: Monte Carlo variance of scrambled net quadrature. SIAM J. Numer. Anal. **34**(5), 1884–1910 (1997)
22. Stein, M.L.: Large sample properties of simulations using Latin hypercube sampling. Technometrics **29**, 143–151 (1987)
23. Pereira, M.V.F., Pinto, L.M.V.G.: Multi-stage stochastic optimization applied to energy planning. Math. Program. **52**, 359–375 (1991)
24. Philpott, A.B., Guan, Z.: On the convergence of stochastic dual dynamic programming and related methods. Oper. Res. Lett. **36**, 450–455 (2008)
25. Shapiro, A.: Analysis of stochastic dual dynamic programming method. Eur. J. Oper. Res. **209**, 63–72 (2011)
26. Shapiro, A., Tekaya, W., da Costa, J.P., Soares, M.P.: Risk neutral and risk averse stochastic dual dynamic programming method. Eur. J. Oper. Res. **224**(2), 375–391 (2013)
27. Hobeika, A.G., Kim, C.: Comparison of traffic assignments in evacuation modeling. IEEE Trans. Eng. Manage. **45**, 192–198 (1998)
28. Donnell, E.T., Hines, S.C., Mahoney, K.M., Porter, R.J., McGee, H.: Speed concepts: informational guide. Technical Report No. FHWA-SA-10-001, U.S. Department of Transportation, Federal Highway Administration (2009)
29. Erdik, M., Sesetyan, K., Hancilar, U., Demircioglu, M.B.: Earthquake risk assessment of an urban area: Istanbul. Unpublished manuscript obtained through private communication from M. Erdik, Boğaziçi University Kandilli Observatory and Earthquake Research Center, Istanbul, Turkey (2011)
30. Unpublished data obtained through private communication from A. Ansal, Boğaziçi University Kandilli Observatory and Earthquake Research Center, Istanbul, Turkey
31. Turkish Statistical Institute: http://www.turkstat.gov.tr
32. Law, A.M.: Simulation Modeling and Analysis, 4th edn. McGraw-Hill, New York (2007)

Chapter 11
Optimal Stock Allocation in Single Echelon Inventory Systems Subject to a Service Constraint

Annalisa Cesaro and Dario Pacciarelli

11.1 Introduction

Single echelon inventory systems are experiencing an increasing interest in practice, in particular for the management of expensive spare parts. In such a context, the supply chain involves at least three actors: equipment users, logistics companies and equipment suppliers. The users need spare parts to carry on their business without interruptions. Intermediate logistic companies are in charge of replenishing spare parts in the short term, by guaranteeing the contractual service level to the users at minimum cost. The suppliers are responsible for supplying new components and/or repaired items to the logistic companies.

This chapter addresses the problem of spare parts allocation in a single echelon inventory system with complete pooling characterized by expensive spares, long repairing time and strict requirements of operational availability (i.e., the fraction of time during which all operational sites are working). Our work is motivated by a practical problem faced by a large Italian logistics company. The company handles 17 warehouses supporting the daily activity of 38 civil airports spread over the Italian territory. Each site is coupled with one regional warehouse. The base stock quantities are computed by the company through the VARIMETRIC algorithm of Sherbrooke [14], based on a stiff hierarchic structure. However, in operation lateral transshipments take place between stocking points whenever there is an emergency requirement for parts, using couriers and overnight carriers to rapidly move parts. The company is therefore interested in determining the potential savings deriving from explicit inclusion of lateral transshipments in the model.

A. Cesaro (✉) • D. Pacciarelli
Dipartimento di Ingegneria, Università Roma Tre, Via della Vasca Navale, 79, Rome I-00146, Italy
e-mail: cesaro@dia.uniroma3.it; pacciarelli@dia.uniroma3.it

G. Dellino, C. Meloni (eds.), *Uncertainty Management in Simulation-Optimization of Complex Systems*, Operations Research/Computer Science Interfaces Series 59,
DOI 10.1007/978-1-4899-7547-8_11

To this aim, we propose and evaluate a new branch and bound procedure for stock level definition and spare parts allocation. The procedure exploits the particular cost structure of the maintenance supply chain under study and is very effective in this context. However, the method is general and we discuss the algorithm performance in a more general context.

The literature on inventory management deals with the analysis of many different models. Extensive surveys of inventory models with lateral transshipments can be found in [5, 13]. In these surveys, the existing approaches are classified according to a number of characteristics related to the inventory system, the ordering policy, the modeling of transshipments and other issues (e.g., the number of items, echelons, the number and role of locations, the unsatisfied demand, the timing of regular orders, the order policy, the type of transshipments, pooling, decision making).

Huiskonen [8] and Kennedy et al. [9] focus on review models for spare part management. They observe that the logistics of spare parts differs from those of other materials in several ways. Equipments may have remarkable costs, long repairing times and sporadic failures. The latter are difficult to forecast and may cause relevant financial effects, due to the economical implications of a lack of equipment at the operational sites. In such cases, continuous review policies are typically adopted to reduce both reaction time to stockouts and inventory levels [1, 7, 11].

We next present the most relevant references for our study. Several heuristic procedures can be found in the literature for allocating spares to warehouses in a single echelon context with complete pooling [2, 11]. In such a context, Wong et al. [17] develop a solution procedure based on Lagrangian relaxation to obtain both a lower bound and an upper bound on the optimal total cost. Koutanoglu and Mahajan [12] consider a model to allocate stock levels at warehouses in a two echelon context. They use approximate models for estimating the performance of a specific allocation of spare parts and exploit it to implicitly enumerate all possible allocations of spares.

In this chapter, we describe a new branch and bound algorithm to compute the optimal base stock quantities that minimize the expected average total cost in a multi-location single echelon transshipment system. The algorithm makes use of a new lower bound based on Lagrangian relaxation. The computational experiments carried on practical instances show the effectiveness of the algorithm.

This chapter is organized as follows. Relevant notation is described in Sect. 11.2. Section 11.4 describes the single echelon one-for-one ordering model with complete pooling and the spare parts allocation problem is formulated as a non-convex integer program. In Sect. 11.3 the Markov chain model used for computing transshipment costs and times. Heuristic and exact allocation algorithms are described in Sect. 11.6. Section 11.5 studies the mathematical structure of the optimization problem. Computational experiments are presented in Sect. 11.7, based on practical data from the airport maintenance context. Some conclusions follow in Sect. 11.8.

11.2 Notation and Assumptions

In order to formally define the problem, let us introduce the following notation. Let $A = \{1, 2, \ldots, a\}$ be a set of operational sites (e.g., airports) where working equipments are located. We assume that operational sites are grouped on a regional basis, with a warehouse of spare parts for each region. Let $W = \{1, 2, \ldots, w\}$ be the set of regional warehouses. Let s_i be the number of spare parts to allocate to each warehouse $i \in W$, $S = \sum_{i \in W} s_i$ be the total stock level and $s = (s_1, \ldots, s_w)$ be an allocation of spares to warehouses, i.e., the vector of decision variables. We denote with $MTTR$ the Mean Time To Return, i.e. the average replenishment time of a spare part by the external supplier, with $MTBF$ the Mean Time Between Failures of the overall system composed by all equipment installed at all sites, with OS the Order and Ship time. Therefore, $MTTR + OS$ is the total time elapsed from the failure of a part to its replenishment in the warehouse. We denote with $MCMT$ the Mean Corrective Maintenance Time and with OA the Operational Availability of all the a sites.

We say that the overall system is in *emergency conditions* when all base stock levels are equal to 0. In fact, an airport is in emergency when working without some equipment for more than a given time limit, and this situation occurs when there is a failure and no spare part is available at any warehouse. In this case, several emergency procedures must be carried out, which increase the management cost and reduce the airport capacity. We denote with MET the Mean Emergency Time, i.e., the mean time needed to replenish a part in emergency conditions, from the failure to the replenishment. In this chapter we assume $MET = MTTR + OS$, which corresponds to the assumption that the order and ship time and the mean time to return from the supplier do not vary in emergency conditions and in the normal operations. This choice corresponds to overestimate the MET, which in practice is often smaller than $MTTR + OS$. We keep $MET = MTTR + OS$ since in our application the operational availability requirements are very strict and it is preferable to overestimate the blocking probability with respect to its underestimation. With this hypothesis, the service rate of a server at warehouse h is $\mu = \frac{1}{MTTR+OS}$. Let T_{hi} be the transfer time for a spare from warehouse h to warehouse i and $T_s(j, h)$ be the substitution time, i.e., the time needed to transfer a spare part to the site $j \in A$ from the warehouse $h \in W$ and to physically replace the failed item. Let λ_{jh} be the mean rate of failures from site j to warehouse h, let $\lambda_h = \sum_{j \in A} \lambda_{jh}$ be the arrival rate at warehouse h and let $\Lambda = \sum_{h \in W} \lambda_h$. Thus, $MTBF = \frac{1}{\Lambda}$. Given an allocation s, the network blocking probability is the probability that a failure occurs at some site and no warehouse can satisfy the spare demand. We denote the network blocking probability as $P_B(S)$ since, as it will be shown in Sect. 11.3, it only depends on the total stock level S rather than on the particular allocation s.

In this chapter we study the system in steady state conditions. Given an allocation s, let $\pi_{hi}(s)$ be the steady state probability of the event: there are no spares in warehouse $h \in W$ and $i \in W$ is the closest warehouse with available spares (i.e., every warehouse l such that $T_{hl} < T_{hi}$, including the case $l = h$, is in stockout condition). Ties are broken arbitrarily, i.e., if there are two warehouses at the same distance, one is considered closer than the other. This choice corresponds to a common administrative procedure: to each warehouse is given an ordered list of warehouses for checking the availability of a spare part and the search must be carried out in strictly sequential order.

Let $n = (n_1, \ldots, n_w, n_{w+1})$ be a vector representing the state of the network, in which n_i is the number of outstanding requests at warehouse $i \in W$, and n_{w+1} is the number of outstanding emergency requests to the external supplier. Let $p(n)$ be the probability that the warehouse network is in state n, and let c^h be the inventory holding cost for warehouse h, c^t_{ij} be the cost for a lateral transshipment from warehouse j to warehouse i, in stockout condition, and c^e be the emergency transshipment cost.

We assume a Poisson distribution for the demand process, which is a typical assumption for modeling low demand processes [15]. The replenishment time of the external supplier is a random variable, exponentially distributed, with known mean value MTTR. The capacity of the supplier repair shop is assumed to be infinite. It follows that also the number of replenishments from the external supplier follows the Poissonian distribution. These common assumptions make possible to use the Markovian analysis for modeling the multi-dimensional inventory system. Finally, we make the following assumptions.

1. Lateral transshipment is always more convenient than emergency shipment, i.e., the time and cost needed for a transshipment from warehouse i to warehouse j is always smaller than the time and cost required for an emergency shipment from warehouse j:

$$\max_{i,j \in W} \{T_{ij}\} < MET \tag{11.1}$$

$$\max_{i,j \in W} \{c^t_{ij}\} < c^e \tag{11.2}$$

2. The cost for a lateral transshipment from warehouse i to warehouse j increases linearly with the transfer time T_{ij}, i.e.,

$$c^t_{ij} = \alpha T_{ij} \tag{11.3}$$

11.3 Multi-Dimensional Markovian Model

In this section, we compute the probability $p(n)$ of each state $n = (n_1, \ldots, n_w, n_{w+1})$ of the associated Markov chain for a given spare part allocation. In case of blocked network, the first repaired item returned by the external supplier is used for replacing a failed item in some operative site, if any. There are direct transitions among states just in case of a single arrival event (i.e. a request for a spare at some warehouse) or a single departure event (i.e. the replenishment of a repaired item by the external supplier). Let e^i be a vector with $w+1$ elements, all equal to 0 but the element in position i that is equal to 1, and let $\psi(h,i)$ be equal to 1 if ($n_i < s_i$ and $n_l = s_l$ for each $l \in W$ such that $T_{lh} < T_{ih}$, included $l = h$) and be equal to 0 otherwise. With this notation, $n + e_i$ is the state of the Markov chain representing an arrival at the i-th warehouse (if $i \in W$ and $n_i < s_i$), due either to a failure in the i-th service region or to a re-forwarded request from some other warehouse h in stockout conditions, i.e., such that $\psi(h,i) = 1$. Similarly, $n - e_i$ is the state obtained from n when a repaired item is shipped from the external supplier to the i-th warehouse (if $i \in W$ and $n_i > 0$). For the external supplier, $n + e_{w+1}$ represents a new emergency request (if $n_i = s_i$ for each $i \in W$) and $n - e_{w+1}$ represents the fulfillment of an emergency request (if $n_{w+1} > 0$). The transition rate $q(n,m)$ from state n towards state $m = n \pm e_i$ and $n \pm e_{w+1}$ is as follows.

- $q(n, n+e_i) = \lambda_i + \sum_{h \in W-\{i\}} \psi(h,i)\lambda_h$, for $i \in W$ and $n_i = 0, 1, \ldots, s_i - 1$;
- $q(n, n+e_{w+1}) = \sum_{i \in W} \lambda_i$, if $n_i = s_i$ $\forall i \in W$;
- $q(n, n-e_i) = \sum_{i=1}^{w+1} n_i \mu$, for $i \in W$ and $n_i > 0$ and $n_{w+1} = 0$;
- $q(n, n-e_{w+1}) = \sum_{i=1}^{w+1} n_i \mu$, for $n_i = s_i$ $\forall i \in W$ and $n_{w+1} \geq 1$.

Figure 11.1a shows the Markov chain for two warehouses, the first having two spares and the second having three available spares. Steady state probabilities can be computed for each state in the Markov chain by solving a linear system. Note that, to this aim the proposed Markov chain is equivalent to the one shown in Fig. 11.1b, having a finite number of states. In the latter Markov chain, all states in which all warehouses are in stockout condition are grouped in one single state with different departure transition rates.

Let n_B be the state in the original model in which $(n_B)_i = s_i$, $\forall i \in W$, and $(n_B)_{w+1} = 0$ (see Fig. 11.1a). In the equivalent finite state model, the transition rates from state n_B after a replenishment is: $q(n_B, n_B - e_i) = (n_B)_i \mu F$, where $F = \frac{p(n_B)}{P_B(S)}$ (see Fig. 11.1b). As proved in [4], quantities $p(n_B)$ and $P_B(S)$ can be easily computed by using the equivalence of the original model with the simple birth death model associated to a single queue with infinitely many servers (see Fig. 11.1c). Specifically, let $\rho = \frac{\sum_{i \in W} \lambda_i}{\mu}$ and consider a set W of warehouses, with total stock level S, in which the service process is exponentially distributed with average rate μ for each server and the demand flow to warehouse $i \in W$ is Poissonian with average rate λ_i. Then, the blocking probability of all warehouses is:

$$P_B(S) = 1 - \sum_{k=0}^{S-1} \frac{\rho^k}{k!} e^{-\rho}, \tag{11.4}$$

while $p(n_B)$ is equal to $\frac{\rho^{N_B}}{N_B!} e^{-\rho}$, where $N_B = \sum_{i=1}^{w+1} (n_B)_i$.

By directly solving the finite state Markov chain model we can compute the steady state probability $p(n)$ of each state n and use them to compute the system cost and performance associated to a given allocation. Since the direct computation

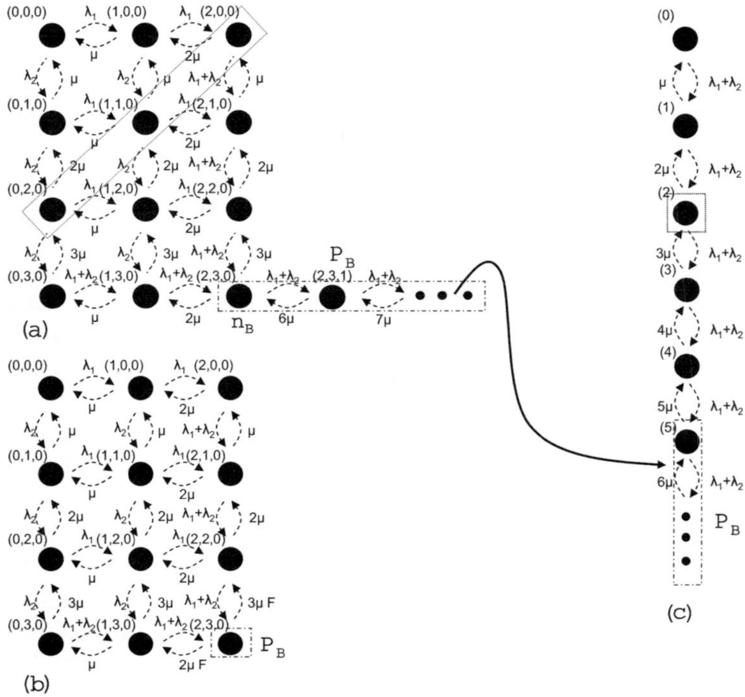

Fig. 11.1 The infinite state space Markov chain for a system of two warehouses (**a**) and finite space state model (**b**) and the aggregated birth death model (**c**)

of state probabilities is expensive in terms of computational effort, we wish to carry out this computation for a limited number of allocations only. In [4] different heuristic methods for estimating costs and performance in such a context have been proposed and compared in terms of estimation accuracy, computation time and memory efforts with the exact Markov chain computation. In Sect. 11.6, we make use of the most effective of such methods to develop a heuristic procedure for spare allocation. On the other hand, we cannot use these heuristic methods to compute exact solutions. Therefore, in what follows we focus on the exact solution of the original Markov chain model.

The Markov chain model that we use is very similar to that of Wong et al. [16, 17]. However, while Wong et al. [16, 17] assume that the demand in state n_B is lost (i.e., the arrival rate in n_B is zero), we assume that this demand is backordered to an external supplier (i.e., we explicitly include the external supplier in the Markov chain). Note that the resulting overall blocking probability in our case is strictly greater than in [16, 17]. The latter property is specifically important for our application, in which operational availability requirements are very strict.

11.4 The Problem

In our model, a logistic company aims to compute the stock level s_i of each warehouse $i \in W$ such that a minimum level of service is granted at the operational sites and the overall cost is minimum. Costs are related to inventory holding, transshipments and emergency shipments.

Given an allocation s of spares to warehouses, the model used to compute the level of service is a single, reparable item, single echelon, w-locations, continuous review, one-for-one replenishment policy inventory system, with lateral and emergency shipments, complete pooling and non-negligible transshipment times.

The Spares Allocation Problem is the problem of finding an allocation s which minimizes the overall cost for inventory holding, lateral and emergency shipments, subject to a constraint on the minimum operational availability of the system.

The contractual service level to grant is the operational availability OA of all operational sites for each item, computed as in [14].

$$OA = \frac{MTBF}{MTBF + MCMT}. \tag{11.5}$$

In Eq. (11.5), MCMT is the average time occurring from the failure of an item to its physical substitution. This is the substitution time if the spare is available at the regional warehouse. If no spares are locally available, the request is forwarded to the closest warehouse with available spares and MCMT increases by the deterministic transfer time between the two warehouses. When no warehouse has spares available, MCMT equals the substitution time plus the replenishment time from the external supplier. The MCMT can be therefore computed as follows:

$$\begin{aligned} MCMT &= \textstyle\sum_{h\in W}\sum_{j\in A}\frac{\lambda_{jh}}{\Lambda}T_s(j,h) \\ &\quad +\textstyle\sum_{h\in W}\left(\frac{\lambda_h}{\Lambda}\sum_{i\in W}\pi_{hi}(s)T_{ih}\right) \\ &\quad +P_B(S)MET \end{aligned} \tag{11.6}$$

We observe that the first term $\sum_{h\in W}\sum_{j=1}^{A}\lambda_{jh}T_s(j,h)$ of Eq. (11.6) only depends on the failure process and on the distance between the sites and their respective regional warehouses. In other words, it does not depend on the specific spare parts management policy being used. Therefore, for sake of simplicity we assume it negligible in our model and omit its computation in the rest of this chapter. As for the quantity $\pi_{hi}(s)$, we assume that a strict deterministic nearest chosen neighbor rule is adopted for sourcing a lateral transshipment, as in Kukreja [11]. Differently from [11], we compute the quantity $\pi_{hi}(s)$ by directly using its definition. In fact, we compute the probability $p(n)$ of each state $n = (n_1, \ldots, n_w, n_{w+1})$ by solving the associated Markov chain defined in Sect. 11.2 exactly and use these probabilities for computing the quantity $\pi_{hi}(s)$ as follows:

Comment. 1. *by denoting with* E *the set of all the states* n *with no spares in warehouse* $h \in W$ *and* $i \in W$ *as the closest warehouse with available spares (i.e., every warehouse* l *such that* $T_{hl} < T_{hi}$*, including the case* $l = h$*, is in stockout condition), the following holds:*

$$\pi_{hi}(s) = \sum_{n \in \Phi} p(n) \tag{11.7}$$

where $\Phi = \{n : n_i < s_i, n_l = s_l \forall l : T_{hl} < T_{hi}\}$.

Comment. 2. *Differently from [11], we use equation (11.8) to compute this value, which directly follows from the definition of* $\pi_{hi}(s)$*.*

$$\pi_{hi}(s) = (1 - p^i(s_i)) \prod_{l:T_{hl}<T_{hi}} (p^l(s_l)). \tag{11.8}$$

For the purpose of formulating the spare allocation problem, let L be the minimum operational availability level to be achieved by a feasible allocation. According to expression (11.5), the minimum operational availability constraint is as follows.

$$\frac{MTBF}{MTBF + \sum_{i \in W}\left[\left(\frac{\lambda_i}{\Lambda}\sum_{j \in W}\pi_{ij}(s)T_{ji}\right)\right] + P_B(S)(MET)} \geq L.$$

This expression is equivalent to

$$MTBF \geq L\left[MTBF + \sum_{i \in W}\left[\left(\frac{\lambda_i}{\Lambda}\sum_{j \in W}\pi_{ij}(s)T_{ji}\right)\right] + P_B(S)(MET)\right]$$

which, in turn, can be expressed as

$$\sum_{i \in W}\left[\left(\frac{\lambda_i}{\Lambda}\sum_{j \in W}\pi_{ij}(s)T_{ji}\right)\right] + P_B(S)(MET) \leq \frac{(1-L)MTBF}{L}.$$

The latter inequality formulates the constraint by allowing a maximum waiting time $\frac{(1-L)MTBF}{L}$ to substitute all the failed items. In view of this expression, the Spares Allocation Problem P_0 can be formulated as the following integer program with non-convex objective function:

Problem P_0:

$$
\begin{aligned}
&\min \ \sum_{i=1}^{w} c^h s_i + \lambda_i \sum_{j\in W} \pi_{ij}(s) c^t_{ji} + \lambda_i P_B(S) c^e \\
&s.t.: \\
&\sum_{i=1}^{w} [\tfrac{\lambda_i}{\Lambda} \sum_{j\in W} \pi_{ij}(s) T_{ji}] + P_B(S)(MET) \leq \tfrac{(1-L)MTBF}{L}
\end{aligned}
\tag{11.9}
$$

Let $f_1(S) = \sum_{i=1}^{w} c^h s_i$ be the total inventory holding cost, let $f_2(s)$ be the cost for lateral transshipments, i.e., $f_2(s) = \left\{\sum_{i=1}^{w} \lambda_i \sum_{j\in W} \pi_{ij}(s) c^t_{ji}\right\}$. Let also $f_3(S) = \sum_{i=1}^{w} \lambda_i P_B(S) c^e$ be the cost for the emergency shipments. Similarly, for the waiting times we let $t_2(s) = \left\{\sum_{i=1}^{w} \frac{\lambda_i}{\Lambda} \sum_{j\in W} \pi_{ij}(s) T_{ji}\right\}$ be the waiting times due to lateral transshipments and $t_3(S) = P_B(S)(MET)$ be the emergency waiting times. Problem P_0 is very similar to that of Wong et al. [17]. The main difference is in the service level constraint. Due to the needs of our practical case study, we assume a single service level constraint for all locations, while in Wong et al. [16, 17] there is a constraint for each location.

11.5 Problem Structure

In this section, we exploit the special structure of problem P_0. Let us first analyze the three functions $f_1(S)$, $f_2(s)$, $f_3(S)$. $f_1(S)$ is clearly linear and increasing with the total stock level S. As shown in [10], $f_3(S)$ is convex and decreasing with S for $S \geq \rho - 1$. Unfortunately, $f_2(s)$ is non-convex. The latter property can be easily shown by observing that $f_2(s)$ equals zero when $s = 0$ or when $s_i \to \infty$ for all $i = 1, \ldots w$, since there are no transshipments in these two cases. On the other hand, $f_2(s) > 0$ otherwise, thus implying that $f_2(s)$ is non-convex. Similarly, it can be easily proved that $t_3(S)$ is convex with S for $S \geq \rho - 1$ and $t_2(s)$ is non-convex. We next show that the quantities $t_2(s) + t_3(S)$ and $f_2(s) + f_3(S)$ are decreasing. To this aim, let us consider an allocation s and a warehouse $i \in W$. Denote with $\hat{s}$ the allocation such that $\hat{s}_i = s_i + 1$ and $\hat{s}_h = s_h$ for all $h \in W, h \neq i$. Let also denote $S = \sum_{i=1}^{w} s_i$ and $\hat{S} = \sum_{i=1}^{w} \hat{s}_i = S + 1$.

Let us first observe that when passing from s to $\hat{s}$ the number of spares at each warehouse does not decrease and therefore the probability that a failed equipment at some airport is replaced with the local stock of the associated regional warehouse cannot decrease. Specifically, the following properties must hold.

- $P_B(S) > P_B(\hat{S})$.
- As for warehouse i, the probability that the arrival rate λ_i (without transshipments) is satisfied by the local stock increases when passing from s_i to $s_i + 1$. Thus, the probability of re-forwarding the demand towards warehouse $j \neq i$ cannot increase, i.e. $\pi_{ij}(\hat{s}) \leq \pi_{ij}(s)$ for all $j \neq i$. It follows that $\sum_{j\in W} \pi_{ij}(s) T_{ji} + P_B(S)(MET) > \sum_{j\in W} \pi_{ij}(\hat{s}) T_{ji} + P_B(\hat{S})(MET)$.

- For what concerns warehouse $h \neq i$ the probability of re-forwarding the request to warehouse i cannot decrease and, therefore, the probability of re-forwarding the request to a more far warehouse (or to the external supplier) cannot increase. Thus, it holds: $\sum_{j \in W} \pi_{hj}(s)T_{jh} + P_B(S)(MET) > \sum_{j \in W} \pi_{hj}(\hat{s})T_{jh} + P_B(\hat{S})(MET)$.

In conclusion,

$$t_2(s) + t_3(S) - t_2(\hat{s}) - t_3(\hat{S})$$

$$= \sum_{i=1}^{w} \frac{\lambda_i}{\Lambda} \left[\sum_{j \in W} \left(\pi_{ij}(s) - \pi_{ij}(\hat{s}) \right) T_{ji} \right] + \left(P_B(S) - P_B(\hat{S}) \right)(MET) > 0.$$

Using assumption (11.2), a similar discussion for the costs leads to $f_2(s) + f_3(S) > f_2(\hat{s}) + f_3(\hat{S})$.

Given an upper bound UB on the optimum of problem P_0, an upper bound MAX on the total stock level S of an optimal solution can be efficiently computed by considering only the terms $f_1(S)$ and $f_3(S)$ of the objective function.

$$MAX = \min\{S : f_1(S) + f_3(S) \geq UB\} \tag{11.10}$$

This value is quite close to the optimal stock level S^* when the transshipment cost $f_2(s^*)$ is small with respect to $f_1(S^*) + f_3(S^*)$. Similarly, a lower bound MIN on S^* can be efficiently computed by considering only the term $t_3(S)$, decreasing with S, in the constraint of the problem.

$$MIN = \min\left\{ S : t_3(s) \leq \frac{(1-L)MTBF}{L} \right\} \tag{11.11}$$

These bounds can be used to refine the formulation of Problem P_0, thus leading to the new formulation P_1.

Problem P_1:

$$\begin{aligned} \min \quad & f_1(S) + f_2(s) + f_3(S) \\ s.t.: & \\ & t_2(s) + t_3(S) \leq \tfrac{(1-L)MTBF}{L} \end{aligned} \tag{11.12}$$

$$MIN \leq S \leq MAX$$

We observe that, if $MIN = \min\left\{S : t_3(s) \leq \frac{(1-L)MTBF}{L}\right\} \geq \rho - 1$, then $f_3(S)$ and $t_3(S)$ are convex [10]. In the remaining part of this chapter we assume that this condition is always satisfied. In fact, this condition holds for all the instances we tested and, more in general, it is a mild condition since, for example, even for $L \geq 0.5$ it can be easily checked that $MIN \geq \rho - 1$ for a wide range of ρ values (up to more than 100).

We next introduce a Lagrangian relaxation $P_2(\gamma)$ of problem P_1 by relaxing the waiting time constraint. We use the notation γ to denote the Lagrangian multiplier.

Problem $P_2(\gamma)$:

$$\begin{aligned} &\min \ f_1(S) + f_2(s) + f_3(S) + \gamma \left(t_2(s) + t_3(S) - \tfrac{(1-L)MTBF}{L} \right) \\ &s.t.: \\ &\qquad MIN \leq S \leq MAX \end{aligned} \tag{11.13}$$

It is well known that, for varying γ, $P_2(\gamma)$ is a concave, piecewise linear function. Calling breakpoint the values of $P_2(\gamma)$ in which the slope of $P_2(\gamma)$ changes, there is an optimal solution γ^* for the Lagrangian dual $\max\{P_2(\gamma) : \gamma \geq 0\}$ which is a breakpoint. If we let $\overline{s}$ be an optimal allocation for $P_2(\overline{\gamma})$, and $\overline{\gamma}$ is not a breakpoint, then the slope of $P_2(\gamma)$ in $\overline{\gamma}$ is [6]:

$$t_2(\overline{s}) + t_3(\overline{S}) - \tfrac{(1-L)MTBF}{L} \tag{11.14}$$

Theorem 1. *If $\overline{\gamma}$ is not a breakpoint there is a single optimal stock level for $P_2(\overline{\gamma})$.*

Proof. By contradiction, let us suppose that in $\overline{\gamma}$ there are two optimal allocations s and $\overline{s}$ with different stock levels S and $\overline{S}$, respectively. Therefore:

$$\begin{aligned} &f_1(S) + f_2(s) + f_3(S) + \overline{\gamma} \left(t_2(s) + t_3(S) - \frac{(1-L)MTBF}{L} \right) \\ &\quad = f_(\overline{S}) + f_2(\overline{s}) + f_3(\overline{S}) + \overline{\gamma} \left(t_2(\overline{s}) + t_3(\overline{S}) - \frac{(1-L)MTBF}{L} \right). \end{aligned}$$

From Eq. (11.14) it follows that the constraint violation is the same for s and $\overline{s}$, i.e., $t_2(s) + t_3(S) = t_2(\overline{s}) + t_3(\overline{S})$. It follows from the proportionality assumption (11.3) that also $f_2(s) + f_3(S) = f_2(\overline{s}) + f_3(\overline{S})$ must hold. Hence, we obtain $f_1(S) = f_1(\overline{S})$, i.e., $c^h S = c^h \overline{S}$. This implies the thesis $S = \overline{S}$. □

Theorem 2. *If $\overline{\gamma}$ is a breakpoint and the slope of $P_2(\overline{\gamma})$ decreases from $t_2(s^1) + t_3(S^1) - \frac{(1-L)MTBF}{L}$ to $t_2(s^2) + t_3(S^2) - \frac{(1-L)MTBF}{L}$, then $S^2 > S^1$.*

Proof. At the breakpoint $\overline{\gamma}$ there are at least the two optimal solutions s^1 and s^2 for problem $P_2(\overline{\gamma})$, i.e.,

$$\begin{aligned} &f_1(S^1) + f_2(s^1) + f_3(S^1) + \overline{\gamma} \left(t_2(s^1) + t_3(S^1) - \frac{(1-L)MTBF}{L} \right) \\ &\quad = f_1(S^2) + f_2(s^2) + f_3(S^2) + \overline{\gamma} \left(t_2(s^2) + t_3(S^2) - \frac{(1-L)MTBF}{L} \right). \end{aligned}$$

Since the slope of $P_2(\gamma)$ decreases, then $t_2(s^1) + t_3(S^1) > t_2(s^2) + t_3(S^2)$ and, from the proportionality assumption (11.3), also $f_2(s^1) + f_3(S^1) > f_2(s^2) + f_3(S^2)$ must hold. Hence, it follows that $f_1(S^1) < f_1(S^2)$, which implies the thesis $S^1 < S^2$. □

Theorem 3. *If the breakpoint γ^* is an optimal solution of the Lagrangian dual $\max\{P_2(\gamma) : \gamma \geq 0\}$ and the slope of $P_2(\gamma^*)$ decreases from $t_2(s^1) + t_3(S^1) - \frac{(1-L)MTBF}{L} \geq 0$ to $t_2(s^2) + t_3(S^2) - \frac{(1-L)MTBF}{L} \leq 0$, then:*

1. *s^2 is feasible for problem P_1;*
2. *either s^2 is optimal for P_1 or S^2 is greater than the optimal stock level for P_1.*

Proof. The feasibility of s^2 directly follows from $t_2(s^2) + t_3(S^2) - \frac{(1-L)MTBF}{L} \leq 0$. If s^2 is not optimal, let s^* be an optimal allocation and S^* be the corresponding stock level. From the optimality of S^* it follows that:

$$f_1(S^*) + f_2(s^*) + f_3(S^*) < f_1(S^2) + f_2(s^2) + f_3(S^2) \tag{11.15}$$

On the other hand at γ^* the objective function of the Lagrangian relaxation computed in s^* must be greater or equal than in s^2, i.e.,

$$f_1(S^*) + f_2(s^*) + f_3(S^*) + \gamma^* \left(t_2(s^*) + t_3(S^*) - \frac{(1-L)MTBF}{L} \right) \geq$$
$$= f_1(S^2) + f_2(s^2) + f_3(S^2) + \gamma^* \left(t_2(s^2) + t_3(S^2) - \frac{(1-L)MTBF}{L} \right).$$

Therefore, $t_2(s^*) + t_3(S^*) > t_2(s^2) + t_3(S^2)$ must hold. From assumption (11.3) it must hold also $f_2(s^*) + f_3(S^*) > f_2(s^2) + f_3(S^2)$. Therefore, from inequality (11.15), $f_1(S^*) < f_1(S^2)$, i.e., $S^* < S^2$. □

Despite the nice properties of $P_2(\gamma^*)$ shown in Theorem 3, the computation of $P_2(\gamma^*)$ requires the computation of quantity $f_2(s^*) + \gamma^* t_2(s^*)$, which is computationally expensive. In order to efficiently compute a lower bound to $P_2(\gamma^*)$, let us introduce problem $P_3(\gamma)$:

Problem $P_3(\gamma)$:

$$\begin{aligned}
\min \quad & f_1(S) + x + f_3(S) + \gamma \left(y + t_3(S) - \tfrac{(1-L)MTBF}{L} \right) \\
s.t.: \quad & \\
& MIN \leq S \leq MAX \\
& x \leq f_2(s) \\
& y \leq t_2(s)
\end{aligned} \tag{11.16}$$

Suitable values for x and y can be computed by exploiting the properties that $f_3(S)$ and $f_2(s) + f_3(S)$ are decreasing with S. Given any feasible allocation s and the corresponding $S = \sum_{i=1}^{w} s_i$, the following must hold:

$$\begin{aligned}
& f_3(S) \leq f_3(MIN) \\
& t_3(S) \leq t_3(MIN) \\
& f_2(s) + f_3(S) \geq \min_{\bar{s}:\sum_{i=1}^{w} \bar{s}_i = MAX} \{f_2(\bar{s})\} + f_3(MAX) \\
& t_2(s) + t_3(S) \geq \min_{\bar{s}:\sum_{i=1}^{w} \bar{s}_i = MAX} \{t_2(\bar{s})\} + t_3(MAX)
\end{aligned} \tag{11.17}$$

Therefore, the values $x = \min_{\overline{s}:\sum_{i=1}^{w}\overline{s}_i=MAX}\{f_2(\overline{s})\} + f_3(MAX) - f_3(MIN)$ and $y = \min_{\overline{s}:\sum_{i=1}^{w}\overline{s}_i=MAX}\{t_2(\overline{s})\} + t_3(MAX) - t_3(MIN)$ guarantee that constraints $x \leq f_2(s)$ and $y \leq t_2(s)$ are satisfied by any allocation s such that $MIN \leq \sum_{i=1}^{w} s_i \leq MAX$. In what follows, we fix x and y to these values and omit the two latter constraints from the formulation of Problem $P_3(\gamma)$, which can be written as follows:

Problem $P_3(\gamma, MIN, MAX)$:

$$\begin{aligned}
\min\quad & f_1(S) + \min_{\overline{s}:\sum_{i=1}^{w}\overline{s}_i=MAX}\{f_2(\overline{s})\} + f_3(MAX) - f_3(MIN) + f_3(S)\\
& +\gamma\left(\min_{\overline{s}:\sum_{i=1}^{w}\overline{s}_i=MAX}\{t_2(\overline{s})\} + t_3(MAX) - t_3(MIN) + t_3(S) - \tfrac{(1-L)MTBF}{L}\right)\\
s.t.:&\\
& MIN \leq S \leq MAX \qquad (11.18)
\end{aligned}$$

Since $f_1(S)$ is linearly increasing while $f_3(S)$ and $t_3(S)$ are convex and decreasing with S, the objective function of Problem $P_3(\gamma, MIN, MAX)$ is convex for any given $\gamma \geq 0$. Therefore, given the values x and y, the optimal S can be efficiently computed by using a binary search approach in the interval $[MIN, MAX]$. We compute x as in [16]. The next theorem shows that computing y is not necessary in order to compute the maximum of $P_3(\gamma, MIN, MAX)$.

Theorem 4. *The value* $\gamma = 0$ *maximizes* $P_3(\gamma, MIN, MAX)$.

Proof. To prove the theorem it is sufficient to prove that quantity

$$\min_{\overline{s}:\sum_{i=1}^{w}\overline{s}_i=MAX}\{t_2(\overline{s})\} + t_3(MAX) - t_3(MIN) + t_3(S) - \frac{(1-L)MTBF}{L}$$

is always non positive for $MIN \leq S \leq MAX$. This property follows by observing that $t_3(S) \leq t_3(MIN)$ and that a feasible solution exists for $S = MAX$, i.e.,

$$\min_{\overline{s}:\sum_{i=1}^{w}\overline{s}_i=MAX}\{t_2(\overline{s})\} + t_3(MAX) \leq \frac{(1-L)MTBF}{L}.$$

□

11.6 Solution Procedure

In this section, a branch-and-bound algorithm for finding an optimal allocation of spares to warehouses is described. At each node of the enumeration tree the lower bound is computed by solving $P_3(0, MIN, MAX)$, where MIN and MAX are computed according to Eqs. (11.11) and (11.10) at the root node and then updated by the branching rule. The heuristic algorithm described in Sect. 11.6.1 provides an initial upper bound UB, then updated whenever a new feasible solution is found, and a sketch of the branch and bound procedure is presented in Sect. 11.6.2.

```
Procedure ISA
    set S = 0 and s_i = 0,      i = 1, ..., w.
    set rhs = (1-L)MTBF / L and k = 1.
    repeat
        repeat
            set S = S + 1, s_k = s_k + 1 and k = k + 1;
            if (k = |W̄| then set k = 1;
        until Σ_{i=1}^{w} [λ_i/Λ Σ_{j∈W} π̂_ij(s)T_ji] + P_B(S)(MET) ≤ rhs
        if Σ_{i=1}^{w} [λ_i/Λ Σ_{j∈W} π_ij(s)T_ji] + P_B(S)(MET) > (1-L)MTBF / L
        then rhs = rhs - Σ_{i=1}^{w} [λ_i/Λ Σ_{j∈W} (π_ij(s) - π̂_ij(s)) T_ji]
    until Σ_{i=1}^{w} [λ_i/Λ Σ_{j∈W} π_ij(s)T_ji] + P_B(S)(MET) ≤ (1-L)MTBF / L
    return s.
```

Fig. 11.2 Pseudocode of the heuristic for initial spares allocation

11.6.1 Upper-Bound Computation

A simple upper bound to Problem P_0 is computed by distributing spare parts among warehouses with positive demand and by giving preference to warehouses with larger demand. In fact, simulation experiments carried out in [3] show that avoiding concentration of spares in few warehouses is an effective allocation policy. The heuristic procedure ISA (Initial Spares Allocation), sketched in Fig. 11.2, finds an allocation s, feasible for P_0, by greedily allocating one spare at a time to warehouses in the set $\overline{W} = \{i \in W : \lambda_i > 0\}$. Without loss of generality we assume that the warehouses are numbered for decreasing value of λ_i, i.e., $\lambda_1 \geq \lambda_2 \geq \ldots \geq \lambda_{|\overline{W}|}$. ISA terminates when the quantity $\sum_{i=1}^{w}[\frac{\lambda_i}{\Lambda}\sum_{j\in W}\pi_{ij}(s)T_{ji}] + P_B(S)(MET)$ becomes smaller than $\frac{(1-L)MTBF}{L}$. In order to speed up the computation of state probabilities $\pi_{ij}(s)$ at each step of the procedure, the heuristic computes approximate values $\hat{\pi}_{ij}(s)$, by using estimated values for the state probabilities of the associated Markov chain. Such values are computed with the fast multidimensional scaling down method described in [4]. The main idea of this method is to replace the original Markov chain with an equivalent one with a smaller number of states but with similar behavior in terms of operational availability. The reduced Markov chain is obtained by scaling the demand, the replenishment time and the stock level of each warehouse using a *scale factor* K. When

$$\sum_{i=1}^{w}\left[\frac{\lambda_i}{\Lambda}\sum_{j\in W}\hat{\pi}_{ij}(s)T_{ji}\right] + P_B(S)(MET) \leq \frac{(1-L)MTBF}{L} \tag{11.19}$$

in the reduced chain, the feasibility of allocation s is checked by solving the original Markov chain exactly. In case of a feasible solution, Procedure ISA stops and returns the feasible allocation s, otherwise the constraint (11.19) is strengthened by replacing the right-hand side $\frac{(1-L)MTBF}{L}$ with the smaller value

$$\frac{(1-L)MTBF}{L} - \sum_{i=1}^{w}\left[\frac{\lambda_i}{\Lambda}\sum_{j\in W}\left(\pi_{ij}(s) - \hat{\pi}_{ij}(s)\right)T_{ji}\right].$$

Procedure ISA then continues allocating one spare at a time and checking feasibility with the multi-dimensional scaling down method until a new apparently feasible solution is found. The procedure stops when the first feasible solution is found.

11.6.2 Branch and Bound Algorithm

Our BB (Branch and Bound) procedure, sketched in Fig. 11.3, maintains a queue $\mathcal{Q}$ of intervals $[MIN, MAX]$ for the stock level S, each corresponding to an instance of P_1.

Procedure BB

Find an allocation $BestSol = ISA$
set $UB = f_1(BestSol) + f_2(BestSol) + f_3(BestSol)$
$MIN = \min\left\{S : t_3(s) \leq \frac{(1-L)MTBF}{L}\right\}$
$MAX = \min\left\{S : f_1(S) + f_3(S) \geq UB\right\}$
push $[MIN, MAX]$ in queue $\mathcal{Q}$
while $\mathcal{Q} \neq \emptyset$ **do**
  pop $[x, y]$ from $\mathcal{Q}$
  if $P_3(0, x, y) < UB$ **then**
    let S^* be the optimal solution to $P_3(0, x, y)$
    set $s^* = \text{argmin}\{t_2(s) : \sum_{i=1}^{w} s_i = S^*\}$
    if $t_2(s^*) + t_3(S^*) \leq \frac{(1-L)MTBF}{L}$ **then**
      if $f_1(S^*) + f_2(s^*) + f_3(S^*) < UB$ **then**
        set $BestSol = s^*$ and $UB = f_1(S^*) + f_2(s^*) + f_3(S^*)$
        set $y = \min\{y; \min\{S : f_1(S) + f_3(S) \geq UB\}\}$
      end if
      push $[x, S^* - 1]$ in $\mathcal{Q}$
      push $[S^* + 1, y]$ in $\mathcal{Q}$
    else
      push $[S^* + 1, y]$ in $\mathcal{Q}$
    end if
  end if
end while
Return UB and $Bestsol$

Fig. 11.3 Pseudocode of the BB algorithm

Procedure ISA provides an initial solution $Bestsol$, from which the first upper bound UB on the optimum is derived. At the root node, $\mathcal{Q}$ is initialized with one open problem in which MIN and MAX are computed according to (11.11) and (11.10).

At each iteration of the BB procedure an open problem is removed from $\mathcal{Q}$ according to First In First Out rule and an optimal solution S^* to $P_3(0, MIN, MAX)$ is computed. If the lower bound $P_3(0, MIN, MAX) \geq UB$ the problem is closed. Otherwise, an allocation $s^* = \text{argmin}\{t_2(s) : \sum_{i=1}^{w} s_i = S^*\}$ is computed as in [16].

If $t_2(s^*) + t_3(S^*) \leq \frac{(1-L)MTBF}{L}$, then s^* is feasible for P_0 and, in view of assumption (11.3), it is also an optimal allocation for the restricted version of P_1 in which $S = S^*$. In this case, two new open problems are added to $\mathcal{Q}$ with $MIN \leq S \leq S^* - 1$ and $S^* + 1 \leq S \leq MAX$, respectively, and the upper bound UB is updated if $f_1(S^*) + f_2(s^*) + f_3(S^*) < UB$.

If $t_2(s^*) + t_3(S^*) > \frac{(1-L)MTBF}{L}$, then s^* is infeasible for P_1. Thus, for all values $MIN \leq S \leq S^*$ there is no feasible solution to P_0 and only the open problem with $S^* + 1 \leq S \leq MAX$ is added to $\mathcal{Q}$. The procedure terminates when $\mathcal{Q}$ is empty and the current allocation $Bestsol$ is an optimal solution to P_0.

11.7 Case Study from the Corrective Airport Maintenance Context

In this section, we report on our computational experiments with the algorithms for spares allocation presented in Sect. 11.6 applied to solve the practical problem from the airport maintenance context described in the introduction of the chapter. The case study originates from the practical needs of an Italian logistics company supporting the activity of 38 civil airports spread over the Italian territory. The company manages the overall processes of purchasing, holding and replacing failed items, ensuring that the overall reliability of safety equipments is always within contractual limits. The aim of the company is therefore to grant the prescribed quality of service at minimum cost. While the company currently follows a two echelon policy for spare part management, the company managers are interested in evaluating the potential benefits deriving from the adoption of a single echelon policy, which is generally acknowledged to achieve better performance in similar contexts. To this aim, the algorithms have been tested on a set of twelve instances from our case study, each based on the warehouse locations and demand rates of a particular item. However, in order to test the algorithms on a wider context than the real situation, we generated several scenarios by varying holding, transshipment and emergency costs of each item. For the replenishment time of an item we use the exponential distribution with average (OS + MTTR) equal to three months for all items and scenarios while for the transshipment time and cost we use a deterministic value proportional to the distance between warehouses. Each pair holding-emergency cost defines a scenario for each of the twelve items. We consider 21 scenarios by choosing the cost of an item from the interval [200, 1,200] and fixing the emergency cost equal to 7,000. The latter cost is a realistic one when emergency costs are the weighty ones, such as in contexts where safety is also involved. Fourteen additional scenarios are defined in order to analyze the influence of the emergency cost on the algorithms performance. In this second set of scenarios the item cost is fixed equal to 300 for each item while the emergency cost varies from 200 to 200,000. Not all the emergency costs are realistic, since our purpose with the second set of scenarios is to investigate the effects of increasing emergency costs. In total we studied a set of 420 instances. Table 11.1 summarizes the values of the main parameters used in the computational experiment.

Tables 11.2, 11.3 and 11.4 report the results obtained for the 12 instances and the 35 scenarios. Table 11.2 shows the solutions and the computation time (in seconds)

Table 11.1 Parameter values for the computational experiment

Parameter name	Unit	Values
Warehouses with positive demand		2,3,4,5,6,7,8,9
Number of installed items		3,5,8,9,10,11,16,18
$MTBF_{eq}$	Hours	16,000, 17,000, 26,000, 38,000, 61,000, 79,000, 81,000, 94,000, 101,000, 132,000, 191,000, 200,000
Holding cost	Euros	200, 250, 300, ..., 1,000, 1,150, 1,200
Emergency cost	Euros	200, 300, ..., 700, 1,000, 2,000, ..., 5,000, 7,000, 50,000, 100,000, 200,000
Min-Max average transshipment lead time	Hours	[5, 37.5]
OS + MTTR	Hours	2,160

Table 11.2 Performance of ISA and BB algorithms for the 12 items

Item	# wareh.	BB cost values			ISA value	$\frac{ISA-BB}{BB}$	Computation time	
		Holding	Transshipment	Emergency			ISA	BB
1	2	1,607.96	107.98	15.95	1,915.79	0.11	0.15	0.82
2	3	1,232.31	360.45	25.13	3,167.76	0.96	0.17	0.94
3	4	1,709.10	456.66	8.09	3,086.06	0.43	0.15	1.40
4	4	2,221.00	517.70	41.56	2,794.14	0.05	0.15	2.00
5	4	1,474.52	563.24	22.42	3,101.16	0.60	0.15	1.39
6	5	1,345.48	668.23	37.11	2,436.62	0.20	0.16	1.80
7	6	1,904.55	869.60	70.29	3,060.88	0.10	0.19	30.80
8	6	1,450.23	914.24	60.45	3,588.61	0.50	0.16	68.09
9	7	1,512.84	1,095.64	22.60	2,694.90	0.10	0.15	1,743.62
10	7	1,528.90	1,086.95	28.10	2,980.42	0.12	0.16	1,867.27
11	8	2,068.41	1,350.92	15.43	3,788.17	0.10	0.17	1,047.60
12	9	1,984.05	1,300.86	38.01	4,036.73	0.23	0.14	4.494.06

Table 11.3 Performance of ISA and BB for different holding costs

Holding cost	Emergency cost	BB cost values			ISA value	$\frac{ISA-BB}{BB}$	# spares	
		Holding	Transshipment	Emergency			BB	ISA
200	7,000	1,050.00	225.57	2.40	1,769.05	0.40	5.2	2.5
250	7,000	1,229.17	302.33	2.71	1,898.21	0.30	4.9	2.5
300	7,000	1,250	511.14	3.38	2,027.38	0.16	4.1	2.5
350	7,000	1,341.67	608.98	12.51	2,156.55	0.10	3.8	2.5
400	7,000	1,433.33	702.55	13.23	2,285.71	0.10	3.5	2.5
450	7,000	1,537.50	770.17	15.87	2,414.88	0.10	3.4	2.5
500	7,000	1,541.67	914.79	29.99	2,544.05	0.05	3.0	2.5
550	7,000	1,604.17	985.84	45.09	2,673.21	0.05	2.9	2.5
600	7,000	1,700.00	1,030.90	49.58	2,852.38	0.05	2.8	2.5
650	7,000	1,733.33	1,125.55	56.92	3,112.70	0.06	2.5	2.5
700	7,000	1,866.67	1,125.55	56.92	3,260.71	0.07	2.5	2.5
750	7,000	1,937.50	1,182.59	62.38	3,389.88	0.07	2.5	2.5
800	7,000	2,066.67	1,182.59	62.38	3,539.05	0.07	2.5	2.5
850	7,000	2,195.83	1,182.59	62.38	3,668.21	0.07	2.5	2.5
900	7,000	2,325.00	1,182.59	62.38	3,877.38	0.08	2.5	2.5
1000	7,000	2,454.17	1,182.59	62.38	4,006.75	0.08	2.5	2.5
1050	7,000	2,583.33	1,182.59	62.38	4,164.88	0.08	2.5	2.5
1100	7,000	2,712.50	1,182.59	62.38	4,394.05	0.11	2.5	2.5
1150	7,000	2,841.67	1,182.59	62.38	4,623.21	0.13	2.5	2.5
1200	7,000	2,875	1,182.59	62.38	4,652.38	0.13	2.5	2.5

of ISA and BB and the relative error of ISA, computed as the average over all instances of the values $\frac{ISA-BB}{BB}$. Each row in table shows the average results obtained for an item by varying the costs over the 35 scenarios. We observe that the BB algorithm is able to find the optimal solution within less than 100 s of computation for eight of the twelve items, while the optimum is found within approximately 30 min for other three items. ISA always finds a feasible solution within less than 1 s. The ISA value turns out to be the optimal solution for 72 out of 420 instances and the average error over the 35 scenarios varies in the range $[0.10, 0.96]$. These experiments show that ISA provides good solutions within short computation time, even if it is worth using the exact algorithm to find better solutions.

In Table 11.3 we analyze the performance of ISA and BB for varying the holding cost of the items. Each row in table reports the average results over the 12 items for one of the first 21 scenarios. We also show the three components of the optimum cost, i.e., holding, transshipment and emergency cost. It can be observed that the transshipment cost is often comparable with the holding cost, and therefore it cannot be neglected in the solution of the problem. For a holding cost lower than 700 the number of spares allocated by ISA is smaller than the optimal value, while for holding costs higher than 350 ISA always allocates a number of spares optimal or

Table 11.4 Performance of ISA and BB for different emergency costs

Holding cost	Emergency cost	BB cost values			ISA value	$\frac{ISA-BB}{BB}$	# spares	
		Holding	Transshipment	Emergency			BB	ISA
300	200	1,200	556.27	0.16	1,966.78	0.12	4	2.5
300	300	1,200	556.27	0.31	1,967.67	0.12	4	2.5
300	400	1,200	556.27	0.47	1,968.56	0.12	4	2.5
300	500	1,200	556.27	0.63	1,969.46	0.12	4	2.5
300	600	1,200	556.27	0.78	1,970.35	0.12	4	2.5
300	700	1,200	556.27	0.94	1,971.24	0.12	4	2.5
300	1,000	1,200	556.27	1.57	1,973.91	0.12	4	2.5
300	2,000	1,200	556.27	3.15	1,982.82	0.12	4	2.5
300	3,000	1,200	556.27	4.72	1,991.73	0.13	4	2.5
300	4,000	1,200	556.27	6.30	2,000.64	0.14	4	2.5
300	5,000	1,250	511.14	2.41	2,009.56	0.14	4.17	2.5
300	7,000	1,250	511.14	3.38	2,027.38	0.15	4.17	2.5
300	50,000	1,250	511.14	24.12	2,410.56	0.35	4.17	2.5
300	100,000	1,325	442.93	38.76	2,856.13	0.60	4.42	2.5
300	200,000	1,400	406.72	15.40	3,747.26	1.05	4.67	2.5

slightly greater than the optimal one. In fact, we observe that the number of spares allocated by ISA does not depend on the spare holding cost and therefore the number of spares allocated by ISA is always the same for all scenarios. A consequence of this behavior is that the gap between ISA and the optimum is influenced by the holding cost. When the holding cost of an item increases from 200 to 500 the error decreases from 40 % down to 5 %. For larger holding costs the error increases regularly until 13 %. Smaller errors are attained when the number of spares allocated by ISA is close to the optimal one and the holding cost is small. In these cases the error only depends on the warehouses to which spares are allocated. As the holding cost increases, the cost related to the different allocation becomes more and more relevant and the relative gap between ISA and BB increases.

In Table 11.4 we analyze the performance of ISA and BB for varying the item emergency costs. Each row in table shows the average results over the 12 instances for one of the 15 scenarios. Similarly to the previous scenario, the number of spares allocated by ISA is the same for all scenarios since this value does not depend on the spare emergency cost. The gap between ISA and the optimum depends therefore on the emergency cost, even if the emergency cost has a smaller influence on the error of ISA with respect to the holding cost. When the emergency cost varies in the range $[200 - 2,000]$, the error remains the same. In order to observe relevant errors, the emergency cost must increase up to more than 50,000.

As a concluding observation, computational experiments show that the overall behavior of ISA is acceptable as an initial solution for subsequent optimization. In general, the performance of ISA depends on the specific holding and emergency costs being considered and, therefore, it may be quite erratic. BB algorithm seems to be more promising, since it finds the proven optimum within acceptable computation time for all tested instances.

11.8 Conclusions

In this chapter we propose and evaluate a solution methodology for optimizing inventory stock allocation of repairable spare parts in a single echelon, w-locations system, where lateral and emergency shipments occur in response to stockouts. We model our problem as a non-convex integer program and develop a new heuristic and a new branch and bound algorithm for allocating the spare parts optimally. Both algorithms are evaluated by using practical data from the Italian airport corrective maintenance context. Computational experiments demonstrate that the branch and bound technique is able to optimally solve almost all tested instances within reasonable computation time. The heuristic algorithm finds sub-optimal solutions within very limited computation time, thus being a promising approach for finding feasible solutions to difficult instances.

Future research should address a deeper structural analysis of the functions studied in this chapter, relaxing some of the assumptions made in this chapter. For example, extending the BB algorithm to the case $MET < MTTR + OS$ would enlarge the range of applicability of the proposed technique. To this aim, the convexity of function $f_3(S)$ has to be investigated.

Future research should also address the development of faster exact methods and effective metaheuristics for the solution of large and difficult instances, as well as on the application of the ideas proposed in this chapter to manage the maintenance of different critical infrastructures, such as medical equipments in hospitals or communication or energy distribution networks and so on.

References

1. Alfredsson, P., Verrijdt, J.: Modeling emergency supply flexibility in a two echelon inventory system. Manage. Sci. **45**, 1416–1431 (1999)
2. Axsater, S.: Modelling emergency lateral transshipments in inventory systems. Manage. Sci. **6**, 1329–1338 (1990)
3. Cesaro, A., Pacciarelli, D.: Evaluation of peaked lateral transshipment in inventory system subject to a service constraint. MSOM 2007 Conference, 18–19 June 2007
4. Cesaro, A., Pacciarelli, D.: Performance assessment for single echelon airport spare part management. Comput. Ind. Eng. **61**, 150–160 (2011)
5. Chiou, C.C.: Transshipment problems in supply chain systems: review and extensions. In: Kordic, V. (ed.) Supply Chains, Theory and Application. I-Tech Education and Publishing, Vienna (2008)
6. Fisher, M.L.: The Lagrangian relaxation method for solving integer programming problems. Manage. Sci. **27**, 1–18 (1981)

7. Grahovac, J., Chakravarty, A.: Sharing and lateral transshipment of inventory in a supply chain with expensive low-demand items. Manage. Sci. **47**, 579–594 (2001)
8. Huiskonen, J.: Maintenance spare parts logistics: special characteristics and strategic choices. Int. J. Prod. Econ. **71**, 125–133 (2001)
9. Kennedy, W.J., Wayne Patterson, J., Fredendall, L.D.: An overview of recent literature on spare parts inventories. Int. J. Prod. Econ. **76**, 201–215 (2002)
10. Kranenburg, A.A., Van Houtum, G.J.: Service differentiation in spare parts inventory management. J. Oper. Res. Soc. **59**(7), 946–955 (2008)
11. Kukreja, A., Schmidt, C.P., Miller, D.M.: Stocking decisions for low-usage items in a multilocation inventory system. Manage. Sci. **47**, 1371–1383 (2001)
12. Kutanoglu, E., Mahajan, M.: An inventory sharing and allocation method for a multi location service parts logistics network with time based service levels. Eur. J. Oper. Res. **194**, 728–742 (2009)
13. Paterson, C., Kiesmuller, G., Teunter, R., Glazebrook, K.: Inventory models with later transshipments: a review. Eur. J. Oper. Res. **210**, 125–136 (2011)
14. Sherbrooke, C.C.: Optimal Inventory Modeling of Systems: Multi-Echelon Techniques. Wiley, New York (2004)
15. Taragas, G., Vlachos, D.: Effectiveness of stock transshipment under various demand distributions and nonnegligible transshipment times. Prod. Oper. Manage. **11**, 183–198 (2002)
16. Wong, H., Cattrysse, D., Van Oudeusden, D.: Inventory pooling of repairable spare parts with non-zero lateral transshipment time and delayed lateral transshipments. Eur. J. Oper. Res. **165**, 207–218 (2005)
17. Wong, H., Van Houtum, G.J., Cattrysse, D., Van Oudheusden, D.: Multi-item spare part systems with lateral transshipments and waiting time constraints. Eur. J. Oper. Res. **171**, 1071–1093 (2006)

MIX
Papier aus verantwortungsvollen Quellen
Paper from responsible sources
FSC® C105338

If you have any concerns about our products,
you can contact us on
ProductSafety@springernature.com

In case Publisher is established outside the EU,
the EU authorized representative is:
Springer Nature Customer Service Center GmbH
Europaplatz 3, 69115 Heidelberg, Germany

Printed by Libri Plureos GmbH
in Hamburg, Germany